A Writer's Reader

A WRITER'S READER

FOURTH EDITION

Donald Hall

D. L. Emblen
Santa Rosa Junior College

 **LITTLE, BROWN AND COMPANY**
Boston   Toronto

Library of Congress Cataloging in Publication Data
Main entry under title:

A Writer's reader.

 Includes indexes.
 1. College readers. 2. English language — Rhetoric.
I. Hall, Donald, 1928– . II. Emblen, D. L. (Donald
Lewis), 1918– .
PE1417.W67 1985   808'.0427   84-21784
ISBN 0-316-33995-4

Library of Congress Card No. 84-21784

ISBN 0-316-33995-4

HAL

Published simultaneously in Canada
by Little, Brown & Company (Canada) Limited

Printed in the United States of America

For William R. Booth

Preface

Reading well precedes writing well. Of all the ancestors claimed by a fine piece of prose, the most important is the prose from which the writer learned his craft. Writers learn craft, not by memorizing rules about restrictive clauses, but by striving to equal a standard formed from reading.

A composition course, then, must be two courses: one in reading, another in writing. If students lack practice in writing, they are usually unpracticed readers as well. Most students lack quality of reading as well as quantity; and if we assert that good models help us, we admit that bad models hurt us. People who read bad prose twelve hours a week — newspapers, popular fiction, textbooks — are as ill-served as people who read nothing at all. Surely most textbooks, from freshman handbooks through the text for Psych 101, encourage the illusion that words merely stand in for ideas, or carry information on their backs — that words exist for the convenience of thinking much as turnpikes exist for the sake of automobiles.

This barbarism underlies the vogue of speed reading, which urges us to scan lines for comprehension, ignoring syntax and metaphor, ignoring image and feeling and sound. If we are to grow and to learn — and surely if we are to write well — we must learn to read slowly and intimately, and to read good writing. We must learn to read actively, even aggressively, without the passivity derived from watching television. The active reader questions as he reads, subjects each author's ideas to skeptical scrutiny, and engages the writer in dialogue as part of the reading process.

For language embodies the human psyche. Learning to read — that privilege so recently extended to the ancestors of most of us — allows us to enter human history. In books we perceive the gesture, the pulse, the heartbeat, the pallor, the eye movement, the pitch, and the tone of people who lived before us, or who live now in other places, in other skins, in other habits, customs, beliefs, and ideas.

Language *embodies* the human psyche, which includes ideas and the feelings that properly accompany ideas. There is no sleight-of-mind by which the idea may be separated from its body and remain alive. The body of good writing is rhythm and image, metaphor and syntax, order of phrase and order of paragraph.

A NOTE TO THE SECOND EDITION

Many teachers helped us prepare the second edition of *A Writer's Reader* — in letters, in conversations at colleges all over the country, in responses to a Little, Brown survey of users. We thank more people than we can list.

We have added considerable material, far more than we have cut, and we are pleased with what we have come up with. We believe that we have made a representative sampling of good prose. We like some pieces more than others, heaven knows, but we believe that all of them provide something to learn from. We have included a wide variety of American prose, not only contemporary but historical, with high points of our history represented in their own style and syntax. We hope that young Americans will attach themselves to the body of their history by immersion in its significant utterances.

We have numbered paragraphs for ease of reference. Although *A Writer's Reader* is a collection of essays, we have again violated coherence by including fiction, feeling that the contrast afforded by a few short stories among the essays was useful and refreshing. For this edition, we have gone further afield and included several poems, for the same reason. Perhaps we should make an argument for including poems — but let us just say that we enjoy them, and we hope you do too. To satisfy students' curiosity, we have included headnotes to the poems; but we have stopped short of suggesting questions after them, lest we seem to surround a landscape garden with a hundred-foot-high concrete wall.

We have chosen to arrange our essays, stories, and poems alphabetically by author. This arrangement makes for random juxtaposition, irrational sequence, and no sense at all — which is why we chose it. We expect no one to teach these pieces in alphabetical order. (We expect teachers to find their own order — which they would do whatever order we attempted to impose.) In our first edition we struggled to make a stylistic organization, listing some essays as examples of "Sentences," others as examples of "Paragraphs." For the editors themselves, a year after deciding on our organization, it was no longer clear why essay X was to be studied for its sentences, essay Y for its paragraphs. With a rhetorical organization, one runs into another sort of problem. Although an essay may contain Division, or Process Analysis, or an example of Example, the same essay is likely to use three or four other patterns as well. No piece of real prose is ever so pure as our systems of classification. Thematic organizations, which have their attractions, have similar flaws; is E. B. White's theme, in "Once More to the Lake," Mortality? Aging? Youth and Age? or, How I Spent My Summer Vacation?

Our arrangement is more arbitrary than an arrangement by style or rhetoric or theme, and presents itself only to be ignored. At the same time, there are dozens of ways in which these essays (and poems and stories) can be used together. Our Instructor's Manual suggests several combinations. Our Rhetorical Index, printed as an appendix to the text itself, lists single-paragraph examples of rhetorical patterns as well as longer units. We hope that students will find the Rhetorical Index useful. Freshmen who return to their rooms from class, set to write a paper using Comparison and Contrast, sometimes find themselves in need of a concrete example of the assigned pattern to imitate.

Thus, we have tried to supply some useful maps to go with our arbitrary arrangement.

We must admit that we take pleasure in the strange juxtapositions the alphabet imposes. We enjoy beginning our book with Henry Adams, James Agee, Woody Allen, Maya Angelou. . . .

A NOTE TO THE THIRD EDITION

Still more teachers have contributed their experience to making the third edition of *A Writer's Reader.* Although our principles have remained the same, we have made changes in our selections; no one wants to teach the same essays year after year. We have made a new Rhetorical Index for this edition and have added a Thematic Index. Following suggestions from several teachers, we have chosen to represent a few authors by small clusters of their work. Thus, we include more than one example of George Orwell, Flannery O'Connor, Langston Hughes, and Sylvia Plath.

A NOTE TO THE FOURTH EDITION

The fourth edition responds to advice from still more instructors. Because the clusters we introduced in the third edition proved popular, we have added groups by Lewis Thomas, Wendell Berry, and Stephen Jay Gould. With Thomas and Gould, we have expanded our representation of writing by scientists. In response to many suggestions, we have looked for short, complete essays in exposition and argument on a variety of topics. Perforce we have dropped essays we admire, which our users assigned infrequently.

If we have omitted essays or authors you miss, please let us know. If there are authors we overlook, whom you would recommend, we solicit your help. Although we intend to remain alert, to good prose and to the needs of the classroom, we need help from the outside.

ACKNOWLEDGMENTS

We thank the following users of the first, second, and third editions for their helpful comments: Louise Ackley, Maureen Andrews, Jane Berk, Meredith Berman, Charles E. Bolton, Patrick Broderick, Ed Buckley, Sandra Burns, Jon Burton, Suzanne Carlson, Marti Carpenter, Richard Cloyed, Edythe Colello, Steven Connelly, Randy Conine, Roger Conner, Charles L. Cornwell, Valecia Crisafulli, Garber Davidson, Virginia de Araujo, Loretta Denner, Salli and Robert Duxbury, Lee Engdahl, Elizabeth Failla, Ralph Farve, Gala Fitzgerald, Frances B. Foreman, Peggy Gledhill, Barbara Hamilton, Walter Harrison, John Huntington, Donald Kansch, Gregory Keeler, Jeff Kluewer, John Larner, Karen LeFerre, Richard H. Lerner, Opal A. Lovett, Nellie McCrory, Sherry McGuire, Andrew Makarushka, Steven J. Masello, Richard Maxwell, Deanne Milan, Molly Moore-Kehler, Barbara Olive, Stephen O'Neil, Patrick Pacheco, Beverly Palmer, Ray Peterson, Martha Rainbolt, James Rosen, Harriet Susskind Rosenblum, Robert Schwegler, Terry Shelton, Donald K. Skiles, Thomas Skmetzo, Marilyn Smith, Arnold Solkov, Andrew Solomon, Richard Speakes, David A. Spurr, Helen Stauffer, Art Suchoki, Bernard Sugarman, Kathleen Sullivan, Jane Bamblin Thomas, Darlene Unrue, Sara Varhus, Craig Watson, Richard Webster, Shirley and Russell White, Richard A. Widmayer, Gary Williams, Suzanne Wilson, George Wymer, and Robert Lee Zimmerman. We thank Carolyn Potts, Virginia Pye, and Billie Ingram at Little, Brown, for their efforts on the book's behalf.

Contents

1 HENRY ADAMS
Winter and Summer   1

"Winter and summer, then, were two hostile lives, and
bred two separate natures. Winter was always the effort
to live; summer was tropical license."

2 JAMES AGEE
Knoxville: Summer 1915   7

"We are talking now of summer evenings in Knoxville,
Tennessee, in the time that I lived there so successfully
disguised to myself as a child."

3 WOODY ALLEN
Death Knocks   12

"Death: I remind him of Moe Lefkowitz. I'm one of the
most terrifying figures you could possibly imagine, and
him I remind of Moe Lefkowitz."

4 MAYA ANGELOU
Mr. Red Leg   21

"So during the age when Mother was exposing us to
certain facts of life, like personal hygiene, proper
posture, table manners, good restaurants and tipping
practices, Daddy Clidell taught me to play poker,
blackjack, tonk and high, low, Jick, Jack and the Game."

5 MARY AUSTIN
The Scavengers   27

"So wide is the range of the scavengers that it is never
safe to say, eyewitness to the contrary, that there are
few or many in such a place."

6   JAMES BALDWIN
Autobiographical Notes   33

"One writes out of one thing only — one's own experience. Everything depends on how relentlessly one forces from this experience the last drop, sweet or bitter, it can possibly give."

7   WENDELL BERRY
A Good Scythe   39

"Apologists for such expensive technological solutions love to say that 'you can't turn back the clock.' But when it makes perfect sense to do so — as when the clock is wrong — of *course* you can!"

8   WENDELL BERRY
In Defense of Literacy   44

"In a country in which everybody goes to school, it may seem absurd to offer a defense of literacy, and yet I believe that such a defense is in order . . ."

9   WENDELL BERRY
The Reactor and the Garden   48

"On June 3, 1979, I took part in an act of nonviolent civil disobedience at the site of a nuclear power plant being built at Marble Hill, near Madison, Indiana."

10 AMBROSE BIERCE
Some Devil's Definitions   57

"*Education, n.* That which discloses to the wise and disguises from the foolish their lack of understanding."

11 CAROLINE BIRD
Where College Fails Us   62

"Too many young people are in college reluctantly, because everyone told them they ought to go, and there didn't seem to be anything better to do."

12 ELIZABETH BISHOP
The Fish   73

"I caught a tremendous fish and held him beside the boat . . ."

13 JOHN N. BLEIBTREU
The Moment of Being   **76**

"The extraordinary preparedness of this creature for that
moment of time during which it will re-enact the
purpose of its life contrasts strikingly with the
probability that this moment will ever occur."

14 BRUCE CATTON
Grant and Lee: A Study in Contrasts   **79**

"They were two strong men, these oddly different
generals, and they represented the strengths of two
conflicting currents that, through them, had come into
final collision."

15 FRANK CONROY
A Yo-Yo Going Down   **84**

"The witty nonsense of Eating Spaghetti, the surprise of
The Twirl, the complex neatness of Cannonball,
Backwards round the World, or Halfway round the
World — I could do them all. . . ."

16 EMILY DICKINSON
There's a certain Slant of light   **92**

"When it comes, the Landscape listens —
Shadows — hold their breath . . ."

17 JOAN DIDION
On Keeping a Notebook   **94**

"It is a good idea, then, to keep in touch, and I suppose
that keeping in touch is what notebooks are all about."

18 ANNIE DILLARD
Strangers to Darkness   **102**

"But shadows spread and deepened and stayed. After
thousands of years we're still strangers to darkness,
fearful aliens in an enemy camp with our arms crossed
over our chests."

19 ANNIE DILLARD
Sojourners   105

"The planet itself is a sojourner in airless space, a wet
ball flung across nowhere. The few objects in the
universe scatter."

20 FREDERICK DOUGLASS
Plantation Life   109

"As I received my first impressions of slavery on this
plantation, I will give some description of it, and of
slavery as it there existed."

21 LOREN EISELEY
More Thoughts on Wilderness   115

"Nothing grows among its pinnacles; there is no shade
except under great toadstools of sandstone whose bases
have been eaten to the shape of wine glasses by the
wind."

22 RALPH ELLISON
On Becoming a Writer   118

"Like Huck, we observed, we judged, we imitated and
evaded as we could the dullness, corruption, and
blindness of 'civilization.' "

23 NORA EPHRON
A Few Words about Breasts: Shaping Up Absurd   126

"Even though I was outwardly a girl and had many of
the trappings generally associated with the field of
girldom — a girl's name, for example, and dresses, my
own telephone, an autograph book — I spent the early
years of my adolescence absolutely certain that I might
at any point gum it up."

24 WILLIAM FAULKNER
A Rose for Emily   135

"When Miss Emily Grierson died, our whole town went
to her funeral: the men through a sort of respectful
affection for a fallen monument, the women mostly out
of curiosity to see the inside of her house. . . ."

25 JULES FEIFFER
Superman 145

"What made Superman extraordinary was his point of origin: Clark Kent."

26 ROBERT FROST
The Gift Outright 149

"The land was ours before we were the land's."

27 MARTIN GANSBERG
38 Who Saw Murder Didn't Call the Police 150

"For more than half an hour 38 respectable, law-abiding citizens in Queens watched a killer stalk and stab a woman in three separate attacks in Kew Gardens."

28 STEPHEN JAY GOULD
The Politics of Census 154

"The census has always been controversial because it was established as a political device, not as an expensive frill to satisfy curiosity and feed academic mills."

29 STEPHEN JAY GOULD
The Phyletic Size Decrease in Hershey Bars 161

"The publicity people at Hershey's mentioned something about a ten-pound free sample. But I guess I've blown it."

30 STEPHEN JAY GOULD
Wide Hats and Narrow Minds 167

"The thought of France's finest anthropologists arguing passionately about the meaning of a dead colleague's hat could easily provoke the most misleading and dangerous inference of all about history — a view of the past as a domain of naive half-wits . . ."

31 JOHN HAINES
Lost 174

". . . two or three years later someone hunting in the back-country came upon a pair of legbones and some scraps of blue wool cloth with metal buttons."

32 LILLIAN HELLMAN
Runaway   178

"I had four dollars and two bits, but that wasn't much
when you meant it to last forever and when you knew it
would not be easy for a fourteen-year-old girl to find
work in a city where too many people knew her."

33 ERNEST HEMINGWAY
Hills Like White Elephants   186

" 'Would you do something for me now?'
'I'd do anything for you.'
'Would you please please please please please please
please stop talking?' "

34 LANGSTON HUGHES
Salvation   192

"God had not struck Westley dead for taking his name
in vain or for lying in the temple. So I decided that
maybe to save further trouble, I'd better lie, too, and say
that Jesus had come, and get up and be saved."

35 LANGSTON HUGHES
Two Poems   195

"Cause you don't love me
Is awful, awful hard."

36 LANGSTON HUGHES
Feet Live Their Own Life   197

"The socks that these feet have bought could build a
knitting mill. The corns I've cut away would dull a
German razor. The bunions I forgot would make you
ache from now till Judgment day."

37 JANE JACOBS
Paradoxes of Size   201

"The biggest and most thoroughly centralized
governments have always, finally, required the special
environment of oppression to continue to maintain
themselves."

38 THOMAS JEFFERSON
The Declarations of Jefferson and of the Congress 208

"I will state the form of the declaration as originally
reported. The parts struck out by Congress shall be
distinguished by a black line drawn under them; &
those inserted by them shall be placed in the margin or
in a concurrent column."

39 ROBIN LAKOFF
You Are What You Say 214

"Having learned our linguistic lesson well, we go out in
the world, only to discover that we are communicative
cripples — damned if we do, and damned if we don't."

40 D. H. LAWRENCE
Pornography 222

"What is pornography to one man is the laughter of
genius to another."

41 ABRAHAM LINCOLN
The Gettysburg Address 228

"The world will little note, nor long remember what we
say here, but it can never forget what they did here."

42 JOHN McPHEE
Ancestors of the Jump Shot 230

"Bradley's graceful hook shot is a masterpiece of
eclecticism."

43 NORMAN MAILER
A Walk on the Moon 234

"They were looking at a terrain which lived in a clarity
of focus unlike anything they had ever seen on earth.
There was no air, of course, and so no wind, nor clouds,
nor dust, nor even the finest scattering of light. . . ."

44 ANDREW MARVELL
To His Coy Mistress 243

"The grave's a fine and private place,
But none, I think, do there embrace."

45 H. L. MENCKEN
Gamalielese   245

"... I rise to pay my small tribute to Dr. Harding. ... he writes the worst English that I have ever encountered. ... It is rumble and bumble. It is flap and doodle. It is balder and dash.
  But I grow lyrical."

46 ALICE B. MORGAN
Exam-Week Unrealities   250

"Yet a course's conclusion has a gratifying unreality, offering us an option we so rarely have elsewhere — a clean break."

47 WRIGHT MORRIS
Odd Balls   252

"All ball games feature hitting and socking, chopping and slicing, smashing, slamming, stroking, and whacking, but only in football are these blows diverted from the ball to the opponent."

48 ANAÏS NIN
Journal Entry   259

"The doctor comes near and looks with amazement. The nurses are silent. Drum drum drum drum drum in soft circles, in soft quiet circles. 'Like a savage,' they whisper. The mystery."

49 FLANNERY O'CONNOR
The Total Effect and the Eighth Grade   262

"Like the college student who wrote in her paper on Lincoln that he went to the movies and got shot, many students go to college unaware that the world was not made yesterday. ..."

50 FLANNERY O'CONNOR
A Good Man Is Hard to Find   267

" '... it's nothing for you to do but enjoy the few minutes you got left the best you can — by killing somebody or burning down his house or doing some other meanness to him. No pleasure but meanness,' he said. ...'"

51 FLANNERY O'CONNOR
From Flannery O'Connor's Letters 283

"The interpretation of your ninety students and three
teachers is fantastic and about as far from my intentions
as it could get to be."

52 GEORGE ORWELL
Politics and the English Language 293

"But if thought corrupts language, language can also
corrupt thought. A bad usage can spread by tradition and
imitation, even among people who should and do know
better."

53 GEORGE ORWELL
Shooting an Elephant 308

"And suddenly I realized I should have to shoot the
elephant after all. The people expected it of me and I had
got to do it. . . ."

54 GEORGE ORWELL
A Hanging 316

"It is curious; but till that moment I had never realized
what it means to destroy a healthy, conscious man."

55 ROBERT M. PIRSIG
The Church of Reason 322

"The real University, he said, has no specific location. It
owns no property, pays no salaries and receives no
material dues. The real University is a state of mind."

56 SYLVIA PLATH
Journal Entries: Charlie Pollard and the Beekeepers 325

"They began looking for the old queen. Slide after slide
was lifted, examined on both sides. To no avail. Myriads
of crawling, creeping bees."

57 SYLVIA PLATH
The Bee Meeting 330

"The villagers are moving the virgins, there will be no
    killing.
The old queen does not show herself, is she so
    ungrateful?"

58 KATHERINE ANNE PORTER
The Necessary Enemy   333

"It is true that if we say I love you, it may be received
with doubt, for there are times when it is hard to
believe. Say I hate you, and the one spoken to believes it
instantly, once for all."

59 JAMES C. RETTIE
"But a Watch in the Night": A Scientific Fable   339

"The Copernicans, it seems, had time-lapse cameras
some 757 million years ago and they also had
superpowered telescopes that gave them a clear view of
what was happening upon this Earth."

60 RICHARD RODRIGUEZ
Does America Still Exist?   347

"Centuries later, in a San Francisco restaurant, a
Mexican-American lawyer of my acquaintance says, in
English, over *salade nicoise,* that he does not intend to
assimilate into gringo society."

61 CARL SAGAN
The Measure of Eratosthenes   352

"Sticks, shadows, reflections in wells, the position of
the sun — of what possible importance could such
simple, everyday matters be? But Eratosthenes was a
scientist. . . ."

62 E. F. SCHUMACHER
Production in Service to Life   355

"In the current vocabulary of condemnation there are
few words as final and conclusive as the word
'uneconomic.' "

63 WILLIAM SHAKESPEARE
That time of year thou mayst in me behold   362

"In me thou see'st the twilight of such day
As after sunset fadeth in the west. . . ."

64 DON SHARP
Under the Hood 363

"To be wrong about inflation or the political aspirations of the Albanians doesn't cost anybody anything, but to claim to know why the car won't start and then to be proved wrong is both embarrassing and costly."

65 WILLIAM STAFFORD
A Way of Writing 372

"A writer is not so much someone who has something to say as he is someone who has found a process that will bring about new things he would not have thought of if he had not started to say them."

66 JONATHAN SWIFT
A Modest Proposal 379

"I have been assured by a very knowing American of my acquaintance in London, that a young healthy child well nursed is at a year old a most delicious, nourishing, and wholesome food, whether stewed, roasted, baked, or boiled. . . ."

67 STUDS TERKEL
Phil Stallings, Spot Welder 388

" 'When you go into Ford, first thing they try to do is break your spirit. . . . To me, this is humanely wrong. A job should be a job, not a death sentence.' "

68 LEWIS THOMAS
On Smell 394

"I should think we might fairly gauge the future of biological science, centuries ahead, by estimating the time it will take to reach a complete, comprehensive understanding of odor."

69 LEWIS THOMAS
Ceti 398

". . . physicists and astronomers from various countries . . . are convinced that the odds for the existence of life elsewhere are very high. . . ."

70 LEWIS THOMAS
Notes on Punctuation 402

"Sometimes you get a glimpse of a semicolon coming, a few lines further on, and it is like climbing a steep path through woods and seeing a wooden bench just at a bend in the road ahead. . . ."

71 HENRY DAVID THOREAU
Thinking Like a Bream 406

"How wild it makes the pond and the township to find a new fish in it!"

72 JAMES THURBER
Which 410

"The relative pronoun 'which' can cause more trouble than any other word, if recklessly used. Foolhardy persons sometimes get lost in which-clauses and are never heard of again."

73 CALVIN TRILLIN
Literally 413

"My problem with country living began innocently enough when our well ran dry and a neighbor said some pump priming would be necessary.
'I didn't come up here to discuss economics,' I said."

74 JOHN UPDIKE
Ace in the Hole 417

"He wasn't hungry; his stomach was tight. It used to be like that when he walked to the gymnasium alone in the dark before a game and could see the people from town, kids and parents, crowding in at the lighted doors. But once he was inside, the locker room would be bright and hot, and the other guys would be there, laughing it up and towel-slapping, and the tight feeling would leave. Now there were whole days when it didn't leave."

75 GORE VIDAL
Drugs   426

"It is possible to stop most drug addiction in the United States within a very short time. Simply make all drugs available and sell them at cost."

76 EUDORA WELTY
A Worn Path   429

"Her name was Phoenix Jackson. She was very old and small and she walked slowly in the dark pine shadows, moving a little from side to side in her steps, with the balanced heaviness and lightness of a pendulum in a grandfather clock."

77 EUDORA WELTY
The Point of the Story   438

"The real dramatic force of a story depends on the strength of the emotion that has set it going."

78 E. B. WHITE
Once More to the Lake   442

"Summertime, oh summertime, pattern of life indelible, the fadeproof lake, the woods unshatterable, the pasture with the sweetfern and the juniper forever and ever, summer without end. . . ."

79 E. B. WHITE
Editorial   450

"Our advice to the nations who call themselves united is to go out and buy rings. If there is to be love-in-bloom at the war's end, we should prefer to see it legal this time, if only for a change."

80 THOMAS WOLFE
Journal Entries   453

". . . the ruins of old settlers homesteads, ghost towns and the bleak little facades of long forgotten postoffices lit bawdily by blazing rising sun and the winding mainstreet, the deserted station of the incessant railway. . . ."

81 VIRGINIA WOOLF
If Shakespeare Had Had a Sister   461

"It is a perennial puzzle why no woman wrote a word of
that extraordinary [Elizabethan] literature when
every other man, it seemed, was capable of song or
sonnet."

82 RICHARD WRIGHT
The Library Card   466

"Reading was like a drug, a dope. The novels created
moods in which I lived for days. But I could not
conquer my sense of guilt, my feeling that the white
men around me knew that I was changing, that I
had begun to regard them differently."

A Rhetorical Index   477

A Thematic Index   485

Henry Adams (1838–1918) entertained notions of a political career, in keeping with family traditions, but withdrew from Washington in distaste over the corruption of the Grant administration. For a time, he taught history at Harvard and edited the North American Review. *After publishing two anonymous novels without great success, he undertook and completed the massive* History of the United States During the Administrations of Jefferson and Madison. *His best works are* Mont St. Michel and Chartres *(1904) and his autobiography — written in the third person and called* The Education of Henry Adams *(1907) — from which we take this fragment of reminiscence.*

Hundreds of American writers have recollected visits to grandfather's house; few were grandson to one president and great-grandson to another. Adams's contrasts of style — eighteenth century with nineteenth, Boston with the small town of Quincy, the Brooks grandfather with the Adams grandfather — culminate in an anecdote that illuminates the fundamental contrast of private and public.

1

HENRY ADAMS
Winter and Summer

Boys are wild animals, rich in the treasures of sense, but the New England boy had a wider range of emotions than boys of more equable climates. He felt his nature crudely, as it was meant. To the boy Henry Adams, summer was drunken. Among senses, smell was the strongest — smell of hot pine-woods and sweet-fern in the scorching summer noon; of new-mown hay; of ploughed earth; of box hedges; of peaches, lilacs, syringas; of stables, barns, cow-yards; of salt water and low tide on the marshes; nothing came amiss. Next to smell came taste, and the children knew the taste of everything they saw or touched, from pennyroyal and flagroot to the shell of a pignut and the letters of a spelling book — the taste of A-B, AB, suddenly revived on the boy's tongue sixty years afterwards. Light, line, and color as sensual pleasures, came later and were as crude as the rest. The New England light is glare, and the atmosphere harshens color. The boy was a full man before he ever knew what was meant by atmosphere; his idea of pleasure in light was the blaze of a New England sun. His idea of color was a peony, with the dew of early morning on its petals. The intense blue of the sea, as he saw it a mile or two away, from the Quincy hills; the cumuli in a June afternoon sky; the strong reds and greens and purples of colored prints and children's picture-books, as the American colors then ran; these were ideals. The opposites or antipathies, were the cold grays of November evenings, and the thick, muddy thaws of Boston winter. With such standards, the Bostonian could not but develop a double nature. Life was a double thing. After a January blizzard, the boy who could look with pleasure into the violent snow-glare of the cold white sunshine, with its intense light and shade, scarcely knew what was meant by tone. He could reach it only by education.

2   Winter and summer, then, were two hostile lives, and bred two separate natures. Winter was always the effort to live; summer was tropical license. Whether the children rolled in the grass, or waded in the brook, or swam in the salt ocean, or sailed in the bay, or fished for smelts in the creeks, or netted minnows in the salt-marshes, or took to the pine-woods and the granite quarries, or chased muskrats and hunted snapping-turtles in the swamps, or mushrooms or nuts on the autumn hills, summer and country were always sensual living, while winter was always compulsory learning. Summer was the multiplicity of nature; winter was school.

3   The bearing of the two seasons on the education of Henry Adams was no fancy; it was the most decisive force he ever knew; it ran through life, and made the division between its perplexing, warring, irreconcilable problems, irreducible opposites, with growing emphasis to the last year of study. From earliest childhood the boy was accustomed to feel that, for him, life was double. Winter and summer, town and country, law and liberty, were hostile, and the man who pretended they were not, was in his eyes a schoolmaster — that is, a man employed to tell lies to little boys. Though Quincy was but two hours' walk from Beacon Hill, it belonged in a different world. For two hundred years, every Adams, from father to son, had lived within sight of State Street, and sometimes had lived in it, yet none had ever taken kindly to the town, or been taken kindly by it. The boy inherited his

in which the old man almost necessarily defeated the boy, but instead of leaving, as usual in such defeats, a lifelong sting, left rather an impression of as fair treatment as could be expected from a natural enemy. The boy met seldom with such restraint. He could not have been much more than six years old at the time — seven at the utmost — and his mother had taken him to Quincy for a long stay with the President during the summer. What became of the rest of the family he quite forgot; but he distinctly remembered standing at the house door one summer morning in a passionate outburst of rebellion against going to school. Naturally his mother was the immediate victim of his rage; that is what mothers are for, and boys also; but in this case the boy had his mother at unfair disadvantage, for she was a guest, and had no means of enforcing obedience. Henry showed a certain tactical ability by refusing to start, and he met all efforts at compulsion by successful, though too vehement protest. He was in fair way to win, and was holding his own, with sufficient energy, at the bottom of the long staircase which led up to the door of the President's library, when the door opened, and the old man slowly came down. Putting on his hat, he took the boy's hand without a word, and walked with him, paralyzed by awe, up the road to the town. After the first moments of consternation at this interference in a domestic dispute, the boy reflected that an old gentleman close on eighty would never trouble himself to walk near a mile on a hot summer morning over a shadeless road to take a boy to school, and that it would be strange if a lad imbued with the passion of freedom could not find a corner to dodge around, somewhere before reaching the school door. Then and always, the boy insisted that this reasoning justified his apparent submission; but the old man did not stop, and the boy saw all his strategical points turned, one after another, until he found himself seated inside the school, and obviously the centre of curious if not malevolent criticism. Not till then did the President release his hand and depart.

The point was that this act, contrary to the inalienable rights of boys, and nullifying the social compact, ought to have made him dislike his grandfather for life. He could not recall that it had this effect even for a moment. With a certain maturity of mind, the child must have recognized that the President, though a tool of tyranny, had done his disreputable work with a certain intelligence. He had shown no temper, no irritation, no personal feeling, and had made no display of force. Above all, he had held his tongue. During their long walk he had said nothing; he had uttered no syllable of revolting cant about the duty of obedience and the wickedness of resistance to law; he had shown no concern in the matter; hardly even a consciousness of the boy's existence. Probably his mind at that moment was actually troubling itself little about his grandson's iniquities, and much about the iniquities of President Polk, but the boy could scarcely at that age feel the whole satisfaction of thinking that President Polk was to be the vicarious victim of his own sins, and he gave his grandfather credit for intelligent silence. For this forbearance he felt instinctive respect. He admitted force as a form of right; he admitted even temper, under protest; but the seeds of moral education would at that moment have fallen on the stoniest soil in Quincy, which is, as every one knows, the stoniest glacial and tidal drift known in any Puritan land.

_____ **CONSIDERATIONS** _____

1. Earlier in his autobiography, Adams gives the reader some idea of how the young Henry, because of the peculiar nature of his family and its position, was burdened with expectations growing out of the family's deep involvement in American history and politics. In this excerpt, study his vocabulary and look for words that express his constant awareness of that involvement.

2. Adams chose an unusual point of view for an autobiography — the third person. Change a given paragraph to the first person point of view to see what difference the author's decision on that technical matter can make.

3. What illustrations does Adams use to help the reader understand what is meant by "He felt his nature crudely. . . ."?

4. Adams's essay might fairly be said to be built upon a system of opposites. List several of these opposites to help you understand how a series of contrasts can serve as an organizing principle of an essay.

5. In Paragraph 6, Adams sets forth clearly and firmly his conviction about what education must be. Judging from your educational experience, to what extent can you agree with him?

6. What allowed the boy to respect his grandfather, even as the old man was disciplining him?

*James Agee (1909–1955) was a journalist, critic, poet, and nov-
elist. He was an early critic of film as art, and wrote the script for*
The African Queen, *among other movies. A heart attack killed
him at forty-five, before he had finished his novel* A Death in the
Family. *Editors assembled the final manuscript and included as
a prologue the essay reprinted here. The novel was awarded the
Pulitzer Prize in 1958. His prose evokes lost time; detail is
described with intimate precision, landscape rendered exactly
with a wash of nostalgia.*

2

JAMES AGEE
Knoxville: Summer 1915

We are talking now of summer evenings in Knoxville, Tennessee 1
in the time that I lived there so successfully disguised to myself as a
child. It was a little bit mixed sort of block, fairly solidly lower middle
class, with one or two juts apiece on either side of that. The houses
corresponded: middle-sized gracefully fretted wood houses built in the
late nineties and early nineteen hundreds, with small front and side
and more spacious back yards, and trees in the yards, and porches.
These were softwooded trees, poplars, tulip trees, cottonwoods. There
were fences around one or two of the houses, but mainly the yards ran
into each other with only now and then a low hedge that wasn't doing
very well. There were few good friends among the grown people, and
they were not poor enough for the other sort of intimate acquaintance,
but everyone nodded and spoke, and even might talk short times,
trivially, and at the two extremes of the general or the particular, and

ordinarily nextdoor neighbors talked quite a bit when they happened to run into each other, and never paid calls. The men were mostly small businessmen, one or two very modestly executives, one or two worked with their hands, most of them clerical, and most of them between thirty and forty-five.

2   But it is of these evenings, I speak.

3   Supper was at six and was over by half past. There was still daylight, shining softly and with a tarnish, like the lining of a shell; and the carbon lamps lifted at the corners were on in the light, and the locusts were started, and the fire flies were out, and a few frogs were flopping in the dewy grass, by the time the fathers and the children came out. The children ran out first hell bent and yelling those names by which they were known; then the fathers sank out leisurely in crossed suspenders, their collars removed and their necks looking tall and shy. The mothers stayed back in the kitchen washing and drying, putting things away, recrossing their traceless footsteps like the life-time journeys of bees, measuring out the dry cocoa for breakfast. When they came out they had taken off their aprons and their skirts were dampened and they sat in rockers on their porches quietly.

4   It is not of the games children played in the evening that I want to speak now, it is of a contemporaneous atmosphere that has little to do with them: that of the fathers of families, each in his space of lawn, his shirt fishlike pale in the unnatural light and his face nearly anonymous, hosing their lawns. The hoses were attached at spigots that stood out of the brick foundations of the houses. The nozzles were variously set but usually so there was a long sweet stream of spray, the nozzle wet in the hand, the water trickling the right forearm and the peeled-back cuff, and the water whishing out a long loose and low-curved cone, and so gentle a sound. First an insane noise of violence in the nozzle, then the still irregular sound of adjustment, then the smoothing into steadiness and a pitch as accurately tuned to the size and style of stream as any violin. So many qualities of sound out of one hose: so many choral differences out of those several hoses that were in earshot. Out of any one hose, the almost dead silence of the release, and the short still arch of the separate big drops, silent as a held breath, and the only noise the flattering noise on leaves and the slapped grass at the fall of each big drop. That, and the intense hiss with the intense stream; that, and that same intensity not growing less but growing more quiet and delicate with the turn of the nozzle, up to that extreme tender whisper when the water was just a wide bell of film. Chiefly, though, the hoses were set much alike, in a compro-

mise between distance and tenderness of spray (and quite surely a sense of art behind this compromise, and a quiet deep joy, too real to recognize itself), and the sounds therefore were pitched much alike; pointed by the snorting start of a new hose; decorated by some man playful with the nozzle; left empty, like God by the sparrow's fall, when any single one of them desists: and all, though near alike, of various pitch; and in this unison. These sweet pale streamings in the light lift out their pallors and their voices all together, mothers hushing their children, the hushing unnaturally prolonged, the men gentle and silent and each snail-like withdrawn into the quietude of what he singly is doing, the urination of huge children stood loosely military against an invisible wall, and gentle happy and peaceful, tasting the mean goodness of their living like the last of their suppers in their mouths; while the locusts carry on this noise of hoses on their much higher and sharper key. The noise of the locust is dry, and it seems not to be rasped or vibrated but urged from him as if through a small orifice by breath that can never give out. Also there is never one locust but an illusion of at least a thousand. The noise of each locust is pitched in some classic locust range out of which none of them varies more than two full tones: and yet you seem to hear each locust discrete from all the rest, and there is a long, slow pulse in their noise, like the scarcely defined arch of a long and high set bridge. They are all around in every tree, so that the noise seems to come from nowhere and everywhere at once, from the whole shell heaven, shivering in your flesh and teasing your eardrums, the boldest of all the sounds of night. And yet it is habitual to summer nights, and is of the great order of noises, like the noises of the sea and of the blood her precocious grandchild, which you realize you are hearing only when you catch yourself listening. Meantime from low in the dark, just outside the swaying horizons of the hoses, conveying always grass in the damp of dew and its strong green-black smear of smell, the regular yet spaced noises of the crickets, each a sweet cold silver noise threenoted, like the slipping each time of three matched links of a small chain.

But the men by now, one by one, have silenced their hoses and 5
drained and coiled them. Now only two, and now only one, is left, and you see only ghostlike shirt with the sleeve garters, and sober mystery of his mild face like the lifted face of large cattle enquiring of your presence in a pitchdark pool of meadow; and now he too is gone; and it has become that time of evening when people sit on their porches, rocking gently and talking gently and watching the street and the standing up into their sphere of possession of the trees, of bird-hung

havens, hangars. People go by; things go by. A horse, drawing a buggy, breaking his hollow iron music on the asphalt; a loud auto; a quiet auto; people in pairs, not in a hurry, scuffling, switching their weight of aestival body, talking casually, the taste hovering over them of vanilla, strawberry, pasteboard and starched milk, the image upon them of lovers and horsemen, squared with clowns in hueless amber. A street car raising its iron moan; stopping, belling and starting; stertorous; rousing and raising again its iron increasing moan and swimming its gold windows and straw seats on past and past and past, the bleak spark crackling and cursing above it like a small malignant spirit set to dog its tracks; the iron whine rises on rising speed; still risen, faints; halts; the faint stinging bell; rises again, still fainter; fainting, lifting, lifts, faints forgone: forgotten. Now is the night one blue dew.

> Now is the night one blue dew, my father has drained, he has
>   coiled the hose.
> Low on the length of lawns, a frailing of fire who breathes.
> Content, silver, like peeps of light, each cricket makes his com-
>   ment over and over in the drowned grass.
> A cold toad thumpily flounders.
> Within the edges of damp shadows of side yards are hovering chil-
>   dren nearly sick with joy of fear, who watch the unguarding of a
>   telephone pole.
> Around white carbon corner lamps bugs of all sizes are lifted ellip-
>   tic, solar systems. Big hardshells bruise themselves, assailant:
>   he is fallen on his back, legs squiggling.
> Parents on porches: rock and rock: From damp strings morning
>   glories: hang their ancient faces.
> The dry and exalted noise of the locusts from all the air at once
>   enchants my eardrums.

6   On the rough wet grass of the back yard my father and mother have spread quilts. We all lie there, my mother, my father, my uncle, my aunt, and I too am lying there. First we were sitting up, then one of us lay down, and then we all lay down, on our stomachs, or on our sides, or on our backs, and they have kept on talking. They are not talking much, and the talk is quiet, of nothing in particular, of nothing at all in particular, of nothing at all. The stars are wide and alive, they seem each like a smile of great sweetness, and they seem very near. All my people are larger bodies than mine, quiet, with voices gentle and meaningless like the voices of sleeping birds. One is an artist, he is living at home. One is a musician, she is living at home. One is my mother who is good to me. One is my father who is good to me. By

some chance, here they are, all on this earth; and who shall ever tell the sorrow of being on their earth, lying, on quilts, on the grass, in a summer evening, among the sounds of the night. May God bless my people, my uncle, my aunt, my mother, my good father, oh, remember them kindly in their time of trouble; and in the hour of their taking away.

After a little I am taken in and put to bed. Sleep, soft smiling, draws me unto her: and those receive me, who quietly treat me, as one familiar and well beloved in that home: but will not, oh, will not, not now, not ever; but will not ever tell me who I am.   7

___ CONSIDERATIONS _____

1. Agee is famous for the close attention he pays to the senses. In this piece, which one — seeing, hearing, smelling, tasting, touching — is exercised the most?

2. What do you make of Agee's paragraph sense? Compare, for example, Paragraph 2 with Paragraph 4. Would you recommend breaking the latter into smaller units? Where? Why, or why not?

3. The first sentence of Paragraph 1 offers an opportunity for experimentation. Copy it out *without* the following phrases: "so successfully," "disguised," and "to myself." Then replace the phrases, one at a time, considering how each addition changes the dimension, the direction, or the depth of the story begun. Which of the three works the greatest change? Why?

4. How does the first sentence embody a theme important to the whole story? Is that theme sounded elsewhere in the story?

5. Agee's evocation of a summer evening might seem strange to an apartment-dweller in Knoxville in 1981. Would it be possible to write so serenely about a summer evening in the Knoxville — or Detroit, or Minneapolis, or San Francisco — of today?

6. Agee's attempt to recapture and thus understand his childhood — or at least a moment of it — is similar to and different from the efforts of several other writers in this book. Compare and contrast "Knoxville: Summer 1915" with one of these: Henry Adams (pages 1–6); Frank Conroy (pages 84–91); Lillian Hellman (pages 178–185); Langston Hughes (pages 192–194); or E. B. White (pages 442–449).

Woody Allen (b. 1935) is a universal genius, best known for acting in, writing, and directing movies. His films range from What's New, Pussycat? *(1964) through* Love and Death *(1975) and* Annie Hall *(1977) to* Stardust Memories *(1980) and he has also published short fiction in* Playboy *and* The New Yorker. *In 1978 he won an O. Henry Award for the best American short story of the previous year. His prose is collected in three volumes,* Getting Even *(1972),* Without Feathers *(1975), and* Side Effects *(1980).*

He began his career as a comedy writer for television shows, then became a comedian himself. His first great successes were Broadway plays, Don't Drink the Water *(1966) and* Play It Again, Sam *(1969). This playlet comes from* Getting Even.

3

WOODY ALLEN
Death Knocks

1   *(The play takes place in the bedroom of the Nat Ackermans' two-story house, somewhere in Kew Gardens. The carpeting is wall-to-wall. There is a big double bed and a large vanity. The room is elaborately furnished and curtained, and on the walls there are several paintings and a not really attractive barometer. Soft theme music as the curtain rises. Nat Ackerman, a bald, paunchy fifty-seven-year-old dress manufacturer, is lying on the bed finishing off tomorrow's* Daily News. *He wears a bathrobe and slippers, and reads by a bed light clipped to the white headboard of the bed. The time is near midnight. Suddenly we hear a noise, and Nat sits up and looks at the window.)*

Nat: What the hell is that?

(Climbing awkwardly through the window is a sombre, caped figure. The intruder wears a black hood and skintight black clothes. The hood covers his head but not his face, which is middle-aged and stark white. He is something like Nat in appearance. He huffs audibly and then trips over the windowsill and falls into the room.)

Death *(for it is no one else):* Jesus Christ. I nearly broke my neck.

Nat *(watching with bewilderment):* Who are you? 5

Death: Death.

Nat: Who?

Death: Death. Listen — can I sit down? I nearly broke my neck. I'm shaking like a leaf.

Nat: Who *are* you?

Death: *Death.* You got a glass of water? 10

Nat: Death? What do you mean, Death?

Death: What is wrong with you? You see the black costume and the whitened face?

Nat: Yeah.

Death: Is it Halloween?

Nat: No. 15

Death: Then I'm Death. Now can I get a glass of water — or a Fresca?

Nat: If this is some joke —

Death: What kind of joke? You're fifty-seven? Nat Ackerman? One eighteen Pacific Street? Unless I blew it — where's that call sheet? *(He fumbles through pocket, finally producing a card with an address on it. It seems to check.)*

Nat: What do you want with me?

Death: What do I want? What do you think I want? 20

Nat: You must be kidding. I'm in perfect health.

Death *(unimpressed):* Uh-huh. *(Looking around)* This is a nice place. You do it yourself?

Nat: We had a decorator, but we worked with her.

Death *(looking at the picture on the wall):* I love those kids with the big eyes.

Nat: I don't want to go yet. 25

Death: *You* don't want to go? Please don't start in. As it is, I'm nauseous from the climb.

Nat: What climb?

Death: I climbed up the drainpipe. I was trying to make a dramatic entrance. I see the big windows and you're awake reading.

I figure it's worth a shot. I'll climb up and enter with a little —
you know . . . *(Snaps fingers)* Meanwhile, I get my heel caught on
some vines, the drainpipe breaks, and I'm hanging by a thread.
Then my cape begins to tear. Look, let's just go. It's been a rough
night.

    Nat: You broke my drainpipe?

30   Death: Broke. It didn't break. It's a little bent. Didn't you hear
anything? I slammed into the ground.

    Nat: I was reading.

    Death: You must have really been engrossed. *(Lifting newspaper
Nat was reading)* "NAB COEDS IN POT ORGY." Can I borrow this?

    Nat: I'm not finished.

    Death: Er — I don't know how to put this to you, pal . . .

35   Nat: Why didn't you just ring downstairs?

    Death: I'm telling you, I could have, but how does it look? This
way I get a little drama going. Something. Did you read *Faust?*

    Nat: What?

    Death: And what if you had company? You're sitting there with
important people. I'm Death — I should ring the bell and traipse right
in the front? Where's your thinking?

    Nat: Listen, Mister, it's very late.

40   Death: Yeah. Well, you want to go?

    Nat: Go where?

    Death: Death. It. The Thing. The Happy Hunting Grounds.
(Looking at his own knee) Y'know, that's a pretty bad cut. My first
job, I'm liable to get gangrene yet.

    Nat: Now, wait a minute. I need time. I'm not ready to go.

    Death: I'm sorry. I can't help you. I'd like to, but it's the moment.

45   Nat: How can it be the moment? I just merged with Modiste
Originals.

    Death: What's the difference, a couple of bucks more or less.

    Nat: Sure, what do you care? You guys probably have all your
expenses paid.

    Death: You want to come along now?

    Nat *(studying him):* I'm sorry, but I cannot believe you're Death.

50   Death: Why? What'd you expect — Rock Hudson?

    Nat: No, it's not that.

    Death: I'm sorry if I disappointed you.

    Nat: Don't get upset. I don't know, I always thought you'd be . . .
uh . . . taller.

    Death: I'm five seven. It's average for my weight.

Nat: You look a little like me.   55
Death: Who should I look like? I'm your death.
Nat: Give me some time. Another day.
Death: I can't. What do you want me to say?
Nat: One more day. Twenty-four hours.
Death: What do you need it for? The radio said rain tomorrow.   60
Nat: Can't we work out something?
Death: Like what?
Nat: You play chess?
Death: No, I don't.
Nat: I once saw a picture of you playing chess.   65
Death: Couldn't be me, because I don't play chess. Gin rummy,
maybe.
Nat: You play gin rummy?
Death: Do I play gin rummy? Is Paris a city?
Nat: You're good, huh?
Death: Very good.   70
Nat: I'll tell you what I'll do —
Death: Don't make any deals with me.
Nat: I'll play you gin rummy. If you win, I'll go immediately. If I
win, give me some more time. A little bit — one more day.
Death: Who's got time to play gin rummy?
Nat: Come on. If you're so good.   75
Death: Although I feel like a game . . .
Nat: Come on. Be a sport. We'll shoot for a half hour.
Death: I really shouldn't.
Nat: I got the cards right here. Don't make a production.
Death: All right, come on. We'll play a little. It'll relax me.   80
Nat *(getting cards, pad, and pencil):* You won't regret this.
Death: Don't give me a sales talk. Get the cards and give me a
Fresca and put out something. For God's sake, a stranger drops in, you
don't have potato chips or pretzels.
Nat: There's M&M's downstairs in a dish.
Death: M&M's. What if the President came? He'd get M&M's
too?
Nat: You're not the President.   85
Death: Deal.
(Nat deals, turns up a five.)
Nat: You want to play a tenth of a cent a point to make it inter-
esting?
Death: It's not interesting enough for you?

90   Nat: I play better when money's at stake.
      Death: Whatever you say, Newt.
      Nat: Nat. Nat Ackerman. You don't know my name?
      Death: Newt, Nat — I got such a headache.
      Nat: You want that five?
95   Death: No.
      Nat: So pick.
      Death *(surveying his hand as he picks):* Jesus, I got nothing here.
      Nat: What's it like?
      Death: What's what like?
100   *(Throughout the following, they pick and discard.)*
      Nat: Death.
      Death: What should it be like? You lay there.
      Nat: Is there anything after?
      Death: Aha, you're saving twos.
105   Nat: I'm asking. Is there anything after?
      Death *(absently):* You'll see.
      Nat: Oh, then I will actually see something?
      Death: Well, maybe I shouldn't have put it that way. Throw.
      Nat: To get an answer from you is a big deal.
110   Death: I'm playing cards.
      Nat: All right, play, play.
      Death: Meanwhile, I'm giving you one card after another.
      Nat: Don't look through the discards.
      Death: I'm not looking. I'm straightening them up. What was the
      knock card?
115   Nat: Four. You ready to knock already?
      Death: Who said I'm ready to knock? All I asked was what was
      the knock card.
      Nat: And all I asked was is there anything for me to look forward
      to.
      Death: Play.
      Nat: Can't you tell me anything? Where do we go?
120   Death: We? To tell you the truth, *you* fall in a crumpled heap on
      the floor.
      Nat: Oh, I can't wait for that! Is it going to hurt?
      Death: Be over in a second.
      Nat: Terrific *(Sighs)* I needed this. A man merges with Modiste
      Originals . . .
      Death: How's four points?
125   Nat: You're knocking?
      Death: Four points is good?

Nat: No, I got two.

Death: You're kidding.

Nat: No, you lose.

Death: Holy Christ, and I thought you were saving sixes.　　130

Nat: No. Your deal. Twenty points and two boxes. Shoot. *(Death deals.)* I must fall on the floor, eh? I can't be standing over the sofa when it happens?

Death: No. Play.

Nat: Why not?

Death: Because you fall on the floor! Leave me alone. I'm trying to concentrate.

Nat: Why must it be on the floor? That's all I'm saying! Why　　135 can't the whole thing happen and I'll stand next to the sofa?

Death: I'll try my best. Now can we play?

Nat: That's all I'm saying. You remind me of Moe Lefkowitz. He's also stubborn.

Death: I remind him of Moe Lefkowitz. I'm one of the most terrifying figures you could possibly imagine, and him I remind of Moe Lefkowitz. What is he, a furrier?

Nat: You should be such a furrier. He's good for eighty thousand a year. Passementeries. He's got his own factory. Two points.

Death: What?　　140

Nat: Two points. I'm knocking. What have you got?

Death: My hand is like a basketball score.

Nat: And it's spades.

Death: If you didn't talk so much.

(They redeal and play on.)　　145

Nat: What'd you mean before when you said this was your first job?

Death: What does it sound like?

Nat: What are you telling me — that nobody ever went before?

Death: Sure they went. But I didn't take them.

Nat: So who did?　　150

Death: Others.

Nat: There's others?

Death: Sure. Each one has his own personal way of going.

Nat: I never knew that.

Death: Why should you know? Who are you?　　155

Nat: What do you mean who am I? Why — I'm nothing?

Death: Not nothing. You're a dress manufacturer. Where do you come to knowledge of the eternal mysteries?

Nat: What are you talking about? I make a beautiful dollar. I sent two kids through college. One is in advertising, the other's married. I got my own home. I drive a Chrysler. My wife has whatever she wants. Maids, mink coat, vacations. Right now she's at the Eden Roc. Fifty dollars a day because she wants to be near her sister. I'm supposed to join her next week, so what do you think I am — some guy off the street?

Death: All right. Don't be so touchy.

160   Nat: Who's touchy?

Death: How would you like it if I got insulted quickly?

Nat: Did I insult you?

Death: You didn't say you were disappointed in me?

Nat: What do you expect? You want me to throw you a block party?

165   Death: I'm not talking about that. I mean me personally. I'm too short, I'm this, I'm that.

Nat: I said you looked like me. It's a reflection.

Death: All right, deal, deal.

(They continue to play as music steals in and the lights dim until all is in total darkness. The lights slowly come up again, and now it is later and their game is over. Nat tallies.)

Nat: Sixty-eight . . . one-fifty . . . Well, you lose.

170   Death *(dejectedly looking through the deck):* I knew I shouldn't have thrown that nine. Damn it.

Nat: So I'll see you tomorrow.

Death: What do you mean you'll see me tomorrow?

Nat: I won the extra day. Leave me alone.

Death: You were serious?

175   Nat: We made a deal.

Death: Yeah, but —

Nat: Don't "but" me. I won twenty-four hours. Come back tomorrow.

Death: I didn't know we were actually playing for time.

Nat: That's too bad about you. You should pay attention.

180   Death: Where am I going to go for twenty-four hours?

Nat: What's the difference? The main thing is I won an extra day.

Death: What do you want me to do — walk the streets?

Nat: Check into a hotel and go to a movie. Take a *schvitz*. Don't make a federal case.

Death: Add the score again.

185   Nat: Plus you owe me twenty-eight dollars.

Death: *What?*

Nat: That's right, Buster. Here it is — read it.

Death *(going through pockets):* I have a few singles — not twenty-eight dollars.

Nat: I'll take a check.

Death: From what account?   190

Nat: Look who I'm dealing with.

Death: Sue me. Where do I keep my checking account?

Nat: All right, gimme what you got and we'll call it square.

Death: Listen, I need that money.

Nat: Why should you need money?   195

Death: What are you talking about? You're going to the Beyond.

Nat: So?

Death: So — you know how far that is?

Nat: So?

Death: So where's gas? Where's tolls?   200

Nat: We're going by car!

Death: You'll find out. *(Agitatedly)* Look — I'll be back tomorrow, and you'll give me a chance to win the money back. Otherwise I'm in definite trouble.

Nat: Anything you want. Double or nothing we'll play. I'm liable to win an extra week or a month. The way you play, maybe years.

Death: Meantime I'm stranded.

Nat: See you tomorrow.   205

Death: *(being edged to the doorway):* Where's a good hotel? What am I talking about hotel, I got no money. I'll go sit in Bickford's. *(He picks up the* News.*)*

Nat: Out. Out. That's my paper *(He takes it back.)*

Death *(exiting):* I couldn't just take him and go. I had to get involved in rummy.

Nat *(calling after him):* And be careful going downstairs. On one of the steps the rug is loose.

(And, on cue, we hear a terrific crash. Nat sighs, then crosses to   210
the bedside table and makes a phone call.)

Nat: Hello, Moe? Me. Listen, I don't know if somebody's playing a joke, or what, but Death was just here. We played a little gin . . . No, *Death.* In person. Or somebody who claims to be Death. But, Moe, he's such a *schlep!*

CURTAIN

_____ CONSIDERATIONS _____

1. Death is something most people avoid talking about. Instead they fall back on euphemisms. Make a collection of euphemisms for death and dying and write an essay on the subject.

2. Nat is insulted by the suggestion that he doesn't know anything about death. "I make a beautiful dollar," he protests. "I sent two kids through college . . ." What do you think of the *logic* of his reply?

3. Obviously, dialogue is everything in a play. Study how some of the other writers in this book make use of dialogue in essays and stories. How could you use it in a forthcoming essay?

4. Nat: You want to play a tenth of a cent a point to make it interesting?
    Death: It's not interesting enough for you?
What does this exchange suggest about habitual or superficial vs. real or essential values? Are the same ideas suggested by the hackneyed expression, "The condemned man ate a hearty breakfast"?

5. The Kew Gardens mentioned in the stage-setting for "Death Knocks" is not the site of the Royal Botanical Gardens in London, but a residential section in a suburb of New York City. As you *listen* to the lines of the play, do you hear any clues that the characters are New Yorkers, not Londoners? Can you find other authors in this book who make use of voice in their work?

6. Woody Allen's playlet is a somewhat unusual example of a writer using personification. What are some more common personifications of death — in essays, stories, poems, cartoons, movies? Many other authors in this book use this literary device. Study their examples, then try your hand at personification.

Maya Angelou (b. 1928) told an interviewer, "One would say of my life — born loser — had to be; from a broken family, raped at eight, unwed mother at sixteen . . . it's a fact, but it's not the truth."

When she grew up, Maya Angelou became an actress, a singer, a dancer, a songwriter, a teacher, an editor, and a poet. She sang and danced professionally in Porgy and Bess *with a company that traveled through twenty-two countries of Europe and Asia. She wrote for the* Ghana Times *and she taught modern dance in Rome and in Tel Aviv. Her recent book are* And Still I Rise *(1978) and* The Heart of a Woman *(1981).*

In 1969 she began her autobiography; I Know Why the Caged Bird Sings *was an immediate success. As she says, "I speak to the black experience, but I am always talking about the human condition." The book recounts her early life, with realism and with joy. This section describes a masterful black con man, skill-ful at turning white bigotry into black profits.*

4

MAYA ANGELOU

Mr. Red Leg

Our house was a fourteen-room typical San Franciscan post-Earthquake affair. We had a succession of roomers, bringing and taking their different accents, and personalities and foods. Shipyard workers clanked up the stairs (we all slept on the second floor except Mother and Daddy Clidell) in their steel-tipped boots and metal hats, and gave way to much-powdered prostitutes, who giggled through their makeup 1 and hung their wigs on the door-knobs. One couple (they were college graduates) held long adult conversations with me in the big kitchen downstairs, until the husband went off to war. Then the wife who had been so charming and ready to smile changed into a silent shadow that played infrequently along the walls. An older couple lived with us for a year or so. They owned a restaurant and had no personality to enchant or interest a teenager, except that the husband was called Uncle Jim, and the wife Aunt Boy. I never figured that out.

2   The quality of strength lined with tenderness is an unbeatable combination, as are intelligence and necessity when unblunted by formal education. I was prepared to accept Daddy Clidell as one more faceless name added to Mother's roster of conquests. I had trained myself so successfully through the years to display interest, or at least attention, while my mind skipped free on other subjects that I could have lived in his house without ever seeing him and without his becoming the wiser. But his character beckoned and elicited admiration. He was a simple man who had no inferiority complex about his lack of education and, even more amazing, no superiority complex because he had succeeded despite that lack. He would say often, "I had been to school three years in my life. In Slaten, Texas, times was hard, and I had to help my daddy on the farm."

3   No recriminations lay hidden under the plain statement, nor was there boasting when he said, "If I'm living a little better now, it's because I treats everybody right."

4   He owned apartment buildings and, later, pool halls, and was famous for being that rarity "a man of honor." He didn't suffer, as many "honest men" do, from the detestable righteousness that diminishes their virtue. He knew cards and men's hearts. So during the age when Mother was exposing us to certain facts of life, like personal hygiene, proper posture, table manners, good restaurants and tipping practices, Daddy Clidell taught me to play poker, blackjack, tonk and high, low, Jick, Jack and the Game. He wore expensive tailored suits and a large yellow diamond stickpin. Except for the jewelry, he was a conservative dresser and carried himself with the unconscious pomp of a man of secure means. Unexpectedly, I resembled him, and when he, Mother and I walked down the street his friends often said, "Clidell, that's sure your daughter. Ain't no way you can deny her."

5   Proud laughter followed those declarations, for he had never had   5
children. Because of his late-arriving but intense paternal sense, I was introduced to the most colorful characters in the Black underground. One afternoon, I was invited into our smoke-filled dining room to

make the acquaintance of Stonewall Jimmy, Just Black, Cool Clyde, Tight Coat and Red Leg. Daddy Clidell explained to me that they were the most successful con men in the world, and they were going to tell me about some games so that I would never be "anybody's mark."

To begin, one man warned me, "There ain't never been a mark   6
yet that didn't want something for nothing." Then they took turns showing me their tricks, how they chose their victims (marks) from the wealthy bigoted whites and in every case how they used the victims' prejudice against them.

Some of the tales were funny, a few were pathetic, but all were   7
amusing or gratifying to me, for the Black man, the con man who could act the most stupid, won out every time over the powerful, arrogant white.

I remember Mr. Red Leg's story like a favorite melody.   8

"Anything that works against you can also work for you once   9
you understand the Principle of Reverse.

"There was a cracker in Tulsa who bilked so many Negroes he   10
could set up a Negro Bilking Company. Naturally he got to thinking, Black Skin means Damn Fool. Just Black and I went to Tulsa to check him out. Come to find out, he's a perfect mark. His momma must have been scared in an Indian massacre in Africa. He hated Negroes only a little more than he despised Indians. And he was greedy.

"Black and I studied him and decided he was worth setting up   11
against the store. That means we were ready to put out a few thousand dollars in preparation. We pulled in a white boy from New York, a good con artist, and had him open an office in Tulsa. He was supposed to be a Northern real estate agent trying to buy up valuable land in Oklahoma. We investigated a piece of land near Tulsa that had a toll bridge crossing it. It used to be part of an Indian reservation but had been taken over by the state.

"Just Black was laid out as the decoy, and I was going to be the   12
fool. After our friend from New York hired a secretary and had his cards printed, Black approached the mark with a proposition. He told him that he had heard that our mark was the only white man colored people could trust. He named some of the poor fools that had been taken by that crook. It just goes to show you how white folks can be deceived by their own deception. The mark believed Black.

"Black told him about his friend who was half Indian and half   13
colored and how some Northern white real estate agent had found out that he was the sole owner of a piece of valuable land and the Northerner wanted to buy it. At first the man acted like he smelled a rat,

but from the way he gobbled up the proposition, turns out what he thought he smelled was some nigger money on his top lip.

14   "He asked the whereabouts of the land but Black put him off. He told this cracker that he just wanted to make sure that he would be interested. The mark allowed how he was being interested, so Black said he would tell his friend and they'd get in touch with him. Black met the mark for about three weeks in cars and in alleys and kept putting him off until the white man was almost crazy with anxiety and greed and then accidentally it seemed Black let drop the name of the Northern real estate agent who wanted the property. From that moment on we knew we had the big fish on the line and all we had to do was to pull him in.

15   "We expected him to try to contact our store, which he did. That cracker went to our setup and counted on his whiteness to ally him with Spots, our white boy, but Spots refused to talk about the deal except to say the land had been thoroughly investigated by the biggest real estate concern in the South and that if our mark did not go around raising dust he would make sure that there would be a nice piece of money in it for him. Any obvious inquiries as to the rightful owner-ship of the land could alert the state and they would surely push through a law prohibiting the sale. Spots told the mark he would keep in touch with him. The mark went back to the store three or four times but to no avail, then just before we knew he would crack, Black brought me to see him. That fool was as happy as a sissy in a C.C.C. camp. You would have thought my neck was in a noose and he was about to light the fire under my feet. I never enjoyed taking anybody so much.

16   "Anyhow, I played scary at first but Just Black told me that this was one white man that our people could trust. I said I did not trust no white man because all they wanted was to get a chance to kill a Black man legally and get his wife in the bed. (I'm sorry, Clidell.) The mark assured me that he was the only white man who did not feel like that. Some of his best friends were colored people. In fact, if I didn't know it, the woman who raised him was a colored woman and he still sees her to this day. I let myself be convinced and then the mark began to drag the Northern whites. He told me that they made Negroes sleep in the street in the North and that they had to clean out toilets with their hands in the North and even things worse than that. I was shocked and said, 'Then I don't want to sell my land to that white man who offered seventy-five thousand dollars for it.' Just Black said, 'I wouldn't know what to do with that kind of money,' and I said

that all I wanted was to have enough money to buy a home for my old mom, to buy a business and to make one trip to Harlem. The mark asked how much would that cost and I said I reckoned I could do it on fifty thousand dollars.

"The mark told me no Negro was safe with that kind of money. 17 That white folks would take it from him. I said I knew it but I had to have at least forty thousand dollars. He agreed. We shook hands. I said it would do my heart good to see the mean Yankee go down on some of 'our land.' We met the next morning and I signed the deed in his car and he gave me the cash.

"Black and I had kept most of our things in a hotel over in Hot 18 Springs, Arkansas. When the deal was closed we walked to our car, drove across the state line and on to Hot Springs.

"That's all there was to it." 19

When he finished, more triumphant stories rainbowed around 20 the room riding the shoulders of laughter. By all accounts those story-tellers, born Black and male before the turn of the twentieth century, should have been ground into useless dust. Instead they used their intelligence to pry open the door of rejection and not only became wealthy but got some revenge in the bargain.

It wasn't possible for me to regard them as criminals or be any- 21 thing but proud of their achievements.

The needs of a society determine its ethics, and in the Black 22 American ghettos the hero is that man who is offered only the crumbs from his country's table but by ingenuity and courage is able to take for himself a Lucullan feast. Hence the janitor who lives in one room but sports a robin's-egg-blue Cadillac is not laughed at but admired, and the domestic who buys forty-dollar shoes is not criticized but is appreciated. We know that they have put to use their full mental and physical powers. Each single gain feeds into the gains of the body collective.

Stories of law violations are weighed on a different set of scales 23 in the Black mind than in the white. Petty crimes embarrass the com-munity and many people wistfully wonder why Negroes don't rob more banks, embezzle more funds and employ graft in the unions. "We are the victims of the world's most comprehensive robbery. Life demands a balance. It's all right if we do a little robbing now." This belief appeals particularly to one who is unable to compete legally with his fellow citizens.

My education and that of my Black associates were quite differ- 24 ent from the education of our white schoolmates. In the classroom we all learned past participles, but in the streets and in our homes the Blacks learned to drop *s*'s from plurals and suffixes from past-tense verbs. We were alert to the gap separating the written word from the colloquial. We learned to slide out of one language and into another without being conscious of the effort. At school, in a given situation, we might respond with "That's not unusual." But in the street, meeting the same situation, we easily said, "It be's like that sometimes."

_____ CONSIDERATIONS _____

1. Most of Angelou's essay is devoted to Mr. Red Leg telling a story. Notice how close to pure narration that story is. Compare it with the selections in this book by Annie Dillard (pages 102–108), George Orwell (pages 293–321), or Richard Wright (pages 466–475), and contrast the amount of description and narration in Mr. Red Leg's story to that in one of the others.

2. Compare Angelou's essay with that of Frank Conroy (pages 84–91), who also emphasizes memorable characters. How do the two authors differ in their reasons for devoting so much space to Mr. Red Leg and to Ramos and Ricardo?

3. At the end of her essay, Angelou sets out an important linguistic principle. Paraphrase that idea and provide examples from your own experience or research.

4. "Stories of law violations are weighed on a different set of scales in the Black mind than in the white." Is a similar difference seen in the minds of two generations? Discuss relative justice versus absolute law.

5. Angelou demonstrates her versatility as a writer frequently in this essay by managing two voices. Find examples and discuss.

6. From what you learn of Angelou's upbringing in the essay, compile a *negative report* by a social worker on Angelou's childhood. Are there positive details in the essay that would allow you to refute a negative report?

Mary Austin (1868–1934) was born in Illinois, then moved with her family to Southern California when she was eighteen. The desert landscape dazzled her. After a brief and unhappy marriage, she devoted herself to writing, and before her death had published more than thirty books, including poems, plays, essays, and fiction. She lived for some years in Carmel, California, among a group of artists that included the novelist Jack London. Later she moved to Santa Fe, New Mexico, where she continued her study of Native American culture. Also a feminist, she wrote The Young Woman Citizen, *in 1918, as a political handbook for the recently enfranchised American female.*

"The Scavengers" comes from Austin's first book The Land of Little Rain *(1903) which tenderly preserves the astonishment felt by the eighteen-year-old from Illinois when she arrived in the San Joaquin valley.*

5

MARY AUSTIN

The Scavengers

Fifty-seven buzzards, one on each of fifty-seven fence posts at the rancho El Tejon, on a mirage-breeding September morning, sat solemnly while the white tilted travelers' vans lumbered down the Canada de los Uvas. After three hours they had only clapped their wings, or exchanged posts. The season's end in the vast dim valley of the San Joaquin is palpitatingly hot, and the air breathes like cotton wool. Through it all the buzzards sit on the fences and low hummocks, with wings spread fanwise for air. There is no end to them, and they smell to heaven. Their heads droop, and all their communication is a rare, horrid croak.

The increase of wild creatures is in proportion to the things they 2 feed upon: the more carrion the more buzzards. The end of the third successive dry year bred them beyond belief. The first year quail mated sparingly; the second year the wild oats matured no seed; the third, cattle died in their tracks with their heads towards the stopped water-courses. And that year the scavengers were as black as the plague all across the mesa and up the treeless, tumbled hills. On clear days they betook themselves to the upper air, where they hung motionless for hours. That year there were vultures among them, distinguished by the white patches under the wings. All their offensiveness notwith-standing, they have a stately flight. They must also have what pass for good qualities among themselves, for they are social, not to say clan-nish.

3   It is a very squalid tragedy, — that of the dying brutes and the scavenger birds. Death by starvation is slow. The heavy-headed, rack-boned cattle totter in the fruitless trails; they stand for long, patient intervals; they lie down and do not rise. There is fear in their eyes when they are first stricken, but afterward only intolerable weariness. I suppose the dumb creatures know nearly as much of death as do their betters, who have only the more imagination. Their even-breathing submission after the first agony is their tribute to its inevitableness. It needs a nice discrimination to say which of the basket-ribbed cattle is likest to afford the next meal, but the scavengers make few mistakes. One stoops to the quarry and the flock follows.

4   Cattle once down may be days in dying. They stretch out their necks along the ground, and roll up their slow eyes at longer intervals. The buzzards have all the time, and no beak is dropped or talon struck until the breath is wholly passed. It is doubtless the economy of nature to have the scavengers by to clean up the carrion, but a wolf at the throat would be a shorter agony than the long stalking and sometime perchings of these loathsome watchers. Suppose now it were a man in this long-drawn, hungrily spied upon distress! When Timmie O'Shea was lost on Armogosa Flats for three days without water, Long Tom Basset found him, not by any trail, but by making straight away for the points where he saw buzzards stooping. He could hear the beat of their wings, Tom said, and trod on their shadows, but O'Shea was past recalling what he thought about things after the second day. My friend Ewan told me, among other things, when he came back from San Juan Hill, that not all the carnage of battle turned his bowels as the sight of slant black wings rising flockwise before the burial squad.

5   There are three kinds of noises buzzards make, — it is impossible to call them notes, — raucous and elemental. There is a short crack of

alarm, and the same syllable in a modified tone to serve all the purposes of ordinary conversation. The old birds make a kind of throaty chuckling to their young, but if they have any love song I have not heard it. The young yawp in the nest a little, with more breath than noise. It is seldom one finds a buzzard's nest, seldom that grown-ups find a nest of any sort; it is only children to whom these things happen by right. But by making a business of it one may come upon them in wide, quiet cañons, or on the lookouts of lonely, table-topped mountains, three or four together, in the tops of stubby trees or on rotten cliffs well open to the sky.

It is probable that the buzzard is gregarious, but it seems unlikely   6 from the small number of young noted at any time that every female incubates each year. The young birds are easily distinguished by their size when feeding, and high up in air by the worn primaries of the older birds. It is when the young go out of the nest on their first foraging that the parents, full of a crass and simple pride, make their indescribable chucklings of gobbling, gluttonous delight. The little ones would be amusing as they tug and tussle, if one could forget what it is they feed upon.

One never comes any nearer to the vulture's nest or nestling   7 than hearsay. They keep to the southerly Sierras, and are bold enough, it seems, to do killing on their own account when no carrion is at hand. They dog the shepherd from camp to camp, the hunter home from the hill, and will even carry away offal from under his hand.

The vulture merits respect for his bigness and for his bandit airs,   8 but he is a sombre bird, with none of the buzzard's frank satisfaction in his offensiveness.

The least objectionable of the inland scavengers is the raven,   9 frequenter of the desert ranges, the same called locally "carrion crow." He is handsomer and has such an air. He is nice in his habits and is said to have likable traits. A tame one in a Shoshone camp was the butt of much sport and enjoyed it. He could all but talk and was another with the children, but an arrant thief. The raven will eat most things that come his way, — eggs and young of ground-nesting birds, seeds even, lizards and grasshoppers, which he catches cleverly; and whatever he is about, let a coyote trot never so softly by, the raven flaps up and after; for whatever the coyote can pull down or nose out is meat also for the carrion crow.

And never a coyote comes out of his lair for killing, in the country of the carrion crows, but looks up first to see where they may be   10 gathering. It is a sufficient occupation for a windy morning, on the

lineless, level mesa, to watch the pair of them eying each other fur-
tively, with a tolerable assumption of unconcern, but no doubt with a
certain amount of good understanding about it. Once at Red Rock, in
a year of green pasture, which is a bad time for the scavengers, we saw
two buzzards, five ravens, and a coyote feeding on the same carrion,
and only the coyote seemed ashamed of the company.

11   Probably we never fully credit the interdependence of wild creatures, and their cognizance of the affairs of their own kind. When the
five coyotes that range the Tejon from Pasteria to Tunawai planned a
relay race to bring down an antelope strayed from the band, beside
myself to watch, an eagle swung down from Mt. Pinos, buzzards materialized out of invisible ether, and hawks came trooping like small
boys to a street fight. Rabbits sat up in the chaparral and cocked their
ears, feeling themselves quite safe for the once as the hunt swung near
them. Nothing happens in the deep wood that the blue jays are not all
agog to tell. The hawk follows the badger, the coyote the carrion crow,
and from their aerial stations the buzzards watch each other. What
would be worth knowing is how much of their neighbor's affairs the
new generations learn for themselves, and how much they are taught
of their elders.

12   So wide is the range of the scavengers that it is never safe to say,
eyewitness to the contrary, that there are few or many in such a place.
Where the carrion is, there will the buzzards be gathered together, and
in three days' journey you will not sight another one. The way up from
Mojave to Red Butte is all desertness, affording no pasture and scarcely
a rill of water. In a year of little rain in the south, flocks and herds
were driven to the number of thousands along this road to the perennial pastures of the high ranges. It is a long, slow trail, ankle deep in
bitter dust that gets up in the slow wind and moves along the backs of
the crawling cattle. In the worst of times one in three will pine and
fall out by the way. In the defiles of Red Rock, the sheep piled up a
stinking lane; it was the sun smiting by day. To these shambles came
buzzards, vultures, and coyotes from all the country round, so that on
the Tejon, the Ceriso, and the Little Antelope there were not scavengers enough to keep the country clean. All that summer the dead
mummified in the open or dropped slowly back to earth in the quag-
mires of the bitter springs. Meanwhile from Red Rock to Coyote
Holes, and from Coyote Holes to Haiwai the scavengers gorged and
gorged.

13   The coyote is not a scavenger by choice, preferring his own kill,
but being on the whole a lazy dog, is apt to fall into carrion eating

because it is easier. The red fox and bobcat, a little pressed by hunger, will eat of any other animal's kill, but will not ordinarily touch what dies of itself, and are exceedingly shy of food that has been man-handled.

Very clean and handsome, quite belying his relationship in appearance, is Clark's crow, that scavenger and plunderer of mountain camps. It is permissible to call him by his common name, "Camp Robber:" he has earned it. Not content with refuse, he pecks open meal sacks, filches whole potatoes, is a gormand for bacon, drills holes in packing cases, and is daunted by nothing short of tin. All the while he does not neglect to vituperate the chipmunks and sparrows that whisk off crumbs of comfort from under the camper's feet. The Camp Robber's gray coat, black and white barred wings, and slender bill, with certain tricks of perching, accuse him of attempts to pass himself off among woodpeckers; but his behavior is all crow. He frequents the higher pine belts, and has a noisy strident call like a jay's, and how clean he and the frisk-tailed chipmunks keep the camp! No crumb or paring or bit of eggshell goes amiss.

High as the camp may be, so it is not above timberline, it is not too high for the coyote, the bobcat, or the wolf. It is the complaint of the ordinary camper that the woods are too still, depleted of wild life. But what dead body of wild thing, or neglected game untouched by its kind, do you find? And put out offal away from camp over night, and look next day at the foot tracks where it lay.

Man is a great blunderer going about in the woods, and there is no other except the bear makes so much noise. Being so well warned beforehand, it is a very stupid animal, or a very bold one, that cannot keep safely hid. The cunningest hunter is hunted in turn, and what he leaves of his kill is meat for some other. That is the economy of nature, but with it all there is not sufficient account taken of the works of man. There is no scavenger that eats tin cans, and no wild thing leaves a like disfigurement on the forest floor.

14

15

16

___ CONSIDERATIONS ___

1. Precise as Mary Austin's observations are, her account would not be described today as a scientific report. Find three or four phrases that would be useful in explaining her departure from the objectivity of the scientist.

2. Given that Austin's essay was first published in 1903, what surprisingly modern idea does she introduce and explore briefly in Paragraph 11?

3. A characteristic of Austin's style is her diction — that is, her choice of particular words. Look carefully at such choices as "stoops," in Paragraph 3; "primaries," in Paragraph 6; "nice," in Paragraph 9; and "a lazy dog," in Paragraph 13 as starting points for a study of her diction. What surprises do some of those choices offer?

4. In Paragraph 4, Austin uses an allusion — "San Juan Hill" — to evoke an even more grisly image of the buzzards. A writer runs a certain risk in using allusions, however, as the intended effect is lost if the reader doesn't recognize to what the allusion refers. What can *you* get from San Juan Hill?

5. What does Mary Austin mean by the "economy of nature," and why does she exclude one well-known species from its workings?

James Baldwin (b. 1924) published his first novel, Go Tell It on the Mountain, *when he was still in his twenties. His most recent is* Just Above My Head *(1979). Son of a Harlem minister, he has written three other novels, a book of stories, one play, and several collections of essays. In these pages Baldwin summarizes his life to the age of thirty-one, then concentrates a life's ambition into one sentence.*

6

JAMES BALDWIN
Autobiographical Notes

I was born in Harlem thirty-one years ago. I began plotting novels   1
at about the time I learned to read. The story of my childhood is the
usual bleak fantasy, and we can dismiss it with the restrained observation that I certainly would not consider living it again. In those days
my mother was given to the exasperating and mysterious habit of
having babies. As they were born, I took them over with one hand and
held a book with the other. The children probably suffered, though
they have since been kind enough to deny it, and in this way I read
Uncle Tom's Cabin and *A Tale of Two Cities* over and over and over
again; in this way, in fact, I read just about everything I could get my
hands on — except the Bible, probably because it was the only book I
was encouraged to read. I must also confess that I wrote — a great deal
— and my first professional triumph, in any case, the first effort of
mine to be seen in print, occurred at the age of twelve or thereabouts,
when a short story I had written about the Spanish revolution won
some sort of prize in an extremely short-lived church newspaper. I

remember the story was censored by the lady editor, though I don't remember why, and I was outraged.

2   Also wrote plays, and songs, for one of which I received a letter of congratulations from Mayor La Guardia, and poetry, about which the less said, the better. My mother was delighted by all these goings-on, but my father wasn't, he wanted me to be a preacher. When I was fourteen I became a preacher, and when I was seventeen I stopped. Very shortly thereafter I left home. For God knows how long I struggled with the world of commerce and industry — I guess they would say they struggled with *me* — and when I was about twenty-one I had enough done of a novel to get a Saxton Fellowship. When I was twenty-two the fellowship was over, the novel turned out to be unsalable, and I started waiting on tables in a Village restaurant and writing book reviews — mostly, as it turned out, about the Negro problem, concerning which the color of my skin made me automatically an expert. Did another book, in company with photographer Theodore Pelatowski, about the store-front churches in Harlem. This book met exactly the same fate as my first — fellowship, but no sale. (It was a Rosenwald Fellowship.) By the time I was twenty-four I had decided to stop reviewing books about the Negro problem — which, by this time, was only slightly less horrible in print than it was in life — and I packed my bags and went to France, where I finished, God knows how, *Go Tell It on the Mountain*.

3   Any writer, I suppose, feels that the world into which he was born is nothing less than a conspiracy against the cultivation of his talent — which attitude certainly has a great deal to support it. On the other hand, it is only because the world looks on his talent with such a frightening indifference that the artist is compelled to make his talent important. So that any writer, looking back over even so short a span of time as I am here forced to assess, finds that the things which hurt him and the things which helped him cannot be divorced from each other; he could be helped in a certain way only because he was hurt in a certain way; and his help is simply to be enabled to move from one conundrum to the next — one is tempted to say that he moves from one disaster to the next. When one begins looking for influences one finds them by the score. I haven't thought much about my own, not enough anyway; I hazard that the King James Bible, the rhetoric of the store-front church, something ironic and violent and perpetually understated in Negro speech — and something of Dickens' love for bravura — have something to do with me today; but I wouldn't stake my life on it. Likewise, innumerable people have

helped me in many ways; but finally, I suppose, the most difficult (and most rewarding) thing in my life has been the fact that I was born a Negro and was forced, therefore, to effect some kind of truce with this reality. (Truce, by the way, is the best one can hope for.)

One of the difficulties about being a Negro writer (and this is not special pleading, since I don't mean to suggest that he has it worse than anybody else) is that the Negro problem is written about so widely. The bookshelves groan under the weight of information, and everyone therefore considers himself informed. And this information, furthermore, operates usually (generally, popularly) to reinforce traditional attitudes. Of traditional attitudes there are only two — For or Against — and I, personally, find it difficult to say which attitude has caused me the most pain. I am speaking as a writer; from a social point of view I am perfectly aware that the change from ill-will to good-will, however motivated, however imperfect, however expressed, is better than no change at all.

But it is part of the business of the writer — as I see it — to examine attitudes, to go beneath the surface, to tap the source. From this point of view the Negro problem is nearly inaccessible. It is not only written about so widely; it is written about so badly. It is quite possible to say that the price of a Negro pays for becoming articulate is to find himself, at length, with nothing to be articulate about. ("You taught me language," says Caliban to Prospero, "and my profit on't is I know how to curse.") Consider: the tremendous social activity that this problem generates imposes on whites and Negroes alike the necessity of looking forward, of working to bring about a better day. This is fine, it keeps the waters troubled; it is all, indeed, that has made possible the Negro's progress. Nevertheless, social affairs are not generally speaking the writer's prime concern, whether they ought to be or not; it is absolutely necessary that he establish between himself and these affairs a distance which will allow, at least, for clarity, so that before he can look forward in any meaningful sense, he must first be allowed to take a long look back. In the context of the Negro problem neither whites nor blacks, for excellent reasons of their own, have the faintest desire to look back; but I think that the past is all that makes the present coherent, and further, that the past will remain horrible for exactly as long as we refuse to assess it honestly.

I know, in any case, that the most crucial time in my own development came when I was forced to recognize that I was a kind of bastard of the West; when I followed the line of my past I did not find myself in Europe but in Africa. And this meant that in some subtle

4

5

6

way, in a really profound way, I brought to Shakespeare, Bach, Rembrandt, to the stones of Paris, to the cathedral at Chartres and to the Empire State Building, a special attitude. These were not really my creations, they did not contain my history; I might search in them in vain forever for any reflection of myself. I was an interloper; this was not my heritage. At the same time I had no other heritage which I could possibly hope to use — I had certainly been unfitted for the jungle or the tribe. I would have to appropriate these white centuries, I would have to make them mine — I would have to accept my special attitude, my special place in this scheme — otherwise I would have no place in *any* scheme. What was the most difficult was the fact that I was forced to admit something I had always hidden from myself, which the American Negro has had to hide from himself as the price of his public progress; that I hated and feared white people. This did not mean that I loved black people; on the contrary, I despised them, possibly because they failed to produce Rembrandt. In effect, I hated and feared the world. And this meant, not only that I thus gave the world an altogether murderous power over me, but also that in such a self-destroying limbo I could never hope to write.

7   One writes out of one thing only — one's own experience. Everything depends on how relentlessly one forces from this experience the last drop, sweet or bitter, it can possibly give. This is the only real concern of the artist, to recreate out of the disorder of life that order which is art. The difficulty then, for me, of being a Negro writer was the fact that I was, in effect, prohibited from examining my own experience too closely by the tremendous demands and the very real dangers of my social situation.

8   I don't think the dilemma outlined above is uncommon. I do think, since writers work in the disastrously explicit medium of language, that it goes a little way towards explaining why, out of the enormous resources of Negro speech and life, and despite the example of Negro music, prose written by Negroes has been generally speaking so pallid and so harsh. I have not written about being a Negro at such length because I expect that to be my only subject, but only because it was the gate I had to unlock before I could hope to write about anything else. I don't think that the Negro problem in America can be even discussed coherently without bearing in mind its context; its context being the history, traditions, customs, the moral assumptions and preoccupations of the country; in short, the general social fabric. Appearances to the contrary, no one in America escapes its effects and everyone in America bears some responsibility for it. I believe this the

more firmly because it is the overwhelming tendency to speak of this problem as though it were a thing apart. But in the work of Faulkner, in the general attitude and certain specific passages in Robert Penn Warren, and, most significantly, in the advent of Ralph Ellison, one sees the beginnings — at least — of a more genuinely penetrating search. Mr. Ellison, by the way, is the first Negro novelist I have ever read to utilize in language, and brilliantly, some of the ambiguity and irony of Negro life.

About my interests: I don't know if I have any, unless the morbid   9 desire to own a sixteen-millimeter camera and make experimental movies can be so classified. Otherwise, I love to eat and drink — it's my melancholy conviction that I've scarcely ever had enough to eat (this is because it's *impossible* to eat enough if you're worried about the next meal) — and I love to argue with people who do not disagree with me too profoundly, and I love to laugh. I do *not* like bohemia, or bohemians, I do not like people whose principal aim is pleasure, and I do not like people who are *earnest* about anything. I don't like people who like me because I'm a Negro; neither do I like people who find in the same accident grounds for contempt. I love America more than any other country in the world, and, exactly for this reason, I insist on the right to criticize her perpetually. I think all theories are suspect, that the finest principles may have to be modified, or may even be pulverized by the demands of life, and that one must find, therefore, one's own moral center and move through the world hoping that this center will guide one aright. I consider that I have many responsibilities, but none greater than this: to last, as Hemingway says, and get my work done.

I want to be an honest man and a good writer.   10

_____ CONSIDERATIONS _____

1. Why didn't the young Baldwin read the Bible? In your education, have you ever been affected by similar feelings?

2. Point out specific features of Baldwin's style that account for its slightly ironic tone. What other authors in this book make use of irony? Why?

3. Baldwin finds it difficult, he says, to distinguish the things that helped him as a writer from those that hurt him. Can you draw any parallels with your experience as a student?

4. Baldwin wrote this essay for a book that appeared in 1955, when he was thirty-one years old and had already published two successful novels. How do those facts affect your response to the last sentence in the essay?

5. Many black writers have argued that the black artist must reject all of white culture. How does Baldwin explain his acceptance of Shakespeare, Bach, Rembrandt, the cathedral at Chartres, and the Empire State Building?

6. Note how many years Baldwin covers in the first half-dozen sentences of Paragraph 2. How do you explain the lack of details about those years? Is this a weakness or a strength of the essay?

Wendell Berry (b. 1934) was born and educated in Kentucky, left home to teach in New York and California, and later returned to the home place. A novelist — Nathan Coulter *(1960),* A Place on Earth *(1968; revised and reissued 1983), and* The Memory of Old Jack *(1974) — and a poet with eight volumes of poetry; the most recent is* The Wheel *(1982). He has also published many collections of essays. One of them, issued by the Sierra Club, expresses in its title the range of Wendell Berry's passions:* The Unsettling of America: Culture and Agriculture *(1977).* Recollected Essays *and* The Gift of Good Land *both appeared in 1981, and* Standing by Words *in 1983.*

"A Good Scythe" comes from The Gift of Good Land. *Berry is not only a poet, essayist, and novelist; he is a farmer who raises cattle, horses, and sheep on his Kentucky farm. He does not keep his life in compartments, and he writes essays or novels or poems in the same spirit with which he ploughs a field.*

7

WENDELL BERRY

A Good Scythe

When we moved to our little farm in the Kentucky River Valley in 1965, we came with a lot of assumptions that we have abandoned or changed in response to the demands of place and time. We assumed, for example, that there would be good motor-powered solutions for all of our practical problems.

One of the biggest problems from the beginning was that our place was mostly on a hillside and included a good deal of ground near

Excerpted from *The Gift of Good Land: Further Essays Cultural and Agricultural,* © 1981 by Wendell Berry. Published by North Point Press and reprinted by arrangement. All rights reserved.

the house and along the road that was too steep to mow with a lawn mower. Also, we were using some electric fence, which needed to be moved out once or twice a year.

3   When I saw that Sears Roebuck sold a "power scythe," it seemed the ideal solution, and I bought one. I don't remember what I paid for it, but it was expensive, considering the relatively small amount of work I needed it for. It consisted of a one-cylinder gasoline engine mounted on a frame with a handlebar, a long metal tube enclosing a flexible drive shaft, and a rotary blade. To use it, you hung it from your shoulder by a web strap, and swept the whirling blade over the ground at the desired height.

4   It did a fairly good job of mowing, cutting the grass and weeds off clean and close to the ground. An added advantage was that it readily whacked off small bushes and tree sprouts. But this solution to the mowing problem involved a whole package of new problems:

1. The power scythe was heavy.
2. It was clumsy to use, and it got clumsier as the ground got steeper and rougher. The tool that was supposed to solve the problem of steep ground worked best on level ground.
3. It was dangerous. As long as the scythe was attached to you by the shoulder strap, you weren't likely to fall onto that naked blade. But it *was* a naked blade, and it did create a constant threat of flying rock chips, pieces of glass, etc.
4. It enveloped you in noise, and in the smudge and stench of exhaust fumes.
5. In rank growth, the blade tended to choke — in which case you had to kill the engine in a hurry or it would twist the drive shaft in two.
6. Like a lot of small gas engines not regularly used, this one was temperamental and undependable. And dependence on an engine that won't run is a plague and a curse.

5   When I review my own history, I am always amazed at how slow I have been to see the obvious. I don't remember how long I used that "labor-saving" power scythe before I finally donated it to help enlighten one of my friends — but it was too long. Nor do I remember all the stages of my own enlightenment.

6   The turning point, anyhow, was the day when Harlan Hubbard showed me an old-fashioned, human-powered scythe that was clearly the best that I had ever seen. It was light, comfortable to hold and handle. The blade was very sharp, angled and curved precisely to the

path of its stroke. There was an intelligence and refinement in its design that made it a pleasure to handle and look at and think about. I asked where I could get one, and Harlan gave me an address: The Marugg Company, Tracy City, Tennessee 37387.

I wrote for a price list and promptly received a sheet exhibiting 7 the stock in trade of the Marugg Company: grass scythes, bush scythes, snaths, sickles, hoes, stock bells, carrying yokes, whetstones, and the hammers and anvils used in beating out the "dangle" cutting edge that is an essential feature of the grass scythes.

In due time I became the owner of a grass scythe, hammer and 8 anvil, and whetstone. Learning to use the hammer and anvil properly (the Marugg Company provides a sheet of instructions) takes some effort and some considering. And so does learning to use the scythe. It is essential to hold the point so that it won't dig into the ground, for instance; and you must learn to swing so that you slice rather than hack.

Once these fundamentals are mastered, the Marugg grass scythe 9 proves itself an excellent tool. It is the most satisfying hand tool that I have ever used. In tough grass it cuts a little less uniformly than the power scythe. In all other ways, in my opinion it is a better tool:

1. It is light.
2. It handles gracefully and comfortably even on steep ground.
3. It is far less dangerous than the power scythe.
4. It is quiet and makes no fumes.
5. It is much more adaptable to conditions than the power scythe: in ranker growth, narrow the cut and shorten the stroke.
6. It always starts — provided the user will start. Aside from reasonable skill and care in use, there are no maintenance problems.
7. It requires no fuel or oil. It runs on what you ate for breakfast.
8. It is at least as fast as the power scythe. Where the cutting is either light or extra heavy, it can be appreciably faster.
9. It is far cheaper than the power scythe, both to buy and to use.

Since I bought my power scythe, a new version has come on the 10 market, using a short length of nylon string in place of the metal blade. It is undoubtedly safer. But I believe the other drawbacks remain. Though I have not used one of these, I have observed them in use, and they appear to me to be slower than the metal-bladed power scythe, and less effective on large-stemmed plants.

I have noticed two further differences between the power scythe 11 and the Marugg scythe that are not so practical as those listed above, but which I think are just as significant. The first is that I never took the least pleasure in using the power scythe, whereas in using the Marugg scythe, whatever the weather and however difficult the cutting, I always work with the pleasure that one invariably gets from using a good tool. And because it is not motor driven and is quiet and odorless, the Marugg scythe also allows the pleasure of awareness of what is going on around you as you work.

12   The other difference is between kinds of weariness. Using the Marugg scythe causes the simple bodily weariness that comes with exertion. This is a kind of weariness that, when not extreme, can in itself be one of the pleasures of work. The power scythe, on the other hand, adds to the weariness of exertion the unpleasant and destructive weariness of strain. This is partly because, in addition to carrying and handling it, your attention is necessarily clenched to it; if you are to use it effectively and safely, you *must* not look away. And partly it is because the power scythe, like all motor-driven tools, imposes patterns of endurance that are alien to the body. As long as the motor is running there is a pressure to keep going. You don't stop to consider or rest or look around. You keep on until the motor stops or the job is finished or you have some kind of trouble. (This explains why the tractor soon evolved headlights, and farmers began to do daywork at night.)

13   These differences have come to have, for me, the force of a parable. Once you have mastered the Marugg scythe, what an absurd thing it makes of the power scythe! What possible sense can there be in carrying a heavy weight on your shoulder in order to reduce by a very little the use of your arms? Or to use quite a lot of money as a substitute for a little skill?

14   The power scythe — and it is far from being an isolated or unusual example — is *not* a labor saver or a shortcut. It is a labor maker (you have to work to pay for it as well as to use it) and a long cut. Apologists for such expensive technological solutions love to say that "you can't turn back the clock." But when it makes perfect sense to do so — as when the clock is wrong — of *course* you can!

_____ CONSIDERATIONS _____

1. Berry's discussion of the two types of scythes provides an excellent example of the way a writer can use comparison/contrast to present and organize an essay. What is the most obvious device Berry uses to show the contrast he wants the reader to see?

2. Why does Berry put quotation marks around the phrase "labor-saving" in Paragraph 5? In what way does that punctuation mark indicate Berry's main idea in the essay?

3. According to Berry, what explains the evolution of farm tractor headlights? What has that explanation to do with the subject of his essay?

4. Every trade or craft seems to develop its own distinctive vocabulary. Consider the unusual words in Paragraph 7. Can you add to that list of intriguing farming terms. Draw up a short lexicon of interesting words from another craft, such as printing, plumbing, cooking, carpentry, dressmaking, stenography, or photography.

5. If you know of another technological advance comparable to the invention of the power scythe, which, according to Berry, created more problems than it solved, use it to illustrate an essay on the questionable wisdom of describing every such advance as "progress."

*The farmer who praises a good scythe is the writer who
believes in "a better language"; "literacy . . . is not an ornament"
any more than honest farming is. This essay comes from* A Con-
tinous Harmony *(1972).*

8

WENDELL BERRY
In Defense of Literacy

1   In a country in which everybody goes to school, it may seem
absurd to offer a defense of literacy, and yet I believe that such a
defense is in order, and that the absurdity lies not in the defense, but
in the necessity for it. The published illiteracies of the certified educated are on the increase. And the universities seem bent upon ratify-
ing this state of things by declaring the acceptability, in their
graduates, of adequate — that is to say, of mediocre — writing skills.

2   The schools, then, are following the general subservience to the
"practical," as that term has been defined for us according to the
benefit of corporations. By "practicality" most users of the term now
mean whatever will most predictably and most quickly make a profit.
Teachers of English and literature have either submitted, or are
expected to submit, along with teachers of the more "practical" disciplines, to the doctrine that the purpose of education is the mass production of producers and consumers. This has forced our profession
into a predicament that we will finally have to recognize as a perversion. As if awed by the ascendency of the "practical" in our society,
many of us secretly fear, and some of us are apparently ready to say,
that if a student is not going to become a teacher of his language, he
has no need to master it.

In other words, to keep pace with the specialization —'and the   3
dignity accorded to specialization — in other disciplines, we have
begun to look upon and to teach our language and literature as specialties. But whereas specialization is of the nature of the applied
sciences, it is a perversion of the disciplines of language and literature.
When we understand and teach these as specialties, we submit willy-
nilly to the assumption of the "practical men" of business, and also
apparently of education, that literacy is no more than an ornament:
when one has become an efficient integer of the economy, *then* it is
permissible, even desirable, to be able to talk about the latest novels.
After all, the disciples of "practicality" may someday find themselves
stuck in conversation with an English teacher.

I may have oversimplified that line of thinking, but not much.   4
There are two flaws in it. One is that, among the self-styled "practical
men," the practical is synonymous with the immediate. The long-
term effects of their values and their acts lie outside the boundaries of
their interest. For such people a strip mine ceases to exist as soon as
the coal has been extracted. Short-term practicality is long-term idiocy.

The other flaw is that language and literature are always *about*   5
something else, and we have no way to predict or control what they
may be about. They are about the world. We will understand the
world, and preserve ourselves and our values in it, only insofar as we
have a language that is alert and responsive to it, and careful of it. I
mean that literally. When we give our plows such brand names as
"Sod Blaster," we are imposing on their use conceptual limits which
raise the likelihood that they will be used destructively. When we
speak of man's "war against nature," or of a "peace offensive," we are
accepting the limitations of a metaphor that suggests and even pro-
poses, violent solutions. When students ask for the right of "partici-
patory input" at the meetings of a faculty organization, they are
thinking of democratic process, but they are *speaking* of a convocation
of robots, and are thus devaluing the very traditions that they invoke.

Ignorance of books and the lack of a critical consciousness of   6
language were safe enough in primitive societies with coherent oral
traditions. In our society, which exists in an atmosphere of prepared,
public language — language that is either written or being read — illit-
eracy is both a personal and a public danger. Think how constantly
"the average American" is surrounded by premeditated language, in
newspapers and magazines, on signs and billboards, on TV and radio.
He is forever being asked to buy or believe somebody else's line of
goods. The line of goods is being sold, moreover, by men who are
trained to make him buy it or believe it, whether or not he needs it or

understands it or knows its value or wants it. This sort of selling is an honored profession among us. Parents who grow hysterical at the thought that their son might not cut his hair are *glad* to have him taught, and later employed, to lie about the quality of an automobile or the ability of a candidate.

7   What is our defense against this sort of language — this language-as-weapon? There is only one. We must know a better language. We must speak, and teach our children to speak, a language precise and articulate and lively enough to tell the truth about the world as we know it. And to do this we must know something of the roots and resources of our language; we must know its literature. The only defense against the worst is a knowledge of the best. By their ignorance people enfranchise their exploiters.

8   But to appreciate fully the necessity for the best sort of literacy we must consider not just the environment of prepared language in which most of us now pass most of our lives, but also the utter transience of most of this language, which is meant to be merely glanced at, or heard only once, or read once and thrown away. Such language is by definition, and often by calculation, not memorable; it is language meant to be replaced by what will immediately follow it, like that of shallow conversation between strangers. It cannot be pondered or effectively criticized. For those reasons an unmixed diet of it is destructive of the informed, resilient, critical intelligence that the best of our traditions have sought to create and to maintain — an intelligence that Jefferson held to be indispensable to the health and longevity of freedom. Such intelligence does not grow by bloating upon the ephemeral information and misinformation of the public media. It grows by returning again and again to the landmarks of its cultural birthright, the works that have proved worthy of devoted attention:

9   "Read not the Times. Read the Eternities," Thoreau said. Ezra Pound wrote that "literature is news that STAYS news." In his lovely poem, "The Island," Edwin Muir spoke of man's inescapable cultural boundaries and of his consequent responsibility for his own sources and renewals:

> Men are made of what is made,
> The meat, the drink, the life, the corn,
> Laid up by them, in them reborn.
> And self-begotten cycles close
> About our way; indigenous art
> And simple spells make unafraid
> The haunted labyrinths of the heart . . .

These men spoke of a truth that no society can afford to shirk for   10
long: we are dependent, for understanding, and for consolation and
hope, upon what we learn of ourselves from songs and stories. This
has always been so, and it will not change.

I am saying, then, that literacy — the mastery of language and   11
the knowledge of books — is not an ornament, but a necessity. It is
impractical only by the standards of quick profit and easy power.
Longer perspective will show that it alone can preserve in us the possibility of an accurate judgment of ourselves, and the possibilities of
correction and renewal. Without it, we are adrift in the present, in the
wreckage of yesterday, in the nightmare of tomorrow.

—— CONSIDERATIONS ——————————————

1. Berry rarely writes about matters with which he is not seriously concerned, be it scythes or literature, but he expresses his concerns differently —
sometimes lightly, sometimes soberly, sometimes matter-of-factly, sometimes imaginatively — by skillful changes in tone and voice. Compare closely
his "A Good Scythe" with "In Defense of Literacy" to discover how Berry
effects those changes.

2. What is the connection between Berry's definition of "practical" in
Paragraph 2 and his concern with specialization in Paragraph 3?

3. In Paragraphs 4 and 5, Berry points out "two flaws" in the line of
thinking he described in Paragraphs 2 and 3. Do you agree that they are flaws?
By what standards are those features flaws — those of logic, of common sense,
of science, of history?

4. Berry mentions "Sod Blaster" and "peace offensive" as two examples
of how language can limit or influence the way of thinking about a given
object or act. Compile a short list of similar terms and use it to illustrate a
short essay explaining the relationship of language to thought.

5. Berry's essay is studded with memorable phrases, such as, "The only
defense against the worst is a knowledge of the best," or, ". . . the mastery of
language . . . is not an ornament but a necessity." Isolate a few more and study
them to see what gives such statements — often called "aphorisms" — their
carrying power.

6. Is it accurate to say that the values Berry expresses in his defense of
literacy are reaffirmed by Ralph Ellison in the last few sentences of "On
Becoming a Writer," Paragraph 16 (page 123). Explain.

Because he favors scythes and literacy, Wendell Berry is a conservative of sorts; the question is what sort. In "The Reactor in the Garden," also from The Gift of Land, *this farmer-writer tells about his civil disobedience.*

9

WENDELL BERRY

The Reactor
and the Garden

1   On June 3, 1979, I took part in an act of nonviolent civil disobedience at the site of a nuclear power plant being built at Marble Hill, near Madison, Indiana. At about noon that day, eighty-nine of us crossed a wire fence onto the power company's land, were arrested, and duly charged with criminal trespass.

2   As crimes go, ours was tame almost to the point of boredom. We acted under a well-understood commitment to do no violence and damage no property. The Jefferson County sheriff knew well in advance and pretty exactly what we planned to do. Our trespass was peaceable and orderly. We were politely arrested by the sheriff and his deputies, who acted, as far as I saw, with exemplary kindness. And this nearly eventless event ended in anticlimax: the prosecutor chose to press charges against only one of the eighty-nine who were arrested, and that one was never brought to trial.

3   And yet, for all its tameness, it was not a lighthearted event. Few of us, I think, found it easy to decide to break the law of the land. For me it was difficult for another reason as well: I do not like public

protests or crowd actions of any kind; I dislike and distrust the slogans and the jargon that invariably stick like bubble gum to any kind of "movement."

Why did I do it? 4

For several years, along with a good many other people, I have 5 been concerned about the proliferation of power plants in the Ohio River Valley, where at present more than sixty plants are either working, under construction, or planned. Air pollution from existing coal-fired plants in the valley is already said to be the worst in the country. And the new plants are being constructed or planned without any evident consideration of the possibility of limiting or moderating the consumption of electricity. The people of this area, then, are expected to sacrifice their health — among other things — to underwrite the fantasy of "unlimited economic growth." This is a decision not made by them — but, rather, made *for* them by the power companies in collaboration with various agencies of government.

The coal-fired plants would be bad enough by themselves. But, 6 in addition, some power companies have decided that nuclear power is the best answer to "the energy problem," and two nuclear power plants are now under construction in this part of the Ohio Valley. The arguments in their favor are not good, but they are backed nevertheless by a great deal of money and political power. For example, our local rural electric co-op publishes a magazine which constantly editorializes in favor of nuclear power. The rate payers are thus, in effect, being taxed to promote an energy policy that many of them consider objectionable and dangerous.

Power plants in the Ohio Valley raise another serious problem, 7 this one political. The Ohio River is a state boundary. A power plant on the north side of the river in Indiana will obviously have an effect in Kentucky. But though a plant will necessarily affect at least two states, it is planned and permitted only in one. The people of one state thus become subject to a decision made in another state, in which they are without representation. And so in the behavior of big technology and corporate power, we can recognize again an exploitive colonialism similar to that of George III.

Like the majority of the people, I am unable to deal competently 8 with the technical aspects of nuclear power and its dangers. My worries are based on several facts available to any reader of a newspaper:

1. Nuclear power is extremely dangerous. For this, the elaborate safety devices and backup systems of the plants themselves are evidence enough. Radioactive wastes, moreover, remain dangerous for

many thousands of years, and there is apparently no foreseeable safe way to dispose of them.

2. Dangerous accidents do happen in nuclear power plants. Officials and experts claim that accidents can be foreseen and prevented, but accidents are surprises by definition. If they are foreseen they do not happen.

3. Nuclear experts and plant employees do not always act competently in dealing with these accidents. Nuclear power requires people to act with *perfect* competence if it is to be used safely. But people in nuclear power plants are just as likely to blunder or panic or miscalculate as people anywhere else.

4. Public officials do not always act responsibly. Sometimes they deliberately falsify, distort, or withhold information essential to the public's health or safety.

9   If I had doubts about any of this, they were removed forever by the accident at Three Mile Island. And if I had any lingering faith that the government would prove a trustworthy guardian of public safety, that was removed by the recent hearings on the atomic bomb tests of the 1950s — which have revealed that the government assured the people living near the explosions that there would be no danger from radiation, when in fact it knew that the danger would be great.

10   And so when I climbed the fence at Marble Hill, I considered that I was casting a vote that I had been given no better opportunity to cast. I was voting no. And I was voting no confidence. Marble Hill is only about twenty miles upwind from my house. As a father, a neighbor, and a citizen, I had begun to look on the risk of going to jail as trivial in comparison to the risks of living so near a nuclear power plant.

11   But even though I took part wholeheartedly in the June 3 protest, I am far from believing that such public acts are equal to their purpose, or that they ever will be. They are necessary, but they are not enough, and they subject the minds of their participants to certain dangers.

12   Any effort that focuses on one problem encourages oversimplification. It is easy to drift into the belief that once the nuclear power problem — or the energy problem, or the pollution problem — is solved everything will be all right. It will not, of course. For all these separate problems are merely aspects of the human problem, which never has been satisfactorily solved, and which would provide every one of us a lifetime agenda of work and worry even if *all* the bedeviling problems of twentieth century technology were solved today.

An even greater danger is that of moral oversimplification, or 13
self-righteousness. Protests, demonstrations, and other forms of
"movement" behavior tend to divide people into the ancient categories of "us" and "them." In the midst of the hard work and the risks
of opposing that "we" see as a public danger, it is easy to assume that
if only "they" were as clear-eyed, alert, virtuous, and brave as "we"
are, our problems would soon be solved. This notion, too, is patently
false. In the argument over nuclear power — as in most public arguments — the division between "us" and "them" does not really exist.
In our efforts to correct the way things are, we are almost always,
almost inevitably, opposing what is wrong with ourselves. If we do
not see that, then I think we won't find any of the solutions we are
looking for.

For example, I believe that most people who took part in the June 14
3 demonstration at Marble Hill got there in an automobile. I did, and
I could hardly have got there any other way. Thus the demonstration,
while it pushed for a solution to one aspect of the energy problem, was
itself another aspect of that problem.

And I would be much surprised to learn that most of us did not 15
return home to houses furnished with electric light switches, which
we flipped on more or less thoughtlessly, not worrying overmuch
about the watersheds that are being degraded or destroyed by strip
mines to produce the coal to run the power plants to make the electricity that burns in our light bulbs. I know, anyhow, that I often flip
on my own light switches without any such worries.

Nearly all of us are sponsoring or helping to cause the ills we 16
would like to cure. Nearly all of us have what I can only call cheap-
energy minds; we continue to assume, or to act as if we assume, that
it does not matter how much energy we use.

I do not mean to imply that I know how to solve the problems of 17
the automobile or of the wasteful modern household. Those problems
are enormously difficult, and their difficulty suggests their extreme
urgency and importance. But I am fairly certain that they won't be
solved simply by public protests. The roots of the problems are private
or personal, and the roots of the solutions will be private or personal
too. Public protests are incomplete actions; they speak to the problem,
not to the solution.

Protests are incomplete, I think, because they are by definition 18
negative. You cannot protest *for* anything. The positive thing that
protest is supposed to do is "raise consciousness," but it can raise
consciousness only to the level of protest. So far as protest itself is

concerned, the raised consciousness is on its own. It appears to be possible to "raise" your consciousness without changing it — and so to keep protesting forever.

19   If you have to be negative, there are better negative things to do. You can quit doing something you know to be destructive. It might, for instance, be possible to take a pledge that you will no longer use electricty or petroleum to entertain yourself. My own notion of an ideal negative action is to get rid of your television set. (It is cheating to get rid of it by selling it or giving it away. You should get rid of it by carefully disassembling it with a heavy blunt instrument. Would you try to get rid of any other brain disease by selling it or giving it away?)

20   But such actions are not really negative. When you get rid of something undesirable you are extending an invitation to something desirable. If it is true that nature abhors a vacuum, there is no need to fear. Wherever you make an opening, it will be filled. When you get rid of petroleum-powered or electronic entertainment you are inviting a renewal of that structure of conversation, work, and play that used to be known as "home life." You are inviting such gentle and instructive pleasures as walking and reading.

21   Or it may be possible for some people to walk or ride a bicycle to work — and so to consider doing without a car altogether. Or there may be some kind of motor-powered tool that can be done without. Or perhaps it will prove economical or pleasing to change from fossil fuel heat to a solar collector or a wood stove.*

22   There is, then, a kind of negative action that cannot remain negative. To give up some things is to create problems, which immediately call for solutions — and so the negative action completes itself in an action that is positive. But some actions are probably more complete than others, and the more complete the action, the more effective it is as a protest.

23   What, then, is a complete action? It is, I think, an action which one takes on one's own behalf, which is particular and complex, real not symbolic, which one can both accomplish on one's own and take full responsibility for. There are perhaps many such actions, but certainly among them is any sort of home production. And of the kinds of home production, the one most possible for most people is gardening.

---

* But the use of wood stoves without proper maintenance of wood lots is only another form of mining. It makes trees an exhaustible resource.

Some people will object at this point that it belittles the idea of   24
gardening to think of it as an act of opposition or protest. I agree. That
is exactly my point. Gardening — or the best kind of gardening — is a
complete action. It is so effective a protest because it is so much more
than a protest.

The best kind of gardening is a form of home production capable   25
of a considerable independence of outside sources. It will, then, be
"organic" gardening. One of the most pleasing aspects of this way of
gardening is its independence. For fertility, plant protection, etc., it
relies as far as possible on resources in the locality and in the gardener's mind. Independence can be further enlarged by saving seed and
starting your own seedlings. To work at ways of cutting down the use
of petroleum products and gasoline engines in the garden is at once to
increase independence and to work directly at a real (that is, a permanent) solution to the energy problem.

A garden gives interest a place, and it proves one's place interest-   26
ing and worthy of interest. It works directly against the feeling — the
source of a lot of our "environmental" troubles — that in order to be
diverted or entertained, or to "make life interesting," it is necessary
to draw upon some distant resource — turn on the TV or take a trip.

One of the most important local resources that a garden makes   27
available for use is the gardener's own body. At a time when the
national economy is largely based on buying and selling substitutes
for common bodily energies and functions, a garden restores the body
to its usefulness — a victory for our species. It may take a bit of effort
to realize that perhaps the most characteristic modern "achievement"
is the obsolescence of the human body. Jogging and other forms of
artificial exercise do not restore the usefulness of the body, but are
simply ways of assenting to its uselessness; the body is a diverting pet,
like one's Chihuahua, and must be taken out for air and exercise. A
garden gives the body the dignity of working in its own support. It is a
way of rejoining the human race.

One of the common assumptions, leading to the obsolescence of   28
the body, is that physical work is degrading. That is true if the body is
used as a slave or a machine — if, in other words, it is misused. But
working in one's own garden does not misuse the body, nor does it
dull or "brutalize" the mind. The work of gardening is not "drudgery,"
but is the finest sort of challenge to intelligence. Gardening is not a
discipline that can be learned once for all, but keeps presenting problems that must be directly dealt with. It is, in addition, an agricul-

tural and ecological education, and that sort of education corrects
the cheap-energy mind.

29   A garden is the most direct way to recapture the issue of health,
and to make it a private instead of a governmental responsibility. In
this, as in several other ways I have mentioned, gardening has a power
that is political and even democratic. And it is a political power that
can be applied constantly, whereas one can only vote or demonstrate
occasionally.

30   Finally, because it makes backyards (or front yards or vacant lots)
productive, gardening speaks powerfully of the abundance of the
world. It does so by increasing and enhancing abundance, and by dem-
onstrating that abundance, given moderation and responsible use, is
limitless. We learn from our gardens to deal with the most urgent
question of the time: How much is enough? We don't soup our gardens
up with chemicals because our goal is *enough*, and we know that
enough requires a modest, moderate, conserving technology.

31   Atomic reactors and other big-technological solutions, on the
other hand, convey an overwhelming suggestion of the poverty of the
world and the scarcity of goods. That is because their actuating principle is excessive consumption. They obscure and destroy the vital
distinction between abundance and extravagance. The ideal of "limitless economic growth" is based on the obsessive and fearful conviction that more is always needed. The growth is maintained by the
consumers' panic-stricken suspicion, since they always want more,
that they will never have enough.

32   Enough is everlasting. Too much, despite all the ballyhoo about
"limitless growth," is temporary. And big-technological solutions are
temporary: the lifetime of a nuclear power plant is thirty years! A
garden, given the right methods and the right care, will last as long as
the world.

33   A garden, of course, is not always as comfortable as Kroger's.[1] If
you grow a garden you are going to shed some sweat, and you are going
to spend some time bent over; you will experience some aches and
pains. But it is in the willingness to accept this discomfort that we
strike the most telling blow against the power plants and what they
represent. We have gained a great deal of comfort and convenience by
our dependence on various public utilities and government agencies.
But it is obviously not possible to become dependent without losing
independence — and freedom too. Or to put it another way, we cannot

[1] Supermarket chain — ED.

be free from discomfort without becoming subject to the whims and abuses of centralized power, and to any number of serious threats to our health. We cannot hope to recover our freedom from such perils without discomfort.

Someone is sure to ask how I can suppose that a garden, "whose action is no stronger than a flower," can compete with a nuclear reactor. Well, I am not supposing that exactly. As I said, I think the protests and demonstrations are necessary. I think that jail may be the freest place when you *have no choice* but to breathe poison or die of cancer. But it is futile to attempt to correct a public wrong without correcting the sources of that wrong in yourself.   34

At the same time, I think it may be too easy to underestimate the power of a garden. A nuclear reactor is a proposed "solution" to "the energy problem." But like all big-technological "solutions," this one "solves" a single problem by causing many. The problems of what to do with radioactive wastes and with decommissioned nuclear plants, for example, have not yet been solved; and we can confidently predict that the "solutions," when they come, will cause yet other serious problems that will come as "surprises" to the officials and the experts. In that way, big technology works perpetually against itself. That is the limit of "unlimited economic growth."   35

A garden, on the other hand, is a solution that leads to other solutions. It is a part of the limitless pattern of good health and good sense.   36

_____ CONSIDERATIONS _____

1. "I dislike and distrust the slogans and the jargon that invariably stick like bubble gum to any kind of 'movement,' writes Berry in Paragraph 3. Why is his simile, "like bubble gum," particularly apt in this context?

2. Berry concludes that "a garden is a solution that leads to other solutions." Compare and contrast this with what he calls in his first essay "A Good Scythe" a solution that simply breeds more problems.

3. Was Berry's participation in the anti-nuclear power demonstration a good example of what Henry David Thoreau had in mind in his famous essay "On the Duty of Civil Disobedience" (1849)? Look up that essay in your college library to answer this question.

4. How did geography become political in the controversy over the nuclear power plants in the Ohio Valley?

5. How does Berry attempt to substantiate his statement that the demonstration against the nuclear power plants "was itself another aspect of that problem"?

6. Read all three of the Berry essays, paying particular attention to the writer's characteristic skill in using the particular and the local as vehicles for the general and the universal.

Ambrose Bierce (1842–1914?) was born in a log cabin on Horse Cave Creek in Ohio. He educated himself by reading the books in his father's small library, and as a young man served in the army during the Civil War. Starting as a journalist in California, he made himself an elegant writer of short stories, which were often supernatural or macabre in theme. Because he was writing in the primitive West, in a country still generally primitive, his serious work went generally unrecognized. Melancholy deepened into misanthropy. The definitions in The Devil's Dictionary *(1906) are funny — but the humor is serious, and the wit is bitter.*

In 1913, Bierce put his affairs in order and went to Mexico, which was in the midst of a civil war. He wrote a friend as he left, ". . . if you hear of my being stood up against a Mexican stone wall and shot to rags please know that I think it a pretty good way to depart this life. It beats old age, disease, or falling down a flight of stairs." He was never heard from again.

10

AMBROSE BIERCE
Some Devil's Definitions

Belladonna, n. In Italian a beautiful lady; in English a deadly poison. A striking example of the essential identity of the two tongues. 1

Bigot, n. One who is obstinately and zealously attached to an opinion that you do not entertain. 2

Bore, n. A person who talks when you wish him to listen. 3

Brute, n. See HUSBAND. 4

Cabbage, n. A familiar kitchen-garden vegetable about as large and wise as a man's head. 5

6   *Calamity, n.* A more than commonly plain and unmistakable reminder that the affairs of this life are not of our own ordering. Calamities are of two kinds: misfortune to ourselves, and good fortune to others.

7   *Cannibal, n.* A gastronome of the old school who preserves the simple tastes and adheres to the natural diet of the pre-pork period.

8   *Cannon, n.* An instrument employed in the rectification of national boundaries.

9   *Cat, n.* A soft, indestructible automaton provided by nature to be kicked when things go wrong in the domestic circle.

10   *Christian, n.* One who believes that the New Testament is a divinely inspired book admirably suited to the spiritual needs of his neighbor. One who follows the teachings of Christ in so far as they are not inconsistent with a life of sin.

11   *Claivoyant, n.* A person, commonly a woman, who has the power of seeing that which is invisible to her patron — namely, that he is a blockhead.

12   *Commerce, n.* A kind of transaction in which A plunders from B the goods of C, and for compensation B picks the pocket of D of money belonging to E.

13   *Compromise, n.* Such an adjustment of conflicting interests as gives each adversary the satisfaction of thinking he has got what he ought not to have, and is deprived of nothing except what was justly his due.

14   *Compulsion, n.* The eloquence of power.

15   *Congratulation, n.* The civility of envy.

16   *Conservative, n.* A statesman who is enamored of existing evils, as distinguished from the Liberal, who wishes to replace them with others.

17   *Consul, n.* In American politics, a person who having failed to secure an office from the people is given one by the Administration on condition that he leave the country.

18   *Consult, v. t.* To seek another's approval of a course already decided on.

19   *Corsair, n.* A politician of the seas.

20   *Coward, n.* One who in a perilous emergency thinks with his legs.

21   *Curiosity, n.* An objectionable quality of the female mind. The desire to know whether or not a woman is cursed with curiosity is one of the most active and insatiable passions of the masculine soul.

22   *Cynic, n.* A blackguard whose faulty vision sees things as they

are, not as they ought to be. Hence the custom among the Scythians of plucking out a cynic's eyes to improve his vision.

Dance, v. i. To leap about to the sound of tittering music, preferably with arms about your neighbor's wife or daughter. There are many kinds of dances, but all those requiring the participation of the two sexes have two characteristics in common: they are conspicuously innocent, and warmly loved by the vicious. 23

Debauchee, n. One who has so earnestly pursued pleasure that he has had the misfortune to overtake it. 24

Decalogue, n. A series of commandments, ten in number — just enough to permit an intelligent selection for observance, but not enough to embarrass the choice. 25

Defame, v. t. To lie about another. To tell the truth about another. 26

Dentist, n. A prestidigitator who, putting metal in your mouth, pulls coins out of your pocket. 27

Die, n. The singular of "dice." We seldom hear the word, because there is a prohibitory proverb, "Never say die." 28

Discussion, n. A method of confirming others in their errors. 29

Distance, n. The only thing that the rich are willing for the poor to call theirs, and keep. 30

Duel, n. A formal ceremony preliminary to the reconciliation of two enemies. Great skill is necessary to its satisfactory observance; if awkwardly performed the most unexpected and deplorable consequences sometimes ensue. A long time ago a man lost his life in a duel. 31

Eccentricity, n. A method of distinction so cheap that fools employ it to accentuate their incapacity. 32

Edible, adj. Good to eat, and wholesome to digest, as a worm to a toad, a toad to a snake, a snake to a pig, a pig to a man, and a man to a worm. 33

Education, n. That which discloses to the wise and disguises from the foolish their lack of understanding. 34

Effect, n. The second of two phenomena which always occur together in the same order. The first, called a Cause, is said to generate the other — which is no more sensible than it would be for one who has never seen a dog except in pursuit of a rabbit to declare the rabbit the cause of the dog. 35

36   *Egotist, n.* A person of low taste, more interested in himself than in me.

37   *Erudition, n.* Dust shaken out of a book into an empty skull.

38   *Eulogy, n.* Praise of a person who has either the advantages of wealth and power, or the consideration to be dead.

39   *Female, n.* One of the opposing, or unfair, sex.

40   *Fib, n.* A lie that has not cut its teeth. An habitual liar's nearest approach to truth: the perigee of his eccentric orbit.

41   *Fiddle, n.* An instrument to tickle human ears by friction of a horse's tail on the entrails of a cat.

42   *Friendship, n.* A ship big enough to carry two in fair weather, but only one in foul.

43   *Garter, n.* An elastic band intended to keep a woman from coming out of her stockings and desolating the country.

44   *Ghost, n.* The outward and visible sign of an inward fear.

45   *Glutton, n.* A person who escapes the evils of moderation by committing dyspepsia.

46   *Gout, n.* A physician's name for the rheumatism of a rich patient.

47   *Grammar, n.* A system of pitfalls thoughtfully prepared for the feet of the self-made man, along the path by which he advances to distinction.

48   *Guillotine, n.* A machine which makes a Frenchman shrug his shoulders with good reason.

____ CONSIDERATIONS _____

1. To appreciate the humor in some of Bierce's definitions, you may have to look up in your desk dictionary some of his words, such as "gastronome," "zealously," "adversary," "civility," "insatiable," "prestidigitator," "perigee," "dyspepsia." How do you add words to your working vocabulary?

2. *The Devil's Dictionary* was first published in 1906. Judging from the definitions here, would you say that Bierce's book is dated? Which items strike you as most relevant to our times? Which are least relevant? Why?

3. Do you find a consistent tone or attitude in Bierce's dictionary? Explain and provide ample evidence.

4. George Orwell, in "Politics and the English Language" (pages 293–307), is hard on euphemisms. Would Bierce agree with Orwell?

5. Which of these would most appreciate Bierce's brand of humor: Annie Dillard ("Strangers to Darkness"), Frederick Douglass ("Plantation Life"), Flannery O'Connor ("A Good Man Is Hard to Find"), or George Orwell ("A Hanging")?

6. Compose a page of definitions for your own Devil's Dictionary, perhaps concentrating on words currently popular.

Caroline Bird (b. 1915) was born in New York City, taught at Vassar, and now divides her time between Manhattan and Poughkeepsie. She has been an editor and a teacher, as well as the author of Born Female *(1968),* The Case against College *(1975), and* What Women Want *(1979). She argues the case against college with a clear vigor, a committed pugnacity; only a skilled debater with a good college education could dispute her.*

11

CAROLINE BIRD
Where College Fails Us

1   The case *for* college has been accepted without question for more than a generation. All high school graduates ought to go, says Conventional Wisdom and statistical evidence, because college will help them earn more money, become "better" people, and learn to be more responsible citizens than those who don't go.

2   But college has never been able to work its magic for everyone. And now that close to half our high school graduates are attending, those who don't fit the pattern are becoming more numerous, and more obvious. College graduates are selling shoes and driving taxis; college students sabotage each other's experiments and forge letters of recommendation in the intense competition for admission to graduate school. Others find no stimulation in their studies, and drop out — often encouraged by college administrators.

3   Some observers say the fault is with the young people themselves — they are spoiled, stoned, overindulged, and expecting too much. But

From *Signature Magazine,* Diners Club, Inc. © 1975. Reprinted by permission of the author.

that's mass character assassination, and doesn't explain all campus unhappiness. Others blame the state of the world, and they are partly right. We've been told that young people have to go to college because our economy can't absorb an army of untrained eighteen-year-olds. But disillusioned graduates are learning that it can no longer absorb an army of trained twenty-two-year-olds, either.

Some adventuresome educators and campus watchers have 4 openly begun to suggest that college may not be the best, the proper, the only place for every young person after the completion of high school. We may have been looking at all those surveys and statistics upside down, it seems, and through the rosy glow of our own remembered college experiences. Perhaps college doesn't make people intelligent, ambitious, happy, liberal, or quick to learn new things — maybe it's just the other way around, and intelligent, ambitious, happy, liberal, and quick-learning people are merely the ones who have been attracted to college in the first place. And perhaps all those successful college graduates would have been successful whether they had gone to college or not. This is heresy to those of us who have been brought up to believe that if a little schooling is good, more has to be much better. But contrary evidence is beginning to mount up.

The unhappiness and discontent of young people is nothing new, 5 and problems of adolescence are always painfully intense. But while traveling around the country, speaking at colleges, and interviewing students at all kinds of schools — large and small, public and private — I was overwhelmed by the prevailing sadness. It was as visible on campuses in California as in Nebraska and Massachusetts. Too many young people are in college reluctantly, because everyone told them they ought to go, and there didn't seem to be anything better to do. Their elders sell them college because it's good for them. Some never learn to like it, and talk about their time in school as if it were a sentence to be served.

Students tell us the same thing college counselors tell us — they 6 go because of pressure from parents and teachers, and stay because it seems to be an alternative to a far worse fate. It's "better" than the Army or a dead-end job, and it has to be pretty bad before it's any worse than staying at home.

College graduates say that they don't want to work "just" for the 7 money: They want work that matters. They want to help people and save the world. But the numbers are stacked against them. Not only are there not enough jobs in world-saving fields, but in the current slowdown it has become evident that there never were, and probably never will be, enough jobs requiring higher education to go around.[1]

8   Students who tell their advisers they want to help people, for example, are often directed to psychology. This year the Department of Labor estimates that there will be 4,300 new jobs for psychologists, while colleges will award 58,430 bachelor's degrees in psychology.[2]

9   Sociology has become a favorite major on socially conscious campuses, but graduates find that social reform is hardly a paying occupation. Male sociologists from the University of Wisconsin reported as gainfully employed a year after graduation included a legal assistant, sports editor, truck unloader, Peace Corps worker, publications director, and a stockboy — but no sociologist per se. The highest paid worked for the post office.

10   Publishing, writing, and journalism are presumably the vocational goal of a large proportion of the 104,000 majors in Communications and Letters expected to graduate in 1975.[3] The outlook for them is grim. All of the daily newspapers in the country combined are expected to hire a total of 2,600 reporters this year. Radio and television stations may hire a total of 500 announcers, most of them in local radio stations.[4] Nonpublishing organizations will need 1,100 technical writers, and public-relations activities another 4,400.[5] Even if new graduates could get all these jobs (they can't, of course), over 90,000 of them will have to find something less glamorous to do.

11   Other fields most popular with college graduates are also pathetically small. Only 1,900 foresters a year will be needed during this decade, although schools of forestry are expected to continue graduat-

---

[1] [Editors' Note: Ms. Bird's article appeared in 1975.] According to the Department of Labor Bureau of Statistics, 20.8 million college graduates will enter the work force from 1982 to 1995; the bureau predicts only 16.9 million job openings in traditional jobs for college graduates during that period.

[2] In 1982 figures: approximately 2076 new jobs for psychologists; 41,031 bachelor's degrees in psychology granted.

[3] In 1982 figures: 74,915 graduates in communications and Letters.

[4] The Department of Labor Bureau of Statistics no longer calculates total yearly job openings in each field. Instead, it projects only the number of new jobs created in a field over a 13-year period. (New job openings account for only 10–20% of all job openings, with the other 80–90% resulting from workers vacating already established positions.) All figures quoted in the footnotes represent an estimated annual average based on this projection. For the period 1982–1995, the bureau projects 1153 new jobs in reporting and 1153 new jobs in radio and television announcing each year.

[5] Statistics for technical writers and public relations personnel are not available.

ing twice that many.[6] Some will get sub-professional jobs as forestry aides. Schools of architecture are expected to turn out twice as many as will be needed,[7] and while all sorts of people want to design things, the Department of Labor forecasts that there will be jobs for only 400 new industrial designers[8] a year. As for anthropologists, only 400 will be needed every year in the 1970s[9] to take care of all the college courses, public-health research, community surveys, museums, and all the archaeological digs on every continent. (For these jobs graduate work in anthropology is required.)

Many popular occupations may seem to be growing fast without 12 necessarily offering employment to very many. "Recreation work" is always cited as an expanding field, but it will need relatively few workers who require more special training than life guards. "Urban planning" has exploded in the media, so the U.S. Department of Labor doubled its estimate of the number of jobs to be filled every year in the 1970s — to a big, fat 800.[10] A mere 200 oceanographers[11] a year will be able to do all the exploring of "inner space" — and all that exciting underwater diving you see demonstrated on television — for the entire decade of the 1970s.

Whatever college graduates *want* to do, most of them are going to wind up doing what *there is* to do. During the next few years, according to the Labor Department, the biggest demand will be for stenographers and secretaries, followed by retail-trade salesworkers, hospital attendants, bookkeepers, building custodians, registered nurses, foremen, kindergarten and elementary-school teachers, receptionists, cooks, cosmetologists, private-household workers, manufacturing inspectors, and industrial machinery repairmen.[12] These are the jobs which will eventually absorb the surplus archaeologists, urban planners, oceanographers, sociologists, editors, and college professors.

[6] Projected figures for the 1980s indicate there will be a need for an average of 1400 new foresters each year, while schools of forestry are expected to grant an average of 3000 bachelor's degrees each year.

[7] In 1982, 9728 students graduated with BAs in architecture, while there were an estimated 2615 new job openings in the field that year.

[8] Current projections indicate 550 new job openings for industrial designers each year in the 1980s.

[9] In the 1980s, approximately 350 anthropologists will be needed each year.

[10] This figure remains the same in the 1980s.

[11] Only 150 in the 1980s.

[12] This year, according to the Labor Department, the fastest-growing professions, in terms of new jobs created, are: building custodians, cashiers, secretaries, general office clerks, retail sales workers, registered nurses, waiters and waitresses, kindergarten and

14   Vocationalism is the new look on campus because of the discouraging job market faced by the generalists. Students have been opting for medicine and law in droves. If all those who check "doctor" as their career goal succeed in getting their MDs, we'll immediately have ten times the target ratio of doctors for the population of the United States. Law schools are already graduating twice as many new lawyers every year as the Department of Labor thinks we will need, and the oversupply grows annually.[13]

15   Specialists often find themselves at the mercy of shifts in demand, and the narrower the vocational training, the more risky the long-term prospects. Engineers are the classic example of the "Yo-Yo" effect in supply and demand. Today's shortage is apt to produce a big crop of engineering graduates after the need has crested, and teachers face the same squeeze.

16   Worse than that, when the specialists turn up for work, they often find that they have learned a lot of things in classrooms that they will never use, that they will have to learn a lot of things on the job that they were never taught, and that most of what they have learned is less likely to "come in handy later" than to fade from memory. One disillusioned architecture student, who had already designed and built houses, said, "It's the degree you need, not everything you learn getting it."

17   A diploma saves the employer the cost of screening candidates and gives him a predictable product: He can assume that those who have survived the four-year ordeal have learned how to manage themselves. They have learned how to budget their time, meet deadlines, set priorities, cope with impersonal authority, follow instructions, and stick with a task that may be tiresome without direct supervision.

18   The employer is also betting that it will be cheaper and easier to train the college graduate because he has demonstrated his ability to learn. But if the diploma serves only to identify those who are talented in the art of schoolwork, it becomes, in the words of Harvard's Christopher Jencks, "a hell of an expensive aptitude test." It is unfair to the candidates because they themselves must bear the cost of the screening — the cost of college. Candidates without the funds, the academic

---

elementary school teachers, truck drivers, nursing aides and orderlies, technical sales representatives, automobile mechanics, supervisors of blue collar workers, kitchen helpers, guards and doorkeepers, fast food preparers, and service personnel, store managers, and electric and electronic technicians.

[13] These figures are similar for the 1980s.

temperament, or the patience for the four-year obstacle race are ruled out, no matter how well they may perform on the job. But if "everyone" has a diploma, employers will have to find another way to choose employees, and it will become an empty credential.

(Screening by diploma may in fact already be illegal. The 1971   19
ruling of the Supreme Court in *Griggs* v. *Duke Power Co.* contended that an employer cannot demand a qualification which systematically excludes an entire class of applicants, unless that qualification reliably predicts success on the job. The requiring of a high school diploma was outlawed in the *Griggs* case, and this could extend to a college diploma.)

The bill for four years at an Ivy League college is currently climb-   20
ing toward $25,000; at a state university, a degree will cost the student and his family about $10,000 (with taxpayers making up the difference.).[14]

Not many families can afford these sums, and when they look   21
for financial aid, they discover that someone else will decide how much they will actually have to pay. The College Scholarship Service, which establishes a family's degree of need for most colleges, is guided by noble principles: uniformity of sacrifice, need rather than merit. But families vary in their willingness to "sacrifice" as much as the bureaucracy of the CSS thinks they ought to. This is particularly true of middle-income parents, whose children account for the bulk of the country's college students. Some have begun to rebel against this attempt to enforce the same values and priorities on all. "In some families, a college education competes with a second car, a color television, or a trip to Europe — and it's possible that college may lose," one financial-aid officer recently told me.

Quite so. College is worth more to some middle-income families   22
than to others. It is chilling to consider the undercurrent of resentment that families who "give up everything" must feel toward their college-age children, or the burden of guilt children must bear every time they goof off or receive less than top grades in their courses.

The decline in return for a college degree within the last genera-   23
tion has been substantial. In the 1950s, a Princeton student could pay his expenses for the school year — eating club and all — on less than $3,000. When he graduated, he entered a job market which provided a

[14] According to the National Center for Educational Statistics, the cost of four years at an Ivy League school is now approaching $50,000; the average cost of four years at a public institution is approximately $13,000.

comfortable margin over the earnings of his agemates who had not been to college. To be precise, a freshman entering Princeton in 1956, the earliest year for which the Census has attempted to project life-time earnings, could expect to realize a 12.5 percent return on his investment. A freshman entering in 1972, with the cost nearing $6,000 annually, could expect to realize only 9.3 percent, less than might be available in the money market. This calculation was made with the help of a banker and his computer, comparing college as an investment in future earnings with other investments available in the booming money market of 1974, and concluded that in strictly financial terms, college is not always the best investment a young person can make.

24   I postulated a young man (the figures are different with a young woman, but the principle is the same) whose rich uncle would give him, in cash, the total cost of four years at Princeton — $34,181.[15] (The total includes what the young man would earn if he went to work instead of to college right after high school.) If he did not spend the money on Princeton, but put it in the savings bank at 7.5 percent interest compounded daily, he would have, at retirement age sixty-four, more than five times as much as the $199,000 extra he could expect to earn between twenty-two and sixty as a college man rather than a mere high school graduate. And with all that money accumu-lating in the bank, he could invest in something with a higher return than a diploma. At age twenty-eight, when his nest egg had reached $73,113, he could buy a liquor store, which would return him well over 20 percent on his investment, as long as he was willing to mind the store. He might get a bit fidgety sitting there, but he'd have to be dim-witted to lose money on a liquor store, and right now we're talk-ing only about dollars.

25   If the young man went to a public college rather than Princeton, the investment would be lower, and the payoff higher, of course, because other people — the taxpayers — put up part of the capital for him. But the difference in return between an investment in public and private colleges is minimized because the biggest part of the invest-ment in either case is the money a student might earn if he went to work, not to college — in economic terms, his "foregone income." That he bears himself.

26   Rates of return and dollar signs on education are a fascinating brain teaser, and, obviously, there is a certain unreality to the game.

[15] Students in the class of 1985 will pay $48,352 for four years at Princeton.

But the same unreality extends to the traditional calculations that have always been used to convince taxpayers that college is a worthwhile investment.

The ultimate defense of college has always been that while it   27
may not teach you anything vocationally useful, it will somehow make you a better person, able to do anything better, and those who make it through the process are initiated into the "fellowship of educated men and women." In a study intended to probe what graduates seven years out of college thought their colleges should have done for them, the Carnegie Commission found that most alumni expected the "development of my abilities to think and express myself." But if such respected educational psychologists as Bruner and Piaget are right, specific learning skills have to be acquired very early in life, perhaps even before formal schooling begins.

So, when pressed, liberal-arts defenders speak instead about   28
something more encompassing, and more elusive. "College changed me inside," one graduate told us fervently. The authors of a Carnegie Commission report, who obviously struggled for a definition, concluded that one of the common threads in the perceptions of a liberal education is that it provides "an integrated view of the world which can serve as an inner guide." More simply, alumni say that college should have "helped me to formulate the values and goals of my life."

In theory, a student is taught to develop these values and goals   29
himself, but in practice, it doesn't work quite that way. All but the wayward and the saintly take their sense of the good, the true, and the beautiful from the people around them. When we speak of students acquiring "values" in college, we often mean that they will acquire the values — and sometimes that means only the tastes — of their professors. The values of professors may be "higher" than many students will encounter elsewhere, but they may not be relevant to situations in which students find themselves in college and later.

Of all the forms in which ideas are disseminated, the college   30
professor lecturing a class is the slowest and most expensive. You don't have to go to college to read the great books or learn about the great ideas of Western Man. Today you can find them everywhere — in paperbacks, in the public libraries, in museums, in public lectures, in adult-education courses, in abridged, summarized, or adapted form in magazines, films, and television. The problem is no longer one of access to broadening ideas; the problem is the other way around: how to choose among the many courses of action proposed to us, how to edit the stimulations that pour into our eyes and ears every waking

hour. A college experience that piles option on option and stimulation on stimulation merely adds to the contemporary nightmare.

31   What students and graduates say that they did learn on campus comes under the heading of personal, rather than intellectual, development. Again and again I was told that the real value of college is learning to get along with others, to practice social skills, to "sort out my head," and these have nothing to do with curriculum.

32   For whatever impact the academic experience used to have on college students, the sheer size of many undergraduate classes in the 1970s dilutes faculty-student dialogue, and, more often than not, they are taught by teachers who were hired when colleges were faced with a shortage of qualified instructors, during their years of expansion and when the big rise in academic pay attracted the mediocre and the less than dedicated.

33   On the social side, colleges are withdrawing from responsibility for feeding, housing, policing, and protecting students at a time when the environment of college may be the most important service it could render. College officials are reluctant to "intervene" in the personal lives of the students. They no longer expect to take over from parents, but often insist that students — who have, most often, never lived away from home before — take full adult responsibility for their plans, achievements, and behavior.

34   Most college students do not live in the plush, comfortable country-clublike surroundings their parents envisage, or, in some cases, remember. Open dorms, particularly when they are coeducational, are noisy, usually overcrowded, and often messy. Some students desert the institutional "zoos" (their own word for dorms) and move into run-down, overpriced apartments. Bulletin boards in student centers are littered with notices of apartments to share and the drift of conversation suggests that a lot of money is dissipated in scrounging for food and shelter.

35   Taxpayers now provide more than half of the astronomical sums that are spent on higher education. But less than half of today's high school graduates go on, raising a new question of equity: Is it fair to make all the taxpayers pay for the minority who actually go to college? We decided long ago that it is fair for childless adults to pay school taxes because everyone, parents and nonparents alike, profits by a literate population. Does the same reasoning hold true for state-supported higher education? There is no conclusive evidence on either side.

Young people cannot be expected to go to college for the general   36
good of mankind. They may be more altruistic than their elders, but
no great numbers are going to spend four years at hard intellectual
labor, let alone tens of thousands of family dollars, for "the advance-
ment of human capability in society at large," one of the many purposes invoked by the Carnegie Commission report. Nor do any
considerable number of them want to go to college to beat the Rus-
sians to Jupiter, improve the national defense, increase the Gross
National Product, lower the crime rate, improve automobile safety, or
create a market for the arts — all of which have been suggested at one
time or other as benefits taxpayers get for supporting higher education.

One sociologist said that you don't have to have a reason for   37
going to college because it's an institution. His definition of an institution is something everyone subscribes to without question. The
burden of proof is not on why you should go to college, but why
anyone thinks there might be a reason for not going. The implication
— and some educators express it quite frankly — is that an eighteen-
year-old high school graduate is still too young and confused to know
what he wants to do, let alone what is good for him.

Mother knows best, in other words.   38

It had always been comfortable for students to believe that   39
authorities, like Mother, or outside specialists, like educators, could
determine what was best for them. However, specialists and authorities no longer enjoy the credibility former generations accorded them.
Patients talk back to doctors and are not struck suddenly dead. Clients
question the lawyer's bills and sometimes get them reduced. It is no
longer self-evident that all adolescents must study a fixed curriculum
that was constructed at a time when all educated men could agree on
precisely what it was that made them educated.

The same with college. If high school graduates don't want to   40
continue their education, or don't want to continue it right away, they
may perceive more clearly than their elders that college is not for
them.

College is an ideal place for those young adults who love learning   41
for its own sake, who would rather read than eat, and who like nothing
better than writing research papers. But they are a minority, even at
the prestigious colleges, which recruit and attract the intellectually
oriented.

The rest of our high school graduates need to look at college more   42
closely and critically, to examine it as a consumer product, and decide
if the cost in dollars, in time, in continued dependency, and in future

returns, is worth the very large investment each student — and his family — must make.

—— CONSIDERATIONS ——————————————————————

1. To what extent is Bird's essay an attack on the conviction that universal education is the surest way to cure the ills and injustices of the world?

2. In her first paragraph, the author states three popular justifications for a college education. Examine her essay to see how, for the most part, it is organized around those three reasons.

3. In her final paragraph, Bird urges high school graduates to examine college "as a consumer product." Is that possible? Explain. Read about Richard Wright's struggle to educate himself ("The Library Card," pages 466–475) and try to imagine him examining that experience as "a consumer product."

4. Bird makes extensive use of statistics to prove her first proposition: that college is a poor investment. Does she cite the sources of her figures? Does she use the figures fairly? How can you tell?

5. How many of your college friends have clear ideas of their vocational or educational goals? Do you? What about friends who are not in college?

6. Bird points out, rightly enough, that "you don't have to go to college to read the great books or learn about the great ideas of Western Man." Judging from your experience with self-directed reading programs, how effective is Bird's statement as an argument?

7. What would Wendell Berry think of Bird's essay according to his views in "In Defense of Literacy" (pages 44–47)?

Elizabeth Bishop (1911–1979) was born in Nova Scotia and grew up in Massachusetts. After graduating from college she worked in New York, then spent many years in Brazil, and returned to the United States where she was teaching at Harvard University at the time of her death. Her poems are consistently excellent. North and South *(1946) was her first collection.* The Collected Poems *appeared in 1983, followed by* The Collected Prose *(1984), short stories and essays in reminiscence.*

12

ELIZABETH BISHOP
The Fish

I caught a tremendous fish
and held him beside the boat
half out of water, with my hook
fast in a corner of his mouth.
He didn't fight.   5
He hadn't fought at all.
He hung a grunting weight,
battered and venerable
and homely. Here and there
his brown skin hung in strips   10
like ancient wallpaper,
and its pattern of darker brown
was like wallpaper:
shapes like full-blown roses

15   stained and lost through age.
He was speckled with barnacles,
fine rosettes of lime,
and infested
with tiny white sea-lice,
20   and underneath two or three
rags of green weed hung down.
While his gills were breathing in
the terrible oxygen
— the frightening gills,
25   fresh and crisp with blood,
that can cut so badly —
I thought of the coarse white flesh
packed in like feathers,
the big bones and the little bones,
30   the dramatic reds and blacks
of his shiny entrails,
and the pink swim-bladder
like a big peony.
I looked into his eyes
35   which were far larger than mine
but shallower, and yellowed,
the irises backed and packed
with tarnished tinfoil
seen through the lenses
40   of old scratched isinglass.
They shifted a little, but not
to return my stare.
— It was more like the tipping
of an object toward the light.
45   I admired his sullen face,
the mechanism of his jaw,
and then I saw
that from his lower lip
— if you could call it a lip —
50   grim, wet, and weaponlike,
hung five old pieces of fish-line,
or four and a wire leader
with the swivel still attached,
with all their five big hooks
55   grown firmly in his mouth.

A green line, frayed at the end
where he broke it, two heavier lines,
and a fine black thread
still crimped from the strain and snap
when it broke and he got away.   60
Like medals with their ribbons
frayed and wavering,
a five-haired beard of wisdom
trailing from his aching jaw.
I stared and stared   65
and victory filled up
the little rented boat,
from the pool of bilge
where oil had spread a rainbow
around the rusted engine   70
to the bailer rusted orange,
the sun-cracked thwarts,
the oarlocks on their strings,
the gunnels — until everything
was rainbow, rainbow, rainbow!   75
And I let the fish go.

*John N. Bleibtreu (b. 1926) lives in New York City, where he
works at Arica Institute, an ESP–sensitivity-training center. In*
The Parable of the Beast *(1968) he examines and explains many
types of research on animal behavior. He explores different creatures' orientations to time, to space, and to the community in an
attempt to understand mechanisms that might work in human
beings as they do in animals. His prose explains with meticulous
scientific accuracy, but its simple clarity allows even a layman
to perceive analogies between animal and human psychology.
Exposition that imparts scientific information to the general
reader is particularly difficult to write, and welcome to read.*

13

JOHN N. BLEIBTREU

The Moment of Being

1   The cattle tick is a small, flat-bodied, blood-sucking insect with
a curious life history. It emerges from the egg not yet fully developed,
lacking a pair of legs, and sex organs. In this state it is still capable of
attacking cold-blooded animals such as frogs and lizards, which it
does. After shedding its skin several times, it acquires its missing
organs, mates, and is then prepared to attack warm-blooded animals.

2   The eyeless female is directed to the tip of a twig on a bush by
her photosensitive skin, and there she stays through darkness and
light, through fair weather and foul, waiting for the moment that will
fulfill her existence. In the Zoological Institute, at Rostock, prior to
World War I ticks were kept on the ends of twigs, waiting for this

moment for a period of eighteen years. The metabolism of the insect is sluggish to the point of being suspended entirely. The sperm she received in the act of mating remains bundled into capsules where it, too, waits in suspension until mammalian blood reaches the stomach of the tick, at which time the capsules break, the sperm are released and they fertilize the eggs which have been reposing in the ovary, also waiting in a kind of time suspension.

The signal for which the tick waits is the scent of butyric acid, a substance present in the sweat of all mammals. This is the only experience that will trigger time into existence for the tick.   3

The tick represents, in the conduct of its life, a kind of apotheosis of subjective time perception. For a period as long as eighteen years nothing happens. The period passes as a single moment; but at any moment within this span of literally senseless existence, when the animal becomes aware of the scent of butyric acid it is thrust into a perception of time, and other signals are suddenly perceived.   4

The animal then hurls itself in the direction of the scent. The object on which the tick lands at the end of this leap must be warm; a delicate sense of temperature is suddenly mobilized and so informs the insect. If the object is not warm, the tick will drop off and reclimb its perch. If it is warm, the tick burrows its head deeply into the skin and slowly pumps itself full of blood. Experiments made at Rostock with membranes filled with fluids other than blood proved that the tick lacks all sense of taste, and once the membrane is perforated the animal will drink any fluid, provided it is of the right temperature.   5

The extraordinary preparedness of this creature for that moment of time during which it will re-enact the purpose of its life contrasts strikingly with probability that this moment will ever occur. There are doubtless many bushes on which ticks perch, which are never bypassed by a mammal within range of the tick's leap. As do most animals, the tick lives in an absurdly unfavorable world — at least so it would appear to the compassionate human observer. But this world is merely the environment of the animal. The world it perceives — which experimenters at Rostock called its *umwelt,* its perceptual world — is not at all unfavorable. A period of eighteen years, as measured objectively by the circuit of the earth around the sun, is meaningless to the tick. During this period, it is apparently unaware of temperature changes. Being blind, it does not see the leaves shrivel and fall and then renew themselves on the bush where it is affixed. Unaware of time it is also unaware of space, and the multitudes of forms and colors which appear in space. It waits, suspended in dura-   6 tion for its particular moment of time, a moment distinguished by being filled with a single, unique experience; the scent of butyric acid.

7   Though we consider ourselves far removed as humans from such a lowly insect form as this, we too are both aware and unaware of elements which comprise our environment. We are more aware than the tick of the passage of time. We are subjectively aware of the aging process; we know that we grow older, that time is shortened by each passing moment. For the tick, however, this moment that precedes its burst of volitional activity, the moment when it scents butyric acid and is thrust into purposeful movement, is close to the end of time for the tick. When it fills itself with blood, it drops from its host, lays its eggs, and dies.

_____ CONSIDERATIONS _____

1. Do any sentences or phrases in "The Moment of Being" suggest that Bleibtreu is writing a parable, not a scientific paper? In what ways might a parable qualify as exposition? Who was the most famous user of the parable as a means of explaining?

2. The author describes the life of the cattle tick mechanistically, implying that the tick's life is determined by forces over which it has no control. Look up "naturalism" in a dictionary of literary terms, and see if Bleibtreu's essay is a good illustration.

3. What does Bleibtreu mean by "a kind of apotheosis of subjective time perception"? Have you experienced "subjective time perception"? How else might you express the idea in that phrase? What other kind of time telling is there?

4. How closely can you compare the cycle of human life with that of the cattle tick? Do you find such a comparison attractive? Repellent? Humorous? Depressing? Explain.

5. It is extremely common to use animals in calling attention to traits or habits in man. Think of common expressions such as "a horse laugh," "dirty dog," "snake in the grass," "a bear of a man," "a wolf in sheep's clothing." Think, too, of Aesop's fables. How do you account for such a widespread use of animal imagery?

Bruce Catton (1899–1978) became a historian while working as a newspaper reporter and magazine editor. His books, many on the Civil War, include Mr. Lincoln's Army *(1951) and* A Stillness at Appomattox *(1953). Catton received both the Pulitzer Prize and the National Book Award.*

14

BRUCE CATTON

Grant and Lee: A Study in Contrasts

When Ulysses S. Grant and Robert E. Lee met in the parlor of a modest house at Appomattox Court House, Virginia, on April 9, 1865, to work out the terms for the surrender of Lee's Army of Northern Virginia, a great chapter in American life came to a close, and a great new chapter began. 1

These men were bringing the Civil War to its virtual finish. To be sure, other armies had yet to surrender, and for a few days the fugitive Confederate government would struggle desperately and vainly, trying to find some way to go on living now that its chief support was gone. But in effect it was all over when Grant and Lee signed the papers. And the little room where they wrote out the terms was the scene of one of the poignant, dramatic contrasts in American history. 2

They were two strong men, these oddly different generals, and they represented the strengths of two conflicting currents that, through them, had come into final collision. 3

From *The American Story* ed. Earl Schenk Miers, © 1956 by Broadcast Music, Inc. Used by permission of the copyright holder.

79

4   Back of Robert E. Lee was the notion that the old aristocratic concept might somehow survive and be dominant in American life.

5   Lee was tidewater Virginia, and in his background were family culture, and tradition . . . the age of chivalry transplanted to a New World which was making its own legends and its own myths. He embodied a way of life that had come down through the age of knighthood and the English country squire. America was a land that was beginning all over again, dedicated to nothing much more complicated than the rather hazy belief that all men had equal rights and should have an equal chance in the world. In such a land Lee stood for the feeling that it was somehow of advantage to human society to have a pronounced inequality in the social structure. There should be a leisure class, backed by ownership of land; in turn, society itself should be keyed to the land as the chief source of wealth and influence. It would bring forth (according to this ideal) a class of men with a strong sense of obligation to the community; men who lived not to gain advantage for themselves, but to meet the solemn obligations which had been laid on them by the very fact that they were privileged. From them the country would get its leadership; to them it could look for the higher values — of thought, of conduct, of personal deportment — to give it strength and virtue.

6   Lee embodied the noblest elements of this aristocratic ideal. Through him, the landed nobility justified itself. For four years, the Southern states had fought a desperate war to uphold the ideals for which Lee stood. In the end, it almost seemed as if the Confederacy fought for Lee; as if he himself was the Confederacy . . . the best thing that the way of life for which the Confederacy stood could ever have to offer. He had passed into legend before Appomattox. Thousands of tired, underfed, poorly clothed Confederate soldiers, long since past the simple enthusiasm of the early days of the struggle, somehow considered Lee the symbol of everything for which they had been willing to die. But they could not quite put this feeling into words. If the Lost Cause, sanctified by so much heroism and so many deaths, had a living justification, its justification was General Lee.

7   Grant, the son of a tanner on the Western frontier, was everything Lee was not. He had come up the hard way and embodied nothing in particular except the eternal toughness and sinewy fiber of the men who grew up beyond the mountains. He was one of a body of men who owed reverence and obeisance to no one, who were self-reliant to a fault, who cared hardly anything for the past but who had a sharp eye for the future.

These frontier men were the precise opposites of the tidewater   8
aristocrats. Back of them, in the great surge that had taken people over
the Alleghenies and into the opening Western country, there was a
deep, implicit dissatisfaction with a past that had settled into grooves.
They stood for democracy, not from any reasoned conclusion about
the proper ordering of human society, but simply because they had
grown up in the middle of democracy and knew how it worked. Their
society might have privileges, but they would be privileges each man
had won for himself. Forms and patterns meant nothing. No man was
born to anything except perhaps to a chance to show how far he could
rise. Life was competition.

Yet along with this feeling had come a deep sense of belonging to   9
a national community. The Westerner, who developed a farm, opened
a shop, or set up in business as a trader, could hope to prosper only as
his own community prospered — and his community ran from the
Atlantic to the Pacific and from Canada down to Mexico. If the land
was settled, with towns and highways and accessible markets, he
could better himself. He saw his fate in terms of the nation's own
destiny. As its horizons expanded, so did his. He had, in other words,
an acute dollars-and-cents stake in the continued growth and development of his country.

And that, perhaps, is where the contrast between Grant and Lee   10
becomes most striking. The Virginia aristocrat, inevitably, saw himself in relation to his own region. He lived in a static society which
could endure almost anything except change. Instinctively, his first
loyalty would go to the locality in which that society existed. He
would fight to the limit of endurance to defend it, because in defending
it he was defending everything that gave his own life its deepest meaning.

The Westerner, on the other hand, would fight with an equal   11
tenacity for the broader concept of society. He fought so because
everything he lived by was tied to growth, expansion, and a constantly
widening horizon. What he lived by would survive or fall with the
nation itself. He could not possibly stand by unmoved in the face of
an attempt to destroy the Union. He would combat it with everything
he had, because he could only see it as an effort to cut the ground out
from under his feet.

So Grant and Lee were in complete contrast, representing two   12
diametrically opposed elements in American life. Grant was the modern man emerging; beyond him, ready to come on the stage, was the
great age of steel and machinery, of crowded cities and a restless bur-

geoning vitality. Lee might have ridden down from the old age of chivalry, lance in hand, silken banner fluttering over his head. Each man was the perfect champion of his cause, drawing both his strengths and his weaknesses from the people he led.

13   Yet it was not all contrast, after all. Different as they were — in background, in personality, in underlying aspiration — these two great soldiers had much in common. Under everything else, they were marvelous fighters. Furthermore, their fighting qualities were really very much alike.

14   Each man had, to begin with, the great virtue of utter tenacity and fidelity. Grant fought his way down the Mississippi Valley in spite of acute personal discouragement and profound military handicaps. Lee hung on in the trenches at Petersburg after hope itself had died. In each man there was an indomitable quality . . . the born fighter's refusal to give up as long as he can still remain on his feet and lift his two fists.

15   Daring and resourcefulness they had, too; the ability to think faster and move faster than the enemy. These were the qualities which gave Lee the dazzling campaigns of Second Manassas and Chancellorsville and won Vicksburg for Grant.

16   Lastly, and perhaps greatest of all, there was the ability, at the end, to turn quickly from war to peace once the fighting was over. Out of the way these two men behaved at Appomattox came the possibility of a peace of reconciliation. It was a possibility not wholly realized, in the years to come, but which did, in the end, help the two sections to become one nation again . . . after a war whose bitterness might have seemed to make such a reunion wholly impossible. No part of either man's life became him more than the part he played in their brief meeting in the McLean house at Appomattox. Their behavior there put all succeeding generations of Americans in their debt. Two great Americans, Grant and Lee — very different, yet under everything very much alike. Their encounter at Appomattox was one of the great moments of American history.

____ **CONSIDERATIONS** _____

1. Bruce Catton's "Grant and Lee" is a classic example of the comparison-contrast essay, both in subject matter and organization. Select equally different figures of your own time and write about them, following Catton's organizational method.

2. After studying the contrast Catton offers in Paragraphs 10 and 11, consider an essay on similar trends in modern American life — adherents of no-growth against those who argue for expansion. Compare with Wendell Berry's treatment of two kinds of scythes (pages 39–42).

3. "Two great Americans, Grant and Lee," writes Catton in his last paragraph. Do you find evidence that Catton favored either?

4. In Paragraph 6, Catton describes Lee as a "symbol." A symbol of what? How can you recognize a symbol when you see one? Why would anyone fight for a symbol?

5. Nowhere in his essay does Catton describe physical appearances. A half hour's research in your college library should give you enough description to add at least a paragraph to Catton's essay. Where, in that essay, would you insert such an addition? Do you find that physical description contributes to or confuses the contrast of their natures that Catton presents?

6. Judging by the proportions of this essay, decide whether Catton found the differences between the two men more interesting than their similarities.

Frank Conroy (b. 1936) grew up in various towns along the eastern seaboard, and attended Haverford College. He plays the jazz piano, teaches writing at Brandeis University, and has been director of the literature program at the National Endowment for the Arts since 1982. He writes about his early life in the only book he has published to date, Stop-Time *(1967). His prose has the qualities that make the best reminiscence: details feel exact and bright, though miniature with distance, like the landscape crafted for background to model trains.*

15

FRANK CONROY

A Yo-Yo Going Down

1   The common yo-yo is crudely made, with a thick shank between two widely spaced wooden disks. The string is knotted or stapled to the shank. With such an instrument nothing can be done except the simple up-down movement. My yo-yo, on the other hand, was a perfectly balanced construction of hard wood, slightly weighted, flat, with only a sixteenth of an inch between the halves. The string was not attached to the shank, but looped over it in such a way as to allow the wooden part to spin freely on its own axis. The gyroscopic effect thus created kept the yo-yo stable in all attitudes.

2   I started at the beginning of the book and quickly mastered the novice, intermediate, and advanced stages, practicing all day every day in the woods across the street from my house. Hour after hour of practice, never moving to the next trick until the one at hand was mastered.

3   The string was tied to my middle finger, just behind the nail. As

I threw — with your palm up, make a fist; throw down your hand, fingers unfolding, as if you were casting grain — a short bit of string would tighten across the sensitive pad of flesh at the tip of my finger. That was the critical area. After a number of weeks I could interpret the condition of the string, the presence of any imperfections on the shank, but most importantly the exact amount of spin or inertial energy left in the yo-yo at any given moment — all from that bit of string on my fingertip. As the throwing motion became more and more natural I found I could make the yo-yo "sleep" for an astonishing length of time — fourteen or fifteen seconds — and still have enough spin left to bring it back to my hand. Gradually the basic moves became reflexes. Sleeping, twirling, swinging, and precise aim. Without thinking, without even looking, I could run through trick after trick involving various combinations of the elemental skills, switching from one to the other in a smooth continuous flow. On particularly good days I would hum a tune under my breath and do it all in time to the music.

Flicking the yo-yo expressed something. The sudden, potentially   4
comic extension of one's arm to twice its length. The precise neatness of it, intrinsically soothing, as if relieving an inner tension too slight to be noticeable, the way a man might hitch up his pants simply to enact a reassuring gesture. It felt good. The comfortable weight in one's hand, the smooth, rapid-descent down the string, ending with a barely audible snap as the yo-yo hung balanced, spinning, pregnant with force and the slave of one's fingertip. That it was vaguely masturbatory seems inescapable. I doubt that half the pubescent boys in America could have been captured by any other means, as, in the heat of the fad, half of them were. A single Loop-the-Loop might represent, in some mysterious way, the act of masturbation, but to break down the entire repertoire into the three stages of throw, trick, and return representing erection, climax, and detumescence seems immoderate.

The greatest pleasure in yo-yoing was an abstract pleasure —   5
watching the dramatization of simple physical laws, and realizing they would never fail if a trick was done correctly. The geometric purity of it! The string wasn't just a string, it was a tool in the enactment of theorems. It was a line, an idea. And the top was an entirely different sort of idea, a gyroscope, capable of storing energy and of interacting with the line. I remember the first time I did a particularly lovely trick, one in which the sleeping yo-yo is swung from right to left while the string is interrupted by an extended index finger. Momentum car-

ries the yo-yo in a circular path around the finger, but instead of completing the arc the yo-yo falls on the taut string between the performer's hands, where it continues to spin in an upright position. My pleasure at that moment was as much from the beauty of the experiment as from pride. Snapping apart my hands I sent the yo-yo into the air above my head, bouncing it off nothing, back into my palm.

6   I practiced the yo-yo because it pleased me to do so, without the slightest application of will power. It wasn't ambition that drove me, but the nature of yo-yoing. The yo-yo represented my first organized attempt to control the outside world. It fascinated me because I could see my progress in clearly defined stages, and because the intimacy of it, the almost spooky closeness I began to feel with the instrument in my hand, seemed to ensure that nothing irrelevant would interfere. I was, in the language of jazz, "up tight" with my yo-yo, and finally free, in one small area at least, of the paralyzing sloppiness of life in general.

7   The first significant problem arose in the attempt to do fifty consecutive Loop-the-Loops. After ten or fifteen the yo-yo invariably started to lean and the throws became less clean, resulting in loss of control. I almost skipped the whole thing because fifty seemed excessive. Ten made the point. But there it was, written out in the book. To qualify as an expert you had to do fifty, so fifty I would do.

8   It took me two days, and I wouldn't have spent a moment more. All those Loop-the-Loops were hard on the strings. Time after time the shank cut them and the yo-yo went sailing off into the air. It was irritating, not only because of the expense (strings were a nickel each, and fabricating your own was unsatisfactory), but because a random element had been introduced. About the only unforeseeable disaster in yo-yoing was to have your string break, and here was a trick designed to do exactly that. Twenty-five would have been enough. If you could do twenty-five clean Loop-the-Loops you could do fifty or a hundred. I supposed they were simply trying to sell strings and went back to the more interesting tricks.

9   The witty nonsense of Eating Spaghetti, the surprise of The Twirl, the complex neatness of Cannonball, Backwards Round the World, or Halfway Round the World — I could do them all, without false starts or sloppy endings. I could do every trick in the book. Perfectly.

10   The day was marked on the kitchen calendar (God Gave Us Bluebell Natural Bottled Gas). I got on my bike and rode into town. Pedal-

ing along the highway I worked out with the yo-yo to break in a new string. The twins were appearing at the dime store.

I could hear the crowd before I turned the corner. Kids were coming on bikes and on foot from every corner of town, rushing down the streets like madmen. Three or four policemen were busy keeping the street clear directly in front of the store, and in a small open space around the doors some of the more adept kids were running through their tricks, showing off to the general audience or stopping to compare notes with their peers. Standing at the edge with my yo-yo safe in my pocket, it didn't take me long to see I had them all covered. A boy in a sailor hat could do some of the harder tricks, but he missed too often to be a serious threat. I went inside.

As Ramos and Ricardo performed I watched their hands carefully, noticing little differences in style, and technique. Ricardo was a shade classier, I thought, although Ramos held an edge in the showy two-handed stuff. When they were through we went outside for the contest.

"Everybody in the alley!" Ramos shouted, his head bobbing an inch or two above the others. "Contest starting now in the alley!" A hundred excited children followed the twins into an alley beside the dime store and lined up against the wall.

"Attention all kids!" Ramos yelled, facing us from the middle of the street like a drill sergeant. "To qualify for contest you got to Rock the Cradle. You got to rock yo-yo in cradle four time. Four time! Okay? Three time no good. Okay. Everybody happy?" There were murmurs of disappointment and some of the kids stepped out of line. The rest of us closed ranks. Yo-yos flicked nervously as we waited. "Winner receive grand prize. Special Black Beauty Prize Yo-Yo with Diamonds," said Ramos, gesturing to his brother who smiled and held up the prize, turning it in the air so we could see the four stones set on each side. ("The crowd gasped . . ." I want to write. Of course they didn't. They didn't make a sound, but the impact of the diamond yo-yo was obvious.) We'd never seen anything like it. One imagined how the stones would gleam as it revolved, and how much prettier the tricks would be. The ultimate yo-yo! The only one in town! Who knew what feats were possible with such an instrument? All around me a fierce, nervous resolve was settling into the contestants, suddenly skittish as racehorses.

"Ricardo will show trick with Grand Prize Yo-Yo. Rock the Cradle four time!"

"One!" cried Ramos.

"Two!" the kids joined in.

11

12

13

14

15

16

17

18   "Three!" It was really beautiful. He did it so slowly you would have thought he had all the time in the world. I counted seconds under my breath to see how long he made it sleep.

19   "Four!" said the crowd.

20   "Thirteen" I said to myself as the yo-yo snapped back into his hand. Thirteen seconds. Excellent time for that particular trick.

21   "Attention all kids!" Ramos announced. "Contest start now at head of line."

22   The first boy did a sloppy job of gathering his string but managed to rock the cradle quickly four times.

23   "Okay." Ramos tapped him on the shoulder and moved to the next boy, who fumbled. "Out." Ricardo followed, doing an occasional Loop-the-Loop with the diamond yo-yo. "Out . . . out . . . okay," said Ramos as he worked down the line.

24   There was something about the man's inexorable advance that unnerved me. His decisions were fast, and there was no appeal. To my surprise I felt my palms begin to sweat. Closer and closer he came, his voice growing louder, and then suddenly he was standing in front of me. Amazed, I stared at him. It was as if he'd appeared out of thin air.

25   "What happen boy, you swarrow bubble gum?"

26   The laughter jolted me out of it. Blushing, I threw down my yo-yo and executed a slow Rock the Cradle, counting the four passes and hesitating a moment at the end so as not to appear rushed.

27   "Okay." He tapped my shoulder. "Good."

28   I wiped my hands on my blue jeans and watched him move down the line. "Out . . . out . . . out." He had a large mole on the back of his neck.

29   Seven boys qualified. Coming back, Ramos called out, "Next trick Backward Round the World! Okay? Go!"

30   The first two boys missed, but the third was the kid in the sailor hat. Glancing quickly to see that no one was behind him, he hunched up his shoulder, threw, and just barely made the catch. There was some loose string in his hand, but not enough to disqualify him.

31   Number four missed, as did number five, and it was my turn. I stepped forward, threw the yo-yo almost straight up over my head, and as it began to fall pulled very gentle to add some speed. It zipped neatly behind my legs and there was nothing more to do. My head turned to one side, I stood absolutely still and watched the yo-yo come in over my shoulder and slap into my hand. I added a Loop-the-Loop just to show the tightness of the string.

32   "Did you see that?" I heard someone say.

33   Number seven missed, so it was between myself and the boy in

the sailor hat. His hair was bleached by the sun and combed up over his forehead in a pompadour, held from behind by the white hat. He was a year or two older than me. Blinking his blue eyes nervously, he adjusted the tension of his string.

"Next trick Cannonball! Cannonball! You go first this time," Ramos said to me. 34

Kids had gathered in a circle around us, those in front quiet and attentive, those in back jumping up and down to get a view. "Move back for room," Ricardo said, pushing them back. "More room, please." 35

I stepped into the center and paused, looking down at the ground. It was a difficult trick. The yo-yo had to land exactly on the string and there was a chance I'd miss the first time. I knew I wouldn't miss twice. "Can I have one practice?" 36

Ramos and Ricardo consulted in their mother tongue, and then Ramos held up his hands. "Attention all kids! Each boy have one practice before trick." 37

The crowd was then silent, watching me. I took a deep breath and threw, following the fall of the yo-yo with my eyes, turning slightly, matador-fashion, as it passed me. My finger caught the string, the yo-yo came up and over, and missed. Without pausing I threw again. "Second time," I yelled, so there would be no misunderstanding. The circle had been too big. This time I made it small, sacrificing beauty for security. The yo-yo fell where it belonged and spun for a moment. (A moment I don't rush, my arms widespread, my eyes locked on the spinning toy. The Trick! There it is, brief and magic right before your eyes! My hands are frozen in the middle of a deaf-and-dumb sentence, holding the whole airy, tenuous statement aloft for everyone to see.) With a quick snap I broke up the trick and made my catch. 38

Ramos nodded. "Okay. Very good. Now next boy." 39

Sailor-hat stepped forward, wiping his nose with the back of his hand. He threw once to clear the string. 40

"One practice," said Ramos. 41

He nodded. 42

"C'mon Bobby," someone said. "You can do it." 43

Bobby threw the yo-yo out to the side, made his move, and missed. "Damn," he whispered. (He said "dahyum.") The second time he got halfway through the trick before his yo-yo ran out of gas and fell impotently off the string. He picked it up and walked away, winding slowly. 44

Ramos came over and held my hand in the air. "The winner!" he 45 yelled. "Grand prize Black Beauty Diamond Yo-Yo will now be awarded."

46   Ricardo stood in front of me. "Take off old yo-yo." I loosened the knot and slipped it off. "Put out hand." I held out my hand and he looped the new string on my finger, just behind the nail, where the mark was. "You like Black Beauty," he said, smiling as he stepped back. "Diamond make pretty colors in the sun."

47   "Thank you," I said.

48   "Very good with yo-yo. Later we have contest for whole town. Winner go to Miami for State Championship. Maybe you win. Okay?"

49   "Okay." I nodded. "Thank you."

50   A few kids came up to look at Black Beauty. I threw it once or twice to get the feel. It seemed a bit heavier than my old one. Ramos and Ricardo were surrounded as the kids called out their favorite tricks.

51   "Do Pickpocket! Pickpocket!"

52   "Do the Double Cannonball!"

53   "Ramos! Ramos! Do the Turkish Army!"

54   Smiling, waving their hands to ward off the barrage of requests, the twins worked their way through the crowd toward the mouth of the alley. I watched them moving away and was immediately struck by a wave of fierce and irrational panic. "Wait," I yelled, pushing through after them. "Wait!"

55   I caught them on the street.

56   "No more today," Ricardo said, and then paused when he saw it was me. "Okay. The champ. What's wrong? Yo-yo no good?"

57   "No. It's fine."

58   "Good. You take care of it."

59   "I wanted to ask when the contest is. The one where you get to go to Miami."

60   "Later. After school begins." They began to move away. "We have to go home now."

61   "Just one more thing," I said, walking after them. "What is the hardest trick you know?"

62   Ricardo laughed. "Hardest trick is killing flies in air."

63   "No, no. I mean a real trick."

64   They stopped and looked at me. "There is a very hard trick," Ricardo said. "I don't do it, but Ramos does. Because you won the contest he will show you. But only once, so watch carefully."

65   We stepped into the lobby of the Sunset Theater. Ramos cleared his string. "Watch," he said, and threw. The trick started out like a

Cannonball, and then unexpectedly folded up, opened again, and as I watched breathlessly the entire complex web spun around in the air, propelled by Ramos' two hands making slow circles like a swimmer. The end was like the end of a Cannonball.

"That's beautiful," I said, genuinely awed. "What's it called?"   66

"The Universe."   67

"The Universe," I repeated.   68

"Because it goes around and around," said Ramos, "like the   69 planets."

_____ **CONSIDERATIONS** _____

1. List the several ways in which Conroy says one can get pleasure from the yo-yo.

2. How much of performance is play? Would you use the word performance for the work of a painter, an opera singer, a tennis star, a poet? Are professional athletes paid to play? What is the difference between work and play?

3. One respected writer says that "play is the direct opposite of seriousness," yet writers like Conroy are serious in recalling their childhood play. Can you resolve this apparent contradiction?

4. Conroy's essay might be divided into two major sections. Where would you draw the dividing line? Describe the two sections in terms of the author's intention. In the second section, the author makes constant use of dialogue; in the first, there is none. Why?

5. "I practiced the yo-yo because it pleased me to do so, without the slightest application of will power." Consider the relevance or irrelevance of will power to pleasure. Are they mutually exclusive?

6. In Paragraph 14, Conroy interrupts his narrative with a parenthetical remark about himself as the writer: "('The crowd gasped . . .' I want to write. Of course they didn't. They didn't make a sound, but the impact of the diamond yo-yo was obvious.)" Are such glimpses of the writer conscious of himself writing useful or merely distracting? Discuss.

Emily Dickinson (1830–1886) was little known as a poet in her lifetime, but is now acknowledged as among the greatest American poets. She lived her entire life in Amherst, Massachusetts, and spent her later years as a virtual recluse in the Dickinsons' brick homestead on Main Street. She was always close to her family, and kept contact with the outside world through a huge correspondence.

She published little poetry in her lifetime. After her death more than a thousand poems were discovered neatly arranged in the bureau of the upstairs bedroom where she wrote. In 1955, a definitive edition of The Poems of Emily Dickinson *was published, containing 1,775 poems and fragments.*

16

EMILY DICKINSON

There's a certain Slant of light

There's a certain Slant of light,
Winter Afternoons—
That oppresses, like the Heft
Of Cathedral Tunes—

5   Heavenly Hurt, it gives us—
We can find no scar,
But internal difference,
Where the Meanings, are—

None may teach it—Any—
'Tis the Seal Despair—   10
An imperial affliction
Sent us of the Air—

When it comes, the Landscape listens—
Shadows—hold their breath—
When it goes, 'tis like the Distance   15
On the look of Death—

Joan Didion (b. 1934) worked as an editor in New York for some years, and then returned to her native California where she supports herself by writing. She has collaborated on screenplays, including Panic in Needle Park *(1971) and* A Star Is Born *(1976). Best known for her novels —* Play It As It Lays *appeared in 1971,* A Book of Common Prayer *in 1977, and* Democracy *in 1984 — she is also admired for her essays, collected in* Slouching Towards Bethlehem *(1969), from which we take this essay, and* The White Album *(1979). Her long essay,* Salvador, *appeared as a book in 1983. Students who keep journals or notebooks, or who practice daily writing, may learn a thing or two from Joan Didion.*

17

JOAN DIDION

On Keeping a Notebook

1   " 'That woman Estelle,' " the note reads, " 'is partly the reason why George Sharp and I are separated today.' *Dirty crepe-de-Chine wrapper, hotel bar, Wilmington RR, 9:45* A.M. August Monday morning."

2   Since the note is in my notebook, it presumably has some meaning to me. I study it for a long while. At first I have only the most general notion of what I was doing on an August Monday morning in the bar of the hotel across from the Pennsylvania Railroad station in Wilmington, Delaware (waiting for a train? missing one? 1960? 1961? why Wilmington?), but I do remember being there. The woman in the dirty crepe-de-Chine wrapper had come down from her room for a

beer, and the bartender had heard before the reason why George Sharp and she were separated today. "Sure," he said, and went on mopping the floor. "You told me." At the other end of the bar is a girl. She is talking, pointedly, not to the man beside her but to a cat lying in the triangle of sunlight cast through the open door. She is wearing a plaid silk dress from Peck & Peck, and the hem is coming down.

Here is what it is: the girl has been on the Eastern Shore, and now she is going back to the city, leaving the man beside her, and all she can see ahead are the viscous summer sidewalks and the 3 A.M. long-distance calls that will make her lie awake and then sleep drugged through all the steaming mornings left in August (1960? 1961?). Because she must go directly from the train to lunch in New York, she wishes that she had a safety pin for the hem of the plaid silk dress, and she also wishes that she could forget about the hem and the lunch and stay in the cool bar that smells of disinfectant and malt and make friends with the woman in the crepe-de-Chine wrapper. She is afflicted by a little self-pity, and she wants to compare Estelles. That is what that was all about.

Why did I write it down? In order to remember, of course, but exactly what was it I wanted to remember? How much of it actually happened? Did any of it? Why do I keep a notebook at all? It is easy to deceive oneself on all those scores. The impulse to write things down is a peculiarly compulsive one, inexplicable to those who do not share it, useful only accidentally, only secondarily, in the way that any compulsion tries to justify itself. I suppose that it begins or does not begin in the cradle. Although I have felt compelled to write things down since I was five years old, I doubt that my daughter ever will, for she is a singularly blessed and accepting child, delighted with life exactly as life presents itself to her, unafraid to go to sleep and unafraid to wake up. Keepers of private notebooks are a different breed altogether, lonely and resistant rearrangers of things, anxious malcontents, children afflicted apparently at birth with some presentiment of loss.

My first notebook was a Big Five tablet, given to me by my mother with the sensible suggestion that I stop whining and learn to amuse myself by writing down my thoughts. She returned the tablet to me a few years ago; the first entry is an account of a woman who believed herself to be freezing to death in the Arctic night, only to find, when day broke, that she had stumbled onto the Sahara Desert, where she would die of the heat before lunch. I have no idea what turn of a five-year-old's mind could have prompted so insistently "ironic" and exotic a story, but it does reveal a certain predilection for the extreme which has dogged me into adult life; perhaps if I were analytically inclined I would find it a truer story than any I might have told about Donald Johnson's birthday party or the day my cousin Brenda put Kitty Litter in the aquarium.

6   So the point of my keeping a notebook has never been, nor is it now, to have an accurate factual record of what I have been doing or thinking. That would be a different impulse entirely, an instinct for reality which I sometimes envy but do not possess. At no point have I ever been able successfully to keep a diary; my approach to daily life ranges from the grossly negligent to the merely absent, and on those few occasions when I have tried dutifully to record a day's events, boredom has so overcome me that the results are mysterious at best. What is this business about "shopping, typing piece, dinner with E, depressed"? Shopping for what? Typing what piece? Who is E? Was this "E" depressed, or was I depressed? Who cares?

7   In fact I have abandoned altogether that kind of pointless entry; instead I tell what some would call lies. "That's simply not true," the members of my family frequently tell me when they come up against my memory of a shared event. "The party was *not* for you, the spider was *not* a black widow, *it wasn't that way at all.*" Very likely they are right, for not only have I always had trouble distinguishing between what happened and what merely might have happened, but I remain unconvinced that the distinction, for my purposes, matters. The cracked crab that I recall having for lunch the day my father came home from Detroit in 1945 must certainly be embroidery, worked into the day's pattern to lend verisimilitude; I was ten years old and would not now remember the cracked crab. The day's events did not turn on cracked crab. And yet it is precisely that fictitious crab that makes me see the afternoon all over again, a home movie run all too often, the father bearing gifts, the child weeping, an exercise in family love and guilt. Or that is what it was to me. Similarly, perhaps it never did snow that August in Vermont; perhaps there never were flurries in the night wind, and maybe no one else felt the ground hardening and summer already dead even as we pretended to bask in it, but that was how it felt to me, and it might as well have snowed, could have snowed, did snow.

8   *How it felt to me:* that is getting closer to the truth about a notebook. I sometimes delude myself about why I keep a notebook, imagine that some thrifty virtue derives from preserving everything

observed. See enough and write it down, I tell myself, and then some morning when the world seems drained of wonder, some day when I am only going through the motions of doing what I am supposed to do, which is write — on that bankrupt morning I will simply open my notebook and there it will all be, a forgotten account with accumulated interest, paid passage back to the world out there: dialogue overheard in hotels and elevators and at the hat-check counter in Pavillon (one middle-aged man shows his hat check to another and says, "That's my old football number"); impressions of Bettina Aptheker and Benjamin Sonnenberg and Teddy ("Mr. Acapulco") Stauffer; careful *aperçus* about tennis bums and failed fashion models and Greek shipping heiresses, one of whom taught me a significant lesson (a lesson I could have learned from F. Scott Fitzgerald, but perhaps we must meet the very rich for ourselves) by asking, when I arrived to interview her in her orchid-filled sitting room on the second day of a paralyzing New York blizzard, whether it was snowing outside.

9   I imagine, in other words, that the notebook is about other people. But of course it is not. I have no real business with what one stranger said to another at the hat-check counter in Pavillon; in fact I suspect that the line "That's my old football number" touched not my own imagination at all, but merely some memory of something once read, probably "The Eighty-Yard Run." Nor is my concern with a woman in a dirty crepe-de-Chine wrapper in a Wilmington bar. My stake is always, of course, in the unmentioned girl in the plaid silk dress. *Remember what it was to be me:* that is always the point.

10   It is a difficult point to admit. We are brought up in the ethic that others, any others, all others, are by definition more interesting than ourselves; taught to be diffident, just this side of self-effacing. ("You're the least important person in the room and don't forget it," Jessica Mitford's governess would hiss in her ear on the advent of any social occasion; I copied that into my notebook because it is only recently that I have been able to enter a room without hearing some such phrase in my inner ear.) Only the very young and the very old may recount their dreams at breakfast, dwell upon self, interrupt with memories of beach picnics and favorite Liberty lawn dresses and the rainbow trout in a creek near Colorado Springs. The rest of us are expected, rightly, to affect absorption in other people's favorite dresses, other people's trout.

11   And so we do. But our notebooks give us away, for however dutifully we record what we see around us, the common denominator of all we see is always, transparently, shamelessly, the implacable

"I." We are not talking here about the kind of notebook that is patently for public consumption, a structural conceit for binding together a series of graceful *pensées:* we are talking about something private, about bits of the mind's string too short to use, an indiscriminate and erratic assemblage with meaning only for its maker.

12   And sometimes even the maker has difficulty with the meaning. There does not seem to be, for example, any point in my knowing for the rest of my life that, during 1964, 720 tons of soot fell on every square mile of New York City, yet there it is in my notebook, labeled "FACT." Nor do I really need to remember that Ambrose Bierce liked to spell Leland Stanford's[1] name "£eland $tanford" or that "smart women almost always wear black in Cuba," a fashion hint without much potential for practical application. And does not the relevance of these notes seem marginal at best?:

> In the basement museum of the Inyo County Courthouse in Independence, California, sign pinned to a mandarin coat: "This MANDARIN COAT was often worn by Mrs. Minnie S. Brooks when giving lectures on her TEAPOT COLLECTION."

> Redhead getting out of car in front of Beverly Wilshire Hotel, chinchilla stole, Vuitton bags with tags reading:
>
>
> MRS LOU FOX
> HOTEL SAHARA
> VEGAS
>

13   Well perhaps not entirely marginal. As a matter of fact, Mrs. Minnie S. Brooks and her MANDARIN COAT pull me back into my own childhood, for although I never knew Mrs. Brooks and did not visit Inyo County until I was thirty, I grew up in just such a world, in houses cluttered with Indian relics and bits of gold ore and ambergris and the souvenirs my Aunt Mercy Farnsworth brought back from the Orient. It is a long way from that world to Mrs. Lou Fox's world, where we all live now, and is it not just as well to remember that? Might not Mrs. Minnie S. Brooks help me to remember what I am? Might not Mrs. Lou Fox help me to remember what I am not?

14   But sometimes the point is harder to discern. What exactly did I have in mind when I noted down that it cost the father of someone I know $650 a month to light the place on the Hudson in which he lived before the Crash? What use was I planning to make of this line by Jimmy Hoffa: "I may have my faults, but being wrong ain't one of

---

[1] Railroad magnate (1834–1893) who founded the university. — ED.

them"? And although I think it interesting to know where the girls
who travel with the Syndicate have their hair done when they find
themselves on the West Coast, will I ever make suitable use of it?
Might I not be better off just passing it on to John O'Hara? What is a
recipe for sauerkraut doing in my notebook? What kind of magpie
keeps this notebook? *"He was born the night the Titanic went down."*
That seems a nice enough line, and I even recall who said it, but is it
not really a better line in life than it could ever be in fiction?

But of course that is exactly it: not that I should ever use the   15
line, but that I should remember the woman who said it and the
afternoon I heard it. We were on her terrace by the sea, and we were
finishing the wine left from lunch, trying to get what sun there was, a
California winter sun. The woman whose husband was born the night
the *Titanic* went down wanted to rent her house, wanted to go back
to her children in Paris. I remember wishing that I could afford the
house, which cost $1,000 a month. "Someday you will," she said
lazily. "Someday it all comes." There in the sun on her terrace it
seemed easy to believe in someday, but later I had a low-grade afternoon hangover and ran over a black snake on the way to the supermarket and was flooded with inexplicable fear when I heard the
checkout clerk explaining to the man ahead of me why she was finally
divorcing her husband. "He left me no choice," she said over and over
as she punched the register. "He has a little seven-month-old baby by
her, he left me no choice." I would like to believe that my dread then
was for the human condition, but of course it was for me, because I
wanted a baby and did not then have one and because I wanted to own
the house that cost $1,000 a month to rent and because I had a hang-
over.

It all comes back. Perhaps it is difficult to see the value in having   16
one's self back in that kind of mood, but I do see it; I think we are well
advised to keep on nodding terms with the people we used to be,
whether we find them attractive company or not. Otherwise they turn
up unannounced and surprise us, come hammering on the mind's door
at 4 A.M. of a bad night and demand to know who deserted them, who
betrayed them, who is going to make amends. We forget all too soon
the things we thought we could never forget. We forget the loves and
the betrayals alike, forget what we whispered and what we screamed,
forget who we were. I have already lost touch with a couple of people
I used to be; one of them, a seventeen-year-old, presents little threat,
although it would be of some interest to me to know again what it
feels like to sit on a river levee drinking vodka-and-orange-juice and

listening to Les Paul and Mary Ford and their echoes sing "How High the Moon" on the car radio. (You see I still have the scenes, but I no longer perceive myself among those present, no longer could even improvise the dialogue.) The other one, a twenty-three-year-old, bothers me more. She was always a good deal of trouble, and I suspect she will reappear when I least want to see her, skirts too long, shy to the point of aggravation, always the injured party, full of recriminations and little hurts and stories I do not want to hear again, at once saddening me and angering me with her vulnerability and ignorance, an apparition all the more insistent for being so long banished.

17   It is a good idea, then, to keep in touch, and I suppose that keeping in touch is what notebooks are all about. And we are all on our own when it comes to keeping those lines open to ourselves: your notebook will never help me, nor mine you. *"So what's new in the whiskey business?"* What could that possibly mean to you? To me it means a blonde in a Pucci bathing suit sitting with a couple of fat men by the pool at the Beverly Hills Hotel. Another man approaches, and they all regard one another in silence for a while. "So what's new in the whiskey business?" one of the fat men finally says by way of welcome, and the blonde stands up, arches one foot and dips it in the pool, looking all the while at the cabaña where Baby Pignatari is talking on the telephone. That is all there is to that, except that several years later I saw the blonde coming out of Saks Fifth Avenue in New York with her California complexion and a voluminous mink coat. In the harsh wind that day she looked old and irrevocably tired to me, and even the skins in the mink coat were not worked the way they were doing them that year, not the way she would have wanted them done, and there is the point of the story. For a while after that I did not like to look in the mirror, and my eyes would skim the newspapers and pick out only the deaths, the cancer victims, the premature coronaries, the suicides, and I stopped riding the Lexington Avenue IRT because I noticed for the first time that all the strangers I had seen for years — the man with the seeing-eye dog, the spinster who read the classified pages every day, the fat girl who always got off with me at Grand Central — looked older than they once had.

18   It all comes back. Even that recipe for sauerkraut: even that brings it back. I was on Fire Island when I first made that sauerkraut, and it was raining, and we drank a lot of bourbon and ate the sauerkraut and went to bed at ten, and I listened to the rain and the Atlantic and felt safe. I made the sauerkraut again last night and it did not make me feel any safer, but that is, as they say, another story.

_____ **CONSIDERATIONS** _____

1. What is the difference between the selection by Didion and those by Anaïs Nin (pages 259–261), Thomas Wolfe (pages 453–460), and Sylvia Plath (pages 325–329)?

2. How far must you read in Didion's piece before you know her real reason for keeping a journal? Why does she delay that announcement so long? Might such a delay work well in one of your essays?

3. "You're the least important person in the room and don't forget it" is a line from Didion's journal. Does she believe that statement? If not, why does she include it in her essay?

4. The randomness of a notebook is one of Didion's topics. How does she use this randomness or lack of order or purpose to bring order and purpose to her essay? Take Paragraphs 14 and 15, and study the method she derives from her seeming madness.

5. In Paragraph 16, Didion says she has already "lost touch with a couple of people I used to be." Is such an awareness related to the last line of James Agee's "Knoxville: Summer 1915" (pages 7–11)? Have you ever had similar feelings about some of the people you used to be? What significant details in your memory come to mind?

6. Using a periodical index in your college library, see how quickly you can locate one of Didion's many journalistic essays.

*Annie Dillard (b. 1945), who now lives in Connecticut, was
born in Pittsburgh, went to Hollins College, and lived for a while
in Virginia in the Roanoke Valley — the area she describes so
well. In 1974, she published her first book of poems,* Tickets for a
Prayer Wheel, *and her first book of prose,* Pilgrim at Tinker
Creek, *which won a Pulitzer Prize. In 1977 she published* Holy
the Firm, *and in 1982* Living by Fiction.

This passage of description comes from Pilgrim at Tinker
Creek. *A walk in failing light, with the eyes of the body wide
open, takes on the fears of nightmare.*

18

ANNIE DILLARD
Strangers to Darkness

1   Where Tinker Creek flows under the sycamore log bridge to the
tear-shaped island, it is slow and shallow, fringed thinly in cattail
marsh. At this spot an astonishing bloom of life supports vast breeding
populations of insects, fish, reptiles, birds, and mammals. On windless
summer evenings I stalk along the creek bank or straddle the sycamore
log in absolute stillness, watching for muskrats. The night I stayed too
late I was hunched on the log staring spellbound at spreading, reflected
stains of lilac on the water. A cloud in the sky suddenly lighted as if
turned on by a switch; its reflection just as suddenly materialized on
the water upstream, flat and floating, so that I couldn't see the creek
bottom, or life in the water under the cloud. Downstream, away from
the cloud on the water, water turtles smooth as beans were gliding

down with the current in a series of easy, weightless push-offs, as men bound on the moon. I didn't know whether to trace the progress of one turtle I was sure of, risking sticking my face in one of the bridge's spider webs made invisible by the gathering dark, or take a chance on seeing the carp, or scan the mudbank in hope of seeing a muskrat, or follow the last of the swallows who caught at my heart and trailed it after them like streamers as they appeared from directly below, under the log, flying upstream with their tails forked, so fast.

But shadows spread and deepened and stayed. After thousands of years we're still strangers to darkness, fearful aliens in an enemy camp with our arms crossed over our chests. I stirred. A land turtle on the bank, startled, hissed the air from its lungs and withdrew to its shell. An uneasy pink here, an unfathomable blue there, gave great suggestion of lurking beings. Things were going on. I couldn't see whether that rustle I heard was a distant rattlesnake, slit-eyed, or a nearby sparrow kicking in the dry flood debris slung at the foot of a willow. Tremendous action roiled the water everywhere I looked, big action, inexplicable. A tremor welled up beside a gaping muskrat burrow in the bank and I caught my breath, but no muskrat appeared. The ripples continued to fan upstream with a steady, powerful thrust. Night was knitting an eyeless mask over my face, and I still sat transfixed. A distant airplane, a delta wing out of nightmare, made a gliding shadow on the creek's bottom that looked like a stingray cruising upstream. At once a black fin slit the pink cloud on the water, shearing it in two. The two halves merged together and seemed to dissolve before my eyes. Darkness pooled in the cleft of the creek and rose, as water collects in a well. Untamed, dreaming lights flickered over the sky. I saw hints of hulking underwater shadows, two pale splashes out of the water, and round ripples rolling close together from a blackened center.

At last I stared upstream where only the deepest violet remained of the cloud, a cloud so high its underbelly still glowed, its feeble color reflected from a hidden sky lighted in turn by a sun halfway to China. And out of that violet, a sudden enormous black body arced over the water. Head and tail, if there was a head and tail, were both submerged in cloud. I saw only one ebony fling, a headlong dive to darkness; then the water closed, and the lights went out.

I walked home in a shivering daze, up hill and down. Later I lay openmouthed in bed, my arms flung wide at my sides to steady the whirling darkness. At this latitude I'm spinning 836 miles an hour round the earth's axis; I feel my sweeping fall as a breakneck arc like the dive of dolphins, and the hollow rushing of wind raises the hairs on my neck and the side of my face. In orbit around the sun I'm moving 64,800 miles an hour. The solar system as a whole, like a merry-go-round unhinged, spins, bobs, and blinks at the speed of 43,200 miles an hour along a course set east of Hercules. Someone has piped, and we are dancing a tarantella until the sweat pours. I open my eyes and I see dark, muscled forms curl out of water, with flapping gills and flattened eyes. I close my eyes and I see stars, deep stars giving way to deeper stars, deeper stars bowing to deepest stars at the crown of an infinite cone.

_____ CONSIDERATIONS _____

1. Like exposition and argument, description and narration are encountered together more often than they are encountered separately. Still, there are real differences between describing something and following a sequence of actions. To see this difference, compare and contrast Dillard's descriptive writing with a clearly narrative selection in this book: Martin Gansberg, Lillian Hellman, Norman Mailer, George Orwell ("Shooting an Elephant"), James C. Rettie, Eudora Welty ("A Worn Path"), or Thomas Wolfe.

2. Telling what she saw that night along Tinker Creek, Dillard uses many literal and figurative images; list them and discuss their differences. In your own essays, do you use phrases that appeal to the senses?

3. Toward the end of this short selection, Dillard suddenly injects facts — the speed of the earth's rotation, for instance. How does this information contribute to her attempt to evoke wonder in us?

4. "Night was knitting an eyeless mask over my face. . . . " Many might describe such language as fancy, flowery, or indirect, and protest that the writer should "just come out and say what she means." Discuss these complaints, thinking of what Dillard intends to accomplish.

5. Dillard describes the effects of one evening on one small creek in one rural neighborhood. Why, then, does she refer to China and the solar system?

Teaching a Stone to Talk (1982) gathers Annie Dillard's mis-cellaneous essays from periodicals. Book reviewers often conde-scend to such collections; in her introduction to the work Annie Dillard wants to be certain that readers understand and tells us ". . . this is my real work." The brief essay is her literary form, and she masters it as Chekhov mastered the short story.

19

ANNIE DILLARD
Sojourner

If survival is an art, then mangroves are artists of the beautiful: not only that they exist at all — smooth-barked, glossy-leaved, thick-ets of lapped mystery — but that they can and do exist as floating islands, as trees upright and loose, alive and homeless on the water. 1

I have seen mangroves, always on tropical ocean shores, in Flor-ida and in the Galápagos. There is the red mangrove, the yellow, the button, and the black. They are all short, messy trees, waxy-leaved, laced all over with aerial roots, woody arching buttresses, and weird leathery berry pods. All this tangles from a black muck soil, a black muck matted like a mud-sopped rag, a muck without any other plants, shaded, cold to the touch, tracked at the water's edge by herons and nosed by sharks. 2

It is these shoreline trees which, by a fairly common accident, can become floating islands. A hurricane flood or a riptide can wrest a tree from the shore, or from the mouth of a tidal river, and hurl it into the ocean. It floats. It is a mangrove island, blown. 3

4   There are floating islands on the planet; it amazes me. Credulous Pliny described some islands thought to be mangrove islands floating on a river. The people called these river islands *the dancers,* "because in any consort of musicians singing, they stir and move at the stroke of the feet, keeping time and measure."

5   Trees floating on rivers are less amazing than trees floating on the poisonous sea. A tree cannot live in salt. Mangrove trees exude salt from their leaves; you can see it, even on shoreline black mangroves, as a thin white crust. Lick a leaf and your tongue curls and coils; your mouth's a heap of salt.

6   Nor can a tree live without soil. A hurricane-born mangrove island may bring its own soil to the sea. But other mangrove trees make their own soil — and their own islands — from scratch. These are the ones which interest me. The seeds germinate in the fruit on the tree. The germinated embryo can drop anywhere — say, onto a dab of floating muck. The heavy root end sinks; a leafy plumule unfurls. The tiny seedling, afloat, is on its way. Soon aerial roots shooting out in all directions trap debris. The sapling's networks twine, the interstices narrow, and water calms in the lee. Bacteria thrive on organic broth; amphipods swarm. These creatures grow and die at the trees' wet feet. The soil thickens, accumulating rainwater, leaf rot, seashells, and guano; the island spreads.

7   More seeds and more muck yield more trees on the new island. A society grows, interlocked in a tangle of dependencies. The island rocks less in the swells. Fish throng to the backwaters stilled in snarled roots. Soon, Asian mudskippers — little four-inch fish — clamber up the mangrove roots into the air and peer about from periscope eyes on stalks, like snails. Oysters clamp to submersed roots, as do starfish, dog whelk, and the creatures that live among tangled kelp. Shrimp seek shelter there, limpets a holdfast, pelagic birds a rest.

8   And the mangrove island wanders on, afloat and adrift. It walks teetering and wanton before the wind. Its fate and direction are random. It may bob across an ocean and catch on another mainland's shores. It may starve or dry while it is still a sapling. It may topple in a storm, or pitchpole. By the rarest of chances, it may stave into another mangrove island in a crash of clacking roots, and mesh. What it is most likely to do is drift anywhere in the alien ocean, feeding on death and growing, netting a makeshift soil as it goes, shrimp in its toes and terns in its hair.

9   We could do worse.

10   I alternate between thinking of the planet as home — dear and

familiar stone hearth and garden — and as a hard land of exile in which we are all sojourners. Today I favor the latter view. The word "sojourner" occurs often in the English Old Testament. It invokes a nomadic people's sense of vagrancy, a praying people's knowledge of estrangement, a thinking people's intuition of sharp loss: "For we are strangers before thee, and sojourners, as were all our fathers: our days on the earth are as a shadow, and there is none abiding."

We don't know where we belong, but in times of sorrow it 11
doesn't seem to be here, here with these silly pansies and witless mountains, here with sponges and hard-eyed birds. In times of sorrow the innocence of the other creatures — from whom and with whom we evolved — seems a mockery. Their ways are not our ways. We seem set among them as among lifelike props for a tragedy — or a broad lampoon — on a thrust rock stage.

It doesn't seem to be here that we belong, here where space is 12
curved, the earth is round, we're all going to die, and it seems as wise to stay in bed as budge. It is strange here, not quite warm enough, or too warm, too leafy, or inedible, or windy, or dead. It is not, frankly, the sort of home for people one would have thought of — although I lack the fancy to imagine another.

The planet itself is a sojourner in airless space, a wet ball flung 13
across nowhere. The few objects in the universe scatter. The coherence of matter dwindles and crumbles toward stillness. I have read, and repeated, that our solar system as a whole is careering through space toward a point east of Hercules. Now I wonder: what could that possibly mean, east of Hercules? Isn't space curved? When we get "there," how will our course change, and why? Will we slide down the universe's inside arc like mud slung at a wall? Or what sort of welcoming shore is this east of Hercules? Surely we don't anchor there, and disembark, and sweep into dinner with our host. Does someone cry, "Last stop, last stop"? At any rate, east of Hercules, like east of Eden, isn't a place to call home. It is a course without direction; it is "out." And we are cast.

These are enervating thoughts, the thoughts of despair. They 14
crowd back, unbidden, when human life as it unrolls goes ill, when we lose control of our lives or the illusion of control, and it seems that we are not moving toward any end but merely blown. Our life seems cursed to be a wiggle merely, and a wandering without end. Even nature is hostile and poisonous, as though it were impossible for our vulnerability to survive on these acrid stones.

Whether these thoughts are true or not I find less interesting than 15 the possibilities for beauty they may hold. We are down here in time, where beauty grows. Even if things are as bad as they could possibly be, and as meaningless, then matters of truth are themselves indifferent; we may as well please our sensibilities and, with as much spirit as we can muster, go out with a buck and wing.

16   The planet is less like an enclosed spaceship — spaceship earth — than it is like an exposed mangrove island beautiful and loose. We the people started small and have since accumulated a great and solacing muck of soil, of human culture. We are rooted in it; we are bearing it with us across nowhere. The word "nowhere" is our cue: the consort of musicians strikes up, and we in the chorus stir and move and start twirling our hats. A mangrove island turns drift to dance. It creates its own soil as it goes, rocking over the salt sea at random, rocking day and night and round the sun, rocking round the sun and out toward east of Hercules.

___ CONSIDERATIONS _____

1. In many passages, Annie Dillard's prose verges on poetry, particularly in her high degree of compression in alluding to persons ("Pliny," Paragraph 4), places ("Galápagos," Paragraph 2; "east of Hercules," Paragraph 13), and sources (see Psalms 39 for the quotation in Paragraph 10) that may not be immediately recognizable to the hurried reader. You will enjoy her essay more and appreciate her skill if you take the time to determine the significance of these allusions.

2. One of the hallmarks of an accomplished writer like Dillard is the ability to integrate the various materials of an essay. As one example, study her closing paragraph to see how tightly she brings together elements she has introduced earlier.

3. Explain why a reader would be foolish to conclude that Dillard's essay is simply a study of the mangrove islands, of interest only to students of natural history. What would you suspect might account for such a conclusion?

4. Dillard's diction (choice of words) mixes vocabularies. Find a few other contrasts, such as the scientific ("plumule," "amphipods," "pelagic") vs. the imaginative ("matted like a mud-sopped rag," or "shrimp in its toes and terns in its hair") vs. the nautical ("pitchpole," "stave," "lee") and discuss the delights and difficulties for a reader encountering such diversity.

5. Does Dillard offer any consolation for the sense of despairing rootlessness she expresses in Paragraph 13? Explain in a short essay based on your own ideas about the destiny or purpose of humankind's presence on the planet.

Frederick Douglass (1817–1895) was born a slave in Maryland, escaped to Massachusetts in 1838, lectured against slavery, and wrote out of his experience. "Plantation Life" comes from A Narrative of the Life of Frederick Douglass, an American Slave, Written by Himself *(1845). During the Civil War he organized two regiments of black troops in Massachusetts; in the Reconstruction period he worked for the government.*

20

FREDERICK DOUGLASS
Plantation Life

My master's family consisted of two sons, Andrew and Richard;   1
one daughter, Lucretia, and her husband, Captain Thomas Auld. They
lived in one house, upon the home plantation of Colonel Edward
Lloyd. My master was Colonel Lloyd's clerk and superintendent. He
was what might be called the overseer of the overseers. I spent two
years of childhood on this plantation in my old master's family. . . .
As I received my first impressions of slavery on this plantation, I will
give some description of it, and of slavery as it there existed. The
plantation is about twelve miles north of Easton, in Talbot county,
and is situated on the border of Miles River. The principal products
raised upon it were tobacco, corn, and wheat. These were raised in
great abundance; so that, with the products of this and the other farms
belonging to him, he was able to keep in almost constant employment
a large sloop, in carrying them to market at Baltimore. This sloop was
named Sally Lloyd, in honor of one of the colonel's daughters. My
master's son-in-law, Captain Auld, was master of the vessel; she was
otherwise manned by the colonel's own slaves. Their names were
Peter, Isaac, Rich, and Jake. These were esteemed very highly by the

109

other slaves, and looked upon as the privileged ones of the plantation; for it was no small affair, in the eyes of the slaves, to be allowed to see Baltimore.

2 Colonel Lloyd kept from three to four hundred slaves on his home plantation, and owned a large number more on the neighboring farms belonging to him. The names of the farms nearest to the home plantation were Wye Town and New Design. "Wye Town" was under the overseership of a man named Noah Willis. New Design was under the overseership of a Mr. Townsend. The overseers of these, and all the rest of the farms, numbering over twenty, received advice and direction from the managers of the home plantation. This was the great business place. It was the seat of government for the whole twenty farms. All disputes among the overseers were settled here. If a slave was convicted of any high misdemeanor, became unmanageable, or evinced a determination to run away, he was brought immediately here, severely whipped, put on board the sloop, carried to Baltimore, and sold to Austin Woolfolk, or some other slave-trader, as a warning to the slaves remaining.

3 Here, too, the slaves of all the other farms received their monthly allowance of food, and their yearly clothing. The men and women slaves received, as their monthly allowance of food, eight pounds of pork, or its equivalent in fish, and one bushel of corn meal. Their yearly clothing consisted of two coarse linen shirts, one pair of linen trousers, like the shirts, one jacket, one pair of trousers for winter, made of coarse negro cloth, one pair of stockings, and one pair of shoes; the whole of which could not have cost more than seven dollars. The allowance of the slave children was given to their mothers, or the old women having the care of them. The children unable to work in the field had neither shoes, stockings, jackets, nor trousers, given to them; their clothing consisted of two coarse linen shirts per year. When these failed them, they went naked until the next allowance-day. Children from seven to ten years old, of both sexes, almost naked, might be seen at all seasons of the year.

4 There were no beds given the slaves, unless one coarse blanket be considered such, and none but the men and women had these. This, however, is not considered a very great privation. They find less difficulty from the want of beds, than from the want of time to sleep; for when their day's work in the field is done, the most of them having their washing, mending, and cooking to do, and having few or none of the ordinary facilities for doing either of these, very many of their sleeping hours are consumed in preparing for the field the coming day; and when this is done, old and young, male and female, married and

single, drop down side by side, on one common bed, — the cold, damp floor, — each covering himself or herself with their miserable blankets; and here they sleep till they are summoned to the field by the driver's horn. At the sound of this, all must rise, and be off to the field. There must be no halting; every one must be at his or her post; and woe betides them who hear not this morning summons to the field; for if they are not awakened by the sense of hearing, they are by the sense of feeling: no age nor sex finds any favor. Mr. Severe, the overseer, used to stand by the door of the quarter, armed with a large hickory stick and heavy cowskin, ready to whip any one who was so unfortunate as not to hear, or, from any other cause, was prevented from being ready to start for the field at the sound of the horn.

Mr. Severe was rightly named: he was a cruel man. I have seen   5 him whip a woman, causing the blood to run half an hour at the time; and this, too, in the midst of her crying children, pleading for their mother's release. He seemed to take pleasure in manifesting his fiendish barbarity. Added to his cruelty, he was a profane swearer. It was enough to chill the blood and stiffen the hair of an ordinary man to hear him talk. Scarce a sentence escaped him but that was commenced or concluded by some horrid oath. The field was the place to witness his cruelty and profanity. His presence made it both the field of blood and of blasphemy. From the rising till the going down of the sun, he was cursing, raving, cutting, and slashing among the slaves of the field, in the most frightful manner. His career was short. He died very soon after I went to Colonel Lloyd's; and he died as he lived, uttering, with his dying groans, bitter curses and horrid oaths. His death was regarded by the slaves as the result of a merciful providence.

Mr. Severe's place was filled by a Mr. Hopkins. He was a very   6 different man. He was less cruel, less profane, and made less noise, than Mr. Severe. His course was characterized by no extraordinary demonstrations of cruelty. He whipped, but seemed to take no pleasure in it. He was called by the slaves a good overseer.

The home plantation of Colonel Lloyd wore the appearance of a   7 country village. All the mechanical operations for all the farms were performed here. The shoemaking and mending, the blacksmithing, cartwrighting, coopering, weaving, and grain-grinding, were all performed by the slaves on the home plantation. The whole place wore a business-like aspect very unlike the neighboring farms. The number of houses, too, conspired to give it advantage over the neighboring farms. It was called by the slaves the *Great House Farm.* Few privileges were esteemed higher, by the slaves of the out-farms, than that of being selected to do errands at the Great House Farm. It was associated in their minds with greatness. A representative could not be prouder of his election to a seat in the American Congress, than a slave on one of the out-farms would be of his election to do errands at the Great House Farm. They regarded it as evidence of great confidence reposed in them by their overseers; and it was on this account, as well as a constant desire to be out of the field from under the driver's lash, that they esteemed it a high privilege, one worth careful living for. He was called the smartest and most trusty fellow, who had this honor conferred upon him the most frequently. The competitors for this office sought as diligently to please their overseers, as the office-seekers in the political parties seek to please and deceive the people. The same traits of character might be seen in Colonel Lloyd's slaves, as are seen in the slaves of the political parties.

8   The slaves selected to go to the Great House Farm, for the monthly allowance for themselves and their fellow-slaves, were peculiarly enthusiastic. While on their way, they would make the dense old woods, for miles around, reverberate with their wild songs, revealing at once the highest joy and the deepest sadness. They would compose and sing as they went along, consulting neither time nor tune. The thought that came up, came out — if not in the word, in the sound; — and as frequently in the one as in the other. They would sometimes sing the most pathetic sentiment in the most rapturous tone, and the most rapturous sentiment in the most pathetic tone. Into all of their songs they would manage to weave something of the Great House Farm. Especially would they do this, when leaving home. They would then sing most exultingly the following words:—

> I am going away to the Great House Farm!
> O, yea! O, yea! O!

This they would sing, as a chorus, to words which to many would seem unmeaning jargon, but which, nevertheless, were full of meaning to themselves. I have sometimes thought that the mere hearing of those songs would do more to impress some minds with the horrible character of slavery, than the reading of whole volumes of philosophy on the subject could do.

9   I did not, when a slave, understand the deep meaning of those rude and apparently incoherent songs. I was myself within the circle; so that I neither saw nor heard as those without might see and hear. They told a tale of woe which was then altogether beyond my feeble comprehension; they were tones loud, long, and deep; they breathed

the prayer and complaint of souls boiling over with the bitterest anguish. Every tone was a testimony against slavery, and a prayer to God for deliverance from chains. The hearing of those wild notes always depressed my spirit, and filled me with ineffable sadness. I have frequently found myself in tears while hearing them. The mere recurrence of those songs, even now, afflicts me; and while I am writing these lines, an expression of feeling has already found its way down my cheek. To those songs I trace my first glimmering conception of the dehumanizing character of slavery. I can never get rid of that conception. Those songs still follow me, to deepen my hatred of slavery, and quicken my sympathies for my brethren in bonds. If any one wishes to be impressed with the soul-killing effects of slavery, let him go to Colonel Lloyd's plantation, and, on allowance-day, place himself in the deep pine woods, and there let him, in silence, analzye the sounds that shall pass through the chambers of his soul, — and if he is not thus impressed, it will only be because "there is no flesh in his obdurate heart."

I have often been utterly astonished, since I came to the north, to find persons who could speak of the singing, among slaves, as evidence of their contentment and happiness. It is impossible to conceive of a greater mistake. Slaves sing most when they are most unhappy. The songs of the slave represent the sorrows of his heart; and he is relieved by them, only as an aching heart is relieved by its tears. At least, such is my experience. I have often sung to drown my sorrow, but seldom to express my happiness. Crying for joy, and singing for joy, were alike uncommon to me while in the jaws of slavery. The singing of a man cast away upon a desolate island might be as appropriately considered as evidence of contentment and happiness, as the singing of a slave; the songs of the one and of the other are prompted by the same emotion.

10

_____ CONSIDERATIONS _____

1. Is there anything to suggest, at the end of Paragraph 7, that Douglass had a talent for satire?

2. In Paragraphs 2 and 7, Douglass sketches the operations of the home plantation and its relationship to the outlying farms owned by the same man. Does the arrangement sound feudal? How did the plantation system differ from feudalism?

3. "I was myself within the circle; so that I neither saw nor heard as those without might see and hear," writes Douglass in Paragraph 9. Is a fish

aware that its medium is water? Can a freshman writer understand what he is doing with his own language?

4. What single phenomenon, according to Douglass, taught him the most moving and enduring lesson about the dehumanizing character of slavery? In what way did that lesson surprise those who had not had Douglass's experience?

5. Paragraph 5 offers a good example of Douglass's typical sentence structure: a linear series of independent clauses, with little or no subordination, all of which produces a blunt, stop-and-go effect. Without losing any of the information provided, rewrite the paragraph, reducing the number of sentences from twelve to six. Do this by converting some of the sentences to phrases, modifying clauses, or, in some cases, single-word modifiers.

Loren Eiseley (1907–1977) was an anthropologist who taught at the University of Pennsylvania, and a writer of unusual ability, author of two books of poems and numerous collections of prose including The Night Country *(1971) and* All the Strange Hours *(1975). Eiseley was a scientist-poet, a human brooder over the natural world, determined never to distort the real world by his brooding dream, an objective anthropologist with a talent for subjective response.*

Imagination and chemistry equally inform "More Thoughts on Wilderness." When Eiseley writes about an experience in the badlands of Nebraska and South Dakota, he combines not only imagination and chemistry, not only archaeology and imagery, but religious feeling and scientific thought.

21

LOREN EISELEY
More Thoughts on Wilderness

On the maps of the old voyageurs it is called *Mauvaises Terres*, 1 the evil lands, and, slurred a little with the passage through many minds, it has come down to us anglicized as the badlands. The soft shuffle of moccasins has passed through its canyons on the grim business of war and flight, but the last of those slight disturbances of immemorial silences died out almost a century ago. The land, if one can call it a land, is a waste as lifeless as that valley in which lie the kings of Egypt. Like the Valley of the Kings, it is a mausoleum, a place of dry bones in what once was a place of life. Now it has silences as deep as those in the moon's airless chasms.

2   Nothing grows among its pinnacles; there is no shade except under great toadstools of sandstone whose bases have been eaten to the shape of wine glasses by the wind. Everything is flaking, cracking, disintegrating, wearing away in the long, imperceptible weather of time. The ash of ancient volcanic outbursts still sterilizes its soil, and its colors in that waste are the colors that flame in the lonely sunsets on dead planets. Men come there but rarely, and for one purpose only, the collection of bones.

3   It was a late hour on a cold, wind-bitten autumn day when I climbed a great hill spined like a dinosaur's back and tried to take my bearings. The tumbled waste fell away in waves in all directions. Blue air was darkening into purple along the bases of the hills. I shifted my knapsack, heavy with the petrified bones of long-vanished creatures, and studied my compass. I wanted to be out of there by nightfall, and already the sun was going sullenly down in the west.

4   It was then that I saw the flight coming on. It was moving like a little close-knit body of black specks that danced and darted and closed again. It was pouring from the north and heading toward me with the undeviating relentlessness of a compass needle. It streamed through the shadows rising out of monstrous gorges. It rushed over towering pinnacles in the red light of the sun or momentarily sank from sight within their shade. Across that desert of eroding clay and windworn stone they came with a faint wild twittering that filled all the air about me as those tiny living bullets hurtled past into the night.

5   It may not strike you as a marvel. It would not, perhaps, unless you stood in the middle of a dead world at sunset, but that was where I stood. Fifty million years lay under my feet, fifty million years of bellowing monsters moving in a green world now gone so utterly that its very light was traveling on the farther edge of space. The chemicals of all that vanished age lay about me in the ground. Around me still lay the shearing molars of dead titanotheres, the delicate sabers of soft-stepping cats, the hollow sockets that had held the eyes of many a strange, outmoded beast. Those eyes had looked out upon a world as real as ours: dark, savage brains had roamed and roared their challenges into the steaming night.

6   Now they were still here, or, put it as you will, the chemicals that made them were here about me in the ground. The carbon that had driven them ran blackly in the eroding stone. The stain of iron was in the clays. The iron did not remember the blood it had once moved within, the phosphorus had forgot the savage brain. The little individual moment had ebbed from all those strange combinations of

chemicals as it would ebb from our living bodies into the sinks and runnels of oncoming time.

I had lifted up a fistful of that ground. I held it while that wild flight of south-bound warblers hurtled over me into the oncoming dark. There went phosphorus, there went iron, there went carbon, there beat the calcium in those hurrying wings. Alone on a dead planet I watched that incredible miracle speeding past. It ran by some true compass over field and waste land. It cried its individual ecstasies into the air until the gullies rang. It swerved like a single body, it knew itself, and, lonely, it bunched close in the racing darkness, its individual entities feeling about them the rising night. And so, crying to each other their identity, they passed away out of my view.

I dropped my fistful of earth. I heard it roll inanimate back into the gully at the base of the hill: iron, carbon, the chemicals of life. Like men from those wild tribes who had haunted these hills before me seeking visions. I made my sign to the great darkness. It was not a mocking sign, and I was not mocked. As I walked into my camp late that night, one man, rousing from his blankets beside the fire, asked sleepily, "What did you see?"

"I think, a miracle," I said softly, but I said it to myself. Behind me that vast waste began to glow under the rising moon.

—— CONSIDERATIONS ——

1. Eiseley's style attracts readers to his essays because he enlivens his expository prose with figures of speech. Write a brief study of his figurative writing, beginning, perhaps, with the half-dozen examples presented in Paragraphs 2 and 3.

2. As a professional anthropologist and archaeologist, Eiseley had many occasions to write the "process essay," that is, the step-by-step explanation of the workings of a particular process. To what extent could "More Thoughts on Wilderness" be called a process essay? Why would that term be unsatisfactory as a complete description of the piece?

3. Eiseley's reflections take him to the chemical elements of life — carbon, iron, phosphorus. How does he escape the sterile kind of analysis and categorization that Henry David Thoreau criticizes in "Thinking Like a Bream," (pages 406–409)?

4. What prompts Eiseley to conclude that what he had seen was a miracle? Explain.

5. Using the passage of long periods of time, as Eiseley does, write a short, descriptive essay in which you reflect on a landscape you know well.

Ralph Ellison (b. 1914), born in Oklahoma, won the National Book Award in 1953 for his novel The Invisible Man. Shadow and Act *(1964) collected his essays. For thirty years, Ellison has lectured and written on literature and race.*

22

RALPH ELLISON
On Becoming A Writer

1   In the beginning writing was far from a serious matter; it was a reflex of reading, an extension of a source of pleasure, escape, and instruction. In fact, I had become curious about writing by way of seeking to understand the aesthetic nature of literary power, the devices through which literature could command my mind and emotions. It was not, then, the *process* of writing which initially claimed my attention, but the finished creations, the artifacts, poems, plays, novels. The act of learning writing technique was, therefore, an amusing investigation of what seemed at best a secondary talent, an exploration, like dabbling in sculpture, of one's potentialities as a "Renaissance Man." This, surely, would seem a most unlikely and even comic concept to introduce here; and yet, it is precisely because I come from where I do (the Oklahoma of the years between World War I and the Great Depression) that I must introduce it, and with a straight face.

2   Anything and everything was to be found in the chaos of Oklahoma; thus the concept of the Renaissance Man has lurked long within the shadow of my past, and I shared it with at least a half dozen of my Negro friends. How we actually acquired it I have never learned,

and since there is no true sociology of the dispersion of ideas within the American democracy, I doubt if I ever shall. Perhaps we breathed it in with the air of the Negro community of Oklahoma City, the capital of that state whose Negroes were often charged by exasperated white Texans with not knowing their "place." Perhaps we took it defiantly from one of them. Or perhaps I myself picked it up from some transplanted New Englander whose shoes I had shined of a Saturday afternoon. After all, the most meaningful tips do not always come in the form of money, nor are they intentionally extended. Most likely, however, my friends and I acquired the idea from some book or some idealistic Negro teacher, some dreamer seeking to function responsibly in an environment which at its most normal took on some of the mixed character of nightmare and of dream.

One thing is certain, ours was a chaotic community, still char- 3
acterized by frontier attitudes and by that strange mixture of the naive and sophisticated, the benign and malignant, which makes the American past so puzzling and its present so confusing; that mixture which often affords the minds of the young who grow up in the far provinces such wide and unstructured latitude, and which encourages the individual's imagination — up to the moment "reality" closes in upon him — to range widely and, sometimes, even to soar.

We hear the effects of this in the Southwestern jazz of the 30's, 4
that joint creation of artistically free and exuberantly creative adventurers, of artists who had stumbled upon the freedom lying within the restrictions of their musical tradition as within the limitations of their social background, and who in their own unconscious way have set an example for any Americans, Negro or white, who would find themselves in the arts. They accepted themselves and the complexity of life as they knew it, they loved their art and through it they celebrated American experience definitively in sound. Whatever others thought or felt, this was their own powerful statement, and only non-musical assaults upon their artistic integrity — mainly economically inspired changes of fashion — were able to compromise their vision.

Much of so-called Kansas City jazz was actually brought to per- 5
fection in Oklahoma by Oklahomans. It is an important circumstance for me as a writer to remember, because while these musicians and their fellows were busy creating out of tradition, imagination, and the sounds and emotions around them, a freer, more complex, and driving form of jazz, my friends and I were exploring an idea of human versatility and possibility which went against the barbs or over the palings of almost every fence which those who controlled social and political

power had erected to restrict our roles in the life of the country. Looking back, one might say that the jazzmen, some of whom we idolized, were in their own way better examples for youth to follow than were most judges and ministers, legislators and governors (we were stuck with the notorious Alfalfa Bill Murray). For as we viewed these pillars of society from the confines of our segregated community we almost always saw crooks, clowns, or hypocrites. Even the best were revealed by their attitudes toward us as lacking the respectable qualities to which they pretended and for which they were accepted outside by others, while despite the outlaw nature of their art, the jazzmen were less torn and damaged by the moral compromises and insincerities which have so sickened the life of our country.

6   Be that as it may, our youthful sense of life, like that of many Negro children (though no one bothers to note it — especially the specialists and "friends of the Negro" who view our Negro-American life as essentially non-human) was very much like that of Huckleberry Finn, who is universally so praised and enjoyed for the clarity and courage of his moral vision. Like Huck, we observed, we judged, we imitated and evaded as we could the dullness, corruption, and blindness of "civilization." We were undoubtedly comic because, as the saying goes, we weren't supposed to know what it was all about. But to ourselves we were "boys," members of a wild, free, outlaw tribe which transcended the category of race. Rather we were Americans born into the forty-sixth state, and thus, into the context of Negro-American post-Civil War history, "frontiersmen." And isn't one of the implicit functions of the American frontier to encourage the individual to a kind of dreamy wakefulness, a state in which he makes — in all ignorance of the accepted limitations of the possible — rash efforts, quixotic gestures, hopeful testings of the complexity of the known and the given?

7   Spurring us on in our controlled and benign madness was the voracious reading of which most of us were guilty and the vicarious identification and empathetic adventuring which it encouraged. This was due, in part, perhaps to the fact that some of us were fatherless — my own father had died when I was three — but most likely it was because boys are natural romantics. We were seeking examples, patterns to live by, out of a freedom which for all its being ignored by the sociologists and subtle thinkers, was implicit in the Negro situation. Father and mother substitutes also have a role to play in aiding the child to help create himself. Thus we fabricated our own heroes and ideals catch-as-catch-can; and with an outrageous and irreverent sense

of freedom. Yes, and in complete disregard of ideas of respectability or the surreal incongruity of some of our projections. Gamblers and scholars, jazz musicians and scientists, Negro cowboys and soldiers from the Spanish-American and First World Wars, movie stars and stunt men, figures from the Italian Renaissance and literature, both classical and popular, were combined with the special virtues of some local bootlegger, the eloquence of some Negro preacher, the strength and grace of some local athlete, the ruthlessness of some businessman-physician, the elegance in dress and manners of some head-waiter or hotel doorman.

Looking back through the shadows upon this absurd activity, I realize now that we were projecting archetypes, recreating folk figures, legendary heroes, monsters even, most of which violated all ideas of social hierarchy and order and all accepted conceptions of the hero handed down by cultural, religious, and racist tradition. But we, remember, were under the intense spell of the early movies, the silents as well as the talkies; and in our community, life was not so tightly structured as it would have been in the traditional South — or even in deceptively "free" Harlem. And our imaginations processed reality and dream, natural man and traditional hero, literature and folklore, like maniacal editors turned loose in some frantic film-cutting room. Remember, too, that being boys, yet in the play-stage of our development, we were dream-serious in our efforts. But serious nevertheless, for *culturally* play is a preparation, and we felt that somehow the human ideal lay in the vague and constantly shifting figures — sometimes comic but always versatile, picaresque, and self-effacingly heroic — which evolved from our wildly improvisatory projections: figures neither white nor black, Christian nor Jewish, but representative of certain desirable essences, of skills and powers, physical, aesthetic, and moral. 8

The proper response to these figures was, we felt, to develop ourselves for the performance of many and diverse roles, and the fact that certain definite limitations had been imposed upon our freedom did not lessen our sense of obligation. Not only were we to prepare but we were to perform — not with mere competence but with an almost reckless verve; with, may we say (without evoking the quaint and questionable notion of *négritude*) Negro-American style? Behind each artist there stands a traditional sense of style, a sense of the felt tension indicative of expressive completeness; a mode of humanizing reality and of evoking a feeling of being at home in the world. It is something which the artist shares with the group, and part of our 9 boyish activity expressed a yearning to make any and everything of quality *Negro-American;* to appropriate it, possess it, recreate it in our own group and individual images.

10   And we recognized and were proud of our group's own style wherever we discerned it, in jazzmen and prize-fighters, ballplayers, and tap dancers; in gesture, inflection, intonation, timbre, and phrasing. Indeed, in all those nuances of expression and attitude which reveal a culture. We did not fully understand the cost of that style, but we recognized within it an affirmation of life beyond all question of our difficulties as Negroes.

11   Contrary to the notion currently projected by certain specialists in the "Negro problem" which characterizes the Negro American as self-hating and defensive, we did not so regard ourselves. We felt, among ourselves at least, that we were supposed to be whoever we would and could be and do anything and everything which other boys did, and do it better. Not defensively, because we were ordered to do so; nor because it was held in the society at large that we were naturally, as Negroes, limited — but because we demanded it of ourselves. Because to measure up to our own standards was the only way of affirming our notion of manhood.

12   Hence it was no more incongruous, as seen from our own particular perspective in this land of incongruities, for young Negro Oklahomans to project themselves as Renaissance men than for white Mississippians to see themselves as ancient Greeks or noblemen out of Sir Walter Scott. Surely our fantasies have caused far less damage to the nation's sense of reality, if for no other reason than that ours were expressive of a more democratic ideal. Remember, too, as William Faulkner made us so vividly aware, that the slaves often took the essence of the aristocratic ideal (as they took Christianity) with far more seriousness than their masters, and that we, thanks to the tight telescoping of American history, were but two generations from that previous condition. Renaissance men, indeed!

13   I managed, by keeping quiet about it, to cling to our boyish ideal during three years in Alabama, and I brought it with me to New York, where it not only gave silent support to my explorations of what was then an unknown territory, but served to mock and caution me when I became interested in the Communist ideal. And when it was suggested that I try my hand at writing it was still with me.

14   The act of writing requires a constant plunging back into the shadow of the past where time hovers ghostlike. When I began writing

in earnest I was forced, thus, to relate myself consciously and imaginatively to my mixed background as American, as Negro-American,
and as a Negro from what in its own belated way was a pioneer background. More important, and inseparable from this particular effort,
was the necessity of determining my true relationship to that body of
American literature to which I was most attracted and through which,
aided by what I could learn from the literatures of Europe, I would find
my own voice and to which I was challenged, by way of achieving
myself, to make some small contribution, and to whose composite
picture of reality I was obligated to offer some necessary modifica-
tions.

This was no matter of sudden insight but of slow and blundering   15
discovery, of a struggle to stare down the deadly and hypnotic temptation to interpret the world and all its devices in terms of race. To
avoid this was very important to me, and in light of my background
far from simple. Indeed, it was quite complex, involving as it did, a
ceaseless questioning of all those formulas which historians, politicians, sociologists, and an older generation of Negro leaders and writers — those of the so-called "Negro Renaissance" — had evolved to
describe my group's identity, its predicament, its fate, and its relation
to the larger society and the culture which we share.

Here the question of reality and personal identity merge. Yes,   16
and the question of the nature of the reality which underlies American
fiction and thus the human truth which gives fiction viability. In this
quest, for such it soon became, I learned that nothing could go unchal-
lenged; especially that feverish industry dedicated to telling Negroes
who and what they are, and which can usually be counted upon to
deprive both humanity and culture of their complexity. I had under-
gone, not too many months before taking the path which led to writing, the humiliation of being taught in a class in sociology at a Negro
college (from Park and Burgess, the leading textbook in the field) that
Negroes represented the "lady of the races." This contention the
Negro instructor passed blandly along to us without even bothering to
wash his hands, much less his teeth. Well, I had no intention of being
bound by any such humiliating definition of my relationship to American literature. Not even to those works which depicted Negroes neg-
atively. Negro Americans have a highly developed ability to abstract
desirable qualities from those around them, even from their enemies,
and my sense of reality could reject bias while appreciating the truth
revealed by achieved art. The pleasure which I derived from reading
had long been a necessity, and in the *act* of reading, that marvelous

collaboration between the writer's artful vision and the reader's sense of life, I had become acquainted with other possible selves; freer, more courageous and ingenuous and, during the course of the narrative at least, even wise.

17   At the time I was under the influence of Ernest Hemingway, and his description, in *Death in the Afternoon*, of his thinking when he first went to Spain became very important as translated in my own naïve fashion. He was trying to write, he tells us,

> and I found the greatest difficulty aside from knowing truly what you really felt, rather than what you were supposed to feel, and had been taught to feel, was to put down what really happened in action; what the actual things were which produced the emotion that you experienced. . . .

18   His statement of moral and aesthetic purpose which followed focused my own search to relate myself to American life through literature. For I found the greatest difficulty for a Negro writer was the problem of revealing what he truly felt, rather than serving up what Negroes were supposed to feel, and were encouraged to feel. And linked to this was the difficulty, based upon our long habit of deception and evasion, of depicting what really happened within our areas of American life, and putting down with honesty and without bowing to ideological expediencies the attitudes and values which give Negro-American life its sense of wholeness and which render it bearable and human and, when measured by our own terms, desirable.

19   I was forced to this awareness through my struggles with the craft of fiction; yes, and by my attraction (soon rejected) to Marxist political theory, which was my response to the inferior status which society sought to impose upon me (I did not then, now, or ever *consider* myself inferior).

20   I did not know my true relationship to America — what citizen of the U.S. really does? — but I did know and accept how I felt inside. And I also knew, thanks to the old Renaissance Man, what I expected of myself in the matter of personal discipline and creative quality. Since by the grace of the past and the examples of manhood picked willy-nilly from the continuing-present of my background, I rejected all negative definitions imposed upon me by others, there was nothing to do but search for those relationships which were fundamental.

21   In this sense fiction became the agency of my efforts to answer the questions, Who am I, what am I, how did I come to be? What shall I make of the life around me, what celebrate, what reject, how con-

front the snarl of good and evil which is inevitable? What does American society *mean* when regarded out of my *own* eyes, when informed by my *own* sense of the past and viewed by my *own* complex sense of the present? How, in other words, should I think of myself and my pluralistic sense of the world, how express my vision of the human predicament, without reducing it to a point which would render it sterile before that necessary and tragic — though enhancing — reduction which must occur before the fictive vision can come alive? It is quite possible that much potential fiction by Negro Americans fails precisely at this point: through the writers' refusal (often through provincialism or lack of courage or through opportunism) to achieve a vision of life and a resourcefulness of craft commensurate with the complexity of their actual situation. Too often they fear to leave the uneasy sanctuary of race to take their chances in the world of art.

—— CONSIDERATIONS ————————————————

1. Ellison's opening statement that writing was "a reflex of reading" points to the similar experience of many other students and writers (see Richard Wright's "The Library Card," pages 467–475) and implies an important relationship between the two activities. Are reading and writing two sides of the same coin?

2. Look in a good dictionary for a definition of "Renaissance man" and explain why that concept is central to an understanding of Ellison's essay.

3. How, in Paragraph 7, does Ellison specify, and thus clarify, what he means by "ours was a chaotic community" in Paragraph 3?

4. At several points in his essay, Ellison is critical of "specialists and 'friends of the Negro.'" What is his primary criticism of their efforts?

5. Does Ellison's remark "boys are natural romantics" in Paragraph 7 help explain his first sentence in Paragraph 8? Do you think that sentence is limited to the boys of one race or class? Use your own experience to write an essay on the subject.

6. Would Eiseley's short essay "More Thoughts on Wilderness" (pages 115–117) be an example of what Ellison expresses in the first sentence of his Paragraph 14?

Nora Ephron (b. 1941), daughter of two screen writers, grew up in Hollywood wanting to come to New York and become a writer. She did. She began by working for Newsweek, *and soon was contributing articles to* New Yorker *and a monthly column to* Esquire. *Most of her writing is about women, and manages to be funny and serious, profound and irreverent — and on occasion outrageous. In 1983 she published a novel entitled* Heartburn. *She has collected her essays in* Wallflower at the Orgy *(1970) and* Crazy Salad *(1975), from which we take this essay on growing up flat-chested.*

23

NORA EPHRON

A Few Words about Breasts: Shaping Up Absurd

1   I have to begin with a few words about androgyny. In grammar school, in the fifth and sixth grades, we were all tyrannized by a rigid set of rules that supposedly determined whether we were boys or girls. The episode in *Huckleberry Finn* where Huck is disguised as a girl and gives himself away by the way he threads a needle and catches a ball — that kind of thing. We learned that the way you sat, crossed your legs, held a cigarette and looked at your nails, your wristwatch, the way you did these things instinctively was absolute proof of your sex. Now obviously most children did not take this literally, but I did. I thought that just one slip, just one incorrect cross of my legs or flick of an imaginary cigarette ash would turn me from whatever I was into the other thing; that would be all it took, really. Even though I was

outwardly a girl and had many of the trappings generally associated with the field of girldom — a girl's name, for example, and dresses, my own telephone, an autograph book — I spent the early years of my adolescence absolutely certain that I might at any point gum it up. I did not feel at all like a girl. I was boyish. I was athletic, ambitious, outspoken, competitive, noisy, rambunctious. I had scabs on my knees and my socks slid into my loafers and I could throw a football. I wanted desperately not to be that way, not to be a mixture of both things but instead just one, a girl, a definite indisputable girl. As soft and as pink as a nursery. And nothing would do that for me, I felt, but breasts.

I was about six months younger than everyone in my class, and   2 so for about six months after it began, for six months after my friends had begun to develop — that was the word we used, develop — I was not particularly worried. I would sit in the bathtub and look down at my breasts and know that any day now, any second now, they would start growing like everyone else's. They didn't. "I want to buy a bra," I said to my mother one night. "What for?" she said. My mother was really hateful about bras, and by the time my third sister had gotten to the point where she was ready to want one, my mother had worked the whole business into a comedy routine. "Why not use a Band-Aid instead?" she would say. It was a source of great pride to my mother that she had never even had to wear a brassiere until she had her fourth child, and then only because her gynecologist made her. It was incomprehensible to me that anyone would ever be proud of something like that. It was the 1950's, for God's sake. Jane Russell. Cashmere sweaters. Couldn't my mother see that? *"I am too old to wear an undershirt."* Screaming. Weeping. Shouting. "Then don't wear an undershirt," said my mother. "But I want to buy a bra." "What for?"

I suppose that for most girls, breasts, brassieres, that entire thing,   3 has more trauma, more to do with the coming of adolescence, of becoming a woman, than anything else. Certainly more than getting your period, although that too was traumatic, symbolic. But you could *see* breasts; they were there; they were visible. Whereas a girl could claim to have her period for months before she actually got it and nobody would ever know the difference. Which is exactly what I did. All you had to do was make a great fuss over having enough nickels for the Kotex machine and walk around clutching your stomach and moaning for three to five days a month about The Curse and you could convince anybody. There is a school of thought somewhere in the women's lib/women's mag/gynecology establishment that claims that menstrual cramps are purely psychological, and I lean toward it. Not that I didn't have them finally. Agonizing cramps, heating-pad cramps, go-down-to-the-school-nurse-and-lie-on-the-cot cramps. But unlike any pain I have ever suffered, I adored the pain of cramps, welcomed it, wallowed in it, bragged about it. "I can't go. I have cramps." "I can't do that. I have cramps." And most of all, gigglingly, blushingly: "I can't swim. I have cramps." Nobody ever used the hard-core word. Menstruation. God, what an awful word. Never that. "I have cramps."

4   The morning I first got my period, I went into my mother's bedroom to tell her. And my mother, my utterly-hateful-about-bras mother, burst into tears. It was really a lovely moment, and I remember it so clearly not just because it was one of the two times I ever saw my mother cry on my account (the other was when I was caught being a six-year-old kleptomaniac), but also because the incident did not mean to me what it meant to her. Her little girl, her firstborn, had finally become a woman. That was what she was crying about. My reaction to the event, however, was that I might well be a woman in some scientific, textbook sense (and could at least stop faking every month and stop wasting all those nickels). But in another sense — in a visible sense — I was as androgynous and as liable to tip over into boyhood as ever.

5   I started with a 28AA bra. I don't think they made them any smaller in those days, although I gather that now you can buy bras for five year olds that don't have any cups whatsoever in them; trainer bras they are called. My first brassiere came from Robinson's Department Store in Beverly Hills. I went there alone, shaking, positive they would look me over and smile and tell me to come back next year. An actual fitter took me into the dressing room and stood over me while I took off my blouse and tried the first one on. The little puffs stood out on my chest. "Lean over," said the fitter (to this day I am not sure what fitters in bra departments do except to tell you to lean over). I leaned over, with the fleeing hope that my breasts would miraculously fall out of my body and into the puffs. Nothing.

6   "Don't worry about it," said my friend Libby some months later, when things had not improved. "You'll get them after you're married."

7   "What are you talking about?" I said.

8   "When you get married," Libby explained, "your husband will touch your breasts and rub them and kiss them and they'll grow."

9   That was the killer. Necking I could deal with. Intercourse I could deal with. But it had never crossed my mind that a man was

going to touch my breasts, that breasts had something to do with all that, petting, my God they never mentioned petting in my little sex manual about the fertilization of the ovum. I became dizzy. For I knew instantly — as naïve as I had been only a moment before — that only part of what she was saying was true: the touching, rubbing, kissing part, not the growing part. And I knew that no one would ever want to marry me. I had no breasts. I would never have breasts.

My best friend in school was Diana Raskob. She lived a block   10 from me in a house full of wonders. English muffins, for instance. The Raskobs were the first people in Beverly Hills to have English muffins for breakfast. They also had an apricot tree in the back, and a badminton court, and a subscription to *Seventeen* magazine, and hundreds of games like Sorry and Parcheesi and Treasure Hunt and Anagrams. Diana and I spent three or four afternoons a week in their den reading and playing and eating. Diana's mother's kitchen was full of the most colossal assortment of junk food I have ever been exposed to. My house was full of apples and peaches and milk and homemade chocolate-chip cookies — which were nice, and good for you, but-not-right-before-dinner-or-you'll-spoil-your-appetite. Diana's house had nothing in it that was good for you, and what's more, you could stuff it in right up until dinner and nobody cared. Bar-B-Q potato chips (they were the first in them, too), giant bottles of ginger ale, fresh popcorn with melted butter, hot fudge sauce on Baskin-Robbins jamoca ice cream, powdered-sugar doughnuts from Van de Kamps. Diana and I had been best friends since we were seven; we were about equally popular in school (which is to say, not particularly), we had about the same success with boys (extremely intermittent) and we looked much the same. Dark. Tall. Gangly.

It is September, just before school begins. I am eleven years old,   11 about to enter the seventh grade, and Diana and I have not seen each other all summer. I have been to camp and she has been somewhere like Banff with her parents. We are meeting, as we often do, on the street midway between our two houses and we will walk back to Diana's and eat junk and talk about what has happened to each of us that summer. I am walking down Walden Drive in my jeans and my father's shirt hanging out and my old red loafers with the socks falling into them and coming toward me is . . . I take a deep breath . . . a young woman. Diana. Her hair is curled and she has a waist and hips and a bust and she is wearing a straight skirt, an article of clothing I have been repeatedly told I will be unable to wear until I have the hips

to hold it up. My jaw drops, and suddenly I am crying, crying hysteri-
cally, can't catch my breath sobbing. My best friend has betrayed me.
She has gone ahead without me and done it. She has shaped up.

12   Here are some things I did to help:

13   Bought a Mark Eden Bust Developer.

14   Slept on my back for four years.

15   Splashed cold water on them every night because some French
actress said in *Life* magazine that that was what *she* did for her perfect
bustline.

16   Ultimately, I resigned myself to a bad toss and began to wear
padded bras. I think about them now, think about all those years in
high school I went around in them, my three padded bras, every single
one of them with different sized breasts. Each time I changed bras I
changed sizes: one week nice perky but not too obtrusive breasts, the
next medium-sized slightly pointed ones, the next week knockers,
true knockers; all the time, whatever size I was, carrying around this
rubberized appendage on my chest that occasionally crashed into a
wall and was poked inward and had to be poked outward — I think
about all that and wonder how anyone kept a straight face through it.
My parents, who normally had no restraints about needling me — why
did they say nothing as they watched my chest go up and down? My
friends, who would periodically inspect my breasts for signs of growth
and reassure me — why didn't they at least counsel consistency?

17   And the bathing suits. I die when I think about the bathing suits.
That was the era when you could lay an uninhabited bathing suit on
the beach and someone would make a pass at it. I would put one on,
an absurd swimsuit with its enormous bust built into it, the bones
from the suit stabbing me in the rib cage and leaving little red welts
on my body, and there I would be, my chest plunging straight downward absolutely vertically from my collarbone to the top of my suit
and then suddenly, wham, out came all that padding and material and
wiring absolutely horizontally.

18   Buster Klepper was the first boy who ever touched them. He was
my boyfriend my senior year of high school. There is a picture of him
in my high-school yearbook that makes him look quite attractive in a
Jewish, horn-rimmed glasses sort of way, but the picture does not
show the pimples, which were air-brushed out, or the dumbness. Well,
that isn't really fair. He wasn't dumb. He just wasn't terribly bright.
His mother refused to accept it, refused to accept the relentlessly

average report cards, refused to deal with her son's inevitable destiny in some junior college or other. "He was tested," she would say to me, apropos of nothing, "and it came out 145. That's near-genius." Had the word underachiever been coined, she probably would have lobbed that one at me, too. Anyway, Buster was really very sweet — which is, I know, damning with faint praise, but there it is. I was the editor of the front page of the high-school newspaper and he was editor of the back page; we had to work together, side by side, in the print shop, and that was how it started. On our first date, we went to see *April Love* starring Pat Boone. Then we started going together. Buster had a green coupe, a 1950 Ford with an engine he had handchromed until it shone, dazzled, reflected the image of anyone who looked into it, anyone usually being Buster polishing it or the gas-station attendants he constantly asked to check the oil in order for them to be overwhelmed by the sparkle on the valves. The car also had a boot stretched over the back seat for reasons I never understood; hanging from the rearview mirror, as was the custom, was a pair of angora dice. A previous girl friend named Solange who was famous throughout Beverly Hills High School for having no pigment in her right eyebrow had knitted them for him. Buster and I would ride around town, the two of us seated to the left of the steering wheel. I would shift gears. It was nice.

There was necking. Terrific necking. First in the car, overlooking   19
Los Angeles from what is now the Trousdale Estates. Then on the bed of his parents' cabana at Ocean House. Incredibly wonderful, frustrating necking, I loved it, really, but no further than necking, please don't, please, because there I was absolutely terrified of the general implications of going-a-step-further with a near-dummy and also terrified of his finding out there was next to nothing there (which he knew, of course; he wasn't that dumb).

I broke up with him at one point. I think we were apart for about   20
two weeks. At the end of that time I drove down to see a friend at a boarding school in Palos Verdes Estates and a disc jockey played *April Love* on the radio four times during the trip. I took it as a sign. I drove straight back to Griffith Park to a golf tournament Buster was playing in (he was the sixth-seeded teen-age golf player in Southern California) and presented myself back to him on the green of the 18th hole. It was all very dramatic. That night we went to a drive-in and I let him get his hand under my protuberances and onto my breasts. He really didn't seem to mind at all.

"Do you want to marry my son?" the woman asked me.   21
"Yes," I said.   22

23   *I was nineteen years old, a virgin, going with this woman's son,
this big strange woman who was married to a Lutheran minister in
New Hampshire and pretended she was Gentile and had this son, by
her first husband, this total fool of a son who ran the hero-sandwich
concession at Harvard Business School and whom for one moment
one December in New Hampshire I said — as much out of politeness
as anything else — that I wanted to marry.*

24   *"Fine," she said. "Now, here's what you do. Always make sure
you're on top of him so you won't seem so small. My bust is very
large, you see, so I always lie on my back to make it look smaller, but
you'll have to be on top most of the time."*

25   *I nodded. "Thank you," I said.*

26   *"I have a book for you to read," she went on. "Take it with you
when you leave. Keep it." She went to the bookshelf, found it, and
gave it to me. It was a book on frigidity.*

27   *"Thank you," I said.*

28   That is a true story. Everything in this article is a true story, but
I feel I have to point out that that story in particular is true. It happened on December 30, 1960. I think about it often. When it first
happened, I naturally assumed that the woman's son, my boyfriend,
was responsible. I invented a scenario where he had had a little heart-
to-heart with his mother and had confessed that his only objection to
me was that my breasts were small; his mother then took it upon
herself to help out. Now I think I was wrong about the incident. The
mother was acting on her own, I think: that was her way of being cruel
and competitive under the guise of being helpful and maternal. You
have small breasts, she was saying; therefore you will never make him
as happy as I have. Or you have small breasts; therefore you will
doubtless have sexual problems. Or you have small breasts; therefore
you are less woman than I am. She was, as it happens, only the first of
what seems to me to be a never-ending string of women who have
made competitive remarks to me about breast size. "I would love to
wear a dress like that," my friend Emily says to me, "but my bust is
too big." Like that. Why do women say these things to me? Do I attract
these remarks the way other women attract married men or alcoholics
or homosexuals? This summer, for example. I am at a party in East
Hampton and I am introduced to a woman from Washington. She is a
minor celebrity, very pretty and Southern and blonde and outspoken
and I am flattered because she has read something I have written. We
are talking animatedly, we have been talking no more than five minutes, when a man comes up to join us. "Look at the two of us," the
woman says to the man, indicating me and her. "The two of us

together couldn't fill an A cup." Why does she say that? It isn't even true, dammit, so why? Is she even more addled than I am on this subject? Does she honestly believe there is something wrong with her size breasts, which, it seems to me, now that I look hard at them, are just right. Do I unconsciously bring out competitiveness in women? In that form? What did I do to deserve it?

As for men.

There were men who minded and let me know they minded. There were men who did not mind. In any case, I always minded.

And even now, now that I have been countlessly reassured that my figure is a good one, now that I am grown up enough to understand that most of my feelings have very little to do with the reality of my shape, I am nonetheless obsessed by breasts. I cannot help it. I grew up in the terrible Fifties — with rigid stereotypical sex roles, the insistence that men be men and dress like men and women be women and dress like women, the intolerance of androgyny — and I cannot shake it, cannot shake my feelings of inadequacy. Well, that time is gone, right? All those exaggerated examples of breast worship are gone, right? Those women were freaks, right? I know all that. And yet, here I am, stuck with the psychological remains of it all, stuck with my own peculiar version of breast worship. You probably think I am crazy to go on like this: here I have set out to write a confession that is meant to hit you with the shock of recognition and instead you are sitting there thinking I am thoroughly warped. Well, what can I tell you? If I had had them, I would have been a completely different person. I honestly believe that.

After I went into therapy, a process that made it possible for me to tell total strangers at cocktail parties that breasts were the hang-up of my life, I was often told that I was insane to have been bothered by my condition. I was also frequently told, by close friends, that I was extremely boring on the subject. And my girl friends, the ones with nice big breasts, would go on endlessly about how their lives had been far more miserable than mine. Their bra straps were snapped in class. They couldn't sleep on their stomachs. They were stared at whenever the word "mountain" cropped up in geography. And *Evangeline,* good God what they went through every time someone had to stand up and recite the Prologue to Longfellow's *Evangeline:* ". . . *stand like druids of eld . . . / With beards that rest on their bosoms."* It was much worse for them, they tell me. They had a terrible time of it, they assure me. I don't know how lucky I was, they say.

I have thought about their remarks, tried to put myself in their place, considered their point of view. I think they are full of shit.

29
30
31
32
33

—— CONSIDERATIONS ——————————————

1. Nora Ephron's account offends some readers and attracts others for the same reason — the frank and casual exploration of a subject that generations have believed unmentionable. This problem is worth investigating: Are there, in fact, subjects that should not be discussed in the popular press? Are there words a writer must not use? Why? And who should make the list of things not to be talked about?

2. Imagine an argument about Ephron's article between a feminist and an antifeminist. What ammunition could each find in the article? Write the dialogue as you hear it.

3. Ephron reports that from a very early age she worried that she might not be "a girl, a definite indisputable girl." Is this anxiety as uncommon as she thought it was? Is worry about one's sex an exclusively female problem?

4. Are our ideas about masculinity and femininity changing? How are such ideas determined? How important are they in shaping personality and in channeling thoughts?

5. Ephron's article is a good example of the very informal essay. What does she do that makes it so informal? Consider both diction and sentence structure.

6. How can one smile at others' problems — or at one's own disappointments, for that matter? How can Ephron see humor now in what she thought of as tragic then?

William Faulkner (1897–1962) was a great novelist, born in Mississippi, who supported himself much of his life by screen-writing and by writing short fiction for magazines. He received the Nobel Prize for literature in 1950. Among his novels are The Sound and the Fury *(1929),* As I Lay Dying *(1930),* Light in August *(1932), and a comic series:* The Hamlet *(1940),* The Town *(1957), and* The Mansion *(1960). "A Rose for Emily" is an expert piece of magazine fiction; remarkably, it also makes an emblem for the disease and decease of a society.*

24

WILLIAM FAULKNER
A Rose for Emily

I

When Miss Emily Grierson died, our whole town went to her funeral: the men through a sort of respectful affection for a fallen monument, the women mostly out of curiosity to see the inside of her house, which no one save an old manservant — a combined gardener and cook — had seen in at least ten years.

It was a big, squarish frame house that had once been white, decorated with cupolas and spires and scrolled balconies in the heavily lightsome style of the seventies, set on what had once been our most select street. But garages and cotton gins had encroached and obliterated even the august names of that neighborhood; only Miss Emily's house was left, lifting its stubborn and coquettish decay above the cotton wagons and the gasoline pumps — an eyesore among eyesores. And now Miss Emily had gone to join the representatives of those august names where they lay in the cedar-bemused cemetery among the ranked and anonymous graves of Union and Confederate soldiers who fell at the battle of Jefferson.

3   Alive, Miss Emily had been a tradition, a duty, and a care; a sort of hereditary obligation upon the town, dating from that day in 1894 when Colonel Sartoris, the mayor — he who fathered the edict that no Negro woman should appear on the streets without an apron — remitted her taxes, the dispensation dating from the death of her father on into perpetuity. Not that Miss Emily would have accepted charity. Colonal Sartoris invented an involved tale to the effect that Miss Emily's father had loaned money to the town, which the town, as a matter of business, preferred this way of repaying. Only a man of Colonel Sartoris' generation and thought could have invented it, and only a woman could have believed it.

4   When the next generation, with its more modern ideas, became mayors and aldermen, this arrangement created some little dissatisfaction. On the first of the year they mailed her a tax notice. February came, and there was no reply. They wrote her a formal letter, asking her to call at the sheriff's office at her convenience. A week later the mayor wrote her himself, offering to call or to send his car for her, and received in reply a note on paper of an archaic shape, in a thin, flowing calligraphy in faded ink, to the effect that she no longer went out at all. The tax notice was also enclosed, without comment.

5   They called a special meeting of the Board of Aldermen. A deputation waited upon her, knocked at the door through which no visitor had passed since she ceased giving china-painting lessons eight or ten years earlier. They were admitted by the old Negro into a dim hall from which a staircase mounted into still more shadow. It smelled of dust and disuse — a close, dank smell. The Negro led them into the parlor. It was furnished in heavy, leather-covered furniture. When the Negro opened the blinds of one window, a faint dust rose sluggishly about their thighs, spinning with slow motes in the single sun-ray. On a tarnished gilt easel before the fireplace stood a crayon portrait of Miss Emily's father.

6   They rose when she entered — a small, fat woman in black, with a thin gold chain descending to her waist and vanishing into her belt, leaning on an ebony cane with a tarnished gold head. Her skeleton was small and spare; perhaps that was why what would have been merely plumpness in another was obesity in her. She looked bloated, like a body long submerged in motionless water, and of that pallid hue. Her eyes, lost in the fatty ridges of her face, looked like two small

pieces of coal pressed into a lump of dough as they moved from one face to another while the visitors stated their errand.

She did not ask them to sit. She just stood in the door and listened 7 quietly until the spokesman came to a stumbling halt. Then they could hear the invisible watch ticking at the end of the gold chain.

Her voice was dry and cold. "I have no taxes in Jefferson. Colonel 8 Sartoris explained it to me. Perhaps one of you can gain access to the city records and satisfy yourselves."

"But we have. We are the city authorities, Miss Emily. Didn't 9 you get a notice from the sheriff, signed by him?"

"I received a paper, yes," Miss Emily said. "Perhaps he considers 10 himself the sheriff. . . . I have no taxes in Jefferson."

"But there is nothing on the books to show that, you see. We 11 must go by the —"

"See Colonel Sartoris. I have no taxes in Jefferson." 12

"But, Miss Emily —" 13

"See Colonel Sartoris." (Colonel Sartoris had been dead almost 14 ten years.) "I have no taxes in Jefferson. Tobe!" The Negro appeared. "Show these gentlemen out."

II

So she vanquished them, horse and foot, just as she had van- 15 quished their fathers thirty years before about the smell. That was two years after her father's death and a short time after her sweetheart — the one we believed would marry her — had deserted her. After her father's death she went out very little; after her sweetheart went away, people hardly saw her at all. A few of the ladies had the temerity to call, but were not received, and the only sign of life about the place was the Negro man — a young man then — going in and out with a market basket.

"Just as if a man — any man — could keep a kitchen properly," 16 the ladies said; so they were not surprised when the smell developed. It was another link between the gross, teeming world and the high and mighty Griersons.

A neighbor, a woman, complained to the mayor, Judge Stevens, 17 eighty years old.

"But what will you have me do about it, madam?" he said. 18

"Why, send her word to stop it," the woman said. "Isn't there a 19 law?"

"I'm sure that won't be necessary," Judge Stevens said. "It's prob- 20 ably just a snake or a rat that nigger of hers killed in the yard. I'll speak to him about it."

21 The next day he received two more complaints, one from a man who came in diffident deprecation. "We really must do something about it, Judge. I'd be the last one in the world to bother Miss Emily, but we've got to do something." That night the Board of Aldermen met — three gray-beards and one younger man, a member of the rising generation.

22 "It's simple enough," he said. "Send her word to have her place cleaned up. Giver her a certain time to do it in, and if she don't . . ."

23 "Dammit, sir," Judge Stevens said, "will you accuse a lady to her face of smelling bad?"

24 So the next night, after midnight, four men crossed Miss Emily's lawn and slunk about the house like burglars, sniffing along the base of the brickwork and at the cellar openings while one of them performed a regular sowing motion with his hand out of a sack slung from his shoulder. They broke open the cellar door and sprinkled lime there, and in all the out-buildings. As they recrossed the lawn, a window that had been dark was lighted and Miss Emily sat in it, the light behind her, and her upright torso motionless as that of an idol. They crept quietly across the lawn and into the shadow of the locusts that lined the street. After a week or two the smell went away.

25 That was when people had begun to feel really sorry for her. People in our town remembering how old lady Wyatt, her great-aunt, had gone completely crazy at last, believed that the Griersons held themselves a little too high for what they really were. None of the young men were quite good enough for Miss Emily and such. We had long thought of them as a tableau: Miss Emily a slender figure in white in the background, her father a spraddled silhouette in the foreground, his back to her and clutching a horsewhip, the two of them framed by the back-flung front door. So when she got to be thirty and was still single, we were not pleased exactly, but vindicated; even with insanity in the family she wouldn't have turned down all of her chances if they had really materialized.

26 When her father died, it got about that the house was all that was left to her; and in a way, people were glad. At last they could pity Miss Emily. Being left alone, and a pauper, she had become humanized. Now she too would know the old thrill and the old despair of a penny more or less.

27 The day after his death all the ladies prepared to call at the house and offer condolence and aid, as is our custom. Miss Emily met them at the door, dressed as usual and with no trace of grief on her face.

She told them that her father was not dead. She did that for three days, with the ministers calling on her, and the doctors trying to persuade her to let them dispose of the body. Just as they were about to resort to law and force, she broke down, and they buried her father quickly.

We did not say she was crazy then. We believed she had to do that. We remembered all the young men her father had driven away, and we knew that with nothing left, she would have to cling to that which had robbed her, as people will. 28

III

She was sick for a long time. When we saw her again, her hair was cut short, making her look like a girl, with a vague resemblance to those angels in colored church windows — sort of tragic and serene. 29

The town had just let the contracts for paving the sidewalks, and in the summer after her father's death they began to work. The construction company came with niggers and mules and machinery, and a foreman named Homer Barron, a Yankee — a big, dark, ready man, with a big voice and eyes lighter than his face. The little boys would follow in groups to hear him cuss the niggers, and the niggers singing in time to the rise and fall of picks. Pretty soon he knew everybody in town. Whenever you heard a lot of laughing anywhere about the square, Homer Barron would be in the center of the group. Presently we began to see him and Miss Emily on Sunday afternoons driving in the yellow-wheeled buggy and the matched team of bays from the livery stable. 30

At first we were glad that Miss Emily would have an interest, because the ladies all said, "Of course a Grierson would not think seriously of a Northerner, a day laborer." But there were still others, older people, who said that even grief could not cause a real lady to forget *noblesse oblige* — without calling it *noblesse oblige.* They just said, "Poor Emily. Her kinsfolk should come to her." She had some kin in Alabama; but years ago her father had fallen out with them over the estate of old lady Wyatt, the crazy woman, and there was no communication between the two families. They had not even been represented at the funeral. 31

And as soon as the old people said, "Poor Emily," the whispering began. "Do you suppose it's really so?" they said to one another. "Of course it is. What else could . . ." This behind their hands; rustling of craned silk and satin behind jalousies closed upon the sun of Sunday 32 afternoon as the thin, swift clop-clop-clop of the matched team passed: "Poor Emily."

33   She carried her head high enough — even when we believed that she was fallen. It was as if she demanded more than ever the recognition of her dignity as the last Grierson; as if it had wanted that touch of earthiness to reaffirm her imperviousness. Like when she bought the rat poison, the arsenic. That was over a year after they had begun to say "Poor Emily," and while the two female cousins were visiting her.

34   "I want some poison," she said to the druggist. She was over thirty then, still a slight woman, though thinner than usual, with cold, haughty black eyes in a face the flesh of which was strained across the temples and about the eyesockets as you imagine a lighthouse-keeper's face ought to look. "I want some poison," she said.

35   "Yes, Miss Emily. What kind? For rats and such? I'd recom —"

36   "I want the best you have. I don't care what kind."

37   The druggist named several. "They'll kill anything up to an elephant. But what you want is —"

38   "Arsenic," Miss Emily said. "Is that a good one?"

39   "Is . . . arsenic? Yes ma'am. But what you want —"

40   "I want arsenic."

41   The druggist looked down at her. She looked back at him, erect, her face like a strained flag. "Why, of course," the druggist said. "If that's what you want. But the law requires you to tell what you are going to use it for."

42   Miss Emily just stared at him, her head tilted back in order to look him eye for eye, until he looked away and went and got the arsenic and wrapped it up. The Negro delivery boy brought her the package; the druggist didn't come back. When she opened the package at home there was written on the box, under the skull and bones: "For rats."

IV

43   So the next day we all said, "She will kill herself"; and we said it would be the best thing. When she had first begun to be seen with Homer Barron, we had said, "She will marry him." Then we said, "She will persuade him yet," because Homer himself had remarked — he liked men, and it was known that he drank with the younger men in the Elk's Club — that he was not a marrying man. Later we said, "Poor Emily," behind the jalousies as they passed on Sunday afternoon in the glittering buggy, Miss Emily with her head high and Homer Barron

with his hat cocked and a cigar in his teeth, reins and whip in a yellow glove.

Then some of the ladies began to say that it was a disgrace to the town and a bad example to the young people. The men did not want to interfere, but at last the ladies forced the Baptist minister — Miss Emily's people were Episcopal — to call upon her. He would never divulge what happened during that interview, but he refused to go back again. The next Sunday they again drove about the streets and the following day the minister's wife wrote to Miss Emily's relations in Alabama. 44

So she had blood-kin under her roof again and we sat back to watch developments. At first nothing happened. Then we were sure that they had to be married. We learned that Miss Emily had been to the jeweler's and ordered a man's toilet set in silver, with the letters H.B. on each piece. Two days later we learned that she had bought a complete outfit of men's clothing, including a nightshirt, and we said, "They are married." We were really glad. We were glad because the two female cousins were even more Grierson than Miss Emily had ever been. 45

So we were surprised when Homer Barron — the streets had been finished some time since — was gone. We were a little disappointed that there was not a public blowing-off, but we believed that he had gone on to prepare for Miss Emily's coming, or to give a chance to get rid of the cousins. (By that time it was a cabal, and we were all Miss Emily's allies to help circumvent the cousins.) Sure enough, after another week they departed. And, as we had expected all along, within three days Homer Barron was back in town. A neighbor saw the Negro man admit him at the kitchen door at dusk one evening. 46

And that was the last we saw of Homer Barron. And of Miss Emily for some time. The Negro man went in and out with the market basket, but the front door remained closed. Now and then we would see her at a window for a moment, as the men did that night when they sprinkled the lime, but for almost six months she did not appear on the streets. Then we knew that this was to be expected too; as if that quality of her father which had thwarted her woman's life so many times had been too virulent and too furious to die. 47

When we next saw Miss Emily, she had grown fat and her hair was turning gray. During the next few years it grew grayer and grayer until it attained an even pepper-and-salt iron-gray, when it ceased turning. Up to the day of her death at seventy-four it was still that vigorous iron-gray, like the hair of an active man. 48

From that time on her front door remained closed, save for a 49 period of six or seven years, when she was about forty, during which she gave lessons in china-painting. She fitted up a studio in one of the downstairs rooms, where the daughters and granddaughters of Colonel Sartoris' contemporaries were sent to her with the same regularity and in the same spirit that they were sent on Sundays with a twenty-five cent piece for the collection plate. Meanwhile her taxes had been remitted.

50   Then the newer generation became the backbone and the spirit of the town, and the painting pupils grew up and fell away and did not send their children to her with boxes of color and tedious brushes and pictures cut from the ladies' magazines. The front door closed upon the last one and remained closed for good. When the town got free postal delivery Miss Emily alone refused to let them fasten the metal numbers above her door and attach a mailbox to it. She would not listen to them.

51   Daily, monthly, yearly we watched the Negro grow grayer and more stooped, going in and out with the market basket. Each December we sent her a tax notice, which would be returned by the post office a week later, unclaimed. Now and then we would see her in one of the downstairs windows — she had evidently shut up the top floor of the house — like the carven torso of an idol in a niche, looking or not looking at us, we could never tell which. Thus she passed from generation to generation — dear, inescapable, impervious, tranquil, and perverse.

52   And so she died. Fell ill in the house filled with dust and shadows, with only a doddering Negro man to wait on her. We did not even know she was sick; we had long since given up trying to get any information from the Negro. He talked to no one, probably not even to her, for his voice had grown harsh and rusty, as if from disuse.

53   She died in one of the downstairs rooms, in a heavy walnut bed with a curtain, her gray head propped on a pillow yellow and moldy with age and lack of sunlight.

V

54   The Negro met the first of the ladies at the front door and let them in, with their hushed, sibilant voices and their quick, curious glances, and then he disappeared. He walked right through the house and out the back and was not seen again.

55   The two female cousins came at once. They held the funeral on the second day, with the town coming to look at Miss Emily beneath

a mass of bought flowers, with the crayon face of her father musing profoundly above the bier and the ladies sibilant and macabre; and the very old men — some in their brushed Confederate uniforms — on the porch and the lawn, talking of Miss Emily as if she had been a contemporary of theirs, believing that they had danced with her and courted her perhaps, confusing time with its mathematical progression, as the old do, to whom all the past is not a diminishing road, but, instead, a huge meadow which no winter ever quite touches, divided from them now by the narrow bottleneck of the most recent decade of years.

Already we knew that there was one room in the region above 56 stairs which no one had seen in forty years, and which would have to be forced. They waited until Miss Emily was decently in the ground before they opened it.

The violence of breaking down the door seemed to fill this room 57 with pervading dust. A thin, acrid pall as of the tomb seemed to lie everywhere upon this room decked and furnished as for a bridal: upon the valance curtains of faded rose color, upon the rose-shaded lights, upon the dressing table, upon the delicate array of crystal and the man's toilet things backed with tarnished silver, silver so tarnished that the monogram was obscured. Among them lay a collar and tie, as if they had just been removed, which, lifted, left upon the surface a pale crescent in the dust. Upon a chair hung the suit, carefully folded; beneath it the two mute shoes and the discarded socks.

The man himself lay in the bed. 58

For a long while we just stood there, looking down at the pro- 59 found and fleshless grin. The body had apparently once lain in the attitude of an embrace, but now the long sleep that outlasts love, that conquers even the grimace of love, had cuckolded him. What was left of him, rotted beneath what was left of the nightshirt, had become inextricable from the bed in which he lay; and upon him and upon the pillow beside him lay that even coating of the patient and biding dust.

Then we noticed that in the second pillow was the indentation 60 of a head. One of us lifted something from it, and leaning forward, that faint and invisible dust dry and acrid in the nostrils, we saw a long strand of iron-gray hair.

___ CONSIDERATIONS _____

1. The art of narration, some say, is the successful management of a significant sequence of actions through time. But "through time" does not

necessarily imply chronological order. Identify the major events of Faulkner's story according to when they actually happened, then arrange them in the order in which they are given by the author. Try the same technique with the story by Eudora Welty (pages 429–437).

2. Faulkner uses the terms "Negro" and "nigger" to refer to nonwhite persons in the story. Does he intend distinction between the two words? If he were writing the story today, instead of in 1930, might he substitute the word "black"? Why? Can you think of parallel terms used to designate other minority peoples, say, Jews, Catholics, Italians, or Japanese? Of what significance is the variety of such terms?

3. In what ways, if any, is Emily Grierson presented as a sympathetic character? Why?

4. In Part III, Faulkner puts considerable emphasis on the phrase *noblesse oblige.* Look up the meaning of that phrase, then comment on the author's use of it.

5. Who is the "we" in the story? Does "we" play any significant part?

6. Obviously, death is an important feature in this story. Could Faulkner also have had in mind the death of a particular society or a way of life? Does the story invite you to think of symbols?

Jules Feiffer (b. 1929) is a writer, cartoonist, and playwright who first came to public attention through his cartoons in the Village Voice. *A versatile artist, he has written successful novels, including* Harry, the Rat with Women *(1963); plays, like* Little Murders *(1967); and a book on* The Great Comic Book Heroes *(1965), from which we take this appreciation of the greatest of them all.*

25

JULES FEIFFER

Superman

The advent of the super-hero was a bizarre comeuppance for the American dream. Horatio Alger could no longer make it on his own. He needed "Shazam!" Here was fantasy with a cynically realistic base: once the odds were appraised honestly it was apparent you had to be super to get on in this world. 1

The particular brilliance of Superman lay not only in the fact that he was the first of the super-heroes, but in the concept of his alter ego. What made Superman different from the legion of imitators to follow was not that when he took off his clothes he could beat up everybody — they all did that. What made Superman extraordinary was his point of origin: Clark Kent. 2

Remember, Kent was not Superman's true identity as Bruce Wayne was the Batman's or (on radio) Lamont Cranston the Shadow's. Just the opposite. Clark Kent was the fiction. Previous heroes — the Shadow, the Green Hornet, The Lone Ranger — were not only more vulnerable; they were fakes. I don't mean to criticize; it's just a state- 3 ment of fact. The Shadow had to cloud men's minds to be in business. The Green Hornet had to go through the fetishist fol-de-rol of donning costume, floppy hat, black mask, gas gun, menacing automobile, and insect sound effects before he was even ready to go out in the street. The Lone Ranger needed an accoutremental white horse, an Indian, and an establishing cry of Hi-Yo Silver to separate him from all those other masked men running around the West in days of yesteryear.

4   But Superman had only to wake up in the morning to be Superman. In his case, Clark Kent was the put-on. The fellow with the eyeglasses and the acne and the walk girls laughed at wasn't real, didn't exist, was a sacrificial disguise, an act of discreet martyrdom. *Had they but known!*

5   And for what purpose? Did Superman become Clark Kent in order to lead a normal life, have friends, be known as a nice guy, meet girls? Hardly. There's too much of the hair shirt in the role, too much devotion to the imprimatur of impotence — an insight, perhaps, into the fantasy life of the Man of Steel. Superman as a secret masochist? Field for study there. For if it was otherwise, if the point, the only point, was to lead a "normal life," why not a more typical identity? How can one be a cowardly star reporter, subject to fainting spells in time of crisis, and not expect to raise serious questions?

6   The truth may be that Kent existed not for the purposes of the story but for the reader. He is Superman's opinion of the rest of us, a pointed caricature of what we, the noncriminal element, were really like. His fake identity was our real one. That's why we loved him so. For if that wasn't really us, if there were no Clark Kents, only lots of glasses and cheap suits which, when removed, revealed all of us in our true identities — what a hell of an improved world it would have been!

7   In drawing style, both in figure and costume, Superman was a simplified parody of Flash Gordon. But if Alex Raymond was the Dior for Superman, Joe Shuster set the fashion from then on. Everybody else's super-costumes were copies from his shop. Shuster represented the best of old-style comic book drawing. His work was direct, unprettied — crude and vigorous; as easy to read as a diagram. No creamy lines, no glossy illustrative effects, no touch of that bloodless prefabrication that passes for professionalism these days. Slickness, thank God, was beyond his means. He could not draw well, but he drew single-mindedly — no one could ghost that style. It was the man. When assistants began "improving" the appearance of the strip it promptly went downhill. It looked as though it were being drawn in a bank.

But, oh, those early drawings! Superman running up the sides of   8
dams, leaping over anything that stood in his way (No one drew sky-
scrapers like Shuster. Impressionistic shafts, Superman poised over
them, his leaping leg tucked under his ass, his landing leg tautly
pointed earthward), cleaning and jerking two-ton get-away cars and
pounding them into the sides of cliffs — and all this done lightly,
unportentously, still with that early Slam Bradley exuberance. What
matter that the stories quickly lost interest; that once you've made a
man super you've plotted him out of believable conflicts; that even
super-villains, super-mad scientists and, yes, super-orientals were dull
and lifeless next to the overwhelming image of that which Clark Kent
became when he took off his clothes. So what if the stories were
boring, the villains blah? This was the Superman Show — a touring
road company backing up a great star. Everything was a stage wait
until he came on. Then it was all worthwhile.

Besides, for the alert reader there were other fields of interest. It   9
seems that among Lois Lane, Clark Kent, and Superman there existed
a schizoid and chaste *ménage à trois*. Clark Kent loved but felt abashed
with Lois Lane; Superman saved Lois Lane when she was in trouble,
found her a pest the rest of the time. Since Superman and Clark Kent
were the same person this behavior demands explanation. It can't be
that Kent wanted Lois to respect him for himself, since himself was
Superman. Then, it appears, he wanted Lois to respect him for his fake
self, to love him when he acted the coward, to be there when he
pretended he needed her. She never was — so, of course, he loved her.
A typical American romance. Superman never needed her, never
needed anybody — in any event, Lois chased *him* — so, of course, he
didn't love her. He had contempt for her. Another typical American
romance.

Love is really the pursuit of a desired object, not pursuit by it.   10
Once you've caught the object there is no longer any reason to love it,
to have it hanging around. There must be other desirable objects out
there, somewhere. So Clark Kent acted as the control for Superman.
What Kent wanted was just that which Superman didn't want to be
bothered with. Kent wanted Lois, Superman didn't — thus marking
the difference between a sissy and a man. A sissy wanted girls who
scorned him; a man scorned girls who wanted him. Our cultural opposite of the man who didn't make out with women has never been the
man who did — but rather the man who could if he wanted to, but
still didn't. The ideal of masculine strength, whether Gary Cooper's,
Lil Abner's, or Superman's, was for one to be so virile and handsome,

to be in such a position of strength, that he need never go near girls. Except to help them. And then get the hell out. Real rapport was not for women. It was for villains. That's why they got hit so hard.

_____ CONSIDERATIONS _____

1. Study Feiffer's diction in his essay, particularly such word choices as "bizarre comeuppance" (Paragraph 1), "fetishist fol-de-rol" and "accoutremental white horse" (Paragraph 3), "imprimatur of impotence" (Paragraph 5), and "a schizoid and chaste *ménage à trois*" (Paragraph 9). Do such combinations attract or repel you as a reader? What does Feiffer accomplish with such combinations of words?

2. In Paragraphs 9 and 10, Feiffer describes what he calls a "typical American romance," and then defines "love." Write a short essay setting forth your agreement or disagreement with his understanding of that all-engrossing subject.

3. To what extent is the popularity of such comic book heroes as Superman dependent upon a macho view of the sex roles?

4. One of the attractions of Superman, and many other "super-heroes," is his appeal to our fondness for fantasy, particularly that common form of fantasy in which we cast ourselves in favorable roles. Write an essay in which you compare and contrast your own favorite fantasy of this sort with the public one produced by Joe Shuster, creator of Superman.

Robert Frost (1874–1963) was born in California and became the great poet of New England. He published many books of poems, and won the Pulitzer Prize three times. A popular figure, Frost was admired as a gentle, affectionate, avuncular figure given to country sayings. The private Frost was another man —guilty, jealous, generous, bitter, sophisticated, occasionally triumphant, and always complicated.

26

ROBERT FROST
The Gift Outright

The land was ours before we were the land's.
She was our land more than a hundred years
Before we were her people. She was ours
In Massachusetts, in Virginia,
But we were England's, still colonials,   5
Possessing what we still were unpossessed by,
Possessed by what we now no more possessed.
Something we were withholding made us weak
Until we found out that it was ourselves
We were withholding from our land of living,   10
And forthwith found salvation in surrender.
Such as we were we gave ourselves outright
(The deed of gift was many deeds of war)
To the land vaguely realizing westward,
But still unstoried, artless, unenhanced,   15
Such as she was, such as she would become.

From *The Poetry of Robert Frost* edited by Edward Connery Lathem. Copyright 1942 by Robert Frost. Copyright © 1969 by Holt, Rinehart and Winston. Copyright © 1970 by Lesley Frost Ballantine. Reprinted by permission of Holt, Rinehart and Winston.

Martin Gansberg (b. 1920) has edited and reported for The
New York Times *for forty years. This story, written in 1964, has
been widely reprinted. Largely because of Gansberg's account,
the murder of Kitty Genovese has become a well-known example
of citizen apathy. When Gansberg returned to the neighborhood
fifteen years afterward, revisiting the place of the murder with a
television crew, the people had not changed: still, no one wanted
to get involved.*

27

MARTIN GANSBERG

38 Who Saw Murder Didn't Call the Police

1   For more than half an hour 38 respectable, law-abiding citizens
in Queens watched a killer stalk and stab a woman in three separate
attacks in Kew Gardens.

2   Twice their chatter and the sudden glow of their bedroom lights
interrupted him and frightened him off. Each time he returned, sought
her out, and stabbed her again. Not one person telephoned the police
during the assault; one witness called after the woman was dead.

3   That was two weeks ago today.

4   Still shocked is Assistant Chief Inspector Frederick M. Lussen,
in charge of the borough's detectives and a veteran of 25 years of
homicide investigations. He can give a matter-of-fact recitation on
many murders. But the Kew Gardens slaying baffles him — not
because it is a murder, but because the "good people" failed to call the
police.

"As we have reconstructed the crime," he said, "the assailant 5
had three chances to kill this woman during a 35-minute period. He
returned twice to complete the job. If we had been called when he first
attacked, the woman might not be dead now."

This is what the police say happened beginning at 3:20 A.M. in 6
the staid, middle-class, tree-lined Austin Street area:

Twenty-eight-year-old Catherine Genovese, who was called 7
Kitty by almost everyone in the neighborhood was returning home
from her job as manager of a bar in Hollis. She parked her red Fiat in a
lot adjacent to the Kew Gardens Long Island Rail Road Station, facing
Mowbray Place. Like many residents of the neighborhood, she had
parked there day after day since her arrival from Connecticut a year
ago, although the railroad frowns on the practice.

She turned off the lights of her car, locked the door, and started 8
to walk the 100 feet to the entrance of her apartment at 82–70 Austin
Street, which is in a Tudor building, with stores in the first floor and
apartments on the second.

The entrance to the apartment is in the rear of the building 9
because the front is rented to retail stores. At night the quiet neighborhood is shrouded in the slumbering darkness that marks most residential areas.

Miss Genovese noticed a man at the far end of the lot, near a 10
seven-story apartment house at 82–40 Austin Street. She halted.
Then, nervously, she headed up Austin Street toward Lefferts Boulevard, where there is a call box to the 102nd Police Precinct in nearby
Richmond Hill.

She got as far as a street light in front of a bookstore before the 11
man grabbed her. She screamed. Lights went on in the 10-story apartment house at 82–67 Austin Street, which faces the bookstore. Windows slid open and voices punctuated the early-morning stillness.

Miss Genovese screamed: "Oh, my God, he stabbed me! Please 12
help me! Please help me!"

From one of the upper windows in the apartment house, a man 13
called down: "Let that girl alone!"

The assailant looked up at him, shrugged and walked down Aus- 14
tin Street toward a white sedan parked a short distance away. Miss
Genovese struggled to her feet.

Lights went out. The killer returned to Miss Genovese, now 15
trying to make her way around the side of the building by the parking
lot to get to her apartment. The assailant stabbed her again.

"I'm dying!" she shrieked. "I'm dying!" 16

17   Windows were opened again, and lights went on in many apartments. The assailant got into his car and drove away. Miss Genovese staggered to her feet. A city bus, O–10, the Lefferts Boulevard line to Kennedy International Airport, passed. It was 3:35 A.M.

18   The assailant returned. By then, Miss Genovese had crawled to the back of the building, where the freshly painted brown doors to the apartment house held out hope for safety. The killer tried the first door; she wasn't there. At the second door, 82–62 Austin Street, he saw her slumped on the floor at the foot of the stairs. He stabbed her a third time — fatally.

19   It was 3:50 by the time the police received their first call, from a man who was a neighbor of Miss Genovese. In two minutes they were at the scene. The neighbor, a 70-year-old woman, and another woman were the only persons on the street. Nobody else came forward.

20   The man explained that he had called the police after much deliberation. He had phoned a friend in Nassau County for advice and then he had crossed the roof of the building to the apartment of the elderly woman to get her to make the call.

21   "I didn't want to get involved," he sheepishly told the police.

22   Six days later, the police arrested Winston Moseley, a 29-year-old business-machine operator, and charged him with homicide. Moseley had no previous record. He is married, has two children and owns a home at 133–19 Sutter Avenue, South Ozone Park, Queens. On Wednesday, a court committed him to Kings County Hospital for psychiatric observation.

23   When questioned by the police, Moseley also said that he had slain Mrs. Annie May Johnson, 24, of 146–12 133d Avenue, Jamaica, on Feb. 29 and Barbara Kralik, 15, of 174–17 140th Avenue, Springfield Gardens, last July. In the Kralik case, the police are holding Alvin L. Mitchell, who is said to have confessed that slaying.

24   The police stressed how simple it would have been to have gotten in touch with them. "A phone call," said one of the detectives, "would have done it." The police may be reached by dialing "O" for operator or SPring 7–3100.

25   Today witnesses from the neighborhood, which is made up of one-family homes in the $35,000 to $60,000 range with the exception of the two apartment houses near the railroad station, find it difficult to explain why they didn't call the police.

26   A housewife, knowingly if quite casually, said, "We thought it was a lover's quarrel." A husand and wife both said, "Frankly, we were afraid." They seemed aware of the fact that events might have been

different. A distraught woman, wiping her hands in her apron, said, "I didn't want my husband to get involved."

One couple, now willing to talk about that night, said they heard 27 the first screams. The husband looked thoughtfully at the bookstore where the killer first grabbed Miss Genovese.

"We went to the window to see what was happening," he said, 28 "but the light from our bedroom made it difficult to see the street." The wife, still apprehensive, added: "I put out the light and we were able to see better."

Asked why they hadn't called the police, she shrugged and 29 replied: "I don't know."

A man peeked out from a slight opening in the doorway to his 30 apartment and rattled off an account of the killer's second attack. Why hadn't he called the police at the time? "I was tired," he said without emotion. "I went back to bed."

It was 4:25 A.M. when the ambulance arrived to take the body of 31 Miss Genovese. It drove off. "Then," a solemn police detective said, "the people came out."

_____ CONSIDERATIONS _____

1. Obviously — though not overtly — Gansberg's newspaper account is a condemnation of the failure of ordinary citizens to feel social responsibility. Explain how the writer makes his purpose obvious without openly stating it. Compare his method with Orwell's use of implication in "A Hanging."

2. In Paragraph 7, Gansberg tells us that Catherine Genovese was called Kitty and that she drove a red Fiat. Are these essential details? If not, why does this writer use them?

3. Newspapers use short paragraphs for visual relief. If you were making this story into a narrative essay, how might you change the paragraphing?

4. Is Gansberg's opening sentence a distortion of the facts? Read his account carefully before you answer; then explain and support your answer with reference to other parts of the story.

5. Gansberg's newspaper report was published nearly twenty years ago. Are similar incidents more common now than then? Were they more common then than in the 1940s, 1920s, 1900s? In what way does the coverage by newspapers and television affect your impressions? What sources could you use to find the facts?

Stephen Jay Gould (b. 1941) is a paleontologist who teaches at Harvard and writes scientific essays for the general reader. He calls himself "an evolutionist," for Darwin and the theory of evolution live at the center of his mind. He has written five books, of which three collect his periodical essays: Ever Since Darwin *(1977),* The Panda's Thumb *(1980), and* Hen's Teeth and Horse's Toes *(1983). Gould's lively mind, eager to use scientific method for public thinking, seeks out diverse subjects and often discovers a political flavor in matters not usually perceived as political.*

28

STEPHEN JAY GOULD
The Politics of Census

1   In the constitution of the United States, the same passage that prescribes a census every ten years also includes the infamous statement that slaves shall be counted as three-fifths of a person. Ironically, and however different the setting and motives, black people are still undercounted in the American census because poor people in inner cities are systematically missed.

2   The census has always been controversial because it was established as a political device, not as an expensive frill to satisfy curiosity and feed academic mills. The constitutional passage that ordained the census begins: "Representatives and direct taxes shall be apportioned among the several states which may be included within this union, according to their respective numbers."

Political use of the census has often extended beyond the alloca- 3
tion of taxation and representation. The sixth census of 1840 engen-
dered a heated controversy based upon the correct contention that
certain black people had, for once, been falsely *over*counted. This curious tale illustrates the principle that copious numbers do not guarantee objectivity and that even the most careful and rigorous surveys are
only as good as their methods and assumptions. (William Stanton tells
the story in *The Leopard's Spots*, his excellent book on the history of
scientific attitudes toward race in America during the first half of the
nineteenth century. I have also read the original papers of the major
protagonist, Edward Jarvis.)

The 1840 census was the first to include counts of the mentally 4
ill and deficient, enumerated by race and by state. Dr. Edward Jarvis,
then a young physician but later to become a national authority on
medical statistics, rejoiced that the frustrations of inadequate data
would soon be overcome. He wrote in 1844:

> The statistics of insanity are becoming more and more an object of
> interest to philanthropists, to political economists, and to men of
> science. But all investigations, conducted by individuals or by
> associations, have been partial, incomplete, and far from satisfac-
> tory. . . . They could not tell the numbers of any class or people,
> among whom they found a definite number of the insane. And
> therefore, as a ground of comparison of the prevalence of insanity
> in one country with that of another, or in one class or race of
> people with that in another, their reports did not answer their
> intended purpose.

Jarvis then praised the marshals of the 1840 census as apostles of 5
the new, quantitative order:

> As these functionaries were ordered to inquire from house to
> house, and leave no dwelling — neither mansion nor cabin — nei-
> ther tent nor ship unvisited and unexamined, it was reasonably
> supposed that there would be a complete and accurate account of
> the prevalence of insanity among 17 millions of people. A wider
> field than this had never been surveyed for this purpose in any part
> of the earth, since the world began. . . . Never had the philanthro-
> pist a better promise of truth hitherto undiscovered. . . . Many pro-
> ceeded at once to analyze the tables, in order to show the
> proportion of lunacy in the various states, and among the two
> races, which constitute our population.

As scholars and ideologues of varying stripes scrutinized the tables, one apparent fact rose to obvious prominence in those troubled times. Among blacks, insanity struck free people in northern states far more often than it afflicted slaves in the South. In fact, one in 162 blacks was insane in free states, but only one in 1,558 in slave states. But freedom and the North posed no mental terror for whites, since their relative sanity did not differ in the North and South.

7   Moreover, insanity among blacks seemed to decrease in even gradation from the harsh North to the congenial South. One in 14 of Maine's black population was either insane or idiotic; in New Hampshire, one in 28; in Massachusetts, one in 43; in New Jersey, one in 279. In Delaware, however, the frequency of insanity among blacks suddenly nose-dived. As Stanton writes: "It appeared that Mason and Dixon had surveyed a line not only between Maryland and Pennsylvania but also — surely all unwitting — between Sanity and Bedlam."

8   In his first publication on the 1840 census, Jarvis drew the same conclusion that so many other whites would advance: slavery, if not the natural state of black people, must have a remarkably beneficent effect upon them. It must exert "a wonderful influence upon the development of moral faculties and the intellectual powers." A slave gains equanimity by "refusing many of the hopes and responsibilities which the free, self-thinking and self-acting enjoy and sustain," for bondage "saves him from some of the liabilities and dangers of active self-direction."

9   The basic "fact" of ten times more insanity in freedom than in slavery was widely bruited about in the contemporary press, often in lurid fashion. Stanton quotes a contributor to the *Southern Literary Messenger* (1843) who, concluding that blacks grow "more vicious in a state of freedom," painted a frightful picture of Virginia should it ever become a free state, with "all sympathy on the part of the master to the slave ended." He inquired:

> Where should we find penitentiaries for the thousands of felons? Where, lunatic asylums for the tens of thousands of maniacs? Would it be possible to live in a country where maniacs and felons meet the traveler at every crossroad.

10   But Jarvis was troubled. The disparity between North and South made sense to him, but its extent was puzzling. Could slavery possibly make such an enormous difference? If the information had not been stamped with a governmental imprimatur, who could have believed it? Jarvis wrote:

This was so improbable, so contrary to common experience, there was in it such a strong prima facie evidence of error, that nothing but a document, coming forth with all the authority of the national government, and "corrected in the department of state," could have gained for it the least credence among the inhabitants of the free states, where insanity was stated to abound so plentifully.

Jarvis therefore began to examine the tables and was shocked by what he discovered. Somehow, and in a fashion that could scarcely represent a set of random accidents, the number of insane blacks had been absurdly inflated in reported figures for northern states. Jarvis discovered that twenty-five towns in the twelve free states contained not a single black person of sound mind. The figure for "all blacks" had obviously been recopied or misplaced in the column for "insane blacks." But data for 135 additional towns (including thirty-nine in Ohio and twenty in New York) could not be explained so easily, for these towns actually reported a population of insane blacks greater than the total number of blacks, both sane and unhinged! 11

In a few cases, Jarvis was able to track down the source of error. Worcester, Massachusetts, for example, reported 133 insane in a total black population of 151. Jarvis inquired and discovered that these 133 people were white patients living in the state mental hospital located there. With this single correction, the first among many, black insanity in Massachusetts dropped from one in 43 to one in 129. Jarvis, demoralized and angry, began a decade of unsuccessful campaigning to win an official retraction or correction of the 1840 census. He began: 12

> Such a document as we have described, heavy with its errors and its misstatements, instead of being a messenger of truth to the world to enlighten its knowledge and guide its opinions, it is, in respect to human ailment, a bearer of falsehood to confuse and mislead.

This debate was destined for a more significant fate than persistent bickering in literary and scholarly journals. For Jarvis's disclosures caught the ear of a formidable man: John Quincy Adams, then near eighty, and capping a distinguished carrer as leader of antislavery forces in the House of Representatives. But Adams's opponent was equally formidable. At that time, the census fell under the jurisdiction of the Department of State, and its newly appointed secretary was none other than John C. Calhoun, the cleverest and most vigorous defender of slavery in America. 13

14   Calhoun, in one of his first acts in office, used the incorrect but official census figures in responding to the expressed hope of the British foreign secretary, Lord Aberdeen, that slavery would not be permitted in the new republic (soon to be state) of Texas. The census proved, Calhoun wrote to Aberdeen, that northern blacks had "invariably sunk into vice and pauperism, accompanied by the bodily and mental afflictions incident thereto," while states that had retained what Calhoun called, in genteel euphemism, "the ancient relation" between races, contained a black population that had "improved greatly in every respect — in number, comfort, intelligence, and morals."

15   Calhoun then proceeded to evade the official request from the House, passed on Adams's motion, that the secretary of state report on errors in the census and steps that would be taken to correct them. Adams then accosted Calhoun in his office and recorded the secretary's response in his diary:

> He writhed like a trodden rattlesnake on the exposure of his false report to the House that no material errors had been discovered in the printed Census of 1840, and finally said that there were so many errors they balanced one another, and led to the same conclusion as if they were all correct.

16   Jarvis, meanwhile, had enlisted the support of the Massachusetts Medical Society and the American Statistical Association. Armed with new data and support, Adams again persuaded the House to ask Calhoun for an official explanation. And again Calhoun wriggled out, finally delivering a report full of obfuscation and rhetoric, and still citing the 1840 figures on insanity as proof that freedom would be "a curse instead of a blessing" for black slaves. Jarvis lived until 1884 and assisted in the censuses of 1850, 1860, and 1870. But he never won official rectification of the errors he had uncovered in the 1840 census; the finagled, if not outrightly fraudulent, data on insanity among blacks continued to be cited as an argument for slavery as the Civil War approached.

17   There is a world of difference between the overcount of insane blacks in 1840 and the undercount of poor blacks (and other groups) in central cities in 1980. First, although the source of error in the 1840 census has never been determined, we may strongly suspect some systematic, perhaps conscious manipulation by those charged with putting the raw data in tabular form. I think we can be reasonably confident that, with automated procedures and more deliberate care,

the systematic errors of the 1980 census are at least honest ones. Second, the politics of 1840 left few channels open to critics, and Calhoun's evasive stubbornness finally prevailed. Today, nearly every census is subjected to legal scrutiny and challenge.

Yet behind these legal struggles stands the fact that we still do   18 not know how to count people accurately. Voluminous numbers and extensive tabulation do not guarantee objectivity. If you can't find people, you can't count them — and the American census is, by law, an attempt at exhaustive counting, not a statistical operation based on sampling.

If it were possible (however expensive) to count everyone with   19 confidence, then no valid complaint could be raised. But it is not, and the very attempt to do so engenders a systematic error that guarantees failure. For some people are much harder to find than others, either by their direct resistance to being counted (illegal aliens, for example) or by the complex of unfortunate circumstances that renders the poor more anonymous than other Americans.

Regions with a concentration of poor people will be systemati-   20 cally undercounted, and such regions are not spread across America at random. They are located in the heart of our major cities. A census that assesses populations by direct counting will be a source of endless contention so long as federal money and representation in Congress reach cities as rewards for greater numbers.

Censusing has always been controversial, especially since its his-   21 torical purpose has usually involved taxation or conscription. When David, inveigled by Satan himself, had the chutzpah to "number" Israel (I Chronicles, chapter 21), the Lord punished him by offering some unpleasant alternatives: three years of famine, three months of devastation by enemy armies, or three days of pestilence (all reducing the population, perhaps to countable levels). The legacy of each American census seems to be ten years of contention.

_____ CONSIDERATIONS _____

1. Gould's opening paragraph provides an excellent example of a forthright thesis statement. It unifies his essay and at the same time gives it point and direction. Examine your own compositions to see if they might be improved by more careful attention to the thesis statement.

2. "The Politics of Census" could be called a book review, since Gould's principal source was a book-length account published originally in 1960.

Gould's essay, however, is not a simple retelling of Stanton's book. What additional research has Gould carried out, and how has he brought the account of census-making up-to-date?

3. Although census techniques have greatly improved since the nineteenth century, Gould maintains that a perfect count is still impossible. Why?

4. Is the account of Calhoun's refusal to acknowledge Jarvis's findings a destructive exposé of government corruption or a constructive job of historical research? Explain, in a short essay, the difference between destructive and constructive criticism.

5. Gould refers, in Paragraph 18, to the difference between counting and sampling. How are we affected today by research based on sampling? Setting aside the possibility of dishonesty, how can such research produce what scientists call "skewed" results?

6. Gould was obviously attracted to the story of the 1840 census by the detective story inherent in Jarvis's quest for the truth. Is it sensible to think of research as detective work? Discuss, with examples of your own finding. (An interesting source for examples of researcher-detectives is Richard D. Altick's *The Art of Literary Research.* New York: Norton, 1963.)

Gould's enthusiasm for scientific method carries him a long way from paleontology. Perhaps he would assert that nothing in this world is a long way from anything else. This essay, like "The Politics of Census," comes from Hen's Teeth and Horse's Toes.

29

STEPHEN JAY GOULD

Phyletic Size Decrease in Hershey Bars

The solace of my youth was a miserable concoction of something 1 sweet and gooey, liberally studded with peanuts and surrounded by chocolate — real chocolate, at least. It was called "Whizz" and it cost a nickel. Emblazoned on the wrapper stood its proud motto in rhyme — "the best nickel candy there izz." Sometime after the war, candy bars went up to six cents for a time, and the motto changed without fanfare — "the best candy bar there izz." Little did I suspect that an evolutionary process, persistent in direction and constantly accelerating, had commenced.

I am a paleontologist — one of those oddballs who parlayed his 2 childhood fascination for dinosaurs into a career. We search the history of life for repeated patterns, mostly without success. One generality that works more often than it fails is called "Cope's rule of phyletic size increase." For reasons yet poorly specified, body size tends to increase fairly steadily within evolutionary lineages. Some have cited general advantages of larger bodies — greater foraging range, higher reproductive output, greater intelligence associated with larger brains. Others claim that founders of long lineages tend to be small, and that increasing size is more a drift away from diminutive stature than a positive achievement of greater bulk.

3   The opposite phenomenon of gradual size decrease is surpassingly rare. There is a famous foram (a single-celled marine creature) that got smaller and smaller before disappearing entirely. An extinct, but once major group, the graptolites (floating, colonial marine organisms, perhaps related to vertebrates) began life with a large number of stipes (branches bearing a row of individuals). The number of stipes then declined progressively in several lineages, to eight, four, and two, until finally all surviving graptolites possessed but a single stipe. Then they disappeared. Did they, like the *Incredible Shrinking Man* simply decline to invisibility — for he, having decreased enough to make his final exit through the mesh of a screen in his movie début, must now be down to the size of a muon, but still, I suspect, hanging in there. Or did they snuff it entirely, like the legendary Foo-bird who coursed in ever smaller circles until he flew up his own you-know-what and disappeared. What would a zero-stiped graptolite look like? In any case, they are no longer part of our world.

4   The rarities of nature are often commonplaces of culture; and phyletic size decrease surrounds us in products of human manufacture. Remember the come-on, once emblazoned on the covers of comic books — "52 pages, all comics." And they only cost a dime. And remember when large meant large, rather than the smallest size in a sequence of detergent or cereal boxes going from large to gigantic to enormous.

5   Consider the Hershey bar — a most worthy standard bearer for the general phenomenon of phyletic size decrease in manufactured goods. It is the unadvertised symbol of American quality. It shares with Band-Aids, Kleenex, Jell-o and the Fridge that rare distinction of attaching its brand name to the generic product. It has also been shrinking fast.

6   I have been monitoring informally, and with distress, this process for more than a decade. Obviously, others have followed it as well. The subject has become sufficiently sensitive that an official memo emanated in December 1978 from corporate headquarters at 19 East Chocolate Avenue — in Hershey, Pa. of course. Hershey chose the unmodified hang-out and spilled all the beans, to coin an appropriate metaphor. This three page document is titled "Remember the nickel

bar?" (I do indeed, and ever so fondly, for I started to chomp them avidly in an age of youthful innocence, ever so long before I first heard of the nickel bag.) Hershey defends its shrinking bars and rising prices as a strictly average (or even slightly better than average) response to general inflation. I do not challenge this assertion since I use the bar as a synecdoche for general malaise — as an average, not an egregious, example.

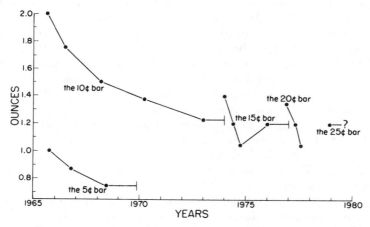

Hershey Bars bite the dust, a quantitative assessment. GRAPH BY L. MESZOLY.

I have constructed the accompanying graph from tabular data in the Hershey memo, including all information from mid-1965 to now. As a paleontologist used to interpreting evolutionary sequences, I spy two general phenomena: gradual phyletic size decrease within each price lineage, and occasional sudden mutation to larger size (and price) following previous decline to dangerous levels. I am utterly innocent of economics, the dismal science. For me, bulls and bears have four legs and are called *Bos taurus* and *Ursus arctos*. But I think I finally understand what an evolutionist would call the "adaptive significance" of inflation. Inflation is a necessary spin-off, or by-product, of a lineage's successful struggle for existence. For this radical explanation of inflation, you need grant me only one premise — that the manufactured products of culture, as fundamentally unnatural, tend to follow life's course in reverse. If organic lineages obey Cope's rule and increase in size, then manufactured lineages have an equally strong propensity for decreasing in size. Therefore, they either follow the fate of the Foo-Bird and we know them no longer, or they periodically restore themselves by sudden mutation to larger size — and, incidentally, fancier prices.

8   We may defend this thesis by extrapolating the tendencies of each price lineage on the graph. The nickel bar weighed an ounce in 1949. And it still weighed an ounce (following some temporary dips to ⅞ oz.) when our story began in September 1965. But it could delay its natural tendency no longer and decline began, to ⅞ oz. in September 1966 and finally to ¾ oz. in May 1968 until its discontinuation on November 24, 1969, a day that will live in infamy. But just as well, for if you extrapolate its average rate of decline (¼ ounce in thirty-two months), it would have become extinct naturally in May 1976. The dime bar followed a similar course, but beginning larger, it held on longer. It went steadily down from 2 oz. in August 1965 to 1.26 oz. in January 1973. It was officially discontinued on January 1, 1974, though I calculate that it would have become extinct on August 17, 1986. The fifteen-cent bar started hopefully at 1.4 oz. in January 1974, but then declined at an alarming rate far in excess of any predecessor. Unexpectedly, it then rallied, displaying the only (though minor) reverse toward larger size within a price lineage since 1965. Nonetheless, it died on December 31, 1976 — and why not, for it could only have lasted until December 31, 1988, and who would have paid fifteen cents for a crumb during its dotage? The twenty-cent bar (I do hope I'm not boring you) arose at 1.35 oz. in December 1976 and immediately experienced the most rapid and unreversed decline of any price lineage. It will die on July 15, 1979. The twenty-five-cent bar, now but a few months old, began at 1.2 oz. in December 1978. *Ave atque vale.*

9   The graph shows another alarming trend. Each time the Hershey Bar mutates to a new price lineage, it gets larger, but never as large as the founding member of the previous price lineage. The law of phyletic size decrease for manufactured goods must operate across related lineages as well as within them — thus ultimately frustrating the strategy of restoration by mutational jump. The ten-cent bar began at 2 oz. and was still holding firm when our story began in late 1965. The fifteen-cent bar arose at 1.4 oz., the twenty-cent bar at 1.35 oz., and the quarter bar at 1.2 oz. We can also extrapolate this rate of decrease across lineages to its final solution. We have seen a decrease of 0.8 oz. in three steps over thirteen years and four months. At this rate, the remaining four and a half steps will take another twenty years. And that ultimate wonder of wonders, the weightless bar, will be introduced in December 1998. It will cost forty-seven and a half cents.

10   The publicity people at Hershey's mentioned something about a

ten-pound free sample. But I guess I've blown it. Still, I would remind everyone of Mark Twain's comment that there are "lies, damned lies and statistics." And I will say this for the good folks in Hershey, Pa. It's still the same damned good chocolate, what's left of it. A replacement of whole by broken almonds is the only compromise with quality I've noticed, while I shudder to think what the "creme" inside a Devil Dog is made of these days.

Still, I guess I've blown it. Too bad. A ten-pound bar titillates my   11
wildest fancy. It would be as good as the 1949 Joe DiMaggio card that I never got (I don't think there was one in the series). And did I ever end up with a stack of pink bubble gum sheets for the effort. But that's another tale, to be told through false teeth at another time.

POSTSCRIPT

I wrote this article (as anyone can tell from internal evidence)   12
early in 1979. Since then, two interesting events have occurred. The first matched my predictions with uncanny accuracy. For the second, that specter of all science, the Great Exception (capital G, capital E), intervened and I have been temporarily foiled. And — as an avid Hershey bar chomper — am I ever glad for it.

The twenty-five cent bar did just about what I said it would. It   13
started at 1.2 oz. in December 1978, where I left it, and then plummeted to 1.05 oz. in March 1980 before becoming extinct in March 1982. But Hershey then added a twist to necessity when it replaced its lamented two-bit bar with the inevitable thirty-cent concoction. Previously, all new introductions had begun (despite their fancier prices) at lower weights than the proud first item of the previous price lineage. (I based my extrapolation to the weightless bar on this pattern.) But, wonder of wonders and salaam to the Great Exception, the thirty-cent bar began at a whopping 1.45 oz., larger than anything we've seen since the ten-cent bar of my long-lost boyhood.

As cynical readers might expect, a tale lies behind this peculiar   14
move. In the *Washington Post* for July 11, 1982 (and with thanks to Ellis Yochelson for sending the article), Randolph E. Bucklin explains all under the title: "Candy Wars: Price Tactic fails Hershey."

It seems that the good folks at (not on) Mars, manufacturers of   15
Three Musketeers, Snickers, and M & M's, and Hershey's chief competitor, had made the unprecedented move of increasing the size of their quarter bars without raising prices. After a while, they snuck the

price up to thirty cents but kept the new size. Hershey tried to hold the line with its shrinking quarter bars. But thousands of mom and pop stores couldn't be bothered charging a quarter for some bars and thirty cents for others (and couldn't remember which were Hershey's and which were Mars's anyway) — and therefore charged thirty cents for both Mars's large bars and Hershey's minuscule offerings. Hershey's sales plummeted: finally, they capitulated to Mars's tactics, raising prices to thirty cents and beefing up sizes to Mars's level and above predictions of the natural trend.

16   As a scientist trained in special pleading, I have a ready explanation for the Great Exception. General trends have an intrinsic character; they continue when external conditions retain their constancy. An unanticipated and unpredictable catastrophe, like the late Cretaceous asteroid of the next essay, or the sneaky sales tactic of Mars and Co., resets the system, and all bets are off. Still, the greater inevitability prevails. The thirty-cent bar will diminish and restitutions at higher prices will shrink as well. The weightless bar may come a few years later than I predicted (even a bit past the millennium) — but I still bet ya it'll cost about four bits.

____ CONSIDERATIONS ____

1. How far do you have to read in Gould's essay before you suspect that he is engaging in mild satire? When and how are your suspicions confirmed?

2. What is a "muon," and why does Gould use such a far-fetched term in Paragraph 3?

3. Gould says in Paragraph 6 that he uses the Hershey bar as a "synecdoche for general malaise." Consult a dictionary for the meaning of synecdoche and decide whether Gould is transferring it justifiably to the field of scientific research.

4. In charting the demise of the nickel Hershey bar, Gould uses an expression — "a day that will live in infamy" — better associated with a somewhat larger event. If you can identify that event, you will better understand one of Gould's satirical techniques. The same applies to the Latin tag, *Ave atque vale*, at the end of Paragraph 8.

5. Study Gould's use of parenthetical remarks, especially in his postscript. How do they contribute to the attractiveness of his essay?

30

STEPHEN JAY GOULD

Wide Hats and Narrow Minds

In 1861, from February to June, the ghost of Baron Georges Cuvier haunted the Anthropological Society of Paris. The great Cuvier, Aristotle of French biology (an immodest designation from which he did not shrink), died in 1832, but the physical vault of his spirit lived on as Paul Broca and Louis Pierre Gratiolet squared off to debate whether or not the size of a brain has anything to do with the intelligence of its bearer.

In the opening round, Gratiolet dared to argue that the best and brightest could not be recognized by their big heads. (Gratiolet, a confirmed monarchist, was no egalitarian. He merely sought other measures to affirm the superiority of white European males.) Broca, founder of the Anthropological Society and the world's greatest craniometrician, or head measurer, replied that "study of the brains of human races would lose most of its interest and utility" if variation in size counted for nothing. Why, he asked, had anthropologists spent

167

so much time measuring heads if the results had no bearing upon what he regarded as the most important question of all — the relative worth of different peoples:

> Among the questions heretofore discussed within the Anthropological Society, none is equal in interest and importance to the question before us now. . . . The great importance of craniology has struck anthropologists with such force that many among us have neglected the other parts of our science in order to devote ourselves almost exclusively to the study of skulls. . . . In such data, we hope to find some information relevant to the intellectual value of the various human races.

3   Broca and Gratiolet battled for five months and through nearly 200 pages of the published bulletin. Tempers flared. In the heat of battle, one of Broca's lieutenants struck the lowest blow of all: "I have noticed for a long time that, in general, those who deny the intellectual importance of the brain's volume have small heads." In the end, Broca won, hands down. During the debate, no item of information had been more valuable to Broca, none more widely discussed or more vigorously contended, than the brain of Georges Cuvier.

4   Cuvier, the greatest anatomist of his time, the man who revised our understanding of animals by classifying them according to function — how they work — rather than by rank in an anthropocentric scale of lower to higher. Cuvier, the founder of paleontology, the man who first established the fact of extinction and who stressed the importance of catastrophes in understanding the history both of life and the earth. Cuvier, the great statesman who, like Talleyrand, managed to serve all French governments, from revolution to monarchy, and die in bed. (Actually, Cuvier passed the most tumultuous years of the revolution as a private tutor in Normandy, although he feigned revolutionary sympathies in his letters. He arrived in Paris in 1795 and never left.) F. Bourdier, a recent biographer, describes Cuvier's corporeal ontogeny, but his words also serve as a good metaphor for Cuvier's power and influence: "Cuvier was short and during the Revolution he was very thin; he became stouter during the Empire; and he grew enormously fat after the Restoration."

5   Cuvier's contemporaries marveled at his "massive head." One admirer affirmed that it "gave to his entire person an undeniable cachet of majesty and to his face an expression of profound meditation." Thus, when Cuvier died, his colleagues, in the interests of science and curiosity, decided to open the great skull. On Tuesday, May

15, 1832, at seven o'clock in the morning, a group of the greatest doctors and biologists of France gathered to dissect the body of Georges Cuvier. They began with the internal organs and, finding "nothing very remarkable," switched their attention to Cuvier's skull. "Thus," wrote the physician in charge, "we were about to contemplate the instrument of this powerful intelligence." And their expectations were rewarded. The brain of Georges Cuvier weighed 1,830 grams, more than 400 grams above average and 200 grams larger than any nondiseased brain previously weighed. Unconfirmed reports and uncertain inference placed the brains of Oliver Cromwell, Jonathan Swift, and Lord Byron in the same range, but Cuvier had provided the first direct evidence that brilliance and brain size go together.

Broca pushed his advantage and rested a good part of his case on Cuvier's brain. But Gratiolet probed and found a weak spot. In their awe and enthusiasm, Cuvier's doctors had neglected to save either his brain or his skull. Moreover, they reported no measures on the skull at all. The figure of 1,830 g for the brain could not be checked; perhaps it was simply wrong. Gratiolet sought an existing surrogate and had a flash of inspiration: "All brains are not weighed by doctors," he stated, "but all heads are measured by hatters and I have managed to acquire, from this new source, information which, I dare to hope, will not appear to you as devoid of interest." In short, Gratiolet presented something almost bathetic in comparison with the great man's brain: he had found Cuvier's hat! And thus, for two meetings, some of France's greatest minds pondered seriously the meaning of a worn bit of felt.

Cuvier's hat. Gratiolet reported, measured 21.8 cm in length and 18.0 cm in width. He then consulted a certain M. Puriau, "one of the most intelligent and widely known hatters of Paris." Puriau told him that the largest standard size for hats measured 21.5 by 18.5 cm. Although very few men wore a hat so big, Cuvier was not off scale. Moreover, Gratiolet reported with evident pleasure, the hat was extremely flexible and "softened by very long usage." It had probably not been so large when Cuvier bought it. Moreover, Cuvier had an exceptionally thick head of hair, and he wore it bushy. "This seems to prove quite clearly," Gratiolet proclaimed, "that if Cuvier's head was very large, its size was not absolutely exceptional or unique."

Gratiolet's opponents preferred to believe the doctors and refused to grant much weight to a bit of cloth. More than twenty years later, in 1883, G. Hervé again took up the subject of Cuvier's brain and discovered a missing item: Cuvier's head had been measured after all, but the figures had been omitted from the autopsy report. The skull was big indeed. Shaved of that famous mat of hair, as it was for the autopsy, its greatest circumference could be equaled by only 6 percent of "scientists and men of letters" (measured in life with their hair at that) and zero percent of domestic servants. As for the infamous hat, Hervé pleaded ignorance, but he did cite the following anecdote: "Cuvier had a habit of leaving his hat on a table in his waiting room. It often happened that a professor or a statesman tried it on. The hat descended below their eyes."

9   Yet, just as the doctrine of more-is-better stood on the verge of triumph, Hervé snatched potential defeat from the jaws of Broca's victory. Too much of a good thing can be as troubling as a deficiency, and Hervé began to worry. Why did Cuvier's brain exceed those of other "men of genius" by so much? He reviewed both details of the autopsy and records of Cuvier's frail early health and constructed a circumstantial case for "transient juvenile hydrocephaly," or water on the brain. If Cuvier's skull had been artificially enlarged by the pressure of fluids early during its growth, then a brain of normal size might simply have expanded — by decreasing in density, not by growing larger — into the space available. Or did an enlarged space permit the brain to grow to an unusual size after all? Hervé could not resolve this cardinal question because Cuvier's brain had been measured and then tossed out. All that remained was the magisterial number, 1,830 grams. "With the brain of Cuvier," wrote Hervé, "science has lost one of the most precious documents it ever possessed."

10   On the surface, this tale seems ludicrous. The thought of France's finest anthropologists arguing passionately about the meaning of a dead colleague's hat could easily provoke the most misleading and dangerous inference of all about history — a view of the past as a domain of naïve half-wits, the path of history as a tale of progress, and the present as sophisticated and enlightened.

11   But if we laugh with derision, we will never understand. Human intellectual capacity has not altered for thousands of years so far as we can tell. If intelligent people invested intense energy in issues that now seem foolish to us, then the failure lies in our understanding of their world, not in their distorted perceptions. Even the standard example of ancient nonsense — the debate about angels on pinheads — makes sense once you realize that theologians were not discussing whether five or eighteen would fit, but whether a pin could house a finite or an infinite number. In certain theological systems, the corporeality or noncorporeality of angels is an important matter indeed.

In this case, a clue to the vital importance of Cuvier's brain for   12
nineteenth-century anthropology lies in the last line of Broca's statement, quoted above: "In such data, we hope to find some information
relevant to the intellectual value of the various human races." Broca
and his school wanted to show that brain size, through its link with
intelligence, could resolve what they regarded as the primary question
for a "science of man" — explaining why some individuals and groups
are more successful than others. To do this, they separated people
according to a priori convictions about their worth — men versus
women, whites versus blacks, "men of genius" versus ordinary folks
— and tried to demonstrate differences in brain size. The brains of
eminent men (literally males) formed an essential link in their argument — and Cuvier was the *crème de la crème.* Broca concluded:

> In general, the brain is larger in men than in women, in eminent
> men than in men of mediocre talent, in superior races than in
> inferior races. Other things equal, there is a remarkable relation-
> ship between the development of intelligence and the volume of
> the brain.

Broca died in 1880, but disciples continued his catalog of eminent   13
brains (indeed, they added Broca's own to the list — although it
weighed in at an undistinguished 1,484 grams). The dissection of
famous colleagues became something of a cottage industry among
anatomists and anthropologists. E.A. Spitzka, the most prominent
American practitioner of the trade, cajoled his eminent friends: "To
me the thought of an autopsy is certainly less repugnant than I imagine the process of cadaveric decomposition in the grave to be." The
two premier American ethnologists, John Wesley Powell and W. J.
McGee made a wager over who had the larger brain — and Spitzka
contracted to resolve the issue for them posthumously. (It was a toss-
up. The brains of Powell and McGee differed very little, no more than
varying body size might require.)

By 1907, Spitzka could present a tabulation of 115 eminent men.   14
As the list grew in length, ambiguity of results increased apace. At
the upper end, Cuvier was finally overtaken when Turgenev broke the
2,000-gram barrier in 1883. But embarrassment and insult stalked the
other end. Walt Whitman managed to hear the varied carols of America singing with only 1,282 g. Franz Josef Gall, a founder of phrenology
— the original "science" of judging mental worth by the size of localized brain areas — could muster only 1,198 g. Later, in 1924, Anatole
France almost halved Turgenev's 2,012 and weighed in at a mere 1,017 g.

15   Spitzka, nonetheless, was undaunted. In an outrageous example of data selected to conform with a priori prejudice, he arranged, in order, a large brain from an eminent white male, a bushwoman from Africa, and a gorilla. (He could easily have reversed the first two by choosing a larger black and a smaller white.) Spitzka concluded, again invoking the shade of Georges Cuvier: "The jump from a Cuvier or a Thackeray to a Zulu or a Bushman is no greater than from the latter to the gorilla or the orang."

16   Such overt racism is no longer common among scientists, and I trust that no one would now try to rank races or sexes by the average size of their brains. Yet our fascination with the physical basis of intelligence persists (as it should), and the naïve hope remains in some quarters that size or some other unambiguous external feature might capture the subtlety within. Indeed, the crassest form of more-is-better — using an easily measured quantity to assess improperly a far more subtle and elusive quality — is still with us. And the method that some men use to judge the worth of their penises or their automobiles is still being applied to brains. This essay was inspired by recent reports on the whereabouts of Einstein's brain. Yes, Einstein's brain was removed for study, but a quarter century after his death, the results have not been published. The remaining pieces — others were farmed out to various specialists — now rest in a Mason jar packed in a cardboard box marked "Costa Cider" and housed in an office in Wichita, Kansas. Nothing has been published because nothing unusual has been found. "So far it's fallen within normal limits for a man his age," remarked the owner of the Mason jar.

17   Did I just hear Cuvier and Anatole France laughing in concert from on high? Are they repeating a famous motto of their native land: *plus ça change, plus c'est la même chose* ("the more things change, the more they remain the same"). The physical structure of the brain must record intelligence in some way, but gross size and external shape are not likely to capture anything of value. I am, somehow, less interested in the weight and convolutions of Einstein's brain than in the near certainty that people of equal talent have lived and died in cotton fields and sweatshops.

_____ **CONSIDERATIONS** _____

1. All three of Gould's essays, "The Politics of Census" (pages 154–160), "Phyletic Size Decrease in Hershey Bars" (pages 161–166), and "Wide

Hats and Narrow Minds" reveal the writer's lively interest in research. What other qualities do they have in common?

2. Why, according to Gould, is the-bigger-the-better the "crassest form" of classifying quality? Cite an example from a current advertisement.

3. Gould's essay might well be taken as a satire if it were not for Paragraph 11. Explain how that passage runs counter to the usual pursuits of satirists.

4. What very specific detail mentioned in Paragraph 16 expresses Gould's opinion of the importance of the research conducted by Gratiolet, Broca, Spitzka and others. Explain. (The detail has nothing to do with brain size.)

5. What does Gould mean in Paragraph 15 when he accuses Spitzka of "an outrageous example of data selected to conform with a priori prejudice"? Concoct your own example in a paragraph satirizing distortion of some recent bit of market or consumer research.

*John Haines (b. 1924) was born in Norfolk, Virginia, and
served in the United States Navy during World War II. In 1947
he went to Alaska as a homesteader; he built his own house
sixty miles from Fairbanks, grew vegetables, and ate moosemeat.
He has lived in Alaska most of his adult life, but occasionally he
has traveled south to teach in tropical Montana.*

His books of poems start with Winter News *(1966) and include
his selected poems,* News from the Glacier *(1982). He has also
published essays —* "On Poetry and Place" in Living Off the
Country *(1981) — and essays about Alaska in* Other Days *(1981)
from which we take* "Lost."

31

JOHN HAINES

Lost

1   Now and then people disappear in the far north and are never
heard from again. For various reasons: they are lost, drowned or frozen
to death. It was common enough in early days when so many were
traveling the country on foot and by water and often alone. Yet in
recent memory whole planeloads of people have dropped out of sight,
the fuselage with its frozen bodies found years later in a snowdrift on
a remote mountainside.

2   I remember one spring morning when a group of men came down
the road at Richardson. We watched them as they searched the roadside thickets and probed the snowdrifts with poles. They were looking
for an old woman who had left her house near Big Delta a few evenings
before, and had not come back. Family and neighbors thought she may

have walked in her half-sleep into the nearby river, to be swept away under the ice. But they couldn't be sure. They went on down the road, a scattered troop of brown and grey soon lost to view in the cold sunlight.

And there was the fellow who disappeared from his Quartz Lake   3 trapline a few winters back. Said to be a little strange in his head and mistrustful of people, he had been long absent in the bush when a search was begun by his brother and the police. Though the country was flown over and searched for weeks, he too was never found alive. But two or three years later someone hunting in the backcountry came upon a pair of legbones and some scraps of blue wool cloth with metal buttons. Most of the bones had been carried off by animals, and it was impossible by then to say who he was or what had happened to him.

There are people lost in more ways than one. Like the man   4 named Abrams, active for a while in the Birch Lake area many years ago. Despondent over something or other, he walked away from camp one late winter day and did not come back. No one followed him then, but he was found eventually in an old cabin up on one of the Salcha River tributaries, dead. He had cut both his wrists, and bled to death lying in a makeshift bunk.

I was told once of the end of a man whose name will have to be   5 Hanson, since I cannot remember his real name. He drove mail by dogsled in an early day, out of Fairbanks and up the Tanana beyond Big Delta. It was sixty below zero one January day when he stopped at Delta on his way upriver. He was urged not to continue, but to stay at the roadhouse for a day or so and wait for a promised break in the weather. An experienced man, he decided to go on. He was well-dressed for it, and carried a good robe on his sled. But his dogs whined in the foggy, windless cold, and would rather have stayed.

A few days later his dogs came back, dragging the sled behind   6 them, but without Hanson. The cold had broken by then, and men went out, following the sled trail back upriver. Some thirty miles on they found Hanson crouched beside a stack of driftwood, his arms folded on his chest, and his head down. He did not move or speak when they walked up on him. One of the men touched him, and found that they had been calling to a stone. At his feet were the charred makings of a fire that had never caught.

Though I have never been lost in the woods, I have known that   7 momentary confusion when a strange trail divided or thinned out before me, and I have stopped there on a hillside in the wind-matted buckbrush and willows, wondering which of the many possible roads

I ought to take. I have come home late through the woods at night and missed my trail underfoot, to stand undecided, listening for something in the darkness: the wind moving aloft in the trees, the sound of a dry leaf skittering over the snowcrust, or the sudden crashing of an animal disturbed.

8   Fred Campbell told me once of being shut in by fog on Buckeye Dome one fall day, a fog so thick he could not see the ground at his feet. He lost all sense of place and time, and wandered that day in an endless and insubstantial whiteness. It seemed to him at times that he was not walking on earth, but was stranded in a still cloud, far from anything he could touch or know. Toward evening the sun burned a hole in the mist, and he found his way down into familiar woods again.

9   That lostness and sinking of things, so close to the ordinariness of our lives. I was mending my salmon net one summer afternoon, leaning over the side of my boat in a broad eddy near the mouth of Tenderfoot. I had drawn the net partway over the gunwale to work on it, when a strong surge in the current pulled the meshes from my hand. As I reached down to grasp the net again I somehow lost hold of my knife, and watched half-sickened as it slipped from my hand and sank out of sight in the restless, seething water.

10   Poling upriver in the fall, maneuvering the nose of my boat through the slack, freezing water; or wading over stones and gravel in the shallowing current, while the boat tugged behind me at the end of a doubled rope; or again, as I floated down on the turbulent summer water, swinging my oars in response to the driftpiles looming swiftly ahead: how easily I might be spilled and swept under, my boat to be found one day lodged in driftwood, an oar washed up on the sand, and myself a sack weighted with silt, turning in an eddy.

11   A drowsy, half-wakeful menace waits for us in the quietness of this world. I have felt it near me while kneeling in the snow, minding a trap on a ridge many miles from home. There, in the cold that gripped my face, in the low, blue light failing around me, and the short day ending, in those familiar and friendly shadows, I was suddenly aware of something that did not care if I lived. Or, as it may be, running the river ice in midwinter: under the sled runners a sudden cracking and buckling that scared the dogs and sent my heart racing. How swiftly the solid bottom of one's life can go.

12   Disappearances, apparitions; few clues, or none at all. Mostly it isn't murder, a punishable crime — the people just vanish. They go away, in sorrow, in pain, in mute astonishment, as of something

decided forever. But sometimes you can't be sure, and a thing will happen that remains so unresolved, so strange, that someone will think of it years later; and he will sit there in the dusk and silence, staring out the window at another world.

_____ **CONSIDERATIONS** _____

1. While John Haines uses no slang or other obvious devices, his prose in "Lost" gives the impression of a seasoned story-teller talking to an avid listener, perhaps in front of a warm fire on a cold night. Study the piece carefully and search for techniques particular to oral rather than written narration.

2. The account of Hanson, in Paragraphs 5 and 6, might bring to mind Jack London's most famous short story "To Build a Fire." Read the story in your college library and then compare and contrast the styles of the two writers.

3. "A pair of legbones and some scraps of blue wool cloth with metal buttons" were all that was found of a missing man (Paragraph 3). Haines's summary is as bare and sparse of sentiment as the ice-bound country itself. Would a reader be correct to conclude that Haines has no feeling for the luckless lost? Defend your answer by referring to other sections of the essay.

4. The arrangement of paragraphs can sometimes tell a reader more than many explanatory sentences. If you can discern the relationship between Paragraphs 9 and 10, you will better understand their individual contributions to the essay.

5. Study Paragraph 12 and try to be precise about the feeling Haines's conclusion gives the reader. Is that feeling merely the product of that last paragraph, or is it supported by the rest of the essay?

Lillian Hellman (1905–1984) was a playwright, born in New Orleans, who grew up in New Orleans and New York City. She graduated from New York University, and went to work in publishing. The Children's Hour *(1934), her first great success on Broadway, was followed by her most famous play,* The Little Foxes *(1939), and* Watch on the Rhine *(1941). She also wrote the book for Leonard Bernstein's musical,* Candide.

Hellman's later works were autobiographical, and include Pentimento *(1973),* Scoundrel Time *(1977), and* An Unfinished Woman, *which won the National Book Award in 1970. These narratives were collected into one volume with new commentary by the author:* Three *(1979). In 1980 she published* Maybe: A Story.

The anecdote below, which is from An Unfinished Woman, *tells of a climactic episode in the transition from childhood to adolescence, and shows the rebelliousness, strong feeling, and independence that become themes of the autobiography.*

32

LILLIAN HELLMAN
Runaway

1   It was that night that I disappeared, and that night that Fizzy said I was disgusting mean, and Mr. Stillman said I would forever pain my mother and father, and my father turned on both of them and said he would handle his family affairs himself without comments from strangers. But he said it too late. He had come home very angry with me: the jeweler, after my father's complaints about his unreliability, had found the lock of hair in the back of the watch. What started out

From *An Unfinished Woman* by Lillian Hellman. Copyright © 1969 by Lillian Hellman. Reprinted by permission of Little, Brown and Co.

178

to be a mild reproof on my father's part soon turned angry when I wouldn't explain about the hair. (My father was often angry when I was most like him.) He was so angry that he forgot that he was attacking me in front of the Stillmans, my old rival Fizzy, and the delighted Mrs. Dreyfus, a new, rich boarder who only that afternoon had complained about my bad manners. My mother left the room when my father grew angry with me. Hannah, passing through, put up her hand as if to stop my father and then, frightened of the look he gave her, went out to the porch. I sat on the couch, astonished at the pain in my head. I tried to get up from the couch, but one ankle turned and I sat down again, knowing for the first time the rampage that could be caused in me by anger. The room began to have other forms, the people were no longer men and women, my head was not my own. I told myself that my head had gone somewhere and I have little memory of anything after my Aunt Jenny came into the room and said to my father, "Don't you remember?" I have never known what she meant, but I knew that soon after I was moving up the staircase, that I slipped and fell a few steps, that when I woke up hours later in my bed, I found a piece of angel cake — an old love, an old custom — left by my mother on my pillow. The headache was worse and I vomited out of the window. Then I dressed, took my red purse, and walked a long way down St. Charles Avenue. A St. Charles Avenue mansion had on its back lawn a famous doll's-house, an elaborate copy of the mansion itself, built years before for the small daughter of the house. As I passed this showpiece, I saw a policeman and moved swiftly back to the doll palace and crawled inside. If I had known about the fantasies of the frightened, that ridiculous small house would not have been so terrible for me. I was surrounded by ornate, carved reproductions of the mansion furniture, scaled for children, bisque figurines in miniature, a working toilet seat of gold leaf in suitable size, small draperies of damask with a sign that said "From the damask of Marie Antoinette," a miniature samovar with small bronze cups, and a tiny Madame Récamier couch on which I spent the night, my legs on the floor. I must have slept, because I woke from a nightmare and knocked over a bisque figurine. The noise frightened me, and since it was now almost light, in one of those lovely mist mornings of late spring when every flower in New Orleans seems to melt and mix with the air, I crawled out. Most of that day I spent walking, although I had a long session in the ladies' room of the railroad station. I had four dollars and two bits, but that wasn't much when you meant it to last forever and when you knew it would not be easy for a fourteen-year-old girl to find work in a city where too many people knew her. Three times I stood in line at the railroad ticket windows to ask where I could go for four dollars, but each time the question seemed too dangerous and I knew no other way of asking.

2 Toward evening, I moved to the French Quarter, feeling sad and envious as people went home to dinner. I bought a few Tootsie Rolls and a half loaf of bread and went to the St. Louis Cathedral in Jackson Square. (It was that night that I composed the prayer that was to become, in the next five years, an obsession, mumbled over and over through the days and nights: "God forgive me, Papa forgive me, Mama forgive me, Sophronia, Jenny, Hannah, and all others, through this time and that time, in life and in death." When I was nineteen, my father, who had made several attempts through the years to find out what my lip movements meant as I repeated the prayer, said, "How much would you take to stop that? Name it and you've got it." I suppose I was sick of the nonsense by that time because I said, "A leather coat and a feather fan," and the next day he bought them for me.) After my loaf of bread, I went looking for a bottle of soda pop and discovered, for the first time, the whorehouse section around Bourbon Street. The women were ranged in the doorways of the cribs, making the first early evening offers to sailors, who were the only men in the streets. I wanted to stick around and see how things like that worked, but the second or third time I circled the block, one of the girls called out to me. I couldn't understand the words, but the voice was angry enough to make me run toward the French Market.

3 The Market was empty except for two old men. One of them called to me as I went past, and I turned to see that he had opened his pants and was shaking what my circle called "his thing." I flew across the street into the coffee stand, forgetting that the owner had known me since I was a small child when my Aunt Jenny would rest from her marketing tour with a cup of fine, strong coffee.

4 He said, in the patois, *"Que faites, ma 'fant? Je suis fermé."*

5 I said, *"Rien. My tante attend"* — Could I have a doughnut?

6 He brought me two doughnuts, saying one was *lagniappe,* but I took my doughnuts outside when he said, *"Mais ou est vo' tante à c'heure?"*

7 I fell asleep with my doughnuts behind a shrub in Jackson Square. The night was damp and hot and through the sleep were many voices and, much later, there was music from somewhere near the river. When all sounds had ended, I woke, turned my head, and knew I was being watched. Two rats were sitting a few feet from me. I urinated

on my dress, crawled backwards to stand up, screamed as I ran up the steps of St. Louis Cathedral and pounded on the doors. I don't know when I stopped screaming or how I got to the railroad station, but I stood against the wall trying to tear off my dress and only knew I was doing it when two women stopped to stare at me. I began to have cramps in my stomach of a kind I had never known before. I went into the ladies' room and sat bent in a chair, whimpering with pain. After a while the cramps stopped, but I had an intimation, when I looked into the mirror, of something happening to me: my face was blotched, and there seemed to be circles and twirls I had never seen before, the straight blonde hair was damp with sweat, and a paste of green from the shrub had made lines on my jaw. I had gotten older.

Sometime during that early morning I half washed my dress, threw away my pants, put cold water on my hair. Later in the morning a cleaning woman appeared, and after a while began to ask questions that frightened me. When she put down her mop and went out of the room, I ran out of the station. I walked, I guess, for many hours, but when I saw a man on Canal Street who worked in Hannah's office, I realized that the sections of New Orleans that were known to me were dangerous for me. 8

Years before, when I was a small child, Sophronia and I would go to pick up, or try on, pretty embroidered dresses that were made for me by a colored dressmaker called Bibettera. A block up from Bibettera's there had been a large ruin of a house with a sign, ROOMS — CLEAN — CHEAP, and cheerful people seemed always to be moving in and out of the house. The door of the house was painted a bright pink. I liked that and would discuss with Sophronia why we didn't live in a house with a pink door. 9

Bibettera was long since dead, so I knew I was safe in this Negro neighborhood. I went up and down the block several times, praying that things would work and I could take my cramps to bed. I knocked on the pink door. It was answered immediately by a small young man. 10

I said, "Hello." He said nothing. 11

I said, "I would like to rent a room, please." 12

He closed the door but I waited, thinking he had gone to get the lady of the house. After a long time, a middle-aged woman put her head out of a second-floor window and said, "What you at?" 13

I said, "I would like to rent a room, please. My mama is a widow and has gone to work across the river. She gave me money and said to come here until she called for me." 14

"Who your mama?" 15

16   "Er. My mama."

17   "What you at? Speak out."

18   "I told you. I have money . . ." But as I tried to open my purse, the voice grew angry.

19   "This is a nigger house. Get you off. *Vite.*"

20   I said, in a whisper, "I know. I'm part nigger."

21   The small young man opened the front door. He was laughing. "You part mischief. Get the hell out of here."

22   I said, "Please" — and then, "I'm related to Sophronia Mason. She told me to come. Ask her."

23   Sophronia and her family were respected figures in New Orleans Negro circles, and because I had some vague memory of her stately bow to somebody as she passed this house, I believed they knew her. If they told her about me I would be in trouble, but phones were not usual then in poor neighborhoods, and I had no other place to go.

24   The woman opened the door. Slowly I went into the hall.

25   I said, "I won't stay long. I have four dollars and Sophronia will give more if . . ."

26   The woman pointed up the stairs. She opened the door of a small room. "Washbasin place down the hall. Toilet place behind the kitchen. Two-fifty and no fuss, no bother."

27   I said, "Yes, ma'am, yes ma'am," but as she started to close the door, the young man appeared.

28   "Where your bag?"

29   "Bag?"

30   "Nobody put up here without no bag."

31   "Oh. You mean the bag with my clothes? It's at the station. I'll go and get it later . . ." I stopped because I knew I was about to say I'm sick, I'm in pain, I'm frightened.

32   He said, "I say you lie. I say you trouble. I say you get out."

33   I said, "And I say you shut up."

34   Years later, I was to understand why the command worked, and to be sorry that it did, but that day I was very happy when he turned and closed the door. I was asleep within minutes.

35   Toward evening, I went down the stairs, saw nobody, walked a few blocks and bought myself an oyster loaf. But the first bite made me feel sick, so I took my loaf back to the house. This time, as I climbed the steps, there were three women in the parlor, and they stopped talking when they saw me. I went back to sleep immediately, dizzy and nauseated.

36   I woke to a high, hot sun and my father standing at the foot of the bed staring at the oyster loaf.

He said, "Get up now and get dressed." 37

I was crying as I said, "Thank you, Papa, but I can't." 38

From the hall, Sophronia said, "Get along up now. *Vite.* The 39
morning is late."

My father left the room. I dressed and came into the hall carrying 40
my oyster loaf. Sophronia was standing at the head of the stairs. She
pointed out, meaning my father was on the street.

I said, "He humiliated me. He did. I won't . . ." 41

She said, "Get you going or I will never see you whenever again." 42

I ran past her to the street. I stood with my father until Sophronia 43
joined us, and then we walked slowly, without speaking, to the street-
car line. Sophronia bowed to us, but she refused my father's hand
when he attempted to help her into the car. I ran to the car meaning
to ask her to take me with her, but the car moved and she raised her
hand as if to stop me. My father and I walked again for a long time.

He pointed to a trash can sitting in front of a house. "Please put 44
that oyster loaf in the can."

At Vanalli's restaurant, he took my arm. "Hungry?" 45

I said, "No, thank you, Papa." 46

But we went through the door. It was, in those days, a New 47
Orleans custom to have an early black coffee, go to the office, and after
a few hours have a large breakfast at a restaurant. Vanalli's was
crowded, the headwaiter was so sorry, but after my father took him
aside, a very small table was put up for us — too small for my large
father, who was accommodating himself to it in a manner most unlike
him.

He said, "Jack, my rumpled daughter would like cold crayfish, a 48
nice piece of pompano, a separate bowl of Béarnaise sauce, don't ask
me why, French fried potatoes . . ."

I said, "Thank you, Papa, but I am not hungry. I don't want to be 49
here."

My father waved the waiter away and we sat in silence until the 50
crayfish came. My hand reached out instinctively and then drew back.

My father said, "Your mother and I have had an awful time." 51

I said, "I'm sorry about that. But I don't want to go home, Papa." 52

He said, angrily, "Yes, you do. But you want me to apologize 53
first. I do apologize but you should not have made me say it."

After a while I mumbled, "God forgive me, Papa forgive me, 54
Mama forgive me, Sophronia, Jenny, Hannah . . ."

"Eat your crayfish." 55

I ate everything he had ordered and then a small steak. I suppose 56
I had been mumbling throughout my breakfast.

57   My father said, "You're talking to yourself. I can't hear you. What are you saying?"

58   "God forgive me, Papa forgive me, Mama forgive me, Sophronia, Jenny . . ."

59   My father said, "Where do we start your training as the first Jewish nun on Prytania Street?"

60   When I finished laughing, I liked him again. I said, "Papa, I'll tell you a secret. I've had very bad cramps and I am beginning to bleed. I'm changing life."

61   He stared at me for a while. Then he said, "Well, it's not the way it's usually described, but it's accurate, I guess. Let's go home now to your mother."

62   We were never, as long as my mother and father lived, to mention that time again. But it was of great importance to them and I've thought about it all my life. From that day on I knew my power over my parents. That was not to be too important: I was ashamed of it and did not abuse it too much. But I found out something more useful and more dangerous: if you are willing to take the punishment, you are halfway through the battle. That the issue may be trivial, the battle ugly, is another point.

_____ CONSIDERATIONS _____

1. Hellman's recollection of running away at fourteen is complicated by her refusal to tell it in strict chronology. Instead, she interrupts the narrative with flashbacks and episodes of later years. How can one justify such interruptions?

2. On page 182, as she is trying to talk her way into the rooming house in the black district, Hellman tells a young man to shut up and then adds, "Years later, I was to understand why the command worked, and to be sorry that it did." What did she later understand?

3. What was the "power over my parents" that Hellman learned from her runaway experience? Do you have such a power?

4. Accounts of childhood escapades often suffer as the author idealizes or glamorizes them. Does Hellman successfully resist the temptation? What is your evidence?

5. The bases the fourteen-year-old runaway touched in her flight were actually part of a familiar world: a doll's house, a cathedral, a market, a railroad station. How then does Hellman give her flight more than a touch of horror?

6. In what specific ways did her first menstrual period heighten and distort some of the things that happened — or seemed to happen — to the fourteen-year-old runaway? Discuss the ways in which physiological and psychological conditions seem to feed upon each other.

Ernest Hemingway (1899–1961) was an ambulance driver and a soldier in World War I, and made use of these experiences in his novel A Farewell to Arms *(1929). One of the Lost Generation of expatriate American writers who lived in Paris in the twenties — a time described in his memoir,* A Moveable Feast *(1964) — he was a great prose stylist and innovator, who received a Nobel Prize for literature in 1954. Other Hemingway novels include* The Sun Also Rises *(1926),* To Have and Have Not *(1937), and* For Whom the Bell Tolls *(1940). His* Selected Letters, *edited by Carlos Baker, appeared in 1981.*

Many critics prefer Hemingway's short stories to his novels, and his early stories — "Hills Like White Elephants" among them — to his later ones. This early prose is plain, simple, and clean. This story is dialogue virtually without narrative or description or interpretation; yet when we have finished it we have met two people whom we will not easily forget.

33

ERNEST HEMINGWAY

Hills Like White Elephants

The hills across the valley of the Ebro were long and white. On this side there was no shade and no trees and the station was between two lines of rails in the sun. Close against the side of the station there was the warm shadow of the building and a curtain, made of strings of bamboo beads, hung across the open door into the bar, to keep out flies. The American and the girl with him sat at a table in the shade, outside the building. It was very hot and the express from Barcelona

would come in forty minutes. It stopped at this junction for two minutes and went on to Madrid.

"What should we drink?" the girl asked. She had taken off her
hat and put it on the table.

"It's pretty hot," the man said.

"Let's drink beer."

"Dos cervezas," the man said into the curtain.

"Big ones?" a woman asked from the doorway.

"Yes. Two big ones."

The woman brought two glasses of beer and two felt pads. She
put the felt pads and the beer glasses on the table and looked at the
man and the girl. The girl was looking off at the line of hills. They
were white in the sun and the country was brown and dry.

"They look like white elephants," she said.

"I've never seen one." The man drank his beer.

"No, you wouldn't have."

"I might have," the man said. "Just because you say I wouldn't
have doesn't prove anything."

The girl looked at the bead curtain. "They've painted something
on it," she said. "What does it say?"

"Anis del Toro. It's a drink."

"Could we try it?"

The man called "Listen" through the curtain.

The woman came out from the bar.

"Four reales."

"We want two Anis del Toros."

"With water?"

"Do you want it with water?"

"I don't know," the girl said. "Is it good with water?"

"It's all right."

"You want them with water?" asked the woman.

"Yes, with water."

"It tastes like licorice," the girl said and put the glass down.

"That's the way with everything."

"Yes," said the girl. "Everything tastes of licorice. Especially all
the things you've waited so long for, like absinthe."

"Oh, cut it out."

"You started it," the girl said. "I was being amused. I was having
a fine time."

"Well, let's try and have a fine time."

"All right. I was trying. I said the mountains looked like white
elephants. Wasn't that bright?"

50   "That was bright."
          "I wanted to try this new drink. That's all we do, isn't it — look
       at things and try new drinks?"
          "I guess so."
          The girl looked across at the hills.
55   "They're lovely hills," she said. "They don't really look like
       white elephants. I just meant the colouring of their skin through the
       trees."
          "Should we have another drink?"
          "All right."
60   The warm wind blew the bead curtain against the table.
          "The beer's nice and cool," the man said.
          "It's lovely," the girl said.
          "It's really an awfully simple operation, Jig," the man said. "It's
       not really an operation at all."
65   The girl looked at the ground the table legs rested on.
          "I know you wouldn't mind it, Jig. It's really not anything. It's
       just to let the air in."
          The girl did not say anything.
          "I'll go with you and I'll stay with you all the time. They just let
70   the air in and then it's all perfectly natural."
          "Then what will we do afterwards?"
          "We'll be fine afterwards. Just like we were before."
          "What makes you think so?"
          "That's the only thing that bothers us. It's the only thing that's
75   made us unhappy."
          The girl looked at the bead curtain, put her hand out and took
       hold of two of the strings of beads.
          "And you think then we'll be all right and be happy."
          "I know we will. You don't have to be afraid. I've known lots of
80   people that have done it."
          "So have I," said the girl. "And afterward they were all so happy."
          "Well," the man said, "if you don't want to you don't have to. I
       wouldn't have you do it if you didn't want to. But I know it's perfectly
       simple."
85   "And you really want to?"
          "I think it's the best thing to do. But I don't want you to do it if
       you don't really want to."
          "And if I do it you'll be happy and things will be like they were
       and you'll love me?"
90   "I love you now. You know I love you."

"I know. But if I do it, then it will be nice again if I say things are like white elephants, and you'll like it?"

"I'll love it. I love it now but I just can't think about it. You know how I get when I worry."

"If I do it you won't ever worry?"

"I won't worry about that because it's perfectly simple."

"Then I'll do it. Because I don't care about me."

"What do you mean?"

"I don't care about me."

"Well, I care about you."

"Oh, yes. But I don't care about me. And I'll do it and then everything will be fine."

"I don't want you to do it if you feel that way."

The girl stood up and walked to the end of the station. Across, on the other side, were fields of grain and trees along the banks of the Ebro. Far away, beyond the river, were mountains. The shadow of a cloud moved across the field of grain and she saw the river through the trees.

"And we could have all this," she said. "And we could have everything and every day we make it more impossible."

"What did you say?"

"I said we could have everything."

"We can have everything."

"No, we can't."

"We can have the whole world."

"No, we can't."

"We can go everywhere."

"No, we can't. It isn't ours any more."

"It's ours."

"No, it isn't. And once they take it away, you never get it back."

"But they haven't taken it away."

"We'll wait and see."

"Come on back in the shade," he said. "You mustn't feel that way."

"I don't feel any way," the girl said. "I just know things."

"I don't want you to do anything that you don't want to do —"

"Nor that isn't good for me," she said. "I know. Could we have another beer?"

"All right. But you've got to realize —"

"I realize," the girl said. "Can't we maybe stop talking?"

They sat down at the table and the girl looked across at the hills on the dry side of the valley and the man looked at her and at the table.

"You've got to realize," he said, "that I don't want you to do it if you don't want to. I'm perfectly willing to go through with it if it means anything to you."

"Doesn't it mean anything to you? We could get along."

"Of course it does. But I don't want anybody but you. I don't want anyone else. And I know it's perfectly simple."

"Yes, you know it's perfectly simple."

"It's all right for you to say that, but I do know it."

"Would you do something for me now?"

"I'd do anything for you."

"Would you please please please please please please please stop talking?"

He did not say anything but looked at the bags against the wall of the station. There were labels on them from all the hotels where they had spent nights.

"But I don't want you to," he said, "I don't care anything about it."

"I'll scream," the girl said.

The woman came out through the curtains with two glasses of beer and put them down on the damp felt pads. "The train comes in five minutes," she said.

"What did she say?" asked the girl.

"That the train is coming in five minutes."

The girl smiled brightly at the woman, to thank her.

"I'd better take the bags over to the other side of the station," the man said. She smiled at him.

"All right. Then come back and we'll finish the beer."

He picked up the two heavy bags and carried them around the station to the other tracks. He looked up the tracks but could not see the train. Coming back, he walked through the bar-room, where people waiting for the train were drinking. He drank an Anis at the bar and looked at the people. They were all waiting reasonably for the train. He went out through the bead curtain. She was sitting at the table and smiled at him.

"Do you feel better?" he asked.

"I feel fine," she said. "There's nothing wrong with me. I feel fine."

_____ **CONSIDERATIONS** _____

1. Nearly all of Hemingway's story is dialogue, often without identifying phrases such as "he said" or "she said." Does the lack of these phrases make it difficult to decide which character is speaking? What, if anything, does Hemingway do to make up for missing dialogue tags? Compare his practice with the way other short story writers in this book handle dialogue.

2. If you have ever questioned the common statement that writers must pay careful attention to *every* word they use, spend a little time examining the way Hemingway uses "it," beginning where the couple start talking about the operation. Try to determine the various possible antecedents for that neutral pronoun in each context where it occurs. Such an effort may help you discover one reason why Hemingway's spare, almost skeletal style is so powerful.

3. Try to put the central conflict of this story in your own words. Imagine yourself the writer suddenly getting the idea for this story and quickly writing a sentence or two to record the idea in your journal. Is that idea anything like the thesis statement of an essay?

4. Why is Hemingway *not* explicit about the kind of operation the two characters are discussing? Is he simply trying to mystify the reader? Does this consideration help you to understand other stories or poems that seem difficult at first?

5. Although Hemingway's description of locale is limited to a few brief passages, he presents a distinct place. How does that place contribute to your understanding the point of the story?

6. Why does Hemingway refuse to describe the two characters? From what the story offers, what do you know about them?

7. Hemingway's story was written in the 1920s. Have the questions he raises about the operation been resolved since then?

Langston Hughes (1902–1967) was a poet, novelist, playwright, and essayist who wrote with wit and energy; he was a leader in the emergence of black American literature in the twentieth century. More than twenty of his books remain in print, including Selected Poems; *his autobiography,* I Wonder as I Wander; *and* The Langston Hughes Reader. *He argues as well as he sings the blues — and he can tell a story.*

34

LANGSTON HUGHES
Salvation

1   I was saved from sin when I was going on thirteen. But not really saved. It happened like this. There was a big revival at my Auntie Reed's church. Every night for weeks there had been much preaching, singing, praying, and shouting, and some very hardened sinners had been brought to Christ, and the membership of the church had grown by leaps and bounds. Then just before the revival ended, they held a special meeting for children, "to bring the young lambs to the fold." My aunt spoke of it for days ahead. That night I was escorted to the front row and placed on the mourners' bench with all the other young sinners, who had not yet been brought to Jesus.

2   My aunt told me that when you were saved you saw a light, and something happened to you inside! And Jesus came into your life! And God was with you from then on! She said you could see and hear and feel Jesus in your soul. I believed her. I had heard a great many old people say the same thing and it seemed to me they ought to know.

So I sat there calmly in the hot, crowded church, waiting for Jesus to come to me.

The preacher preached a wonderful rhythmical sermon, all   3
moans and shouts and lonely cries and dire pictures of hell, and then he sang a song about the ninety and nine safe in the fold, but one little lamb was left out in the cold. Then he said: "Won't you come? Won't you come to Jesus? Young lambs, won't you come?" And he held out his arms to all us young sinners there on the mourners' bench. And the little girls cried. And some of them jumped up and went to Jesus right away. But most of us just sat there.

A great many old people came and knelt around us and prayed,   4
old women with jet-black faces and braided hair, old men with work-gnarled hands. And the church sang a song about the lower lights are burning, some poor sinners to be saved. And the whole building rocked with prayer and song.

Still I kept waiting to *see* Jesus.   5

Finally all the young people had gone to the altar and were saved,   6
but one boy and me. He was a rounder's son named Westley. Westley and I were surrounded by sisters and deacons praying. It was very hot in the church, and getting late now. Finally Westley said to me in a whisper: "God damn! I'm tired o' sitting here. Let's get up and be saved." So he got up and was saved.

Then I was left all alone on the mourners' bench. My aunt came   7
and knelt at my knees and cried, while prayers and songs swirled all around me in the little church. The whole congregation prayed for me alone, in a mighty wail of moans and voices. And I kept waiting serenely for Jesus, waiting, waiting — but he didn't come. I wanted to see him, but nothing happened to me. Nothing! I wanted something to happen to me, but nothing happened.

I heard the songs and the minister saying: "Why don't you come?   8
My dear child, why don't you come to Jesus? Jesus is waiting for you. He wants you. Why don't you come? Sister Reed, what is this child's name?"

"Langston," my aunt sobbed.   9

"Langston, why don't you come? Why don't you come and be   10
saved? Oh, Lamb of God! Why don't you come?"

Now it was really getting late. I began to be ashamed of myself,   11
holding everything up so long. I began to wonder what God thought about Westley, who certainly hadn't seen Jesus either, but who was now sitting proudly on the platform, swinging his knickerbockered

legs and grinning down at me, surrounded by deacons and old women on their knees praying. God had not struck Westley dead for taking his name in vain or for lying in the temple. So I decided that maybe to save further trouble, I'd better lie, too, and say that Jesus had come, and get up and be saved.

12   So I got up.

13   Suddenly the whole room broke into a sea of shouting, as they saw me rise. Waves of rejoicing swept the place. Women leaped in the air. My aunt threw her arms around me. The minister took me by the hand and led me to the platform.

14   When things quieted down, in a hushed silence, punctuated by a few ecstatic "Amens," all the new young lambs were blessed in the name of God. Then joyous singing filled the room.

15   That night, for the last time in my life but one — for I was a big boy twelve years old — I cried. I cried, in bed alone, and couldn't stop. I buried my head under the quilts, but my aunt heard me. She woke up and told my uncle I was crying because the Holy Ghost had come into my life, and because I had seen Jesus. But I was really crying because I couldn't bear to tell her that I had lied, that I had deceived everybody in the church, and I hadn't seen Jesus, and that now I didn't believe there was a Jesus any more, since he didn't come to help me.

_____ **CONSIDERATIONS** _____

1. Hughes tells this critical episode of his childhood in a simple, straightforward, unelaborated fashion, almost as though he were still a child telling the story as it happened. Why is it necessary to say "*almost* as though he were still a child"? How would you go about recounting a critical moment in your childhood? Where does simple childhood memory stop and adult judgment take over?

2. Hughes's disillusionment is an example of what people call "an initiation story." Compare it with the Ernest Hemingway short story (pages 186–191), or John Updike's story (pages 417–425), or the autobiographical essay by Lillian Hellman (pages 178–185). Discuss the *degrees* of awareness noticeable among these varied characters.

3. Why was it so important to the congregation of Auntie Reed's church that everyone, children included, acknowledge that they were saved?

4. Why did Westley finally proclaim that he had been saved?

5. In his final paragraph, Hughes writes, "That night, for the last time in my life but one . . . I cried." He does not tell us, in this account, what that other time was. Read a little more of his life, or simply use your imagination, and write a brief account of the other time.

Langston Hughes's poetry took many forms, and much of it resembled song. If you repeat the first two lines of each stanza of these poems, you will discover the classic form of the blues.

35

LANGSTON HUGHES
Two Poems

BAD LUCK CARD

Cause you don't love me
Is awful, awful hard.
Gypsy done showed me
My bad luck card.   4

There ain't no good left
In this world for me
Gypsy done told me —
Unlucky as can be.   8

I don't know what
Po' weary me can do.
Gypsy says I'd kill my self
If I was you.   12

HOMECOMING

I went back in the alley
And I opened up my door.
All her clothes was gone:
4   She wasn't home no more.

I pulled back the covers.
I made down the bed.
A *whole* lot of room
8   Was the only thing I had.

Langston Hughes's "Simple" stories carry ideas, humor, pain, and wisdom. Hughes draws on folk material — as he does in his poems — and shapes and controls it. In his introduction to a collection of stories about Simple, Hughes wrote: "It is impossible to live in Harlem and not know at least a hundred Simples."

36

LANGSTON HUGHES
Feet Live Their Own Life

"If you want to know about my life," said Simple as he blew the foam from the top of the newly filled glass the bartender put before him, "don't look at my face, don't look at my hands. Look at my feet and see if you can tell how long I been standing on them." 1

"I cannot see your feet through your shoes," I said. 2

"You do not need to see through my shoes," said Simple. "Can't you tell by the shoes I wear — not pointed, not rocking-chair, not French-toed, not nothing but big, long, broad, and flat — that I been standing on these feet a long time and carrying some heavy burdens? They ain't flat from standing at no bar, neither, because I always sets at a bar. Can't you tell that? You know I do not hang out in a bar unless it has stools, don't you?" 3

"That I have observed," I said, "but I did not connect it with your past life." 4

"Everything I do is connected up with my past life," said Simple. "From Virginia to Joyce, from my wife to Zarita, from my mother's milk to this glass of beer, everything is connected up." 5

"I trust you will connect up with that dollar I just loaned you 6 when you get paid," I said. "And who is Virginia? You never told me about her."

7　　"Virginia is where I was borned," said Simple. "I *would* be borned in a state named after that woman. From that day on, women never give me no peace."

8　　"You, I fear, are boasting. If the women were running after you as much as you run after them, you would not be able to sit here on this bar stool in peace. I don't see any women coming to call you out to go home, as some of these fellows' wives do around here."

9　　"Joyce better not come in no bar looking for me," said Simple. "That is why me and my wife busted up — one reason. I do not like to be called out of no bar by a female. It's a man's perogative to just set and drink sometimes."

10　　"How do you connect that prerogative with your past?" I asked.

11　　"When I was a wee small child," said Simple, "I had no place to set and think in, being as how I was raised up with three brothers, two sisters, seven cousins, one married aunt, a common-law uncle, and the minister's grandchild — and the house only had four rooms. I never had no place just to set and think. Neither to set and drink — not even much my milk before some hongry child snatched it out of my hand. I were not the youngest, neither a girl, nor the cutest. I don't know why, but I don't think nobody liked me much. Which is why I was afraid to like anybody for a long time myself. When I did like somebody, I was full-grown and then I picked out the wrong woman because I had no practice in liking anybody before that. We did not get along."

12　　"Is that when you took to drink?"

13　　"Drink took to me," said Simple. "Whiskey just naturally likes me but beer likes me better. By the time I got married I had got to the point where a cold bottle was almost as good as a warm bed, especially when the bottle could not talk and the bed-warmer could. I do not like a woman to talk to me too much — I mean about me. Which is why I like Joyce. Joyce most in generally talks about herself."

14　　"I am still looking at your feet," I said, "and I swear they do not reveal your life to me. Your feet are no open book."

15　　"You have eyes but you see not," said Simple. "These feet have stood on every rock from the Rock of Ages to 135th and Lenox. These feet have supported everything from a cotton bale to a hongry woman. These feet have walked ten thousand miles working for white folks and another ten thousand keeping up with colored. These feet have stood at altars, crap tables, free lunches, bars, graves, kitchen doors, betting windows, hospital clinics, WPA desks, social security railings, and in all kinds of lines from soup lines to the draft. If I just had four feet, I could have stood in more places longer. As it is, I done wore out seven hundred pairs of shoes, eighty-nine tennis shoes, twelve summer sandals, also six loafers. The socks that these feet have bought could build a knitting mill. The corns I've cut away would dull a German razor. The bunions I forgot would make you ache from now till Judgment Day. If anybody was to write the history of my life, they should start with my feet."

"Your feet are not all that extraordinary," I said. "Besides, everything you are saying is general. Tell me specifically some one thing your feet have done that makes them different from any other feet in the world, just one." 16

"Do you see that window in that white man's store across the street?" asked Simple. "Well, this right foot of mine broke out that window in the Harlem riots right smack in the middle. Didn't no other foot in the world break that window but mine. And this left foot carried me off running as soon as my right foot came down. Nobody else's feet saved me from the cops that night but these *two* feet right here. Don't tell me these feet ain't had a life of their own." 17

"For shame," I said, "going around kicking out windows. Why?" 18

"Why?" said Simple. "You have to ask my great-great-grandpa why. He must of been simple — else why did he let them capture him in Africa and sell him for a slave to breed my great-grandpa in slavery to breed my grandpa in slavery to breed my pa to breed me to look at that window and say, 'It ain't mine! Bam-mmm-mm-m!' and kick it out?" 19

"This bar glass is not yours either," I said. "Why don't you smash it?" 20

"It's got my beer in it," said Simple. 21

Just then Zarita came in wearing her Thursday-night rabbit-skin coat. She didn't stop at the bar, being dressed up, but went straight back to a booth. Simple's hand went up, his beer went down, and the glass back to its wet spot on the bar. 22

"Excuse me a minute," he said, sliding off the stool. 23

Just to give him a pause, the dozens, that old verbal game of maligning a friend's female relatives, came to mind. "Wait," I said. "You have told me about what to ask your great-great-grandpa. But I want to know what to ask your great-great-*grandma*." 24

"I don't play the dozens that far back," said Simple, following Zarita into the smoky juke-box blue of the back room. 25

_____ **CONSIDERATIONS** _____

1. In order to get across the extent of his experience, Simple presents some statistics: "I done wore out seven hundred pairs of shoes, eighty-nine tennis shoes, twelve summer sandals . . ." Is that the same technique James C. Rettie uses to imagine a film that would cover 757 million years in a one-year showing? Try concocting statistics of repetitious events or things in your own life as a means of conveying an abstract idea or feeling.

2. "Everything I do is connected up with my past life," says Simple. What sobering truth is expressed by this casual remark?

3. Compare Hughes's use of dialect with Flannery O'Connor's in "A Good Man Is Hard to Find." Why does an author use dialect? What are the problems with dialect?

4. "Your feet are not all that extraordinary," says Simple's companion. Try exercising your powers of observation on a pair of shoes — not your own — and write the biography revealed.

Jane Jacobs (b. 1916) was born in Scranton, Pennsylvania, and came to New York City when she was eighteen. Cities became the focus of her life. She was an editor of Architectural Form *(1952) for a decade, during which she wrote* The Life and Death of Great American Cities *(1961). Later she published* The Economy of Cities *(1969),* The Question of Separatism *(1980) — from which we take "Paradoxes of Size" — and most recently* Cities and the Wealth of Nations *(1984). Like Stephen Jay Gould, she has a mind that will not be shackled by the obvious and that finds similarity in the apparently dissimilar.*

37

JANE JACOBS
Paradoxes of Size

About half a century ago the English biologist J.B.S. Haldane wrote a delightful short essay called "On Being the Right Size." He pointed out, among other things, that sheer size has much to do with the equipment an animal must have. For instance, an insect, being so small, does not need an oxygen-carrying bloodstream. The oxygen its cells require can be absorbed by diffusion. Being larger means an animal must take on an oxygen-distributing and -pumping system to reach all the cells.

A relatively large animal, he also explained, has a relatively large mass in proportion to its surface area. The larger the animal, the greater the disproportion between the mass where the heat from oxidation is generated, and the surface area through which heat can escape. Big animals are thus inherently better equipped to withstand

2

arctic and subarctic cold; they can more easily keep warm than small animals. But it also follows that large animals need special devices to dispose of internally generated heat before it becomes fatal: like sweat glands for cooling by evaporation, or the bizarre ears which increase the elephant's surface, or cooling, area.

3   Haldane presents us with an interesting principle about animal size: big animals are not big because they are complicated; rather, they have to be complicated because they are big. This principle, it seems to me, also applies to institutions, governments, companies, organizations of all sorts. The larger they are, the more complicated they must be. They are big because they produce a huge output of telephones, say, or have a lot of welfare clients, or govern a big population. Whatever the reason for expansion, the large size creates complications. Big organizations need coordinators, liaison people, prescribed channels of communication, administrators, supervisors of supervisors, whole extra departments devoted to serving the organization itself. A small organization can get along without a bureaucracy. A big one cannot.

4   Bigness and the complications that go along with it have their price, but can be worth it. The human brain — with its unfathomable numbers of cells for storing, sorting, cross-referencing and retrieving words, and doing so many other things too — is so complicated that it remains incomprehensible to us. Our brains' intricate capacities exact many prices which animals with smaller brains escape. We must use exorbitant amounts of fuel to maintain our brains and the services for them; we seem to be subjected to more mental illnesses than chickens or cows; we have to be born in an exceedingly helpless state in order to emerge before the head is too big for the birth canal; we have very extended childhoods compared with other animals, which can be hard on parents, and so on.

5   Just so, many jobs in this world can only be done or can best be done by large units. It is as simplistic to jump to the conclusion that something smaller is necessarily better than something bigger as it is to suppose the reverse. The point is that there is always a price to be paid for bigness. It would be too bad, or so I think, if we had only little villages or towns. But big cities exact a price, many prices; the extended and complicated physical, economic and social conditions their very size brings about have to be kept constantly in good working order, on pain of breakdown.

6   People who do not understand what I am calling Haldane's principle are forever being disappointed that making big units out of many

smaller units seldom saves money. They think consolidation gives economies of scale. Sometimes, of course, this works, if the consoli-dated units really are small to begin with, and the aggregation of them not very large. But otherwise, the costs of added complications exact a price. When the government of Metropolitan Toronto was formed, combining some of the previously duplicated functions of government in what is now the city and five boroughs, the cost of government did not decline because of economies of scale. Costs rose. Even though unnecessary duplications of function were eliminated, other new functions and jobs had to be added just to make the larger bureaucra-cies of the larger police, school, traffic and social-service systems work. If all the functions of government in the city and five boroughs were to be amalgamated into a single all-purpose Metro government, we may be sure costs would soar.

In the United States a new President, when he takes office, usu- 7 ally sets forth as one of his aims simplification of the federal bureauc-racy. Much highly skilled effort has gone into those attempts at reorganization and cost cutting. But the notable results have been that the attempts themselves have imposed additional costs and new com-plications. New bureaucracies have to be set up, or old ones expanded, to study the problems of reorganization, work out proposals and try to carry them out. Shift the old arrangements though they may, the reor-ganizations reduce neither costs nor complications of the federal bu-reaucracies. The size of the country and the centralization of its government require very big bureaucracies, which in turn require tre-mendous complications; the repeated reorganization schemes are, themselves, only further manifestations of those complications, not a cure for them. The high costs, the inflexibility of the bureaucracies, and their complexity are prices of scale.

One of the most exasperating and destructive costs of bigness is 8 that sometimes the complications become so excessive that they are stifling: they interfere with the very purposes an organization is intended to serve. A hospital architect has told me that a hospital in Canada can be designed, built and put into operation in roughly two years' less time than a comparable hospital in the United States. The added costs of those two extra years' time and effort are of course large. Furthermore, the hospitals are apt not to be quite comparable in some sense because the same red tape that takes two extra years to untangle in the United States also precludes many sensible decisions, second thoughts and solutions to problems that can sometimes be undertaken in Canada. The differences in red tape, he says, are in large part owing to the fact that in the United States the huge federal government gets into the act with all its own complicated requirements — financing formulas and reviews, for example, all its own necessarily ponderous and complicated ways of doing things — and these are added to whatever complications are injected by the state, the municipality and the hospital administration itself. In Canada, the provincial governments, not Ottawa, take responsibility.

9   An Ontario civil servant told me a few years ago a similar tale about complications, this one concerning the clean-up of Lake Ontario. On our side of the border the work proceeded according to a timetable set up by international agreement. On the American side the similar work of building sewage-treatment plants fell far behind the timetable. The problem, he said, was not lack of money for the American part of the work, nor lack of will or interest either. People there had been working, in their own way, quite as hard as the Canadians. They were struggling with red tape. Red tape is the way we commonly describe complications of size that have become stifling.

10   Many jobs for which we have come to think that very large outfits are necessary — just because that is the way they are being handled — can be done as well by smaller organizations, indeed can sometimes be done better. When the Canadian postal system was smaller, had less mail to handle, it delivered the mail more swiftly and reliably. I think our postal system has become like the human brain in the sense that the post office itself is no longer able to understand its own complications. One of the things I look forward to if Quebec ever does separate is two smaller postal systems instead of what we now have. (Small countries have their own postal system; we do not see that as being extravagant or representing unnecessary duplication.) In the meantime, of course, much important Canadian mail is now no longer entrusted to the postal system. It turns out that small, hence less complicated, courier services are more reliable and swift, and even though they were supposed to be illegal and for a time were hounded and prosecuted, they flourished because they had become a sheer necessity. Some in Toronto now charge only 15 cents a letter in comparison with the official 17 cents, but it is their reliability and speed that make them so valuable. On occasion, to the government's embarrassment, government departments have been caught using them.

11   Many Americans take it for granted that telephone service has to be consolidated in a huge organization to be efficient. When I tell American acquaintances that the province of Alberta has long owned a separate telephone system, and that I can vouch from experience for

its first-rate efficiency, they are amazed. They become downright incredulous when they hear that within Alberta the city of Edmonton owns yet a different and separate telephone system and that it works with first-class efficiency too. I hardly dare tell them that the two systems have an excellent reputation for creating improvements in service and equipment — but they do.

In New York, people have been pointing out for a couple of generations that the amount of money spent per pupil in the public schools is larger than the amount per pupil spent in many fine private schools with smaller classes. At first thought it is hard to imagine, short of assuming embezzlement, how the discrepancies between what is paid for and what is delivered can be explained. But if one explores the New York public school system's administration and sees the burden of overhead the vast consolidated system supports, the costs become understandable. These are costs of size, not corruption. Perhaps we can speak of the corruption of size. Decentralization of the school system was undertaken about a decade ago in New York. But in practice, decentralization meant new layers of administration and complication within the central organization, because the central organization was retained too. As Marshall McLuhan has said, you can't decentralize centrally. 12

Where national governments are concerned, a traditional way of keeping size and its complications under control has been federalism. Most large nations have employed federal systems in one form or another, and so have some very small ones, such as Switzerland. Of course there have been other reasons for federalism too. It provides varying degrees of autonomy for autonomy's own sake, but one use of it has been to try to keep big government and centralized government in hand. 13

Federalism has been falling on bad days in many places. The Soviet Union had federalism in form, but in fact is exceedingly centralized in its management and decisions. The United States has federalism in form, but in fact has converted itself into a unitary state where all but the most minor and inherently local matters — and even some of those — must be traipsed through centralized corridors of power. 14

Centralization of national governments has been gathering force in most of this century and has been intensifying swiftly in our own time. When centralization is combined with increased responsibilities taken on by government, as has also been happening, the result is very big government. 15

Not all countries have embraced this combination. Switzerland 16 and Japan are outstanding exceptions. Both have relatively few national programs. Canada has also resisted extreme centralization because Quebec, Ontario, Alberta and British Columbia have insisted on considerable provincial autonomy. Thus Canada retains a federal system in fact as well as in form. Nevertheless, elephantiasis threatens us, too. Ottawa's employees have increased by more than 50 percent just since 1968.

17   Almost everywhere in the world, bureaucratic complications have now become so intractable as to defy either solution or understanding. Many intelligent, industrious and well-intentioned people in government are spending their lives creating messes, futilities and waste because they cannot avoid doing so. The complications are labyrinthine. The red tape is stifling. The vast, unwieldy organizational bulks are inflexible, impossible to put on the right track when they have nosed onto the wrong. Arrangements like this do not seem to offer a promising future.

18   If we take Haldane's principle seriously, as I think we must, increased centralization of government ought not to be combined with added or multiplied governmental responsibilities. On the contrary, added governmental responsibilities ought logically to be combined with looser federalism, or else with secessions. Certainly it seems that the only promising arrangement for busy governments, if that is what we need or want, is small nations.

19   To go back to the size of animals once more, some become so bulky that no conceivable complications can contend with the hazards of their size. They must have very special environments to survive. In the heat of the day, the hippopotamus immerses itself in water, only its nostrils emerging. The great whales could never have attained their huge size except in water; otherwise their own heat would have killed them. There is an analogy to be found here, appropriately a chilling one. The biggest and most thoroughly centralized governments have always, finally, required the special environment of oppression to continue to maintain themselves. And some could never have attained their great size at all had they not grown in that environment.

_____ **CONSIDERATIONS** _____

1. How does Jane Jacobs avoid writing just another simplistic blast against governmental control?

2. "Paradoxes of Size" begins (Paragraphs 1–4) with an analogy, because

the writer remembered something she read and saw a useful connection between that reading and her present subject. This ability is one of the greatest assets a writer can have. Try your own hand at it by finding a connection between Jacobs's essay and Stephen Jay Gould's "Phyletic Size Decrease in Hershey Bars" (pages 161–166), or Wendell Berry's "A Good Scythe" (pages 39–42).

3. Why does Jacob return to her analogy in her closing paragraph? Provide two good reasons.

4. In Paragraphs 13 and 14, Jacobs, writing from the Canadian side of the border, uses the term "federalism" in a way that may be confusing to American readers accustomed to thinking of federalism as a strongly centralized government. To clarify the matter, read those paragraphs carefully and review the definitions of "federalism" in a good dictionary.

5. Why, according to Jacobs, does it seldom save money to make big units out of many smaller units?

6. Another writer in this text, E. F. Schumacher (pages 355–361), became famous for his best-selling book *Small Is Beautiful* (1973). Would Jacobs agree with the implication that big is terrible? Support your answer with references to her essay.

Thomas Jefferson (1743–1826) was the third president of the United States, and perhaps more truly the Father of his Country than George Washington was; or maybe we would only like to think so, for such paternity flatters the offspring. Jefferson was a politician, philosopher, architect, inventor, and writer. With an energy equal to his curiosity, he acted to improve the world: he wrote the Declaration of Independence; he wrote a life of Jesus; and he founded the University of Virginia, whose original buildings he designed. An arch-republican, fearful of Alexander Hamilton's monarchical reverence for authority, Jefferson withheld support from the Constitution until he saw the Bill of Rights added to it.

We take this text from Garry Wills's Inventing America *(1978); by juxtaposition, Wills demonstrates the revision of a classic.*

38

THOMAS JEFFERSON

The Declarations of Jefferson and of the Congress

I will state the form of the declaration as originally reported. The parts struck out by Congress shall be distinguished by a black line drawn under them; & those inserted by them shall be placed in the margin or in a concurrent column:

A Declaration by the representatives of the United states of America, in [General] Congress assembled. 1

When in the course of human events it becomes necessary for one people to dissolve the political bands which have connected them with another, and to assume among the powers of the earth the separate & equal station to which the laws of nature and 2

Taken from Jefferson's Notes and Proceedings — *Papers*, 1:315–319.

of nature's god entitle them, a decent respect to the opinions of mankind requires that they should declare the causes which impel them to the separation.

3   We hold these truths to be self evident: that all men are created equal; that they are endowed by their creator with ∧ [inher-   certain
ent and] inalienable rights; that among these are life, liberty & the pursuit of happiness: that to secure these rights, governments are instituted among men, deriving their just powers from the consent of the governed; that whenever any form of government becomes destructive of these ends, it is the right of the people to alter or to abolish it, & to institute new government, laying it's foundation on such principles, & organising it's powers in such form, as to them shall seem most likely to effect their safety & happiness. Prudence indeed will dictate that governments long established should not be changed for light & transient causes; and accordingly all experience hath shewn that mankind are more disposed to suffer while evils are sufferable than to right themselves by abolishing the forms to which they are accustomed. But when a long train of abuses & usurpations [begun at a distinguished period and] pursuing invariably the same object, evinces a design to reduce them under absolute despotism it is their right, it is their duty to throw off such government, & to provide new guards for their future security. Such has been the patient sufferance of these colonies; & such is now the necessity which constrains them to ∧ [expunge]   alter
their former systems of government. The history of the present king of Great Britain is a history of ∧ [unremitting] injuries &   repeated
usurpations, [among which appears no solitary fact to contradict the uniform tenor of the rest but all have] ∧ in direct object the   all having
establishment of an absolute tyranny over these states. To prove this let facts be submitted to a candid world [for the truth of which we pledge a faith yet unsullied by falsehood.]

4   He has refused his assent to laws the most wholesome & necessary for the public good.

5   He has forbidden his governors to pass laws of immediate & pressing importance, unless suspended in their operation till his assent should be obtained; & when so suspended, he has utterly neglected to attend to them.

6   He has refused to pass other laws for the accommodation of large districts of people, unless those people would relinquish the right of representation in the legislature, a right inestimable to them, & formidable to tyrants only.

7   He has called together legislative bodies at places unusual, uncomfortable, and distant from the depository of their public records, for the sole purpose of fatiguing them into compliance with his measures.

8   He has dissolved representative houses repeatedly [& contin-

ually] for opposing with manly firmness his invasions on the rights of the people.

He has refused for a long time after such dissolutions to 9
cause others to be elected, whereby the legislative powers, incapable of annihilation, have returned to the people at large for their exercise, the state remaining in the mean time exposed to all the dangers of invasion from without & convulsions within.

He has endeavored to prevent the population of these states; 10
for that purpose obstructing the laws for naturalization of foreigners, refusing to pass others to encourage their migrations hither, & raising the conditions of new appropriations of lands.

obstructed   He has ∧ [suffered] the administration of justice [totally to 11
by   cease in some of these states] ∧ refusing his assent to laws for establishing judiciary powers.

He has made [our] judges dependant on his will alone, for the 12
tenure of their offices, & the amount & paiment of their salaries.

He has erected a multitude of new offices [by a self assumed 13
power] and sent hither swarms of new officers to harrass our people and eat out their substance.

He has kept among us in times of peace standing armies [and 14
ships of war] without the consent of our legislatures.

He has affected to render the military independant of, & 15
superior to the civil power.

He has combined with others to subject us to a jurisdiction 16
foreign to our constitutions & unacknoleged by our laws, giving his assent to their acts of pretended legislation for quartering large bodies of armed troops among us; for protecting them by a mock-trial from punishment for any murders which they should commit on the inhabitants of these states; for cutting off our trade with all parts of the world; for imposing taxes on us without our consent;
in many cases   for depriving us ∧ of the benefits of trial by jury; for transporting us beyond seas to be tried for pretended offences; for abolishing the free system of English laws in a neighboring province, establishing therein an arbitrary government, and enlarging it's boundaries, so as to render it at once an example and fit instrument for
colonies   introducing the same absolute rule into these ∧ [states]; for taking away our charters, abolishing our most valuable laws, and altering fundamentally the forms of our governments; for suspending our own legislatures, & declaring themselves invested with power to legislate for us in all cases whatsoever.

by declaring   He has abdicated government here ∧ [withdrawing his gov- 17
us out of his   ernors, and declaring us out of his allegiance & protection.]
protection &
waging war   He has plundered our seas, ravaged our coasts, burnt our 18
against us.   towns, & destroyed the lives of our people.

19   He is at this time transporting large armies of foreign mercenaries to compleat the works of death, desolation & tyranny already begun with circumstances of cruelty and perfidy ∧ unworthy the head of a civilized nation.   *[margin: scarcely paralleled in the most barbarous ages, & totally]*

20   He has constrained our fellow citizens taken captive on the high seas to bear arms against their country, to become the executioners of their friends & brethren, or to fall themselves by their hands.

21   He has ∧ endeavored to bring on the inhabitants of our frontiers the merciless Indian savages, whose known rule of warfare is an undistinguished destruction of all ages, sexes, & conditions [of existence.]   *[margin: excited domestic insurrections amongst us, & has]*

22   [He has incited treasonable insurrections of our fellow-citizens, with the allurements of forfeiture & confiscation of our property.

23   He has waged cruel war against human nature itself, violating it's most sacred rights of life and liberty in the persons of a distant people who never offended him, captivating & carrying them into slavery in another hemisphere or to incur miserable death in their transportation thither. This piratical warfare, the opprobrium of *infidel* powers, is the warfare of the *Christian* king of Great Britain. Determined to keep open a market where *Men* should be bought & sold, he has prostituted his negative for suppressing every legislative attempt to prohibit or to restrain this execrable commerce. And that this assemblage of horrors might want no fact of distinguished die, he is now exciting those very people to rise in arms among us, and to purchase that liberty of which he has deprived them, by murdering the people on whom he also obtruded them: thus paying off former crimes committed against the *Liberties* of one people, with crimes which he urges them to commit against the *lives* of another.]

24   In every stage of these oppressions we have petitioned for redress in the most humble terms: our repeated petitions have been answered only by repeated injuries. A prince whose character is thus marked by every act which may define a tyrant is unfit to be the ruler of a ∧ people [who mean to be free. Future ages will scarcely believe that the hardiness of one man adventured, within the short compass of twelve years only, to lay a foundation so broad & so undisguised for tyranny over a people fostered & fixed in principles of freedom.]   *[margin: free]*

25   Nor have we been wanting in attentions to our British brethren. We have warned them from time to time of attempts by their legislature to extend ∧ [a] jurisdiction over ∧ [these our states.] We have reminded them of the circumstances of our emigration &   *[margin: an unwarrantable us]*

settlement here, [no one of which could warrant so strange a pretension: that these were effected at the expence of our own blood & treasure, unassisted by the wealth or the strength of Great Britain: that in constituting indeed our several forms of government, we had adopted one common king, thereby laying a foundation for perpetual league & amity with them: but that submission to their parliament was no part of our constitution, nor ever in idea, if history may be credited: and,] we ∧ appealed to their native justice and magnanimity ∧ [as well as to] the ties of our common kindred to disavow these usurpations which ∧ [were likely to] interrupt our connection and correspondence. They too have been deaf to the voice of justice & of consanguinity, [and when occasions have been given them, by the regular course of their laws, of removing from their councils the disturbers of our harmony, they have, by their free election, re-established them in power. At this very time too they are permitting their chief magistrate to send over not only souldiers of our common blood, but Scotch & foreign mercenaries to invade & destroy us. These facts have given the last stab to agonizing affection, and manly spirit bids us to renounce for ever these unfeeling brethren. We must endeavor to forget our former love for them, and to hold them as we hold the rest of mankind enemies in war, in peace friends. We might have been a free and a great people together; but a communication of grandeur & of freedom it seems is below their dignity. Be it so, since they will have it. The road to happiness & to glory is open to us too. We will tread it apart from them, and] ∧ acquiesce in the necessity which denounces our [eternal] separation ∧ !

Left margin:
have
and we have
conjured them
by
would inevitably

Left margin (lower):
we must
therefore
and hold them
as we hold the
rest of mankind,
enemies in war,
in peace friends.

Right margin: 26

We therefore the representatives of the United states of America in General Congress assembled do in the name, & by the authority of the good people of these [states reject & renounce all allegiance & subjection to the kings of Great Britain & all others who may hereafter claim by, through or under them: we utterly dissolve all political connection which may heretofore have subsisted between us & the people or parliament of Great Britain: & finally we do assert & declare these colonies to be free & inde-

We therefore the representatives of the United states of America in General Congress assembled, appealing to the supreme judge of the world for the rectitude of our intentions, do in the name, & by the authority of the good people of these colonies, solemnly publish & declare that these United colonies are & of right ought to be free & independant states; that they are absolved from all allegiance to the British crown, and that all political connection between them & the state of Great Britain is, & ought to be,

pendant states,] & that as free & independent states, they have full power to levy war, conclude peace, contract alliances, establish commerce, & to do all other acts & things which independant states may of right do. And for the support of this declaration we mutually pledge to each other our lives, our fortunes & our sacred honour.

totally dissolved; & that as free & independant states they have full power to levy war, conclude peace, contract alliances, establish commerce & to do all other acts & things which independant states may of right do.

And for the support of this declaration, with a firm reliance on the protection of divine providence we mutually pledge to each other our lives, our fortunes & our sacred honour.

___ **CONSIDERATIONS** ___

1. What part of the original declaration deleted by Congress most surprises you? Why?

2. Make a careful study of the first eight or ten changes imposed by Congress on Jefferson's original declaration. Why do you think each was made? Would any of them have made good examples for George Orwell to use in his "Politics and the English Language"?

3. Garry Wills says in his book, *Inventing America*, that the declaration is easy to misunderstand because it "is written in the lost language of the Enlightenment." What was the Enlightenment? How does the language of that period differ from that of today? Perhaps the declaration should be rewritten in modern English?

4. If you conclude that the declaration should be rewritten, try your hand at it. Try, for instance, rewriting the famous third paragraph: "We hold these truths . . ." Can you be sure you're not writing a parody?

5. How is the declaration organized? Does it break down into distinct parts? If so, what is the function of those parts?

6. For a more thorough exploration of the before-and-after versions of the declaration and of the political and literary motives for the changes, see Carl Becker's *The Declaration of Independence.*

Robin Lakoff (b. 1942) was born in Brooklyn, New York, and received her B.A. and her Ph.D. from Harvard. She is now a professor of linguistics at the University of California at Berkeley. She began book publication with Abstract Syntax and Latin Complementation *(MIT Press, 1968) and followed it in 1975 with* Language and Woman's Place. *In 1984, in collaboration with Raquel Scherr, she published* Face Value: The Politics of Beauty.

39

ROBIN LAKOFF
You Are What You Say

1   "Women's language" is that pleasant (dainty?), euphemistic, never-aggressive way of talking we learned as little girls. Cultural bias was built into the language we were allowed to speak, the subjects we were allowed to speak about, and the ways we were spoken of. Having learned our linguistic lesson well, we go out in the world, only to discover that we are communicative cripples — damned if we do, and damned if we don't.

2   If we refuse to talk "like a lady," we are ridiculed and criticized for being unfeminine. ("She thinks like a man" is, at best, a left-handed compliment.) If we do learn all the fuzzy-headed, unassertive language of our sex, we are ridiculed for being unable to think clearly, unable to take part in a serious discussion, and therefore unfit to hold a position of power.

3   It doesn't take much of this for a woman to begin feeling she deserves such treatment because of inadequacies in her own intelligence and education.

4   "Women's language" shows up in all levels of English. For exam-

From *Ms.* magazine, July 1974. Reprinted by permission of the author.

ple, women are encouraged and allowed to make far more precise discriminations in naming colors than men do. Words like *mauve, beige, ecru, aquamarine, lavender,* and so on, are unremarkable in a woman's active vocabulary, but largely absent from that of most men. I know of no evidence suggesting that women actually *see* a wider range of colors than men do. It is simply that fine discriminations of this sort are relevant to women's vocabularies, but not to men's; to men, who control most of the interesting affairs of the world, such distinctions are trivial — irrelevant.

In the area of syntax, we find similar gender-related peculiarities 5
of speech. There is one construction, in particular, that women use conversationally far more than men: the tag-question. A tag is midway between an outright statement and a yes-no question; it is less assertive than the former, but more confident than the latter.

A *flat statement* indicates confidence in the speaker's knowledge 6
and is fairly certain to be believed; a *question* indicates a lack of knowledge on some point and implies that the gap in the speaker's knowledge can and will be remedied by an answer. For example, if, at a Little League game, I have had my glasses off, I can legitimately ask someone else: "Was the player out at third?" A *tag-question*, being intermediate between statement and question, is used when the speaker is stating a claim, but lacks full confidence in the truth of that claim. So if I say, "Is Joan here?" I will probably not be surprised if my respondent answers "no"; but if I say, "Joan is here, isn't she?" instead, chances are I am already biased in favor of a positive answer, wanting only confirmation. I still want a response, but I have enough knowledge (or think I have) to predict that response. A tag question, then, might be thought of as a statement that doesn't demand to be believed by anyone but the speaker, a way of giving leeway, of not forcing the addressee to go along with the views of the speaker.

Another common use of the tag-question is in small talk when 7
the speaker is trying to elicit conversation: "Sure is hot here, isn't it?"

But in discussing personal feelings or opinions, only the speaker 8
normally has any way of knowing the correct answer. Sentences such as "I have a headache, don't I?" are clearly ridiculous. But there are other examples where it is the speaker's opinions, rather than perceptions, for which corroboration is sought, as in "The situation in Southeast Asia is terrible, isn't it?"

While there are, of course, other possible interpretations of a 9
sentence like this, one possibility is that the speaker has a particular answer in mind — "yes" or "no" — but is reluctant to state it baldly.

This sort of tag-question is much more apt to be used by women than by men in conversation. Why is this the case?

10   The tag-question allows a speaker to avoid commitment, and thereby avoid conflict with the addressee. The problem is that, by so doing, speakers may also give the impression of not really being sure of themselves, or looking to the addressee for confirmation of their views. This uncertainty is reinforced in more subliminal ways, too. There is a peculiar sentence intonation-pattern, used almost exclusively by women, as far as I know, which changes a declarative answer into a question. The effect of using the rising inflection typical of a yes-no question is to imply that the speaker is seeking confirmation, even though the speaker is clearly the only one who has the requisite information, which is why the question was put to her in the first place:

(Q) When will dinner be ready?
(A) Oh . . . around six o'clock . . . ?

11   It is as though the second speaker were saying, "Six o'clock — if that's okay with you, if you agree." The person being addressed is put in the position of having to provide confirmation. One likely consequence of this sort of speech-pattern in a woman is that, often unbeknownst to herself, the speaker builds a reputation of tentativeness, and others will refrain from taking her seriously or trusting her with any real responsibilities, since she "can't make up her mind," and "isn't sure of herself."

12   Such idiosyncrasies may explain why women's language sounds much more "polite" than men's. It is polite to leave a decision open, not impose your mind, or views, or claims, on anyone else. So a tag-question is a kind of polite statement, in that it does not force agreement or belief on the addressee. In the same way a request is a polite command, in that it does not force obedience on the addressee, but rather suggests something be done as a favor to the speaker. A clearly stated order implies a threat of certain consequences if it is not followed, and — even more impolite — implies that the speaker is in a superior position and able to enforce the order. By couching wishes in the form of a request, on the other hand, a speaker implies that if the request is not carried out, only the speaker will suffer; noncompliance cannot harm the addressee. So the decision is really left up to addressee. The distinction becomes clear in these examples:

Close the door.
Please close the door.

Will you close the door?
Will you please close the door?
Won't you close the door?

In the same ways as words and speech patterns used *by* women   13
undermine their image, those used *to describe* women make matters
even worse. Often a word may be used of both men and women (and
perhaps of things as well); but when it is applied to women, it assumes
a special meaning that, by implication rather than outright assertion,
is derogatory to women as a group.

The use of euphemisms has this effect. A euphemism is a substi-   14
tute for a word that has acquired a bad connotation by association
with something unpleasant or embarrassing. But almost as soon as the
new word comes into common usage, it takes on the same old bad
connotations, since feelings about the things or people referred to are
not altered by a change of name; thus new euphemisms must be constantly found.

There is one euphemism for *woman* still very much alive. The   15
word, of course, is *lady*. *Lady* has a masculine counterpart, namely
gentleman, occasionally shortened to *gent*. But for some reason *lady*
is very much commoner than *gent (leman)*.

The decision to use *lady* rather than *woman*, or vice versa, may   16
considerably alter the sense of a sentence, as the following examples
show:

(a) a woman (lady) I know is a dean at Berkeley.
(b) A woman (lady) I know makes amazing things out of shoelaces and
      old boxes.

The use of *lady* in (a) imparts a frivolous, or nonserious, tone to   17
the sentence: the matter under discussion is not one of great moment.
Similarly, in (b), using *lady* here would suggest that the speaker considered the "amazing things" not to be serious art, but merely a hobby
or an aberration. If *woman* is used, she might be a serious sculptor. To
say *lady doctor* is very condescending, since no one ever says *gentleman doctor* or even *man doctor*. For example, mention in the San
Francisco *Chronicle* of January 31, 1972, of Madalyn Murray O'Hair
as the *lady atheist* reduces her position to that of scatterbrained eccentric. Even *woman atheist* is scarcely defensible: sex is irrelevant to
her philosophical position.

Many women argue that, on the other hand, *lady* carries with it   18
overtones recalling the age of chivalry: conferring exalted stature on
the person so referred to. This makes the term seem polite at first, but

we must also remember that these implications are perilous: they suggest that a "lady" is helpless, and cannot do things by herself.

19   *Lady* can also be used to infer frivolousness, as in titles of organizations. Those that have a serious purpose (not merely that of enabling "the ladies" to spend time with one another) cannot use the word *lady* in their titles, but less serious ones may. Compare the *Ladies' Auxiliary* of a men's group, or the *Thursday Evening Ladies' Browning and Garden Society* with *Ladies' Liberation* or *Ladies' Strike for Peace*.

20   What is curious about this split is that *lady* is in origin a euphemism — a substitute that puts a better face on something people find uncomfortable — for *woman*. What kind of euphemism is it that subtly denigrates the people to whom it refers? Perhaps *lady* functions as a euphemism for *woman* because it does not contain the sexual implications present in *woman:* it is not "embarrassing" in that way. If this is so, we may expect that, in the future, *lady* will replace woman as the primary word for the human female, since *woman* will have become too blatantly sexual. That this distinction is already made in some contexts at least is shown in the following examples, where you can try replacing *woman* with *lady:*

(a) She's only twelve, but she's already a woman.
(b) After ten years in jail, Harry wanted to find a woman.
(c) She's my woman, see, so don't mess around with her.

21   Another common substitute for *woman* is *girl*. One seldom hears a man past the age of adolescence referred to as a boy, save in expressions like "going out with the boys," which are meant to suggest an air of adolescent frivolity and irresponsibility. But women of all ages are "girls": one can have a man — not a boy — Friday, but only a girl — never a woman or even a lady — Friday; women have girlfriends, but men do not — in a nonsexual sense — have boyfriends. It may be that this use of *girl* is euphemistic in the same way the use of *lady* is: in stressing the idea of immaturity, it removes the sexual connotations lurking in *woman*. *Girl* brings to mind irresponsibility: you don't send a girl to do a woman's errand (or even, for that matter, a boy's errand). She is a person who is both too immature and too far from real life to be entrusted with responsibilities or with decisions of any serious or important nature.

22   Now let's take a pair of words which, in terms of the possible relationships in an earlier society, were simple male-female equivalents, analogous to *bull: cow*. Suppose we find that, for independent

reasons, society has changed in such a way that the original meanings now are irrelevant. Yet the words have not been discarded, but have acquired new meanings, metaphorically related to their original senses. But suppose these new metaphorical uses are no longer parallel to each other. By seeing where the parallelism breaks down, we discover something about the different roles played by men and women in this culture. One good example of such a divergence through time is found in the pair, *master: mistress.* Once used with reference to one's power over servants, these words have become unusable today in their original master-servant sense as the relationship has become less prevalent in our society. But the words are still common.

Unless used with reference to animals, *master* now generally refers to a man who has acquired consummate ability in some field, normally nonsexual. But its feminine counterpart cannot be used this way. It is practically restricted to its sexual sense of "paramour." We start out with two terms, both roughly paraphrasable as "one who has power over another." But the masculine form, once one person is no longer able to have absolute power over another, becomes usable metaphorically in the sense of "having power over *something.*" *Master* requires as its object only the name of some activity, something inanimate and abstract. But *mistress* requires a masculine noun in the possessive to precede it. One cannot say: "Rhonda is a mistress." One must be *someone's* mistress. A man is defined by what he does, a woman by her sexuality, that is, in terms of one particular aspect of her relationship to men. It is one thing to be an *old master* like Hans Holbein, and another to be an *old mistress.* 23

The same is true of the words *spinster* and *bachelor* — gender words for "one who is not married." The resemblance ends with the definition. While *bachelor* is a neuter term, often used as a compliment, *spinster* normally is used pejoratively, with connotations of prissiness, fussiness, and so on. To be a bachelor implies that one has the choice of marrying or not, and this is what makes the idea of a bachelor existence attractive, in the popular literature. He has been pursued and has successfully eluded his pursuers. But a spinster is one who has not been pursued, or at least not seriously. She is old, unwanted goods. The metaphorical connotations of *bachelor* generally suggest sexual freedom; of *spinster*, puritanism or celibacy. 24

These examples could be multiplied. It is generally considered a *faux pas*, in society, to congratulate a woman on her engagement, while it is correct to congratulate her fiancé. Why is this? The reason seems to be that it is impolite to remind people of things that may be 25 uncomfortable to them. To congratulate a woman on her engagement is really to say, "Thank goodness! You had a close call!" For the man, on the other hand, there was no such danger. His choosing to marry is viewed as a good thing, but not something essential.

26   The linguistic double standard holds throughout the life of the relationship. After marriage, bachelor and spinster become man and wife, not man and woman. The woman whose husband dies remains "John's widow"; John, however, is never "Mary's widower."

27   Finally, why is it that salesclerks and others are so quick to call women customers "dear," "honey," and other terms of endearment they really have no business using? A male customer would never put up with it. But women, like children, are supposed to enjoy these endearments, rather than being offended by them.

28   In more ways than one, it's time to speak up.

_____ **CONSIDERATIONS** _____

1. In this informal essay, Lakoff does not provide the documentation and references that she would in a formal paper. The reader is thus asked to take the writer's word for what she says. Given the importance Lakoff places, for example, on the tag-question (Paragraphs 5 through 10) it might be interesting to make your own objective, systematic observation of the use of that locution. Carefully note tag-question usages — including place, time, sex of speaker, and context — and report your findings to your class. Linguistic field research is fascinating, but it makes severe demands upon your accuracy and honesty.

2. In discussing the word "lady" (Paragraphs 15 through 20) Lakoff points out the connotations of the word that work against women. To study the importance of connotative meanings as opposed to denotative meanings, list associative and implied meanings for the terms "lady," "woman," "female," and "girl." Follow through in the same way for "gentleman," "man," "male," and "boy." What are your conclusions?

3. Lakoff states in Paragraph 23 "It is one thing to be an 'old master' like Hans Holbein, and another to be an 'old mistress.' " Study this paragraph to see how carefully Lakoff leads the reader to accepting the point she makes in this sentence.

4. Lakoff's central point about sexism in language is similar to Wendell Berry's observation in Paragraph 5 of his "In Defense of Literacy" (pages 44–47) about the power of words to impose "conceptual limits." Re-state Lakoff's thesis in your own words and comment on how well her essay supports that thesis.

5. While Lakoff writes informally in this essay, you may find a number

of unfamiliar words such as "euphemism," "syntax," "gender-related," "subliminal," and "denigrates." List all unfamiliar words, then take the trouble to develop a working acquaintance with each one. [Such an exercise could lead to an improved vocabulary.]

6. Would you say that the anxiety suffered by the woman in Katherine Anne Porter's "The Necessary Enemy" (pages 333–337) is heightened by sexism in language as described by Lakoff? Explain.

D. H. Lawrence (1885–1930) was born in Nottinghamshire, in England, son of a coal-miner father brutalized by work and poverty, and a schoolteacher mother who encouraged his writing. The family was poor and Lawrence was sickly, but he studied to become certified as a teacher, and wrote poetry and fiction when he could. In 1911 he published his first novel, **The White Peacock,** *and quit his post as a teacher. The next year, he met Frieda von Richthofen Weekley, German wife of a Professor Weekley, and cousin of the Baron Manfred von Richthofen who was to become the Red Baron of World War I. Lawrence and Frieda fell in love, and Frieda left her husband and children to run away with Lawrence; they remained together, tempestuous and difficult and devoted, until his death.*

His first book of poems appeared in 1913, as did the first of his great novels, **Sons and Lovers.** *Lawrence and Frieda, who were able to marry in 1914, traveled in Germany and Italy, and settled in England when the war started.* **The Prussian Officer,** *a book of stories, appeared in 1914, followed by* **The Rainbow** *(1915). That novel's second half,* **Women in Love,** *was not published until 1920 because publishers feared the response to its relative explictness about sexual feeling.*

Living by his wits, Lawrence published innumerable stories, essays, novels, poems, criticism, and travel books. He and Frieda traveled continually. After World War I, they took off for Italy; two of his travel books are about that country. A journey to Australia resulted in a novel called **Kangaroo** *(1923). In the New World, he delighted in Mexico (*The Plumed Serpent, *1926) and New Mexico. During the last years before his death from tuberculosis, he wrote* **Lady Chatterley's Lover,** *which was suppressed, and his best poetry.*

In Lawrence's novels, his relative explicitness seems mild enough today, but we must remember that he published his first novel before World War I — when Queen Victoria had been dead only ten years. As might be expected, D. H. Lawrence was called a pornographer.

40

D. H. LAWRENCE
Pornography

What is pornography to one man is the laughter of genius to another.   1

The word itself, we are told, means "pertaining to harlots" — the graph of the harlot. But nowadays, what is a harlot? If she was a woman who took money from a man in return for going to bed with him — really, most wives sold themselves, in the past, and plenty of harlots gave themselves, when they felt like it, for nothing. If a woman hasn't got a tiny streak of harlot in her, she's a dry stick as a rule. And probably most harlots had somewhere a streak of womanly generosity. Why be so cut and dried? The law is a dreary thing, and its judgments have nothing to do with life. . . .   2

One essay on pornography, I remember, comes to the conclusion that pornography in art is that which is calculated to arouse sexual desire, or sexual excitement. And stress is laid on the fact, whether the author or artist *intended* to arouse sexual feelings. It is the old vexed question of intention, become so dull today, when we know how strong and influential our unconscious intentions are. And why a man should be held guilty of his conscious intentions, and innocent of his unconscious intentions, I don't know, since every man is more made up of unconscious intentions than of conscious ones. I am what I am, not merely what I think I am.   3

However! We take it, I assume, that *pornography* is something base, something unpleasant. In short, we don't like it. And why don't we like it? Because it arouses sexual feelings?   4

I think not. No matter how hard we may pretend otherwise, most   5 of us rather like a moderate rousing of our sex. It warms us, stimulates us like sunshine on a grey day. After a century or two of Puritanism, this is still true of most people. Only the mob-habit of condemning any form of sex is too strong to let us admit it naturally. And there are, of course, many people who are genuinely repelled by the simplest and most natural stirrings of sexual feeling. But these people are perverts who have fallen into hatred of their fellow-men; thwarted, disappointed, unfulfilled people, of whom, alas, our civilisation contains so many. And they nearly always enjoy some unsimple and unnatural form of sex excitement, secretly.

6   Even quite advanced art critics would try to make us believe that any picture or book which had "sex appeal" was *ipso facto* a bad book or picture. This is just canting hypocrisy. Half the great poems, pictures, music, stories, of the whole world are great by virtue of the beauty of their sex appeal. Titian or Renoir, the Song of Solomon or *Jane Eyre*, Mozart or "Annie Laurie," the loveliness is all interwoven with sex appeal, sex stimulus, call it what you will. Even Michelangelo, who rather hated sex, can't help filling the Cornucopia with phallic acorns. Sex is a very powerful, beneficial and necessary stimulus in human life, and we are all grateful when we feel its warm, natural flow through us, like a form of sunshine. . . .

7   Then what is pornography, after all this? It isn't sex appeal or sex stimulus in art. It isn't even a deliberate intention on the part of the artist to arouse or excite sexual feelings. There's nothing wrong with sexual feelings in themselves, so long as they are straightforward and not sneaking or sly. The right sort of sex stimulus is invaluable to human daily life. Without it the world grows grey. I would give everybody the gay Renaissance stories to read, they would help to shake off a lot of grey self-importance, which is our modern civilised disease.

8   But even I would censor genuine pornography, rigorously. It would not be very difficult. In the first place, genuine pornography is almost always underworld, it doesn't come into the open. In the second, you can recognise it by the insult it offers, invariably, to sex and to the human spirit.

9   Pornography is the attempt to insult sex, to do dirt on it. This is unpardonable. Take the very lowest instance, the picture postcard sold underhand, by the underworld, in most cities. What I have seen of them have been of an ugliness to make you cry. The insult to the human body, the insult to a vital human relationship! Ugly and cheap they make the human nudity, ugly and degraded they make the sexual act, trivial and cheap and nasty.

It is the same with the books they sell in the underworld. They   10
are either so ugly they make you ill, or so fatuous you can't imagine
anybody but a cretin or a moron reading them, or writing them.

It is the same with the dirty limericks that people tell after din-   11
ner, or the dirty stories one hears commercial travellers telling each
other in a smoke-room. Occasionally there is a really funny one, that
redeems a great deal. But usually they are just ugly and repellent, and
the so-called "humour" is just a trick of doing dirt on sex.

Now the human nudity of a great many modern people is just   12
ugly and degraded, and the sexual act between modern people is just
the same, merely ugly and degrading. But this is nothing to be proud
of. It is the castastrophe of our civilisation. I am sure no other civilisation, not even the Roman, has showed such a vast proportion of
ignominious and degraded nudity, and ugly, squalid dirty sex. Because
no other civilisation has driven sex into the underworld, and nudity
to the W.C.

The intelligent young, thank heaven, seem determined to alter   13
in these two respects. They are rescuing their young nudity from the
stuffy, pornographical hole-and-corner underworld of their elders, and
they refuse to sneak about the sexual relation. This is a change the
elderly grey ones of course deplore, but it is in fact a very great change
for the better, and a real revolution.

But it is amazing how strong is the will in ordinary, vulgar peo-   14
ple, to do dirt on sex. It was one of my fond illusions, when I was
young, that the ordinary healthy-seeming sort of men in railway car-
riages, or the smoke-room of an hotel or a pullman, were healthy in
their feelings and had a wholesome rough devil-may-care attitude
towards sex. All wrong! All wrong! Experience teaches that common
individuals of this sort have a disgusting attitude towards sex, a disgusting contempt of it, a disgusting desire to insult it. If such fellows
have intercourse with a woman, they triumphantly feel that they have
done her dirt, and now she is lower, cheaper, more contemptible than
she was before.

It is individuals of this sort that tell dirty stories, carry indecent   15
picture postcards, and know the indecent books. This is the great
pornographical class — the really common men-in-the-street and
women-in-the-street. They have as great a hate and contempt of sex
as the greyest Puritan, and when an appeal is made to them, they are
always on the side of the angels. They insist that a film-heroine shall
be a neuter, a sexless thing of washed-out purity. They insist that real
sex-feeling shall only be shown by the villain or villainess, low lust.

They find a Titian or a Renoir really indecent, and they don't want their wives and daughters to see it.

16   Why? Because they have the grey disease of sex-hatred, coupled with the yellow disease of dirt-lust. The sex functions and the excrementory functions in the human body work so close together, yet they are, so to speak, utterly different in direction. Sex is a creative flow, the excrementory flow is towards dissolution, de-creation, if we may use such a word. In the really healthy human being the distinction between the two is instant, our profoundest instincts are perhaps our instincts of opposition between the two flows.

17   But in the degraded human being the deep instincts have gone dead, and then the two flows become identical. *This* is the secret of really vulgar and of pornographical people: the sex flow and the excrement flow is the same to them. It happens when the psyche deteriorates, and the profound controlling instincts collapse. Then sex is dirt and dirt is sex, and sexual excitement becomes a playing with dirt, and any sign of sex in a woman becomes a show of her dirt. This is the condition of the common, vulgar human being whose name is legion, and who lifts his voice and it is the *Vox populi, vox Dei.* And this is the source of all pornography.

_____ **CONSIDERATIONS** _____

1. How much help can you get from your dictionary in understanding terms like "pornography," "obscenity," "lascivious," "lewd"? Why do their definitions seem to take you in circles rather than in a straight line toward some absolute meaning? Are you frustrated by all definitions?

2. "The law is a dreary thing," writes Lawrence in Paragraph 2, "and its judgments have nothing to do with life." Does the language of law give us this impression? Why does law seem removed from life? Are there advantages in this removal?

3. In Paragraph 3, Lawrence mentions the "old, vexed question of intention." Can we use intention to resolve any matter open to interpretation — in literature, for example? How could we possibly establish Shakespeare's intentions when he wrote the sonnet "That Time of Year Thou Mayst in Me Behold"?

4. Throughout his essay, Lawrence scatters generalizations as freely as one might scatter grass seed across a needy lawn; see the last sentence of Paragraph 5, and the third sentence of Paragraph 6. Most teachers claim that such sweeping remarks weaken rather than strengthen an argument. After studying the whole of Lawrence's essay, can you find any redeeming feature in his tendency to generalize?

5. Can you find any connection between Lawrence's comment on "the mob-habit of condemning any form of sex" and Katherine Anne Porter's discussion of conventional views of marriage in "The Necessary Enemy" (pages 333–337)?

6. Lawrence's diction is a problem for young American readers when he uses terms more familiar to British readers, or terms that have since changed their meanings dramatically, or terms that have double meanings. Find three examples of terms offering difficulty, and analyze the difficulty in each.

Abraham Lincoln (1809–1865) was our sixteenth president, and a consensus of historians ranks him our greatest president — a ranking generally supported by the American people. He grew up self-educated, nurturing his mind on five special books: the King James Version of the Bible, Shakespeare, Parson Weems's Life of Washington, *John Bunyan's* Pilgrim's Progress, *and Daniel Defoe's* Robinson Crusoe. *His speeches and letters are models of a formal, rhythmic, studied English prose. None of his utterances is so known — so parodied, so quoted, so misquoted — as the speech he gave at Gettysburg.*

41

ABRAHAM LINCOLN
The Gettysburg Address

1   Four score and seven years ago our fathers brought forth on this continent, a new nation, conceived in Liberty, and dedicated to the proposition that all men are created equal.

2   Now we are engaged in a great civil war, testing whether that nation, or any nation so conceived and so dedicated, can long endure. We are met on a great battle-field of that war. We have come to dedicate a portion of that field, as a final resting place for those who here gave their lives that that nation might live. It is altogether fitting and proper that we should do this.

3   But, in a larger sense, we can not dedicate — we can not consecrate — we can not hallow — this ground. The brave men, living and dead, who struggled here, have consecrated it, far above our poor power to add or detract. The world will little note, nor long remember what we say here, but it can never forget what they did here. It is for us the living, rather, to be dedicated here to the unfinished work which they who fought here have thus far so nobly advanced. It is

rather for us to be here dedicated to the great task remaining before us — that from these honored dead we take increased devotion to that cause for which they gave the last full measure of devotion — that we here highly resolve that these dead shall not have died in vain — that this nation, under God, shall have a new birth of freedom — and that government of the people, by the people, for the people, shall not perish from the earth.

____ CONSIDERATIONS ____

1. Lincoln's Gettysburg Address was not subjected to the intense study, criticism, and revision that Congress gave Thomas Jefferson's Declaration of Independence (pages 208–213), but neither did Lincoln give his short speech off the top of his head. He reworked the composition before he delivered it. One of the changes occurred in the last sentence of Paragraph 2, which in an earlier version read, "This we may, in all propriety do." What do you think of his decision to change that sentence?

2. Commentators have noted that Lincoln made telling use of repeated sentence structure. Locate a good example in the address, then compose two sentences of your own, on any subject, but built in the same way.

3. Shortly after Lincoln delivered the address, the *Chicago Times* criticized his phrase, "a new birth of freedom" and called it a misrepresentation of the motives of the men slain at Gettysburg. The *Times* argued that the soldiers had died to maintain the government, the Constitution, and the union — not to advance Lincoln's "odious abolition doctrines." Can an objective reading of the address help you determine whether the *Times* attack had any substance?

4. Note how Lincoln's first reference to place is the word "continent"; his second is to "nation"; his third to "battle-field"; and his fourth to "a portion of that field." What do you make of this progressive narrowing of the field of vision? Can you see a use for such a device in your own writing?

5. Lincoln begins Paragraph 3 with a sentence in which he moves from "dedicate" to "consecrate" to "hallow." Are these words synonyms? If so, why does he say the same thing three times? If they have different meanings, is there any significance in the order in which Lincoln arranges them? Consult a good dictionary or collection of synonyms.

42

JOHN McPHEE

Ancestors of the Jump Shot

1   Bradley is not an innovator. Actually, basketball has had only a few innovators in its history — players like Hank Luisetti, of Stanford, whose introduction in 1936 of the running one-hander did as much to open up the game for scoring as the forward pass did for football; and Joe Fulks, of the old Philadelphia Warriors, whose twisting two-handed heaves, made while he was leaping like a salmon, were the beginnings of the jump shot, which seems to be basketball's ultimate weapon. Most basketball players appropriate fragments of other play-

ers' styles, and thus develop their own. This is what Bradley has done, but one of the things that set him apart from nearly everyone else is that the process has been conscious rather than osmotic. His jump shot, for example, has had two principal influences. One is Jerry West, who has one of the best jumpers in basketball. At a summer basketball camp in Missouri some years ago, West told Bradley that he always gives an extra hard bounce to the last dribble before a jump shot, since this seems to catapult him to added height. Bradley has been doing that ever since. Terry Dischinger, of the Detroit Pistons, has told Bradley that he always slams his foot to the floor on the last step before a jump shot, because this stops his momentum and thus prevents drift. Drifting while aloft is the mark of a sloppy jump shot.

Bradley's graceful hook shot is a masterpiece of eclecticism. It 2 consists of the high-lifted knee of the Los Angeles Lakers' Darrall Imhoff, the arms of Bill Russell, of the Boston Celtics, who extends his idle hand far under his shooting arm and thus magically stabilizes the shot, and the general corporeal form of Kentucky's Cotton Nash, a rookie this year with the Lakers. Bradley carries his analyses of shots further than merely identifying them with pieces of other people. "There are five parts to the hook shot," he explains to anyone who asks. As he continues, he picks up a ball and stands about eighteen feet from a basket. "Crouch," he says, crouching, and goes on to demonstrate the other moves. "Turn your head to look for the basket, step, kick, follow through with your arms." Once, as he was explaining this to me, the ball curled around the rim and failed to go in.

"What happened then?" I asked him. 3

"I didn't kick high enough," he said. 4

"Do you always know exactly why you've missed a shot?" 5

"Yes," he said, missing another one. 6

"What happened that time?" 7

"I was talking to you. I didn't concentrate. The secret of shooting 8 is concentration."

His set shot is borrowed from Ed Macauley, who was a St. Louis 9 University All-American in the late forties and was later a star member of the Boston Celtics and the St. Louis Hawks. Macauley runs the basketball camp Bradley first went to when he was fifteen. In describing the set shot, Bradley is probably quoting a Macauley lecture. "Crouch like Groucho Marx," he says. "Go off your feet a few inches. You shoot with your legs. Your arms merely guide the ball." Bradley says that he has more confidence in his set shot than in any other. However, he seldom uses it, because he seldom has to. A set shot is a long shot, usually a twenty-footer, and Bradley, with his speed and footwork, can almost always take some other kind of shot, closer to the basket. He will take set shots when they are given to him, though. Two seasons ago, Davidson lost to Princeton, using a compact zone defense that ignored the remoter areas of the court. In one brief sequence, Bradley sent up seven set shots, missing only one. The missed one happened to rebound in Bradley's direction, and he leaped up, caught it with one hand, and scored.

10   Even his lay-up shot has an ancestral form; he is full of admiration for "the way Cliff Hagan pops up anywhere within six feet of the basket," and he tries to do the same. Hagan is a former Kentucky star who now plays for the St. Louis Hawks. Because opposing teams always do everything they can to stop Bradley, he gets an unusual number of foul shots. When he was in high school, he used to imitate Bob Pettit, of the St. Louis Hawks, and Bill Sharman of the Boston Celtics, but now his free throw is more or less his own. With his left foot back about eighteen inches — "wherever it feels comfortable," he says — he shoots with a deep-bending rhythm of knees and arms, one-handed, his left hand acting as a kind of gantry for the ball until the moment of release. What is most interesting, though, is that he concentrates his attention on one of the tiny steel eyelets that are welded under the rim of the basket to hold the net to the hoop — on the center eyelet, of course — before he lets fly. One night, he scored over twenty points on free throws alone; Cornell hacked at him so heavily that he was given twenty-one free throws, and he made all twenty-one, finishing the game with a total of thirty-seven points.

11   When Bradley, working out alone, practices his set shots, hook shots, and jump shots, he moves systematically from one place to another around the basket, his distance from it being appropriate to the shot, and he does not permit himself to move on until he has made at least ten shots out of thirteen from each location. He applies this standard to every kind of shot, with either hand, from any distance. Many basketball players, including reasonably good ones, could spend five years in a gym and not make ten out of thirteen left-handed hook shots, but that is part of Bradley's daily routine. He talks to himself while he is shooting, usually reminding himself to concentrate but sometimes talking to himself the way every high-school j.v. basketball player has done since the dim twenties — more or less imitating a radio announcer, and saying, as he gathers himself up for a shot, "It's pandemonium in Dillon Gymnasium. The clock is running out. He's up with a jumper. Swish!"

Last summer, the floor of the Princeton gym was being resur- 12
faced, so Bradley had to put in several practice sessions at the Lawrenceville School. His first afternoon at Lawrenceville, he began by
shooting fourteen-foot jump shots from the right side. He got off to a
bad start, and he kept missing them. Six in a row hit the back rim of
the basket and bounced out. He stopped, looking discomfited, and
seemed to be making an adjustment in his mind. Then he went up for
another jump shot from the same spot and hit it cleanly. Four more
shots went in without a miss, and then he paused and said, "You want
to know something? That basket is about an inch and a half low."
Some weeks later, I went back to Lawrenceville with a steel tape,
borrowed a stepladder, and measured the height of the basket. It was
nine feet ten and seven-eighths inches above the floor, or one and one-
eighth inches too low.

____ CONSIDERATIONS _____

1. McPhee treats Bradley's technique as seriously as any student or
critic treats that of a famous musician, author, painter, or sculptor. See, for
example, Ralph Ellison in "On Becoming a Writer." Is it nonsense to write
about the throwing of a basketball as though it were an art?

2. McPhee likes to borrow phrases from one field and apply them to
another. Find at least three examples of this borrowing and evaluate their
appropriateness or effectiveness.

3. Compare this McPhee piece and John Updike's short story, "Ace in
the Hole."

4. To describe the movements of Bradley's jump shot requires close
observation. Go to your college gym or playing field, select a move by a player,
make detailed notes, and write a paragraph in which you reproduce in words
what that player does with his or her body.

5. Does McPhee avoid the jargon known only to people in basketball? Is
his vocabulary obscure, if you do not know the sport? List any special basketball terms McPhee uses, circle those you don't know, and decide how successful he is in making those terms clear to you.

Norman Mailer (b. 1923) grew up in Brooklyn and went to Harvard. As an undergraduate he was already publishing short stories, and his first book was a novel about World War II called The Naked and the Dead *(1948). He has published four novels since —* Barbary Shore *(1951),* The Deer Park *(1955),* An American Dream *(1965), and* Why Are We in Vietnam? *(1967) — but more and more of his writing has been nonfiction.*

He is an eminent practitioner of the New Journalism, nonfiction that employs many devices we used to associate only with fiction — lively description, dialogue, subjective exposition of character, and a tone that combines informality with energy. Early essays appeared in Advertisements for Myself *(1959), along with stories and parts of abandoned novels. In* The Presidential Papers *(1963) he began to go more fully into politics, a subject that returned in* Cannibals and Christians *(1966) and books about the protest movement (*The Armies of the Night, *1968) and about the political campaigns of 1968 and 1972 (*Miami and the Siege of Chicago, *1968;* St. George and the Godfather, *1972). More recently, he is the author of books about Marilyn Monroe and Muhammad Ali. In 1979 he published his "true life novel" about the murderer Gary Gilmore,* The Executioner's Song. *In 1983 appeared* Ancient Evenings, *a long novel set in ancient Egypt.*

Perhaps the best of his nonfiction books is Of a Fire on the Moon *(1971), his account of the first journey to the moon. This book uses some observation and personal experience. Mailer interviewed Werner Von Braun, he watched the Apollo take off. He has used much diligent research in engineering and the sciences, perhaps drawing on memories of his studies for the Bachelor of Science degree in aeronautical engineering that he took at Harvard in 1943. But Mailer's personal style often disguises Mailer's hard work. His novelist's ear for language allows him to describe with brilliance such matters as the difficulty of wedging a bulky space suit through a narrow hatch. Here, he narrates and explains the moments of man's first steps on the moon.*

234

43

NORMAN MAILER

A Walk on the Moon

It was not until nine-forty at night, Houston time, that they got   1
the hatch open at last. In the heat of running almost two hours late,
ensconced in the armor of a man-sized spaceship, could they still have
felt an instant of awe as they looked out that open hatch at a panorama
of theater: the sky is black, but the ground is brightly lit, bright as
footlights on the floor of a dark theater. A black and midnight sky, yet
on the moon ground, "you could almost go out in your shirt-sleeves
and get a suntan," Aldrin would say. "I remember thinking, 'Gee, if I
didn't know where I was, I could believe that somebody had created
this environment somewhere out in the West and given us another
simulation to work in.'" Everywhere on that pitted flat were shadows
dark as the sky above, shadows dark as mine shafts.

What a struggle to push out from that congested cabin, now twice   2
congested in their bulky-wham suits, no feeling of obstacle against
their flesh, their sense of touch dead and numb, spaceman body
manipulated out into the moon world like an upright piano turned by
movers on the corner of the stairs.

"You're lined up on the platform. Put your left foot to the right a   3
little bit. Okay, that's good. Roll left."

Armstrong was finally on the porch. Could it be with any sense   4
of an alien atmosphere receiving the fifteen-layer encapsulations of
the pack and suit on his back? Slowly, he climbed down the ladder.
Archetypal, he must have felt, a boy descending the rungs in the wall
of an abandoned well, or was it Jack down the stalk? And there he was
on the bottom, on the footpad of the leg of the Lem, a metal plate

perhaps three feet across. Inches away was the soil of the moon. But first he jumped up again to the lowest rung of the ladder. A couple of hours later, at the end of the EVA, conceivably exhausted, the jump from the ground to the rung, three feet up, might be difficult in that stiff and heavy space suit, so he tested it now. "It takes," said Armstrong, "a pretty good little jump."

5   Now, with television working, and some fraction of the world peering at the murky image of this instant, poised between the end of one history and the beginning of another, he said quietly, "I'm at the foot of the ladder. The Lem footpads are only depressed in the surface about one or two inches, although the surface appears to be very very fine-grained as you get close to it. It's almost like a powder." One of Armstrong's rare confessions of uneasiness is focused later on this moment. "I don't recall any particular emotion or feeling other than a little caution, a desire to be sure it was safe to put my weight on that surface outside Eagle's footpad."

6   Did his foot tingle in the heavy lunar overshoe? "I'm going to step off the Lem now."

7   Did something in him shudder at the touch of the new ground? Or did he draw a sweet strength from the balls of his feet? Nobody was necessarily going ever to know.

8   "That's one small step for a man," said Armstrong, "one giant leap for mankind." He had joined the ranks of the forever quoted. Patrick Henry, Henry Stanley and Admiral Dewey moved over for him.

9   Now he was out there, one foot on the moon, then the other foot on the moon, the powder like velvet underfoot. With one hand still on the ladder, he comments, "The surface is fine and powdery. I can . . . I can pick it up loosely with my toe." And as he releases his catch, the grains fall back slowly to the soil, a fan of feathers gliding to the floor. "It does adhere in fine layers like powdered charcoal to the sole and sides of my boots. I only go in a small fraction of an inch. Maybe an eighth of an inch. But I can see the footprints of my boots and the treads in the fine sand particles."

10   Capcom: "Neil, this is Houston. We're copying."

11   Yes, they would copy. He was like a man who goes into a wrecked building to defuse a new kind of bomb. He talks into a microphone as he works, for if a mistake is made, and the bomb goes off, it will be easier for the next man if every detail of his activities has been mentioned as he performed them. Now, he released his grip on the

ladder and pushed off for a few steps on the moon, odd loping steps, almost thrust into motion like a horse trotting up a steep slope. It could have been a moment equivalent to the first steps he took as an infant for there was nothing to hold onto and he did not dare to fall — the ground was too hot, the rocks might tear his suit. Yet if he stumbled, he could easily go over for he could not raise his arms above his head nor reach to his knees, his arms in the pressure bladder stood out before him like sausages; so, if he tottered, the weight of the pack could twist him around, or drop him. They had tried to shape up simulations of lunar gravity while weighted in scuba suits at the bottom of a pool, but water was not a vacuum through which to move; so they had also flown in planes carrying two hundred pounds of equipment on their backs. The pilot would take the plane through a parabolic trajectory. There would be a period of twenty-two seconds at the top of the curve when a simulation of one-sixth gravity would be present, and the two hundred pounds of equipment would weigh no more than on the moon, no more than thirty-plus pounds, and one could take loping steps down the aisle of the plane, staggering through unforeseen wobbles or turbulence. Then the parabolic trajectory was done, the plane was diving, and it would have to pull out of the dive. That created the reverse of one-sixth gravity — it multiplied gravity by two and a half times. The two hundred pounds of equipment now weighed five hundred pounds and the astronauts had to be supported by other men straining to help them bear the weight. So simulations gave them time for hardly more than a clue before heavy punishment was upon them. But now he was out in the open endless lunar gravity, his body and the reflexes of his life obliged to adopt a new rhythm and schedule of effort, a new disclosure of grace.

Still, he seemed pleased after the first few steps. "There seems to be no difficulty in moving around as we suspected. It's even perhaps easier than the simulations . . ." He would run a few steps and stop, run a few steps and stop. Perhaps it was not unlike directing the Lem when it hovered over the ground. One moved faster than on earth and with less effort, but it was harder to stop — one had to pick the place to halt from several yards ahead. Yes, it was easier once moving, but awkward at the beginning and the end because of the obdurate plastic bendings of the suit. And once standing at rest, the sense of the vertical was sly. One could be leaning further forward than one knew. Or leaning backward. Like a needle on a dial one would have to oscillate from side to side of the vertical to find position. Conceivably the sensation was not unlike skiing with a child on one's back.

13   It was time for Aldrin to descend the ladder from the Lem to the ground, and Armstrong's turn to give directions: "The shoes are about to come over the sill. Okay, now drop your PLSS down. There you go. You're clear. . . . About an inch clearance on top of your PLSS."

14   Aldrin spoke for future astronauts: "Okay, you need a little bit of arching of the back to come down . . ."

15   When he reached the ground, Aldrin took a big and exuberant leap up the ladder again, as if to taste the pleasures of one-sixth gravity all at once. "Beautiful, beautiful," he exclaimed.

16   Armstrong: "Isn't that something. Magnificent sight out here."

17   Aldrin: "Magnificent desolation."

18   They were looking at a terrain which lived in a clarity of focus unlike anything they had ever seen on earth. There was no air, of course, and so no wind, nor clouds, nor dust, nor even the finest scattering of light from the smallest dispersal of microscopic particles on a clear day on earth, no, nothing visible or invisible moved in the vacuum before them. All light was pure. No haze was present, not even the invisible haze of the finest day — therefore objects did not go out of focus as they receded into the distance. If one's eyes were good enough, an object at a hundred yards was as distinct as a rock at a few feet. And their eyes were good enough. Just as one could not determine one's altitude above the moon, not from fifty miles up nor five, so now along the ground before them no distance was real, for all distances had the faculty to appear equally near if one peered at them through blinders and could not see the intervening details. Again the sense of being on a stage or on the lighted floor of a room so large one could not see where the dark ceiling began must have come upon them, for there were no hints of gathering evanescence in ridge beyond ridge; rather each outline was as severe as the one in front of it, and since the ground was filled with small craters of every size, from antholes to potholes to empty pools, and the horizon was near, four times nearer than on earth and sharp as the line drawn by a pencil, the moon ground seemed to slope and drop in all directions "like swimming in an ocean with six-foot or eight-foot swells and waves," Armstrong said later. "In that condition, you never can see very far away from where you are." But what they could see, they could see entirely — to the depth of their field of view at any instant their focus was complete. And as they swayed from side to side, so a sense of the vertical kept eluding them, the slopes of the craters about them seeming to tilt a few degrees to one side of the horizontal, then the other. On earth, one had only to incline one's body an inch or two and a sense of the

vertical was gone, but on the moon they could lean over, then further over, lean considerably further over without beginning to fall. So verticals slid and oscillated. Rolling from side to side, they could as well have been on water, indeed their sense of the vertical was probably equal to the subtle uncertainty of the body when a ship is rolling on a quiet sea. "I say," said Aldrin, "the rocks are rather slippery."

They were discovering the powder of the moon soil was curious 19 indeed, comparable in firmness and traction to some matter between sand and snow. While the Lem looked light as a kite, for its pads hardly rested on the ground and it appeared ready to lift off and blow away, yet their own feet sometimes sank for two or three inches into the soft powder on the slope of very small craters, and their soles would slip as the powder gave way under their boots. In other places the ground was firm and harder than sand, yet all of these variations were to be found in an area not a hundred feet out from the legs of the Lem. As he explored his footing, Aldrin sent back comments to Mission Control, reporting in the rapt professional tones of a coach instructing his team on the conditions of the turf in a new plastic football field.

Meanwhile Armstrong was transporting the television camera 20 away from the Lem to a position where it could cover most of their activities. Once properly installed, he revolved it through a full panorama of their view in order that audiences on earth might have a clue to what he saw. But in fact the transmission was too rudimentary to give any sense of what was about them, that desert sea of rocks, rubble, small boulders, and crater lips.

Aldrin was now working to set up the solar wind experiment, a 21 sheet of aluminum foil hung on a stand. For the next hour and a half, the foil would be exposed to the solar wind, an invisible, unfelt, but high-velocity flow of noble gases from the sun like argon, krypton, neon and helium. For the astronauts, it was the simplest of procedures, no more difficult than setting up a piece of sheet music on a music stand. At the end of the EVA, however, the aluminum foil would be rolled up, inserted in the rock box, and delivered eventually to a laboratory in Switzerland uniquely equipped for the purpose. There any noble gases which had been trapped in the atomic lattice of the aluminum would be baked out in virtuoso procedures of quantitative analysis, and a closer knowledge of the components of the solar wind would be gained. Since the solar wind, it may be recalled, was diverted by the magnetosphere away from the earth it had not hitherto been available for casual study.

That was the simplest experiment to set up; the other two would 22 be deployed about an hour later. One was a passive seismometer to measure erratic disturbances and any periodic vibrations, as well as moonquakes, and the impact of meteors in the weeks and months to follow; it was equipped to radio this information to earth, the energy for transmission derived from solar panels which extended out to either side, and thereby gave it the look of one of those spaceships of the future with thin extended paperlike wings which one sees in science fiction drawings. In any case it was so sensitive that the steps of the astronauts were recorded as they walked by. Finally there was a Laser Ranging Retro-Reflector, an LRRR (or LRQ, or L R-cubed), and that was a mirror whose face was a hundred quartz crystals, black as coal, cut to a precision never obtained before in glass — one-third of an arc/sec. Since each quartz crystal was a corner of a rectangle, any ray of light striking one of the three faces in each crystal would bounce off the other two in such a way that the light would return in exactly the same direction it had been received. A laser beam sent up from earth would therefore reflect back to the place from which it was sent. The time it required to travel this half-million miles from earth to moon round trip, a journey of less than three seconds, could be measured so accurately that physicists might then discern whether the moon was drifting away from the earth a few centimeters a year, or (by using two lasers) whether Europe and America might be drifting apart some comparable distance, or even if the Pacific Ocean were contracting. These measurements could then be entered into the caverns of Einstein's General Theory of Relativity, and new proof or disproof of the great thesis could be obtained.

23 We may be certain the equipment was remarkable. Still, its packaging and its ease of deployment had probably done as much to advance its presence on the ship as any clear priority over other scientific equipment; the beauty of these items from the point of view of NASA was that the astronauts could set them up in a few minutes while working in their space suits, even set them up with inflated gloves so insensitive that special silicone pads had to be inserted at the fingertips in order to leave the astronauts not altogether numb-fingered in their manipulations. Yet these marvels of measurement would soon be installed on the moon with less effort than it takes to remove a vacuum cleaner from its carton and get it operating.

24 It was at this point that patriotism, the corporation, and the national taste all came to occupy the same head of a pin, for the astronauts next proceeded to set up the flag. But that operation, as always, presented its exquisite problems. There was, we remind our-

selves, no atmosphere for the flag to wave in. Any flag made of cloth would droop, indeed it would dangle. Therefore, a species of starched plastic flag had to be employed, a flag which would stand out, there, out to the nonexistent breeze, flat as a slab of plywood. No, that would not do either. The flag was better crinkled and curled. Waves and billows were bent into it, and a full corkscrew of a curl at the end. There it stands for posterity, photographed in the twists of a high gale on the windless moon, curled up tin flag, numb as a pickled pepper.

Aldrin would hardly agree. "Being able to salute that flag was one   25
of the more humble yet proud experiences I've ever had. To be able to look at the American flag and know how much so many people had put of themselves and their work into getting it where it was. We sensed — we really did — this almost mystical identification of all the people in the world at that instant."

Two minutes after the flag was up, the President of the United   26
States put in his phone call. Let us listen one more time:

"Because of what you have done," said Nixon, "the heavens have   27
become a part of man's world. And as you talk to us from the Sea of Tranquility, it inspires us to redouble our efforts to bring peace and tranquility to earth . . ."

"Thank you, Mr. President. It's a great honor and privilege for us   28
to be here representing not only the United States, but men of peace of all nations . . ."

In such piety is the schizophrenia of the ages.   29

Immediately afterward, Aldrin practiced kicking moon dust, but   30
he was somewhat broken up. Either reception was garbled, or Aldrin was temporarily incoherent. "They seem to leave," he said to the Capcom, referring to the particles, "and most of them have about the same angle of departure and velocity. From where I stand, a large portion of them will impact at a certain distance out. Several — the percentage is, of course, that will impact . . ."

Capcom: "Buzz, this is Houston. You're cutting out on the end   31
of your transmissions. Can you speak a little more forward into your microphone. Over."

Aldrin: "Roger, I'll try that."   32

Capcom: "Beautiful."   33

Aldrin: "Now I had that one inside my mouth that time."   34

Capcom: "It sounded a little wet."   35

And on earth, a handful of young scientists were screaming,   36
"Stop wasting time with flags and presidents — collect some rocks!"

____ CONSIDERATIONS _____

1. Mailer's task — to narrate what the moon-walkers experienced — is complicated by the necessity to describe technical operations, equipment, and navigational procedures. Is Mailer successful in keeping human experience uppermost? Explain.

2. Look closely at Mailer's account of setting up the American flag on the moon and at the remarks immediately following by Aldrin, President Nixon, and Mailer himself. "In such piety is the schizophrenia of the ages," says Mailer. Is this straight reporting? Is it loaded? If so, can you justify it?

3. What are some differences between the astronauts' moon exploration and the travels of others in this book, such as Lillian Hellman (pages 178–185) and Mary Austin (pages 27–31)?

4. "If it were spelled 'mune,' " wrote Jack Spicer, the American poet, "it would not cause madness." The moon has been surrounded by worlds of mythology, superstition, and fond fantasy. Will exact information about the moon affect our way of thinking of or responding to "moon"? Does knowledge affect belief?

5. A man in Houston tells a man on the moon when to put his left foot down. Discuss the remote control feature in moon explorations. Are there parallels in medicine, or oceanographic research, or electronic games?

Andrew Marvell (1621–1678) lived during a time of turmoil in England — during Cromwell's revolution, the beheading of a king, and the restoration of the monarchy. He was a political man, a member of Parliament, and at different times espoused different sides, without ever turning hypocrite. Some of his poems are political; the best are not, unless "To His Coy Mistress" is a manifesto of sexual politics. Many readers find it less concerned with sexuality than with mortality.

44

ANDREW MARVELL

To His Coy Mistress

Had we but world enough, and time,
This coyness, lady, were no crime.
We would sit down, and think which way
To walk, and pass our long love's day.
Thou by the Indian Ganges' side   5
Shouldst rubies find; I by the tide
Of Humber would complain. I would
Love you ten years before the flood,
And you should, if you please, refuse
Till the conversion of the Jews.   10
My vegetable love should grow
Vaster than empires and more slow;
An hundred years should go to praise
Thine eyes, and on thy forehead gaze;
Two hundred to adore each breast,   15
But thirty thousand to the rest;
An age at least to every part,
And the last age should show your heart.

    For, lady, you deserve this state,
20 Nor would I love at lower rate
        But at my back I always hear
    Time's wingéd chariot hurrying near;
    And yonder all before us lie
    Deserts of vast eternity.
25 Thy beauty shall no more be found;
    Nor, in thy marble vault, shall sound
    My echoing song; then worms shall try
    That long-preserved virginity,
    And your quaint honor turn to dust,
30 And into ashes all my lust:
    The grave's a fine and private place,
    But none, I think, do there embrace.
        Now therefore, while the youthful hue
    Sits on thy skin like morning dew,
35 And while thy willing soul transpires
    At every pore with instant fires,
    Now let us sport us while we may,
    And now, like amorous birds of prey,
    Rather at once our time devour
40 Than languish in his slow-chapped° power.
    Let us roll all our strength and all
    Our sweetness up into one ball,
    And tear our pleasures with rough strife
    Thorough the iron gates of life:
45 Thus, though we cannot make our sun
    Stand still, yet we will make him run.

° slow-jawed.

H. L. Mencken (1880–1956), the dominant editor of his day, edited the magazines Smart Set *and* American Mercury, *and wrote funny, intelligent, cantankerous, irascible, mocking essays about American political, artistic, and social mores. He collected the best of his periodical writing in six books of* Prejudices *(1919, 1920, 1922, 1924, 1926, 1927) and in* A Book of Prefaces *(1917). (See Richard Wright's reminiscence of reading Mencken, on pages 245–248.) His* The American Language *(1919) and its two* Supplements *(1945, 1948) looked at the difference between American and English, and argued the vitality of the American language. Later in life he wrote an autobiography in three volumes,* Happy Days *(1940),* Newspaper Days *(1941) and* Heathen Days *(1943).*

"Gamalielese" shows Mencken's talents as a social critic, as a debunker of popular idiocy. It also demonstrates his tight observation of the American language, and his humor. Warren Gamaliel Harding was twenty-ninth president of the United States. On the question of President Harding's intellectual qualifications for office, history has been as unkind as Harding's contemporary.

45

H. L. MENCKEN
Gamalielese

On the question of the logical content of Dr. Harding's harangue of last Friday I do not presume to have views. The matter has been debated at great length by the editorial writers of the Republic, all of them experts in logic; moreover, I confess to being prejudiced. When a man arises publicly to argue that the United States entered the late

From the *Baltimore Sun*, March 7, 1921. Reprinted by permission of the *Baltimore Sun*.

war because of a "concern for preserved civilization," I can only snicker in a superior way and wonder why he isn't holding down the chair of history in some American university. When he says that the U.S. has "never sought territorial aggrandizement through force," the snicker rises to the virulence of a chuckle, and I turn to the first volume of General Grant's memoirs. And when, gaining momentum, he gravely informs the boobery that "ours is a constitutional freedom where the popular will is supreme, and minorities are sacredly protected," then I abandon myself to a mirth that transcends, perhaps, the seemly, and send picture postcards of A. Mitchell Palmer.[1] and the Atlanta Penitentiary to all of my enemies who happen to be Socialists.

2   But when it comes to the style of a great man's discourse, I can speak with a great deal less prejudice, and maybe with somewhat more competence, for I have earned most of my livelihood for twenty years past by translating the bad English of a multitude of authors into measurably better English. Thus qualified professionally, I rise to pay my small tribute to Dr. Harding. Setting aside a college professor or two and half a dozen dipsomaniacal newspaper reporters, he takes the first place in my Valhall of literati. That is to say, he writes the worst English that I have ever encountered. It reminds me of a string of wet sponges; it reminds me of tattered washing on the line; it reminds me of a stale bean-soup, of college yells, of dogs barking idiotically through endless nights. It is so bad that a sort of grandeur creeps into it. It drags itself out of the dark abysm (I was about to write abscess!) of pish, and crawls insanely up the topmost pinnacle of posh. It is rumble and bumble. It is flap and doodle. It is balder and dash.

3   But I grow lyrical. More scientifically, what is the matter with it? Why does it seem so flabby, so banal, so confused and childish, so stupidly at war with sense? If you first read the inaugural address and then hear it intoned, as I did (at least in part), then you will perhaps arrive at an answer. That answer is very simple. When Dr. Harding prepares a speech he does not think it out in terms of an educated reader locked up in jail, but in terms of a great horde of stoneheads gathered around a stand. That is to say, the thing is always a stump speech; it is conceived as a stump speech and written as a stump speech. More, it is a stump speech addressed primarily to the sort of audience that the speaker has been used to all his life, to wit, an audience of small town yokels, of low political serfs, of morons

---

[1] Seventh U.S. attorney general, who ordered arrests in the red scare of 1919 and 1920. — ED.

scarcely able to understand a word of more than two syllables, and wholly unable to pursue a logical idea for more than two centimeters.

Such imbeciles do not want ideas — that is, new ideas, ideas that 4 are unfamiliar, ideas that challenge their attention. What they want is simply a gaudy series of platitudes, of threadbare phrases terrifically repeated, of sonorous nonsense driven home with gestures. As I say, they can't understand many words of more than two syllables, but that is not saying that they do not esteem such words. On the contrary, they like them and demand them. The roll of incomprehensible polysyllables enchants them. They like phrases which thunder like salvos of artillery. Let that thunder sound, and they take all the rest on trust. If a sentence begins furiously and then peters out into fatuity, they are still satisfied. If a phrase has a punch in it, they do not ask that it also have a meaning. If a word slides off the tongue like a ship going down the ways, they are content and applaud it and wait for the next.

Brought up amid such hinds, trained by long practice to engage 5 and delight them, Dr. Harding carries over his stump manner into everything he writes. He is, perhaps, too old to learn a better way. He is, more likely, too discreet to experiment. The stump speech, put into cold type, maketh the judicious to grieve. But roared from an actual stump, with arms flying and eyes flashing and the old flag overhead, it is certainly and brilliantly effective. Read the inaugural address, and it will gag you. But hear it recited though a sound-magnifier, with grand gestures to ram home its periods, and you will begin to understand it.

Let us turn to a specific example. I exhume a sentence from the 6 latter half of the eminent orator's discourse:

"I would like government to do all it can to mitigate; then, in 7 understanding, in mutuality of interest, in concern for the common good, our tasks will be solved."

I assume that you have read it. I also assume that you set it down 8 as idiotic — a series of words without sense. You are quite right; it is. But now imagine it intoned as it was designed to be intoned. Imagine the slow tempo of a public speech. Imagine the stately unrolling of the first clause, the delicate pause upon the word "then" — and then the loud discharge of the phrases "in understanding," "in mutuality of interest," "in concern for the common good," each with its attendant glare and roll of the eyes, each with its sublime heave, each with its gesture of a blacksmith bringing down his sledge upon an egg — imagine all this, and then ask yourself where you have got. You have got, in brief, to a point where you don't know what it is all about. You hear and applaud the phrases, but their connection has already escaped you. And so, when in violation of all sequence and logic, the final phrase, "our tasks will be solved," assaults you, you do not notice its disharmony — all you notice is that, if this or that, already forgotten, is done, "our tasks will be solved." Whereupon, glad of the assurance and thrilled by the vast gestures that drive it home, you give a cheer.

9   That is, if you are the sort of man who goes to political meetings, which is to say, if you are the sort of man that Dr. Harding is used to talking to, which is to say, if you are a jackass.

10   The whole inaugural address reeked with just such nonsense. The thing started off with an error in English in its very first sentence — the confusion of pronouns in the *one-he* combination, so beloved of bad newspaper reporters. It bristled with words misused: *civic* for *civil, luring* for *alluring, womanhood* for *women, referendum* for *reference,* even *task* for *problem.* "The *task* is to be *solved*" — what could be worse? Yet I find it twice. "The expressed views of world opinion" — what irritating tautology! "The expressed conscience of progress" — what on earth does it mean? "This is not selfishness, it is sanctity" — what intelligible idea do you get out of that? "I know that Congress and the administration will favor every wise government policy to aid the resumption and encourage continued progress" — the resumption of what? "Service is the supreme *commitment* of life — *ach, du heiliger!*

11   But is such bosh out of place in a stump speech? Obviously not. It is precisely and thoroughly in place in a stump speech. A tight fabric of ideas would weary and exasperate the audience; what it wants is simply a loud burble of words, a procession of phrases that roar, a series of whoops. This is what it got in the inaugural address of the Hon. Warren Gamaliel Harding. And this is what it will get for four long years — unless God sends a miracle and the corruptible puts on incorruption . . . Almost I long for the sweeter song, the rubber-stamps of more familiar design, the gentler and more seemly bosh of the late Woodrow.

___ **CONSIDERATIONS** _____

1. In his first sentence, Mencken denies having opinions about "the logical content" in Harding's address, promising instead to concentrate on Harding's style. How successful is he in avoiding comment on the content of the Harding speech? What is the relationship between content and style?

2. Can you find two or three phrases that suggest Mencken's irony? What do his ironic twists and turns contribute to his essay?

3. Mencken wrote his review of Harding's address at least twenty years before George Orwell published his "Politics and the English Language" (pages 293–307). Would Orwell applaud or criticize Mencken's treatment of the president?

4. Study the variety of Mencken's words, perhaps setting up two columns, one to list words like "pish" and "posh," and the other for words or phrases like "incomprehensible polysyllables." Do such extremes of diction confuse the reader, enliven the writer's argument, both, or neither?

5. Is Mencken himself guilty of any sins that he attributes to Harding? Explain, with examples.

6. How does Mencken's style support his opinionated view of politicians and political language?

Alice Morgan (b. 1940) took her Ph.D. in English at Harvard, where she later taught expository writing. The notions expressed in this brief article first occurred to her, as we might expect, when she was an undergraduate facing final exams.

46

ALICE B. MORGAN
Exam-Week Unrealities

1   It has long been acceptable to criticize colleges as ivory towers, sheltered from life's harsher realities. To some this is the best thing about college, however, and it is never more evident than during the last days of a course. The very concept of a course enforces the idea: the student isolates one area of study, temporarily, from the rest, commences learning in that area, and finally concludes the process. Both he and the instructor know that subjects are immutably entangled with each other, and that learning does not start and stop on key dates in the academic calendar. Yet a course's conclusion has a gratifying unreality, offering us an option we so rarely have elsewhere — a clean break. If we choose, we can cease to think about this subject, cease to confront this teacher, cease to talk with or even to see the other students in the class. We can end the whole experience, leaving behind only the relatively trivial residue of the grade.

2   How exceptional this is! What a contrast to the usual messy durability of our ideas, our obsessions! As we grow older, we come to recognize that most experiences are hard to conclude, and that they leave behind untidy, unwieldy, and unwanted effects. People do not disappear comfortably; we must repel them, or they must abandon us.

No relationship has so natural an end as that between student and teacher, or between students in the same course. This is not to say that no such relationship can continue, or that knowledge should be forgotten or thinking suspended because a course is over. That, we must hope, rarely happens. The marvelous thing is that it can happen, if that is what we want. In this artificial world of thought and experience, we can close the books, without insult or offense, for good and all.

——— CONSIDERATIONS ———————————————

1. Morgan says that both student and instructor "know that subjects are immutably entangled with each other." Is that your experience? Or are you surprised when you notice that separate courses are interconnected? Write a short essay on the relationship between two courses of interest to you — say, art history and gymnastics, or history and biology, or French and logic.

2. Much of the success of Morgan's mini-essay depends upon the ability of the student to infer much meaning from relatively spare statements — not unlike what has to happen when one reads a poem. Write out two or three inferences that you are able to draw from highly compressed lines in Morgan's essay, and use those examples in a discussion on the joys and/or frustrations of reading such material.

3. Is Morgan's description of college life, "this artificial world of thought and experience," at all related to the common remark that school is a preparation for life? What's wrong — or right — with such a conception of the college years?

4. In what sense is Morgan's essay an argument? An exposition? If it is an argument, does she anticipate the points of her opponents?

Wright Morris (b. 1910) won the National Book Award in 1956 for his novel The Field of Vision, *and in 1981 the American Book Award for his novel* Plains Songs. *Altogether, he has published more than twenty volumes of prose, most of it fiction, most of it set in the Nebraska where he grew up. His most recent book is a memoir called* Solo *(1983).*

In much of his writing, Morris specializes in viewing things with the strange clarity of a Martian visitor. People have written about sports from a variety of points of view; rarely, we believe, have they kept their eye on the ball.

_47

WRIGHT MORRIS

Odd Balls

1   Most games that involve the use of a ball can be described, but seldom explained. Consider the ball itself.

2   We begin with the golf ball, white until soiled, hard as a rock, the surface uniformly pitted with mini-craters, in size about that of a meatball. This ball is stroked with a slender, wandlike shaft, about the length of a cane, the bottom end tipped with a blade, variously tilted, or a fistlike wooden knob. A mystical belief that the club, not the player, directs the ball, and the ball, not the player, determines its direction, is common among most players. With their needs in mind, a ball is promised that will correct the mistakes made by the club. A ball could more easily be drawn to the hole by a magnet, but the excitement generated among the spectators is based on the role in the game that chance plays. No thrill equals the sight of a peerless player missing a nine-inch putt. Golf balls not stroked are often given to

From *The Atlantic Monthly,* June 1978. Reprinted by permission of Russell & Volkening as agents of the author. Copyright © 1978 by Wright Morris.

babies, found in car seats, stored in raincoat pockets, or left where they can be stepped on.

Golf is played in the open, preferably on grass, over a course cunningly strewn with obstructions. Bunkers, sand traps, trees, streams, ponds, and spectators, along with rain, sleet, cold, and lightning, make the game of golf what it is. What it is was not known to many golfers until they saw the game on TV. The mock-ups used by the commentators made clear a fact that many golfers found puzzling. What they were doing was walking up and down, back and forth. Most ball games seem to have in common the going back and forth, rather than going anyplace.

The very smallness of the ball may substantially contribute to the high moral tone of the game. What is there to fight over? Each player has several balls of his own. Although equipped with sticks that would make good clubs, the golf player refrains from striking his opponents, making loud slurring remarks, or coughing or hissing when another player is putting. It is not at all unusual to hear another player described as a great gentleman.

In this game alone the opinion of an official is accepted in a depressed, sportsmanlike manner. The player does not scream and curse, as in baseball, or stage riots, as in football, but accepts without comment or demonstration the fickle finger of fate. Law and order prevail on the links, if viewed on prime time. The game was once played for the health of it, by amateurs (a term currently applied to unemployed track stars); now the lonely, single golfer is burdened with the knowledge that he does for nothing what others are paid for. This condition is technically described as a handicap.

Some players hit the ball and stand, dejected, waiting for it to land; others turn away and leave it up to the caddy. Some enjoy the pain they give to others, some like to torture themselves. Although the physical challenge is substantial — miles and miles of walking, hours of waiting, the possibility of heatstroke or of being stuck by lightning — the crucial element is mental. If not in a seizure of torment and self-doubt, the player must pass hole after hole daydreaming, or wondering why he has so many clubs to choose from. A loss of concentration on the easy holes will invariably cost him the hard ones. In summary we can say that the smallness of the ball is no measure of the effort it takes to stroke it or of the reward it brings.

Between the small golf ball and the palm-sized baseball is the billiard or pool ball. Even those ignorant of the game know what it is to be behind the eight ball. The game is played on an oblong table in a smoke-filled room, off bounds to growing boys and women. The ball is stroked with a long, tapering cue, first rolled on the table to see if the table is flat. If it is not flat, you use a warped cue. The way the chalk is applied to the cue's leather tip, and the green chalk dust is then blown from the fingers, distinguishes men from boys. Pocket billiards is best under lights hung low over the table, in such a manner that one sees only the hands of the players. If smoke conceals the balls, one can hear them rebound on the cushions, click when they collide, or drop into a pocket and rattle down the chute. Without billiards, small boys in YMCA lobbies would have had no cause to grow up and be men.

8   The game is rich in ceremony, symbolic objects, stroking, fondling, thrusting, chalking, cursing, shot-calling, with the dramatic dimness of light necessary to a monastic order. Once identified with masculine odors and pursuits, pool halls, YMCAs, vice dens, conclaves of sleeve-rolled toughs and ward politicians, brazenly sexist, the game will surely interest the new liberated woman. Billiard balls are also used to roll across tile floors, crush the skull of an opponent, or serve as a knob on the sportier type of gearshift. The meaning of being *in front* of the eight ball remains to be explored.

9   Once relatively rare, hidden away in drawers with flannel trousers, like a huge mothball, the snow-white, cotton-fuzzy tennis ball with the visible seams is now commonplace.

10   The aura of breeding and snobbery, so important to tennis, a game played and observed by royalty, is now on the wane as the masses have puzzled out the scoring system. If both players know how to keep score, it comes down to how to psych the opponent. This can be done by hissing at him openly, wearing unmatched socks, varying the bounce of the ball before serving, pretending to sulk, screaming at the linesmen, or delaying the game by blowing softly on the fingers of one hand. These strategies were poorly observed in the past but are now intimately revealed on the TV screen. Many players seem blinded by their own long hair, but this might well be tactical cunning.

11   Nor has tennis stood still, living in the shadow of bygone times and grass-stained balls; it has kept pace with the times with the introduction of the two-handed backhand. Theories vary, but anyone who has played the game badly has experienced the irresistible urge to club the ball with both hands. To everyone's surprise there was nothing in the rules to prevent it. Both ladies and gentlemen whack the ball in this manner, using racquets of wood and metal. Metal rackets are not new: they were used by players in the madcap twenties, one known to

me personally, the steel strings noted for their length of life and the fuzz they removed from the balls. In those days matches were observed by eight or ten girls, seated in Scripps-Booth roadsters, holding the players' sweaters and their racquet presses. Any player with a racquet *and* a press was sure to have a good girl.

In other ball games, the frenzy and enthusiasm of the spectators stimulates the player to greater efforts, but in tennis absolute silence testifies to the moments of crisis. The bong of the ball, the twang of the net cord, the voice of the umpire are all that is heard, unless one of the maverick hot-blooded types is involved in a dispute. This is well known to be bad for tennis, but great for higher receipts.   12

Team tennis, which may puzzle some observers, is for those who dislike tennis but like to bet on winners and identify with places.   13

The baseball is small enough to be thrown and caught by a boy but large enough to be seen from the bleachers by a grownup. The use of a round bat to hit a round ball testifies to native inventive genius. Balls were once made of the materials found under beds, and became lopsided when batted, or split at the seams. Official balls were once made of miles and miles of string wound into a tight ball and covered with horsehide. God knows what they use now. Sensible players are afraid to look.   14

The big games are played in cities that have a ball park. The field is shaped like a large wedge of pie, straight along the sides, curved at the back. There are official positions for nine players, but once the ball is batted they run about wildly. Collisions are common.   15

The rules of the game lull some into feeling that the object of the game is the scoring of runs. *Quelle bêtise!*[1] Observe how one player, crouched as in prayer, holds the bat across his knee in a ceremonial manner. He is calm and assured. His appointed task, surely, is to crouch and wait. Another walks to the box reserved for the batter, his manner both insolent and indecisive. He steps in, then he steps back, he soils his hands with dirt, then he wipes them, he looks to see if the bat is his own, or another's, if it has the proper length, heft, and roundness; if he is assured of all these points, he re-enters the box. With his spikes he paws his own hole to stand in; straddle-legged he threatens the pitcher with his bat. No words are spoken. Both know this is the moment of truth. See how the pitcher rubs, turns, fondles, and conceals the ball; see how he stoops for the resin, note how he discards it, fingers the bill of his cap, strokes away perspiration,   16

---

[1] What stupidity! — ED.

glances slantwise down his cheeks at a potential runner; how he begins and stops, how he delays and stares, how he may rudely turn his back on the batter, actions designed to arouse, to incite, to distract the man at the plate from hitting the ball. In spite of these precautions it sometimes happens, to the relief and consternation of the players. Some may have dozed off, or have thoughts on their minds.

17   There are players, as well as the idly curious, who ask why the game is called "the national pastime." For one thing, if nothing else, time *passes:* sometimes the better part of an afternoon or evening, if you allow two hours or more for the game and at least an hour getting to and from the ball park. In the old days games were called off because of darkness, but in the new days they might go on forever, under the lights. Somebody has to win. That's what it says in the rules.

18   The football is oval in shape, usually thrown in a spiral, and when kicked end over end may prove difficult to catch. If not caught on the fly it bounces around erratically.

19   The apparent intent of the game is to deposit the ball across the opponent's goal line. Any child with a ball of its own might do it, six days a week and most of Sunday morning, but the rules of the game specify it must be done with members of both teams present and on the field. Owing to large-scale substitutions this is often difficult.

20   In the old days people went crazy trying to follow the ball. The players still do, but the viewing public, who are watching the game on TV, can relax and wait for the replay. If anything happens, that's where you'll see it. The disentanglement of bodies on the goal line is one of the finer visual moments available to sports fans. The tight knot bursts open, the arms and legs miraculously return to the point of rest, before the ball was snapped. Some find it unsettling. Is this what it means to be born again?

21   All ball games feature hitting and socking, chopping and slicing, smashing, slamming, stroking, and whacking, but only in football are these blows diverted from the ball to the opponent. And the more the players are helped or carried from the field, the more attendance soars. This truly male game is also enjoyed by women who find group therapy less rewarding. The sacking of the passer by the front four is especially gratifying. Charges that a criminal element threatens the game are a characteristic, but hopeful, exaggeration. What to do with big, mean, boyish-hearted men, long accustomed to horsing around in good clean dormitories, unaccustomed to the rigors of life in the Alaska oilfields, was, until football, a serious national dilemma.

All games are peculiar, one to the other, and defy the comprehen- 22
sion of nonplayers, but none is so bizarre as the game of dunking the
ball through the basket. Until basketball, boys seven feet tall ran off
and hid in the woods or joined a circus. Now the woods are combed in
search of them. If they can dribble and dunk a ball, they've got it made.
Rules are rules, and all the rules say is that the ball has to enter the
basket at the top. The tall boys dunk it. There's nothing against it,
according to the rules.

It may surprise people to learn that basketball was once played 23
by normal, flat-chested boys who shot the ball with two hands. The
show-off who shot the ball with one hand was hooted off the court.
The first change in the game was the one-hand shooter, several known
to me personally. The next change in the game was the dunk shot.
The normal thing to do would be to raise the basket and let the seven-
foot boys mull around beneath it, but what is normal about basketball?
People who watch the game understand this problem, but people who
play it think they're normal. They think of six-foot, long-winded, flat-
chested boys as being handicapped.

The importance of drafting basketball players early is to keep 24
them from playing anything but soccer. If they want to play soccer
they have personal problems they need to work out. Most athletes
have nothing to fear but fear itself, and that's how they feel. When
they run off the field at the half, or between innings, some observers
have the feeling that they won't come back. Why should they, if it's
raining and they're losing? They come back, not because they are paid
to, as you might think, but because of what it says in the rules. Hard
and fast rules are hard to come by, as you may know. When a player
runs off the field and tries to hide in the shower room, he's a free man,
and that scares him. Whose side is he on? Where does he play? Without
his Bank of America or American Express card, who is going to recognize him? Most of the games people play just go on and on without
time-outs, vacations, or free ambulance service, but ball games have a
beginning and an ending. It says so in the rules. In case you've often
wondered, that may account for their strange appeal.

_____ **CONSIDERATIONS** _____

1. How far do you have to read before you suspect that Morris is not
taking his sports very seriously? What are the surest clues to his attitude?

2. What does Morris imply with the final clause of the third sentence of Paragraph 5? Why? How important are the implications to Morris's essay?

3. To what extent are ritual and ceremony important in sports? Collect the several comments Morris makes on this question, add your own observations, and state your conclusion.

4. How does Morris's article differ from McPhee's account of Bradley on the basketball court (pages 230–233)? Consider the difference in voice and tone, using specific examples of each in the two essays.

5. Which of the sports does Morris see as the most bizarre? Does he like one sport more than the others? Using the *Reader's Guide to Periodical Literature,* locate magazine articles on Morris and read them to find out whether he himself is a sportsman of any kind.

6. In what ways are the terms "sports," "recreation," and "play" synonymous? How are they different? If an amateur becomes a professional, must he then call his activity work? How do you distinguish between play and work? Or do you see them as part of the same thing?

Anaïs Nin (1903–1977) was born in Paris. When her father, a Spanish musician and composer, left her mother in 1914, the family sailed to New York. She adored her father and began a diary addressed to him, hoping that some day she would send it to him, and by its excellence win his approval. She continued writing the diary — more than sixty-five volumes — throughout her life. At the age of fifteen she began to support her mother and her brothers, first as a model, and later as a Spanish dancer. For decades her writings were unpublished but attained a reputation among other writers, who read portions privately. She was a friend and confidant of Henry Miller, author of Tropic of Cancer *and other novels. In 1939 she printed her novel* Winter of Artifice *herself, on a foot-powered printing press, and won more readers among a small but powerful elite. Later in the forties, a New York publisher attempted to distribute several of her novels, but without commercial success. In the 1960s, the Swallow Press reissued her novels, and her reputation widened. The publication of her diaries, in seven volumes, greatly increased her audience.*

Many of the entries in the diaries of Anaïs Nin mean little detached from the body of the text, so closely related are the references. Here we print a brief excerpt about her premature delivery of a dead child. It begins in the hospital delivery room after four difficult hours of labor. Images with the fantastic intensity of dream ("Will the ice come . . . ? At the end of the dark tunnel, a knife gleams") are common in Anaïs Nin's writing.

48

ANAÏS NIN

Journal Entry

1   The nurses begin to talk again. I say, "Let me alone." I place my two hands on my stomach and very slowly, very softly, with the tips of my fingers I drum, drum, drum on my stomach, in circles. Round and round, softly, with eyes open in great serenity. The doctor comes near and looks with amazement. The nurses are silent. Drum drum drum drum drum in soft circles, in soft quiet circles. "Like a savage," they whisper. The mystery.

2   Eyes open, nerves quiet, I drum gently on my stomach for a long while. The nurses begin to quiver. A mysterious agitation runs through them. I hear the ticking of the clock. It ticks inexorably, separately. The little nerves awaken, stir. I say, "I can push now!" and I push violently. They are shouting, "A little more! Just a little more!"

3   Will the ice come, and the darkness, before I am through? At the end of the dark tunnel, a knife gleams. I hear the clock and my heart. I say, "Stop!" The doctor holds the instrument, and he is leaning over. I sit up and shout at him. He is afraid again. "Let me alone, all of you!"

4   I lie back so quietly. I hear the ticking. Softly I drum, drum, drum. I feel my womb stirring, dilating. My hands are so weary, they will fall off. They will fall off, and I will lie there in darkness. The womb is stirring and dilating. Drum drum drum drum drum. "I am ready!" The nurse puts her knee on my stomach. There is blood in my eyes. A tunnel. I push into this tunnel. I bite my lips and push. There is fire, flesh ripping and no air. Out of the tunnel! All my blood is spilling out. "Push! Push! It is coming! It is coming!" I feel the slipperiness, the sudden deliverance, the weight is gone. Darkness.

I hear voices. I open my eyes. I hear them saying, "It was a little   5
girl. Better not show it to her." All my strength is coming back. I sit
up. The doctor shouts, "For God's sake, don't sit up, don't move!"

"Show me the child," I say.   6

"Don't show it," says the nurse, "it will be bad for her."   7

The nurses try to make me lie down. My heart is beating so   8
loudly I can hardly hear myself repeating, "Show it to me!" The doctor
holds it up. It looks dark, and small, like a diminutive man. But it is a
little girl. It has long eyelashes on its closed eyes, it is perfectly made,
and all glistening with the waters of the womb. It was like a doll, or
like a miniature Indian, about one foot long, skin on bones, no flesh.
But completely formed. The doctor told me afterwards that it had
hands and feet exactly like mine. The head was bigger than average.
As I looked at the dead child, for a moment I hated it for all the pain
it had caused me, and it was only later that this flare of anger turned
into great sadness.

——— CONSIDERATIONS ———

1. A surprisingly little-used grammatical technique adds to the tension
of the narrative. What is it? How does it add to the drama? Why is it so rarely
used by writers?

2. "At the end of the dark tunnel, a knife gleams." What tunnel?

3. In the first paragraph, Nin describes herself as serene; in the third, "I
sit up and shout at him." How do you account for this apparent contradiction?

4. Notice how repetition raises suspense in this short narrative. How
does Nin adapt her style to make the most of the repetition in the fourth
paragraph? Do you hear that repetition echoed in Paragraph 5?

5. Take a dramatic moment from your own experience and write a short
account of it, imitating Nin's style.

6. How might those either for or against natural childbirth methods
make use of Nin's experience?

Flannery O'Connor (1925–1964) was born in Savannah, and moved with her family to her mother's birthplace, Milledgeville, Georgia, when she was twelve years old. When she was fifteen her father died of the inherited degenerative disease, lupus. She took her B.A. at Milledgeville's Georgia State College for Women (now Georgia College) and then studied the writing of fiction at the University of Iowa. From 1947 until 1951 she moved among New York, Connecticut, and Georgia. When she discovered that she was ill, she returned to live with her mother on the Milledgeville farm called Andalusia, surrounded by pet peacocks and peahens, writing her remarkable fiction and staying in touch with friends by letter. She died of lupus when she was thirty-eight.

Flannery O'Connor wrote essays also, collected after her death in a volume called Mystery and Manners *(1969). This essay appeared in the* Georgia Bulletin *in 1963, addressed to local and immediate problems; in the American eighties its insights remain urgent, as our culture, in O'Connor's word, becomes increasingly "fractured."*

49

FLANNERY O'CONNOR
The Total Effect
and the Eighth Grade

In two recent instances in Georgia, parents have objected to their 1
eighth- and ninth-grade children's reading assignments in modern fiction. This seems to happen with some regularity in cases throughout
the country. The unwitting parent picks up his child's book, glances
through it, comes upon passages of erotic detail or profanity, and takes
off at once to complain to the school board. Sometimes, as in one of
the Georgia cases, the teacher is dismissed and hackles rise in liberal
circles everywhere.

The two cases in Georgia, which involved Steinbeck's *East of* 2
Eden and John Hersey's *A Bell for Adano*, provoked considerable
newspaper comment. One columnist, in commending the enterprise
of the teachers, announced that students do not like to read the fusty
works of the nineteenth century, that their attention can best be held
by novels dealing with the realities of our own time, and that the
Bible, too, is fully of racy stories.

Mr. Hersey himself addressed a letter to the State School Super- 3
intendent in behalf of the teacher who had been dismissed. He pointed
out that his book is not scandalous, that it attempts to convey an
earnest message about the nature of democracy, and that it falls well
within the limits of the principle of "total effect," that principle fol-

lowed in legal cases by which a book is judged not for isolated parts but by the final effect of the whole book upon the general reader.

4   I do not want to comment on the merits of these particular cases. What concerns me is what novels ought to be assigned in the eighth and ninth grades as a matter of course, for if these cases indicate anything, they indicate the haphazard way in which fiction is approached in our high schools. Presumably there is a state reading list which contains "safe" books for teachers to assign; after that it is up to the teacher.

5   English teachers come in Good, Bad, and Indifferent, but too frequently in high schools anyone who can speak English is allowed to teach it. Since several novels can't easily be gathered into one textbook, the fiction that students are assigned depends upon their teacher's knowledge, ability, and taste: variable factors at best. More often than not, the teacher assigns what he thinks will hold the attention and interest of the students. Modern fiction will certainly hold it.

6   Ours is the first age in history which has asked the child what he would tolerate learning, but that is a part of the problem with which I am not equipped to deal. The devil of Educationism that possesses us is the kind that can be "cast out only by prayer and fasting." No one has yet come along strong enough to do it. In other ages the attention of children was held by Homer and Virgil, among others, but, by the reverse evolutionary process, that is no longer possible; our children are too stupid now to enter the past imaginatively. No one asks the student if algebra pleases him or if he finds it satisfactory that some French verbs are irregular, but if he prefers Hersey to Hawthorne, his taste must prevail.

7   I would like to put forward the proposition, repugnant to most English teachers, that fiction, if it is going to be taught in the high schools, should be taught as a subject and as a subject with a history. The total effect of a novel depends not only on its innate impact, but upon the experience, literary and otherwise, with which it is approached. No child needs to be assigned Hersey or Steinbeck until he is familiar with a certain amount of the best work of Cooper, Hawthorne, Melville, the early James, and Crane, and he does not need to be assigned these until he has been introduced to some of the better English novelists of the eighteenth and nineteenth centuries.

8   The fact that these works do not present him with the realities of his own time is all to the good. He is surrounded by the realities of his own time, and he has no perspective whatever from which to view them. Like the college student who wrote in her paper on Lincoln that

he went to the movies and got shot, many students go to college unaware that the world was not made yesterday; their studies began with the present and dipped backward occasionally when it seemed necessary or unavoidable.

There is much to be enjoyed in the great British novels of the   9 nineteenth century, much that a good teacher can open up in them for the young student. There is no reason why these novels should be either too simple or too difficult for the eighth grade. For the simple, they offer simple pleasures; for the more precocious, they can be made to yield subtler ones if the teacher is up to it. Let the student discover, after reading the nineteenth-century British novel, that the nineteenth-century American novel is quite different as to its literary characteristics, and he will thereby learn something not only about these individual works but about the sea-change which a new historical situation can effect in a literary form. Let him come to modern fiction with this experience behind him, and he will be better able to see and to deal with the more complicated demands of the best twentieth-century fiction.

Modern fiction often looks simpler than the fiction that preceded   10 it, but in reality is more complex. A natural evolution has taken place. The author has for the most part absented himself from direct participation in the work and has left the reader to make his own way amid experiences dramatically rendered and symbolically ordered. The modern novelist merges the reader in experience; he tends to raise the passions he touches upon. If he is a good novelist, he raises them to effect by their order and clarity a new experience — the total effect — which is not in itself sensuous or simply of the moment. Unless the child has had some literary experience before, he is not going to be able to resolve the immediate passions the book arouses into any true, total picture.

It is here the moral problem will arise. It is one thing for a child   11 to read about adultery in the Bible or in *Anna Karenina,* and quite another for him to read about it in most modern fiction. This is not only because in both the former instances adultery is considered a sin, and in the latter, at most, an inconvenience, but because modern writing involves the reader in the action with a new degree of intensity, and literary mores now permit him to be involved in any action a human being can perform.

In our fractured culture, we cannot agree on morals; we cannot   12 even agree that moral matters should come before literary ones when there is a conflict between them. All this is another reason why the high schools would do well to return to their proper business of preparing foundations. Whether in the senior year students should be assigned modern novelists should depend both on their parents' consent and on what they have already read and understood.

13   The high-school English teacher will be fulfilling his responsibility if he furnishes the student a guided opportunity, through the best writing of the past, to come, in time, to an understanding of the best writing of the present. He will teach literature, not social studies or little lessons in democracy or the customs of many lands.

14   And if the student finds that this is not to his taste? Well, that is regrettable. Most regrettable. His taste should not be consulted; it is being formed.

———— CONSIDERATIONS ————

1. How far must you read in O'Connor's essay before you know her chief concern? Does it occupy her attention in her first three paragraphs? If not, how can you defend the organization of this essay?

2. O'Connor argues in Paragraph 8 that "it is all to the good" that the so-called classics do not present the child with realities of his own time. Is her argument anything like that of Langston Hughes's character, Simple, who asserts that "Everything I do is connected up with my past life"? Or is it more like the complaint of the historian who describes us today as "prisoners of the present"?

3. To what extent does O'Connor's Paragraph 10 help explain the principle of "total effect" mentioned in Paragraph 3? Do you consider that principle a reasonable means of sorting out acceptable from unacceptable reading matter?

4. Would D. H. Lawrence (in "Pornography") agree or disagree with O'Connor's solution to the moral problem explained in her Paragraph 12? Explain.

5. Write a response to O'Connor's answer to her question at the beginning of Paragraph 14. Try to take into account the rest of her essay as well as your own feelings.

6. What nineteenth-century British and American novels do you remember well enough to compare with modern novels? If your answer is "none," are you in any position to argue with O'Connor?

Flannery O'Connor's first novel, Wise Blood, *appeared in 1952, her second and last,* The Violent Bear It Away, *in 1960. Most readers believe her short stories to be her best fiction; they are available in* The Collected Stories of Flannery O'Connor *(1972). During her lifetime she published one volume of stories, bearing the title of the story that follows. This was the story she usually read aloud when asked to read.*

50

FLANNERY O'CONNOR

A Good Man Is Hard to Find

The grandmother didn't want to go to Florida. She wanted to visit some of her connections in east Tennessee and she was seizing every chance to change Bailey's mind. Bailey was the son she lived with, her only boy. He was sitting on the edge of his chair at the table, bent over the orange sports section of the *Journal.* "Now look here, Bailey," she said, "see here, read this," and she stood with one hand on her thin hip and the other rattling the newspaper at his bald head. "Here this fellow that calls himself The Misfit is aloose from the Federal Pen and headed toward Florida and you read here what it says he did to these people. Just you read it. I wouldn't take my children in any direction with a criminal like that aloose in it. I couldn't answer to my conscience if I did." 1

Bailey didn't look up from his reading so she wheeled around 2 then and faced the children's mother; a young woman in slacks, whose face was as broad and innocent as a cabbage and was tied around with a green headkerchief that had two points on the top like rabbit's ears. She was sitting on the sofa, feeding the baby his apricots out of a jar. "The children have been to Florida before," the old lady said. "You all ought to take them somewhere else for a change so they would see different parts of the world and be broad. They never have been to east Tennessee."

3   The children's mother didn't seem to hear her, but the eight-year-old boy, John Wesley, a stocky child with glasses, said, "If you don't want to go to Florida, why dontcha stay at home?" He and the little girl, June Star, were reading the funny papers on the floor.

4   "She wouldn't stay at home to be queen for a day," June Star said without raising her yellow head.

5   "Yes, and what would you do if this fellow, The Misfit, caught you?" the grandmother asked.

6   "I'd smack his face," John Wesley said.

7   "She wouldn't stay at home for a million bucks," June Star said. "Afraid she'd miss something. She has to go everywhere we go."

8   "All right, Miss," the grandmother said. "Just remember that the next time you want me to curl your hair."

9   June Star said her hair was naturally curly.

10   The next morning the grandmother was the first one in the car, ready to go. She had her big black valise that looked like the head of a hippopotamus in one corner, and underneath it she was hiding a basket with Pitty Sing, the cat, in it. She didn't intend for the cat to be left alone in the house for three days because he would miss her too much and she was afraid he might brush against one of the gas burners and accidentally asphyxiate himself. Her son, Bailey, didn't like to arrive at a motel with a cat.

11   She sat in the middle of the back seat with John Wesley and June Star on either side of her. Bailey and the children's mother and the baby sat in the front and they left Atlanta at eight forty-five with the mileage on the car at 55890. The grandmother wrote this down because she thought it would be interesting to say how many miles they had been when they got back. It took them twenty minutes to reach the outskirts of the city.

12   The old lady settled herself comfortably, removing her white cotton gloves and putting them up with her purse on the shelf in front of the back window. The children's mother still had on slacks and still had her head tied up in a green kerchief, but the grandmother had on

a navy blue straw sailor hat with a bunch of white violets on the brim and a navy blue dress with a small white dot in the print. Her collar and cuffs were white organdy trimmed with lace and at her neckline she had pinned a purple spray of cloth violets containing a sachet. In case of an accident, anyone seeing her dead on the highway would know at once that she was a lady.

She said she thought it was going to be a good day for driving, 13 neither too hot nor too cold, and she cautioned Bailey that the speed limit was fifty-five miles an hour and that the patrolmen hid themselves behind bill-boards and small clumps of trees and sped out after you before you had a chance to slow down. She pointed out interesting details of the scenery: Stone Mountain; the blue granite that in some places came up to both sides of the highway; the brilliant red clay banks slightly streaked with purple; and the various crops that made rows of green lace-work on the ground. The trees were full of silver-white sunlights and the meanest of them sparkled. The children were reading comic magazines and their mother had gone back to sleep.

"Let's go through Georgia fast so we don't have to look at it 14 much," John Wesley said.

"If I were a little boy," said the grandmother, "I wouldn't talk 15 about my native state that way. Tennessee has the mountains and Georgia has the hills."

"Tennessee is just a hillbilly dumping ground," John Wesley said, 16 "and Georgia is a lousy state too."

"You said it," June Star said. 17

"In my time," said the grandmother, folding her thin veined fin- 18 gers, "children were more respectful of their native states and their parents and everything else. People did right then. Oh look at the cute little pickaninny!" she said and pointed to a Negro child standing in the door of a shack. "Wouldn't that make a picture, now?" she asked and they all turned and looked at the little Negro out of the back window. He waved.

"He didn't have any britches on," June Star said. 19

"He probably didn't have any," the grandmother explained. "Lit- 20 tle niggers in the country don't have things like we do. If I could paint, I'd paint that picture," she said.

The children exchanged comic books. 21

The grandmother offered to hold the baby and the children's 22 mother passed him over the front seat to her. She set him on her knee and bounced him and told him about the things they were passing. She rolled her eyes and screwed up her mouth and stuck her leathery thin face into his smooth bland one. Occasionally he gave her a far-away smile. They passed a large cotton field with five or six graves fenced in the middle of it, like a small island. "Look at the graveyard!" the grandmother said, pointing it out. "That was the old family bury-ing ground. That belonged to the plantation."

23   "Where's the plantation?" John Wesley asked.

24   "Gone With the Wind," said the grandmother. "Ha. Ha."

25   When the children finished all the comic books they had brought, they opened the lunch and ate it. The grandmother ate a peanut butter sandwich and an olive and would not let the children throw the box and the paper napkins out the window. When there was nothing else to do they played a game by choosing a cloud and making the other two guess what shape it suggested. John Wesley took one the shape of a cow and June Star guessed a cow and John Wesley said, no, an auto-mobile, and June Star said he didn't play fair, and they began to slap each other over the grandmother.

26   The grandmother said she would tell them a story if they would keep quiet. When she told a story, she rolled her eyes and waved her head and was very dramatic. She said once when she was a maiden lady she had been courted by a Mr. Edgar Atkins Teagarden from Jasper, Georgia. She said he was a very good-looking man and a gentle-man and that he brought her a watermelon every Saturday afternoon with his initials cut in it, E.A.T. Well, one Saturday, she said, Mr. Teagarden brought the watermelon and there was nobody at home and he left it on the front porch and returned in his buggy to Jasper, but she never got the watermelon, she said, because a nigger boy ate it when he saw the initials, E.A.T.! This story tickled John Wesley's funny bone and he giggled and giggled but June Star didn't think it was any good. She said she wouldn't marry a man that just brought her a watermelon on Saturday. The grandmother said she would have done well to marry Mr. Teagarden because he was a gentleman and had bought Coca-Cola stock when it first came out and that he had died only a few years ago, a very wealthy man.

27   They stopped at The Tower for barbecued sandwiches. The Tower was a part-stucco and part-wood filling station and dance hall set in a clearing outside of Timothy. A fat man named Red Sammy Butts ran it and there were signs stuck here and there on the building and for miles up and down the highway saying, TRY RED SAMMY'S FAMOUS BARBECUE. NONE LIKE FAMOUS RED SAMMY'S! RED SAM! THE FAT BOY WITH THE HAPPY LAUGH. A VETERAN! RED SAMMY'S YOUR MAN!

28   Red Sammy was lying on the bare ground outside The Tower

with his head under a truck while a gray monkey about a foot high, chained to a small chinaberry tree, chattered nearby. The monkey sprang back into the tree and got on the highest limb as soon as he saw the children jump out of the car and run toward him.

Inside, The Tower was a long dark room with a counter at one end and tables at the other and dancing space in the middle. They all sat down at a broad table next to the nickelodeon and Red Sam's wife, a tall burnt-brown woman with hair and eyes lighter than her skin, came and took their order. The children's mother put a dime in the machine and played "The Tennessee Waltz," and the grandmother said that tune always made her want to dance. She asked Bailey if he would like to dance but he only glared at her. He didn't have a naturally sunny disposition like she did and trips made him nervous. The grandmother's brown eyes were very bright. She swayed her head from side to side and pretended she was dancing in her chair. June Star said play something she could tap to so the children's mother put in another dime and played a fast number and June Star stepped out onto the dance floor and did her tap routine.   29

"Ain't she cute?" Red Sam's wife said, leaning over the counter. "Would you like to come be my little girl?"   30

"No, I certainly wouldn't," June Star said. "I wouldn't live in a broken-down place like this for a million bucks!" and she ran back to the table.   31

"Ain't she cute?" the woman repeated, stretching her mouth politely.   32

"Aren't you ashamed?" hissed the grandmother.   33

Red Sam came in and told his wife to quit lounging on the counter and hurry up with these people's order. His khaki trousers reached just to his hip bones and his stomach hung over them like a sack of meal swaying under his shirt. He came over and sat down at a table nearby and let out a combination sigh and yodel. "You can't win," he said. "You can't win," and he wiped his sweating red face off with a gray handkerchief. "These days you don't know who to trust," he said. "Ain't that the truth?"   34

"People are certainly not nice like they used to be," said the grandmother.   35

"Two fellers come in here last week," Red Sammy said, "driving a Chrysler. It was an old beat-up car but it was a good one and these boys looked all right to me. Said they worked at the mill and you know I let them fellers charge the gas they bought? Now why did I do that?"   36

37   "Because you're a good man!" the grandmother said at once.

38   "Yes'm, I suppose so," Red Sam said as if he were struck with this answer.

39   His wife brought the orders, carrying the five plates all at once without a tray, two in each hand and one balanced on her arm. "It isn't a soul in this green world of God's that you can trust," she said. "And I don't count nobody out of that, not nobody," she repeated, looking at Red Sammy.

40   "Did you read about that criminal, The Misfit, that's escaped?" asked the grandmother.

41   "I wouldn't be a bit surprised if he didn't attack this place right here," said the woman. "If he hears about it being here, I wouldn't be none surprised to see him. If he hears it's two cent in the cash register, I wouldn't be a tall surprised if he . . ."

42   "That'll do," Red Sam said. "Go bring these people their Co'-Colas," and the woman went off to get the rest of the order.

43   "A good man is hard to find," Red Sammy said. "Everything is getting terrible. I remember the day you could go off and leave your screen door unlatched. Not no more."

44   He and the grandmother discussed better times. The old lady said that in her opinion Europe was entirely to blame for the way things were now. She said the way Europe acted you would think we were made of money and Red Sam said it was no use talking about it, she was exactly right. The children ran outside into the white sunlight and looked at the monkey in the lacy chinaberry tree. He was busy catching fleas on himself and biting each one carefully between his teeth as if it were a delicacy.

45   They drove off again into the hot afternoon. The grandmother took cat naps and woke up every few minutes with her own snoring. Outside of Toombsboro she woke up and recalled an old plantation that she had visited in this neighborhood once when she was a young lady. She said the house had six white columns across the front and that there was an avenue of oaks leading up to it and two little wooden trellis arbors on either side in front where you sat down with your suitor after a stroll in the garden. She recalled exactly which road to turn off to get to it. She knew that Bailey would not be willing to lose any time looking at an old house, but the more she talked about it, the more she wanted to see it once again and find out if the little twin arbors were still standing. "There was a secret panel in this house," she said craftily, not telling the truth but wishing that she were, "and the story went that all the family silver was hidden in it when Sherman came through but it was never found. . . ."

"Hey!" John Wesley said. "Let's go see it! We'll find it! We'll   46
poke all the wood work and find it! Who lives there? Where do you
turn off at? Hey Pop, can't we turn off there?"

"We never have seen a house with a secret panel!" June Star   47
shrieked. "Let's go to the house with the secret panel! Hey, Pop, can't
we go see the house with the secret panel!"

"It's not far from here, I know," the grandmother said. "It   48
wouldn't take over twenty minutes."

Bailey was looking straight ahead. His jaw was as rigid as a horse-   49
shoe. "No," he said.

The children began to yell and scream that they wanted to see   50
the house with the secret panel. John Wesley kicked the back of the
front seat and June Star hung over her mother's shoulder and whined
desperately into her ear that they never had any fun even on their
vacation, that they could never do what THEY wanted to do. The baby
began to scream and John Wesley kicked the back of the seat so hard
that his father could feel the blows in his kidney.

"All right!" he shouted and drew the car to a stop at the side of   51
the road. "Will you all shut up? Will you all just shut up for one
second? If you don't shut up, we won't go anywhere."

"It would be very educational for them," the grandmother mur-   52
mured.

"All right," Bailey said, "but get this. This is the only time we're   53
going to stop for anything like this. This is the one and only time."

"The dirt road that you have to turn down is about a mile back,"   54
the grandmother directed. "I marked it when we passed."

"A dirt road," Bailey groaned.   55

After they had turned around and were headed toward the dirt   56
road, the grandmother recalled other points about the house, the beautiful glass over the front doorway and the candle lamp in the hall. John
Wesley said that the secret panel was probably in the fireplace.

"You can't go inside the house," Bailey said. "You don't know   57
who lives there."

"While you all talk to the people in front, I'll run around behind   58
and get in a window," John Wesley suggested.

"We'll all stay in the car," his mother said.   59

They turned onto the dirt road and the car raced roughly along in   60
a swirl of pink dust. The grandmother recalled the times when there
were no paved roads and thirty miles was a day's journey. The dirt
road was hilly and there were sudden washes in it and sharp curves on
dangerous embankments. All at once they would be on a hill, looking
down over the blue tops of trees for miles around, then the next min-

ute, they would be in a red depression with the dust-coated trees looking down on them.

61   "This place had better turn up in a minute," Bailey said, "or I'm going to turn around."

62   The road looked as if no one had traveled on it in months.

63   "It's not much farther," the grandmother said and just as she said it, a horrible thought came to her. The thought was so embarrassing that she turned red in the face and her eyes dilated and her feet jumped up, upsetting her valise in the corner. The instant the valise moved, the newspaper top she had over the basket under it rose with a snarl and Pitty Sing, the cat, sprang onto Bailey's shoulder.

64   The children were thrown to the floor and their mother, clutching the baby, was thrown out the door onto the ground; the old lady was thrown into the front seat. The car turned over once and landed right-side-up in a gulch on the side of the road. Bailey remained in the driver's seat with the cat — gray-striped with a broad white face and an orange nose — clinging to his neck like a caterpillar.

65   As soon as the children saw they could move their arms and legs, they scrambled out of the car, shouting, "We've had an ACCIDENT!" The grandmother was curled up under the dashboard, hoping she was injured so that Bailey's wrath would not come down on her all at once. The horrible thought she had had before the accident was that the house she had remembered so vividly was not in Georgia but in Tennessee.

66   Bailey removed the cat from his neck with both hands and flung it out the window against the side of a pine tree. Then he got out of the car and started looking for the children's mother. She was sitting against the side of the red gutted ditch, holding the screaming baby, but she only had a cut down her face and a broken shoulder. "We've had an ACCIDENT!" the children screamed in a frenzy of delight.

67   "But nobody's killed," June Star said with disappointment as the grandmother limped out of the car, her hat still pinned to her head but the broken front brim standing up at a jaunty angle and the violet spray hanging off the side. They all sat down in the ditch, except the children, to recover from the shock. They were all shaking.

68   "Maybe a car will come along," said the children's mother hoarsely.

69   "I believe I have injured an organ," said the grandmother, pressing her side, but no one answered her. Bailey's teeth were clattering. He had on a yellow sport shirt with bright blue parrots designed in it and his face was as yellow as the shirt. The grandmother decided that she would not mention that the house was in Tennessee.

The road was about ten feet above and they could see only the   70
tops of the trees on the other side of it. Behind the ditch they were
sitting in there were more woods, tall and dark and deep. In a few
minutes they saw a car some distance away on top of a hill, coming
slowly as if the occupants were watching them. The grandmother
stood up and waved both arms dramatically to attract their attention.
The car continued to come on slowly, disappeared around a bend and
appeared again, moving even slower, on top of the hill they had gone
over. It was a big black battered hearselike automobile. There were
three men in it.

It came to a stop just over them and for some minutes, the driver   71
looked down with a steady expressionless gaze to where they were
sitting, and didn't speak. Then he turned his head and muttered something to the other two and they got out. One was a fat boy in black
trousers and a red sweat shirt with a silver stallion embossed on the
front of it. He moved around on the right side of them and stood
staring, his mouth partly open in a kind of loose grin. The other had
on khaki pants and a blue striped coat and a gray hat pulled down very
low, hiding most of his face. He came around slowly on the left side.
Neither spoke.

The driver got out of the car and stood by the side of it, looking   72
down at them. He was an older man than the other two. His hair was
just beginning to gray and he wore silver-rimmed spectacles that gave
him a scholarly look. He had a long creased face and didn't have on any
shirt or undershirt. He had on blue jeans that were too tight for him
and he was holding a black hat and a gun. The two boys also had guns.

"We've had an ACCIDENT!" the children screamed.   73

The grandmother had the peculiar feeling that the bespectacled   74
man was someone she knew. His face was as familiar to her as if she
had known him all her life but she could not recall who he was. He
moved away from the car and began to come down the embankment,
placing his feet carefully so that he wouldn't slip. He had on tan and
white shoes and no socks, and his ankles were red and thin. "Good
afternoon," he said, "I see you all had you a little spill."

"We turned over twice!" said the grandmother.   75

"Oncet," he corrected. "We see it happen. Try their car and see   76
will it run, Hiram," he said quietly to the boy with the gray hat.

"What you got that gun for?" John Wesley asked. "Whatcha   77
gonna do with that gun?"

"Lady," the man said to the children's mother, "would you mind   78
calling them children to sit down by you? Children make me nervous.
I want all you all to sit down right together there were you're at."

79   "What are you telling us what to do for?" June Star asked.

80   Behind them the line of woods gaped like a dark open mouth. "Come here," said their mother.

81   "Look here now," Bailey began suddenly, "we're in a predicament! We're in . . ."

82   The grandmother shrieked. She scrambled to her feet and stood staring.

83   "You're The Misfit!" she said. "I recognized you at once!"

84   "Yes'm," the man said, smiling slightly as if he were pleased in spite of himself to be known. "But it would have been better for all of you, lady, if you hadn't of reckernized me."

85   Bailey turned his head sharply and said something to his mother that shocked even the children. The old lady began to cry and The Misfit reddened.

86   "Lady," he said, "don't you get upset. Sometimes a man says things he don't mean. I don't reckon he meant to talk to you thataway."

87   "You wouldn't shoot a lady, would you?" the grandmother said and removed a clean handkerchief from her cuff and began to slap at her eyes with it.

88   The Misfit pointed the toe of his shoe into the ground and made a little hole and then covered it up again. "I would hate to have to," he said.

89   "Listen," the grandmother almost screamed, "I know you're a good man. You don't look a bit like you have common blood. I know you must come from nice people!"

90   "Yes mam," he said, "finest people in the world." When he smiled he showed a row of strong white teeth. "God never made a finer woman than my mother and my daddy's heart was pure gold," he said. The boy with the red sweat shirt had come around behind them and was standing with his gun at his hip. The Misfit squatted down on the ground. "Watch them children, Bobby Lee," he said. "You know they make me nervous." He looked at the six of them huddled together in front of him and he seemed to be embarrassed as if he couldn't think of anything to say. "Ain't a cloud in the sky," he remarked, looking up at it. "Don't see no sun but don't see no cloud neither."

91   "Yes, it's a beautiful day," said the grandmother. "Listen," she said, "you shouldn't call yourself The Misfit because I know you're a good man at heart. I can just look at you and tell."

92   "Hush!" Bailey yelled. "Hush! Everybody shut up and let me

handle this!'' He was squatting in the position of a runner about to spring forward but he didn't move.

"I pre-chate that, lady,'' The Misfit said and drew a little circle in the ground with the butt of his gun. 93

"It'll take a half a hour to fix this here car,'' Hiram called, looking over the raised hood of it. 94

"Well, first you and Bobby Lee get him and that little boy to step over yonder with you,'' The Misfit said, pointing to Bailey and John Wesley. "The boys want to ask you something,'' he said to Bailey. "Would you mind stepping back in them woods there with them?'' 95

"Listen,'' Bailey began, "we're in a terrible predicament! Nobody realizes what this is,'' and his voice cracked. His eyes were as blue and intense as the parrots in his shirt and he remained perfectly still. 96

The grandmother reached up to adjust her hat brim as if she were going to the woods with him but it came off in her hand. She stood staring at it and after a second she let it fall on the ground. Hiram pulled Bailey up by the arm as if he were assisting an old man. John Wesley caught hold of his father's hand and Bobby Lee followed. They went off toward the woods and just as they reached the dark edge, Bailey turned and supporting himself against a gray naked pine trunk, he shouted, "I'll be back in a minute, Mamma, wait on me!'' 97

"Come back this instant!'' his mother shrilled but they all disappeared into the woods. 98

"Bailey Boy!'' the grandmother called in tragic voice but she found she was looking at The Misfit squatting on the ground in front of her. "I just know you're a good man,'' she said desperately. "You're not a bit common!'' 99

"Nome, I ain't a good man,'' The Misfit said after a second as if he had considered her statement carefully, "but I ain't the worst in the world neither. My daddy said I was a different breed of dog from my brothers and sisters. 'You know,' Daddy said, 'it's some that can live their whole life out without asking about it and it's others has to know why it is, and this boy is one of the latters. He's going to be into everything!' '' He put on his black hat and looked up suddenly and then away deep into the woods as if he were embarrassed again. "I'm sorry, I don't have on a shirt before you ladies,'' he said, hunching his shoulders slightly. "We buried our clothes that we had on when we escaped and we're just making do until we can get better. We borrowed these from some folks we met,'' he explained. 100

"That's perfectly all right,'' the grandmother said. "Maybe Bailey has an extra shirt in his suitcase.'' 101

102   "I'll look and see terrectly," The Misfit said.

103   "Where are they taking him?" the children's mother screamed.

104   "Daddy was a card himself," The Misfit said. "You couldn't put anything over on him. He never got in trouble with the Authorities though. Just had the knack of handling them."

105   "You could be honest too if you'd only try," said the grandmother. "Think how wonderful it would be to settle down and live a comfortable life and not have to think about somebody chasing you all the time."

106   The Misfit kept scratching in the ground with the butt of his gun as if he were thinking about it. "Yes'm, somebody is always after you," he murmured.

107   The grandmother noticed how thin his shoulder blades were just behind his hat because she was standing up looking down on him. "Do you ever pray?" she asked.

108   He shook his head. All she saw was the black hat wiggle between his shoulder blades. "Nome," he said.

109   There was a pistol shot from the woods, followed closely by another. Then silence. The old lady's head jerked around. She could hear the wind move through the tree tops like a long satisfied insuck of breath. "Bailey Boy!" she called.

110   "I was a gospel singer for a while," The Misfit said. "I been most everything. Been in the arm service, both land and sea, at home and abroad, been twict married, been an undertaker, been with the railroads, plowed Mother Earth, been in a tornado, seen a man burnt alive oncet," and he looked up at the children's mother and the little girl who were sitting close together, their faces white and their eyes glassy; "I even seen a woman flogged," he said.

111   "Pray, pray," the grandmother began, "pray, pray . . ."

112   "I never was a bad boy that I remember of," The Misfit said in an almost dreamy voice, "but somewheres along the line I done something wrong and got sent to the penitentiary. I was buried alive," and he looked up and held her attention to him by a steady stare.

113   "That's when you should have started to pray," she said. "What did you do to get sent to the penitentiary that first time?"

114   "Turn to the right, it was a wall," The Misfit said, looking up again at the cloudless sky. "Turn to the left, it was a wall. Look up it was a ceiling, look down it was a floor. I forgot what I done, lady. I set there and set there, trying to remember what it was I done and I ain't recalled it to this day. Oncet in a while, I would think it was coming to me, but it never come."

"Maybe they put you in by mistake," the old lady said vaguely.   115

"Nome," he said. "It wasn't no mistake. They had the papers on   116
me."

"You must have stolen something," she said.   117

The Misfit sneered slightly. "Nobody had nothing I wanted," he   118
said. "It was a head-doctor at the penitentiary said what I had done
was kill my daddy but I known that for a lie. My daddy died in nineteen ought nineteen of the epidemic flu and I never had a thing to do
with it. He was buried in the Mount Hopewell Baptist churchyard and
you can go there and see for yourself."

"If you would pray," the old lady said, "Jesus would help you."   119

"That's right," The Misfit said.   120

"Well then, why don't you pray?" she asked trembling with   121
delight suddenly.

"I don't want no hep," he said, "I'm doing all right by myself."   122

Bobby Lee and Hiram came ambling back from the woods. Bobby   123
Lee was dragging a yellow shirt with bright blue parrots in it.

"Throw me that shirt, Bobby Lee," The Misfit said. The shirt   124
came flying at him and landed on his shoulder and he put it on. The
grandmother couldn't name what the shirt reminded her of. "No,
lady," The Misfit said while he was buttoning it up, "I found out the
crime don't matter. You can do one thing or you can do another, kill
a man or take a tire off his car, because sooner or later you're going to
forget what it was you done and just be punished for it."

The children's mother had begun to make heaving noises as if   125
she couldn't get her breath. "Lady," he asked, "would you and that
little girl like to step off yonder with Bobby Lee and Hiram and join
your husband?"

"Yes, thank you," the mother said faintly. Her left arm dangled
helplessly and she was holding the baby, who had gone to sleep, in the
other. "Hep that lady up, Hiram," The Misfit said as she struggled to
climb out of the ditch, "and Bobby Lee, you hold onto that little girl's
hand."

"I don't want to hold hands with him," June Star said. "He   127
reminds me of a pig."

The fat boy blushed and laughed and caught her by the arm and   128
pulled her off into the woods after Hiram and her mother.

Alone with The Misfit, the grandmother found that she had lost   129
her voice. There was not a cloud in the sky nor any sun. There was
nothing around her but woods. She wanted to tell him that he must
pray. She opened and closed her mouth several times before anything

came out. Finally she found herself saying, "Jesus. Jesus," meaning, Jesus will help you, but the way she was saying it, it sounded as if she might be cursing.

130   "Yes'm," The Misfit said as if he agreed. "Jesus thrown everything off balance. It was the same case with Him as with me except He hadn't committed any crime and they could prove I had committed one because they had the papers on me. Of course," he said, "they never shown me any papers. That's why I sign myself now. I said long ago, you get you a signature and sign everything you do and keep a copy of it. Then you'll know what you done and you can hold up the crime to the punishment and see do they match and in the end you'll have something to prove you ain't been treated right. I call myself The Misfit," he said, "because I can't make what all I done wrong fit what all I gone through in punishment."

131   There was a piercing scream from the woods, followed closely by a pistol report. "Does it seem right to you, lady, that one is punished a heap and another ain't punished at all?"

132   "Jesus!" the old lady cried. "You've got blood! I know you wouldn't shoot a lady! I know you come from nice people! Pray! Jesus, you ought not to shoot a lady. I'll give you all the money I've got!"

133   "Lady," The Misfit said, looking beyond her far into the woods, "there was never a body that give the undertaker a tip."

134   There were two more pistol reports and the grandmother raised her head like a parched old turkey hen crying for water and called, "Bailey Boy, Bailey Boy!" as if her heart would break.

135   "Jesus was the only One that ever raised the dead," The Misfit continued, "and He shouldn't have done it. He thrown everything off balance. If He did what He said, then it's nothing for you to do but throw away everything and follow Him, and if He didn't then it's nothing for you to do but enjoy the few minutes you got left the best way you can — by killing somebody or burning down his house or doing some other meanness to him. No pleasure but meanness," he said and his voice had become almost a snarl.

136   "Maybe He didn't raise the dead," the old lady mumbled, not knowing what she was saying and feeling so dizzy that she sank down in the ditch with her legs twisted under her.

137   "I wasn't there so I can't say He didn't," The Misfit said. "I wisht I had of been there," he said, hitting the ground with his fist. "It ain't right I wasn't there because if I had of been there I would of known. Listen lady," he said in a high voice, "if I had of been there I would of known and I wouldn't be like I am now." His voice seemed about to

crack and the grandmother's head cleared for an instant. She saw the man's face twisted close to her own as if he were going to cry and she murmured, "Why, you're one of my babies. You're one of my own children!" She reached out and touched him on the shoulder. The Misfit sprang back as if a snake had bitten him and shot her three times through the chest. Then he put his gun down on the ground and took off his glasses and began to clean them.

Hiram and Bobby Lee returned from the woods and stood over   138
the ditch, looking down at the grandmother who half sat and half lay
in a puddle of blood with her legs crossed under her like a child's and
her face smiling up at the cloudless sky.

Without his glasses, The Misfit's eyes were red-rimmed and pale   139
and defenseless-looking. "Take her off and throw her where you
thrown the others," he said, picking up the cat that was rubbing itself
against his leg.

"She was a talker, wasn't she?" Bobby Lee said, sliding down the   140
ditch with a yodel.

"She would of been a good woman," The Misfit said, "if it had   141
been somebody there to shoot her every minute of her life."

"Some fun!" Bobby Lee said.   142

"Shut up, Bobby Lee," The Misfit said. "It's no real pleasure in   143
life."

_____ **CONSIDERATIONS** _____

1. In order to keep the children quiet, the grandmother tells the ridiculous story of Mr. Edgar Atkins Teagarden, who cut his initials, E.A.T., in a watermelon. How do you account for O'Connor's including such an anecdote in a story about a psychopathic murderer?

2. One respected scholar and critic describes O'Connor's story as a "satire on the half-and-half Christian faced with nihilism and death." In what sense would the grandmother qualify as a "half-and-half Christian"? Is there anything in O'Connor's letters to John Hawkes and Alfred Corn (see pages 284–290) that might help you understand what O'Connor thought a real Christian was?

3. Does this story contain characteristics of satire as seen in Jonathan Swift's "A Modest Proposal," Stephen Jay Gould's "Phyletic Size Decrease in Hershey Bars," or Woody Allen's "Death Knocks"?

4. O'Connor borrows a line from her own story to serve as a title. Find the line, study the context and comment on it as a title.

5. When the Misfit tells the grandmother, "it would have been better

for all of you, lady, if you hadn't of reckernized me," what purpose does his warning serve, in furthering the story?

6. Study three elderly women: the grandmother in this story, Faulkner's Emily, and Welty's Phoenix Jackson. Do you think it fair to say that all three are used to convey the point of their respective authors' stories? Explain.

In 1979 a selection of Flannery O'Connor's letters, edited by Sally Fitzgerald, appeared as The Habit of Being. *The letters are affectionate, often funny, rich with literary and religious thought.*

The following excerpts begin with passages from two letters about "A Good Man Is Hard to Find." The letter To a Professor of English is prefaced by Sally Fitzgerald's explanatory note. The other passage comes from a letter addressed to the novelist John Hawkes, a leading writer of O'Connor's generation, author of The Lime Twig, Blood Oranges, *and* The Passion Artist *among other novels. Here O'Connor speaks of the theology of her story. In the letter that follows, also to John Hawkes, O'Connor's Catholicism is clear and certain; Hawkes is of another mind. The last letter is addressed to Alfred Corn, who is now a well-known poet. In 1962 he was an undergraduate at Emory University in Atlanta, Georgia; when he heard Flannery O'Connor speak to an English class, he wrote her about a subject that troubled him.*

51

FLANNERY O'CONNOR

From Flannery O'Connor's Letters

TO JOHN HAWKES

14 April 60

1   Thanks for your letter of some time back. I have been busy keeping my blood pressure down while reading various reviews of my book. Some of the favorable ones are as bad as the unfavorable; most reviewers seem to have read the book in fifteen minutes and written the review in ten. . . . I hope that when yours comes out you'll fare better.

2   It's interesting to me that your students naturally work their way to the idea that the Grandmother in "A Good Man" is not pure evil and may be a medium for Grace. If they were Southern students I would say this was because they all had grandmothers like her at home. These old ladies exactly reflect the banalities of the society and the effect of the comical rather than the seriously evil. But Andrew [Lytle] insists that she is a witch, even down to the cat. These children, yr. students, know their grandmothers aren't witches.

3   Perhaps it is a difference in theology, or rather the difference that ingrained theology makes in the sensibility. Grace, to the Catholic way of thinking, can and does use as its medium the imperfect, purely human, and even hypocritical. Cutting yourself off from Grace is a very decided matter, requiring a real choice, act of will, and affecting the very ground of the soul. The Misfit is touched by the Grace that

comes through the old lady when she recognizes him as her child, as she has been touched by the Grace that comes through him in his particular suffering. His shooting her is a recoil, a horror at her humanness, but after he has done it and cleaned his glasses, the Grace has worked in him and he pronounces his judgment: she would have been a good woman if *he* had been there every moment of her life. True enough. In the Protestant view, I think Grace and nature don't have much to do with each other. The old lady, because of her hypocrisy and humanness and banality couldn't be a medium for Grace. In the sense that I see things the other way, I'm a Catholic writer.

TO A PROFESSOR OF ENGLISH

A professor of English had sent Flannery the following letter: "I am writing as spokesman for three members of our department and some ninety university students in three classes who for a week now have been discussing your story 'A Good Man Is Hard to Find.' We have debated at length several possible interpretations, none of which fully satisfies us. In general we believe that the appearance of the Misfit is not "real" in the same sense that the incidents of the first half of the story are real. Bailey, we believe, imagines the appearance of the Misfit, whose activities have been called to his attention on the night before the trip and again during the stopover at the roadside restaurant. Bailey, we further believe, identifies himself with the Misfit and so plays two roles in the imaginary last half of the story. But we cannot, after great effort, determine the point at which reality fades into illusion or reverie. Does the accident literally occur, or is it a part of Bailey's dream? Please believe me when I say we are not seeking an easy way out of our difficulty. We admire your story and have examined it with great care, but we are convinced that we are missing something important which you intended for us to grasp. We will all be very grateful if you comment on the interpretation which I have outlined above and if you will give us further comments about your intention in writing 'A Good Man Is Hard to Find.' "

She replied:

28 March 61

The interpretation of your ninety students and three teachers is fantastic and about as far from my intentions as it could get to be. If it were a legitimate interpretation, the story would be little more than a trick and its interest would be simply for abnormal psychology. I am not interested in abnormal psychology.

2   There is a change of tension from the first part of the story to the second where the Misfit enters, but this is no lessening of reality. This story is, of course, not meant to be realistic in the sense that it portrays the everyday doings of people in Georgia. It is stylized and its conventions are comic even though its meaning is serious.

3   Bailey's only importance is as the Grandmother's boy and the driver of the car. It is the Grandmother who first recognizes the Misfit and who is most concerned with him throughout. The story is a duel of sorts between the Grandmother and her superficial beliefs and the Misfit's more profoundly felt involvement with Christ's action which set the world off balance for him.

4   The meaning of a story should go on expanding for the reader the more he thinks about it, but meaning cannot be captured in an interpretation. If teachers are in the habit of approaching a story as if it were a research problem for which any answer is believable so long as it is not obvious, then I think students will never learn to enjoy fiction. Too much interpretation is certainly worse than too little, and where feeling for a story is absent, theory will not supply it.

5   My tone is not mean to be obnoxious. I am in a state of shock.

TO JOHN HAWKES

28 November 61

1   I have been fixing to write you ever since last summer when we saw the goat man.[1] We went up to north Georgia to buy a bull and when we were somewhere above Conyers we saw up ahead a pile of rubble some eight feet high on the side of the road. When we got about fifty feet from it, we could begin to make out that some of the rubble was distributed around something like a cart and that some of it was alive. Then we began to make out the goats. We stopped in front of it and looked back. About half the goats were asleep, venerable and exhausted, in a kind of heap. I didn't see Chess. Then my mother located an arm around the neck of one of the goats. We also saw a knee. The old man was lying on the road, asleep amongst them, but we never located his face.

---

[1] The founder of the Free Thinking Christian Mission, a wandering witness who traveled with a cart and a clutch of goats.

That is wonderful about the new baby. I can't equal that but I do have some new additions to my ménage. For the last few years I have been hunting a pair of swans that I could afford. Swans cost $250 a pair and that was beyond me. My friend in Florida, the one I wrote you about once, took upon herself to comb Florida for cheap swans. What she sets out to do, she does. . . . So now I am the owner of a one-eyed swan and her consort. They are Polish, or immutable, swans and very tractable and I radiate satisfaction every time I look at them. 2

I had brief notes from Andrew [Lytle][2] a couple of times lately. In fact he has a story of mine but I haven't heard from him whether he's going to use it or not. He said he had asked you to write an article about my fiction and that if he used my story I might want to send it to you. If he does take it and you write an article and want to see the story ["The Lame Shall Enter First"], I'll send it. It's about one of Tarwater's terrible cousins, a lad named Rufus Johnson, and it will add fuel to your theory though not legitimately I think. 3

You haven't convinced me that I write with the Devil's will or belong in the romantic tradition and I'm prepared to argue some more with you on this if I can remember where we left off at. I think the reason we can't agree on this is because there is a difference in our two devils. My Devil has a name, a history and a definite plan. His name is Lucifer, he's a fallen angel, his sin is pride, and his aim is the destruction of the Divine plan. Now I judge that your Devil is co-equal to God, not his creature; that pride is his virtue, not his sin; and that his aim is not to destroy the Divine plane because there isn't any Divine plan to destroy. My Devil is objective and yours is subjective. You say one becomes "evil" when one leaves the herd. I say that depends entirely on what the herd is doing. 4

The herd has been known to be right, in which case the one who leaves it is doing evil. When the herd is wrong, the one who leaves it is not doing evil but the right thing. If I remember rightly, you put that word, evil, in quotation marks which means the standards you judge it by there are relative; in fact you would be looking at it there with the eyes of the herd. 5

I think I would admit to writing what Hawthorne called "romances," but I don't think that has anything to do with the romantic mentality. Hawthorne interests me considerably. I feel more of a kinship with him than with any other American, though some of what he wrote I can't make myself read through to the end. 6

---

[2] Novelist, editor at this time of the *Sewanee Review*.

7   I didn't write the note to *Wise Blood.* I just let it go as is. I thought here I am wasting my time saying what I've written when I've already written it and I could be writing something else. I couldn't hope to convince anybody anyway. A friend of mine wrote me that he had read a review in one of the university magazines of *The Violent Bear etc.* that said that since the seeds that had opened one at a time in Tarwater's blood were put there in the first place by the great uncle that the book was about homosexual incest. When you have a generation of students who are being taught to think like that, there's nothing to do but wait for another generation to come along and hope it won't be worse. . . .

8   I've introduced *The Lime Twig* to several people and they're all enthusiastic. Somebody has gone off with my copy now. I hope you are at another one.

TO ALFRED CORN

30 May 62

1   I think that this experience you are having of losing your faith, or as you think, of having lost it, is an experience that in the long run belongs to faith; or at least it can belong to faith if faith is still valuable to you, and it must be or you would not have written me about this.

2   I don't know how the kind of faith required of a Christian living in the 20th century can be at all if it is not grounded on this experience that you are having right now of unbelief. This may be the case always and not just in the 20th century. Peter said, "Lord, I believe. Help my unbelief." It is the most natural and most human and most agonizing prayer in the gospels, and I think it is the foundation prayer of faith.

3   As a freshman in college you are bombarded with new ideas, or rather pieces of ideas, new frames of reference, an activation of the intellectual life which is only beginning, but which is already running ahead of your lived experience. After a year of this, you think you cannot believe. You are just beginning to realize how difficult it is to have faith and the measure of a commitment to it, but you are too young to decide you don't have faith just because you feel you can't believe. About the only way we know whether we believe or not is by what we do, and I think from your letter that you will not take the path of least resistance in this matter and simply decide that you have lost your faith and that there is nothing you can do about it.

4   One result of the stimulation of your intellectual life that takes

place in college is usually a shrinking of the imaginative life. This sounds like a paradox, but I have often found it to be true. Students get so bound up with difficulties such as reconciling the clashing of so many different faiths such as Buddhism, Mohammedanism, etc., that they cease to look for God in other ways. Bridges once wrote Gerard Manley Hopkins and asked him to tell him how he, Bridges, could believe. He must have expected from Hopkins a long philosophical answer. Hopkins wrote back, "Give alms." He was trying to say to Bridges that God is to be experienced in Charity (in the sense of love for the divine image in human beings). Don't get so entangled with intellectual difficulties that you fail to look for God in this way.

The intellectual difficulties have to be met, however, and you   5
will be meeting them for the rest of your life. When you get a reasonable hold on one, another will come to take its place. At one time, the clash of the different world religions was a difficulty for me. Where you have absolute solutions, however, you have no need of faith. Faith is what you have in the absence of knowledge. The reason this clash doesn't bother me any longer is because I have got, over the years, a sense of the immense sweep of creation, of the evolutionary process in everything, of how incomprehensible God must necessarily be to be the God of heaven and earth. You can't fit the Almighty into your intellectual categories. I might suggest that you look into some of the works of Pierre Teilhard de Chardin (*The Phenomenon of Man* et al.). He was a paleontologist — helped to discover Peking man — and also a man of God. I don't suggest you go to him for answers but for different questions, for that stretching of the imagination that you need to make you a sceptic in the face of much that you are learning, much of which is new and shocking but which when boiled down becomes less so and takes its place in the general scheme of things. What kept me a sceptic in college was precisely my Christian faith. It always said: wait, don't bite on this, get a wider picture, continue to read.

If you want your faith, you have to work for it. It is a gift, but for   6
very few is it a gift given without any demand for equal time devoted to its cultivation. For every book you read that is anti-Christian, make it your business to read one that presents the other side of the picture; if one isn't satisfactory read others. Don't think that you have to abandon reason to be a Christian. A book that might help you is *The Unity of Philosophical Experience* by Etienne Gilson. Another is Newman's *The Grammar of Assent*. To find out about faith, you have to go to the people who have it and you have to go to the most intelligent ones if you are going to stand up intellectually to agnostics and the

general run of pagans that you are going to find in the majority of people around you. Much of the criticism of belief that you find today comes from people who are judging it from the standpoint of another and narrower discipline. The Biblical criticism of the 19th century, for instance, was the product of historical disciplines. It has been entirely revamped in the 20th century by applying broader criteria to it, and those people who lost their faith in the 19th century because of it, could better have hung on in blind trust.

7   Even in the life of a Christian, faith rises and falls like the tides of an invisible sea. It's there, even when he can't see it or feel it, if he wants it to be there. You realize, I think, that it is more valuable, more mysterious, altogether more immense than anything you can learn or decide upon in college. Learn what you can, but cultivate Christian scepticism. It will keep you free — not free to do anything you please, but free to be formed by something larger than your own intellect or the intellects of those around you.

8   I don't know if this is the kind of answer that can help you, but any time you care to write me, I can try to do better.

_____ **CONSIDERATIONS** _____

Letter to John Hawkes: April 14, 1960

1. What does O'Connor mean when she says that some of the favorable reviews of her book "are as bad as the unfavorable"? How do you go about judging the quality of a book review? As a writer, how do you judge the comments on your own papers when they are returned by your instructors?

2. In Paragraph 2 O'Connor suggests that the grandmother in her story is like a lot of grandmothers in the South, but in her letter to the Professor of English (pages 285–286) she says her story is not realistic in the "everyday" sense. Can you reconcile this apparent contradiction?

3. O'Connor's comments on the term "grace" in Paragraph 3 might be more understandable if you pursued the word itself in a good dictionary where you will find at least a dozen different definitions of the word. Keep in mind that she is using the word according to her own view of Catholic theology.

4. O'Connor says at the end of Paragraph 3 that she is a Catholic writer. Does she mean that Protestant readers are not welcome or that Protestants could not understand her work? Is it possible to disagree with — or even disapprove of — a writer's ideas and still appreciate that writer's work? Explain.

5. While she does not always agree with John Hawkes's reading of her stories, O'Connor's letters to him (see also that of 11/28/61) express a good deal more respect for his ideas than can be found in her letter to a professor of

English. Read a little of the work of John Hawkes to see if you can discover qualities he shares with O'Connor.

Letter to a Professor of English, March 28, 1961

1. O'Connor says her story is realistic, not in an "everyday" but "stylized" sense. Compare a paragraph or two of her story with a passage in Eudora Welty's "The Worn Path" to see if you can determine what O'Connor means by "stylized." You might also get some help on that word by consulting a history of art.

2. Find passages in "A Good Man Is Hard to Find" that will illustrate what O'Connor means by the grandmother's "superficial beliefs" and the Misfit's "more profoundly felt involvement." Does such a close examination of the story push you closer to or further away from O'Connor's belief that the heart of the story is a "duel of sorts" between the grandmother and the Misfit?

3. In Paragraph 4 O'Connor makes an interesting distinction between "meaning" and "interpretation" as she deplores the "habit of approaching a story as if it were a research problem for which any answer is believable so long as it is not obvious." Discuss some experience of your own in which insistence upon a particular interpretation (yours or anyone else's) interfered with the expanded meaning O'Connor mentions.

4. O'Connor says in her last paragraph that her tone in the letter "is not meant to be obnoxious." If you were the professor to whom she had written, what particular lines or words in the letter might you think gave it an obnoxious tone? Can you find any other writers in your text whose tone is obnoxious? Explain.

5. In what sense, if any, do you think a short story (or poem or novel or play or essay for that matter) can be taught? What assistance do you expect or want from your own instructor and/or text in reading a story like O'Connor's?

Letter to John Hawkes, November 28, 1961

1. O'Connor's remarkable versatility in the use of the English language is demonstrated in her letters as well as in her stories. This letter to John Hawkes, for example, shows her ability to shift from one voice to another at will. Find examples.

2. At the end of Paragraph 4, O'Connor tells Hawkes, "You say one becomes 'evil' when one leaves the herd. I say that depends entirely on what the herd is doing." Write an essay on relative versus absolute morality.

3. O'Connor, speaking of her interest in Hawthorne, makes a distinction between writing "romances" and having a "romantic mentality." What did Hawthorne mean by "romances," and why does O'Connor "feel more of a kinship with him than with any other American"?

4. O'Connor's letters are filled with brief reports on local events and people, like the one on the goat man in the letter to John Hawkes. Eudora Welty, in discussing one of her own short stories — see her essay "The Point of the Story" — says that her story began when she observed an old woman in Mississippi. How might O'Connor's observations of her surroundings have contributed to "A Good Man Is Hard to Find"?

Letter to Alfred Corn, May 30, 1962

1. "You can't fit the Almighty into your intellectual categories," says O'Connor. Does she advise her correspondent to ignore the intellectual challenges of college? Study her discussion of the clash between intellectual inquiry and faith, especially in Paragraphs 5 and 6, and write an essay on her conclusions.

2. How, according to O'Connor, can we know whether we believe or not?

3. Look over Consideration 1 regarding O'Connor's 1961 letter to John Hawkes and think about voice. How would you describe the voice in this letter to Alfred Corn? Does O'Connor play with changes of voice in this letter? Why?

4. Read Langston Hughes's essay "Salvation"; how might O'Connor have consoled the disillusioned boy?

George Orwell (1903–1950) was the pen name of Eric Blair, who was born in India of English parents, attended Eton on a scholarship, and returned to the East as a member of the Imperial Police. He quit his position after five years because he wanted to write, and because he came to feel that imperialism was "very largely a racket." For eight years he wrote with small success and in considerable poverty. His first book, **Down and Out in Paris and London** *(1933), described those years. Further memoirs and novels followed, including* **Burmese Days** *(1935) and* **Keep the Aspidistra Flying** *(1938). His last books were the political fable* **Animal Farm** *(1945) and his great anti-utopia* **1984,** *which appeared in 1949, shortly before his death. He died of tuberculosis, his health first afflicted when he was a policeman in Burma, undermined by years of poverty, and further worsened by a wound he received during the civil war in Spain.*

*Best known for his fiction, Orwell was essentially an essayist; even his novels are essays. He made his living most of his adult life by writing reviews and articles for English weeklies. His collected essays, reviews, and letters form an impressive four volumes. Politics is at the center of his work — a personal politics. After his disaffection from imperialism, he became a leftist, and fought on the Loyalist side against Franco in Spain. (*Homage to Catalonia *comes out of this time.) But his experience of Communist duplicity there, and his early understanding of the paranoid totalitarianism of Stalin, turned him anti-Communist. He could swear allegiance to no party. His anti-Communism made him in no way conservative; he considered himself a socialist until his death, but other socialists would have nothing to do with him. He found politics shabby and politicians dishonest. With an empirical, English turn of mind, he looked skeptically at all saviors and panaceas. In this famous essay, he attacks the rhetoric of politics. He largely attacks the left — because his audience was an English intellectual class that was largely leftist.*

52

GEORGE ORWELL
Politics and the English Language

1   Most people who bother with the matter at all would admit that the English language is in a bad way, but it is generally assumed that we cannot by conscious action do anything about it. Our civilization is decadent and our language — so the argument runs — must inevitably share in the general collapse. It follows that any struggle against the abuse of language is a sentimental archaism, like preferring candles to electric light or hansom cabs to aeroplanes. Underneath this lies the half-conscious belief that language is a natural growth and not an instrument which we shape for our own purposes.

2   Now, it is clear that the decline of a language must ultimately have political and economic causes: it is not due simply to the bad influence of this or that individual writer. But an effect can become a cause, reinforcing the original cause and producing the same effect in an intensified form, and so indefinitely. A man may take to drink because he feels himself to be a failure, and then fail all the more completely because he drinks. It is rather the same thing that is happening to the English language. It becomes ugly and inaccurate because our thoughts are foolish, but the slovenliness of our language makes it easier for us to have foolish thoughts. The point is that the process is reversible. Modern English, especially written English, is full of bad habits which spread by imitation and which can be avoided if one is willing to take the necessary trouble. If one gets rid of these

habits one can think more clearly, and to think clearly is a necessary first step towards political regeneration: so that the fight against bad English is not frivolous and is not the exclusive concern of professional writers. I will come back to this presently, and I hope that by that time the meaning of what I have said here will have become clearer. Meanwhile, here are five specimens of the English language as it is now habitually written.

These five passages have not been picked out because they are especially bad — I could have quoted far worse if I had chosen — but because they illustrate various of the mental vices from which we now suffer. They are a little below the average, but are fairly representative samples. I number them so that I can refer back to them when necessary:

3

> (1) I am not, indeed, sure whether it is not true to say that the Milton who once seemed not unlike a seventeenth-century Shelley had not become, out of an experience ever more bitter in each year, more alien [*sic*] to the founder of that Jesuit sect which nothing could induce him to tolerate.
>
>

Professor Harold Laski
[Essay in *Freedom of Expression*].

> (2) Above all, we cannot play ducks and drakes with a native battery of idioms which prescribes such egregious collocations of vocables as the Basic *put up with* for *tolerate* or *put at a loss* for *bewilder*.
>
>

Professor Lancelot Hogben [*Interglossa*].

> (3) On the one side we have the free personality: by definition it is not neurotic, for it has neither conflict nor dream. Its desires, such as they are, are transparent, for they are just what institutional approval keeps in the forefront of consciousness; another institutional pattern would alter their number and intensity, there is little in them that is natural, irreducible, or culturally dangerous. But *on the other side*, the social bond itself is nothing but the mutual reflection of these self-secure integrities. Recall the definition of love. Is not this the very picture of a small academic? Where is there a place in this hall of mirrors for either personality or fraternity?
>
>

Essay on psychology in *Politics* [New York].

> (4) All the "best people" from the gentlemen's clubs, and all the frantic fascist captains, united in common hatred of Socialism and bestial horror of the rising tide of the mass revolutionary movement, have turned to acts of provocation, to foul incendiarism, to

medieval legends of poisoned wells, to legalize their own destruction of proletarian organizations, and rouse the agitated petty-bourgeoisie to chauvinistic fervor on behalf of the fight against the revolutionary way out of the crisis.

Communist pamphlet.

(5) If a new spirit is to be infused into this old country, there is one thorny and contentious reform which must be tackled, and that is the humanization and galvanization of the B.B.C. Timidity here will bespeak canker and atrophy of the soul. The heart of Britain may be sound and of strong beat, for instance, but the British lion's roar at present is like that of Bottom in Shakespeare's *Midsummer Night's Dream* — as gentle as any sucking dove. A virile new Britain cannot continue indefinitely to be traduced in the eyes, or rather ears, of the world by the effete languors of Langham Place brazenly masquerading as "standard English." When the Voice of Britain is heard at nine o'clock, better far and infinitely less ludicrous to hear aitches honestly dropped than the present priggish, inflated, inhibited, school-ma'amish arch braying of blameless bashful mewing maidens!

Letter in Tribune.

4   Each of these passages has faults of its own, but, quite apart from avoidable ugliness, two qualities are common to all of them. The first is staleness of imagery; the other is lack of precision. The writer either has a meaning and cannot express it, or he inadvertently says something else, or he is almost indifferent as to whether his words mean anything or not. This mixture of vagueness and sheer incompetence is the most marked characteristic of modern English prose, and especially of any kind of political writing. As soon as certain topics are raised, the concrete melts into the abstract and no one seems able to think of turns of speech that are not hackneyed: prose consists less and less of *words* chosen for the sake of their meaning, and more and more of *phrases* tacked together like the sections of a prefabricated hen-house. I list below, with notes and examples, various of the tricks by means of which the work of prose-construction is habitually dodged:

DYING METAPHORS

5   A newly invented metaphor assists thought by evoking a visual image, while on the other hand a metaphor which is technically "dead" (e.g. *iron resolution*) has in effect reverted to being an ordinary

word and can generally be used without loss of vividness. But in between these two classes there is a huge dump of worn-out metaphors which have lost all evocative power and are merely used because they save people the trouble of inventing phrases for themselves. Examples are: *Ring the changes on, take up the cudgels for, toe the line, ride roughshod over, stand shoulder to shoulder with, play into the hands of, no axe to grind, grist to the mill, fishing in troubled waters, on the order of the day, Achilles' heel, swan song, hotbed.* Many of these are used without knowledge of their meaning (what is a "rift," for instance?), and incompatible metaphors are frequently mixed, a sure sign that the writer is not interested in what he is saying. Some metaphors now current have been twisted out of their original meaning without those who use them even being aware of the fact. For example, *toe the line* is sometimes written *tow the line.* Another example is *the hammer and the anvil,* now always used with the implication that the anvil gets the worst of it. In real life it is always the anvil that breaks the hammer, never the other way about: a writer who stopped to think what he was saying would be aware of this, and would avoid perverting the original phrase.

OPERATORS OR VERBAL FALSE LIMBS

These save the trouble of picking out appropriate verbs and nouns, and at the same time pad each sentence with extra syllables which give it an appearance of symmetry. Characteristic phrases are *render inoperative, militate against, make contact with, be subjected to, give rise to, give grounds for, have the effect of, play a leading part (role) in, make itself felt, take effect, exhibit a tendency to, serve the purpose of,* etc., etc. The keynote is the elimination of simple verbs. Instead of being a single word, such as *break, stop, spoil, mend, kill* a verb becomes a *phrase,* made up of a noun or adjective tacked on to some general-purpose verb such as *prove, serve, form, play, render.* In addition, the passive voice is wherever possible used in preference to the active, and noun constructions are used instead of gerunds *(by examination of* instead of *by examining).* The range of verbs is further cut down by means of the *-ize* and *de-* formations, and the banal statements are given an appearance of profundity by means of the *not un-* formation. Simple conjunctions and prepositions are replaced by such phrases as *with respect to, having regard to, the fact that, by dint of, in view of, in the interests of, on the hypothesis that;* and the

6

ends of sentences are saved from anticlimax by such resounding commonplaces as *greatly to be desired, cannot be left out of account, a development to be expected in the near future, deserving of serious consideration, brought to a satisfactory conclusion* and so on and so forth.

PRETENTIOUS DICTION

7   Words like *phenomenon, element, individual* (as noun), *objective, categorical, effective, virtual, basic, primary, promote, constitute, exhibit, exploit, utilize, eliminate, liquidate,* are used to dress up simple statements and give an air of scientific impartiality to biased judgments. Adjectives like *epoch-making, epic, historic, unforgettable, triumphant, age-old, inevitable, inexorable, veritable,* are used to dignify the sordid processes of international politics, while writing that aims at glorifying war usually takes on an archaic color, its characteristic words being: *realm, throne, chariot, mailed fist, trident, sword, shield, buckler, banner, jackboot, clarion.* Foreign words and expresssions such as *cul de sac, ancien régime, deux ex machina, mutatis mutandis, status quo, gleichschaltung, weltanschauung,* are used to give an air of culture and elegance. Except for the useful abbreviations *i.e., e.g.,* and *etc.,* there is no real need for any of the hundreds of foreign phrases now current in English. Bad writers, and especially scientific, political and sociological writers, are nearly always haunted by the notion that Latin or Greek words are grander than Saxon ones, and unnecessary words like *expedite, ameliorate, predict, extraneous, deracinated, clandestine, subaqueous* and hundreds of others constantly gain ground from their Anglo-Saxon opposite numbers.[1] The jargon peculiar to Marxist writing *(hyena, hangman, cannibal, petty bourgeois, these gentry, lacquey, flunkey, mad dog, White Guard,* etc.) consists largely of words and phrases translated from Russian, German or French; but the normal way of coining a new word is to use a Latin or Greek root with the appropriate affix and, where neces-

---

[1] An interesting illustration of this is the way in which the English flower names which were in use till very recently are being ousted by Greek ones, *snapdragon* becoming *antirrhinum, forget-me-not* becoming *myosotis,* etc. It is hard to see any practical reason for this change of fashion: it is probably due to an instinctive turning-away from the more homely word and a vague feeling that the Greek is scientific.

sary, the -*ize* formation. It is often easier to make up words of this kind (*deregionalize, impermissible, extramarital, non-fragmentary* and so forth) than to think up the English words that will cover one's meaning. The result, in general, is an increase in slovenliness and vagueness.

MEANINGLESS WORDS

In certain kinds of writing, particularly in art criticism and liter-   8
ary criticism, it is normal to come across long passages which are almost completely lacking in meaning.[2] Words like *romantic, plastic, values, human, dead, sentimental, natural, vitality,* as used in art criticism, are strictly meaningless, in the sense that they not only do not point to any discoverable object, but are hardly ever expected to do so by the reader. When one critic writes, "The outstanding feature of Mr. X's work is its living quality," while another writes, "The immediately striking thing about Mr. X's work is its peculiar dead-ness," the reader accepts this as a simple difference of opinion. If words like *black* and *white* were involved, instead of the jargon words *dead* and *living,* he would see at once that language was being used in an improper way. Many political words are similarly abused. The word *Fascism* has now no meaning in so far as it signifies "something not desirable." The words *democracy, socialism, freedom, patriotic, realistic, justice,* have each of them several different meanings which cannot be reconciled with one another. In the case of a word like *democracy,* not only is there no agreed definition, but the attempt to make one is resisted from all sides. It is almost universally felt that when we call a country democratic we are praising it: consequently the defenders of every kind of régime claim that it is a democracy, and fear that they might have to stop using the word if it were tied down to any one meaning. Words of this kind are often used in a consciously dishonest way. That is, the person who uses them has his own private definition, but allows his hearer to think he means something quite

---

[2] Example: "Comfort's catholicity of perception and image, strangely Whitman-esque in range, almost the exact opposite in aesthetic compulsion, continues to evoke that trembling atmospheric accumulative hinting at a cruel, an inexorably serene time-lessness. . . . Wrey Gardiner scores by aiming at simple bull's-eyes with precision. Only they are not so simple, and through his contented sadness runs more than the surface bitter-sweet of resignation." (Poetry Quarterly.)

different. Statements like *Marshal Pétain was a true patriot, The Soviet Press is the freest in the world, The Catholic Church is opposed to persecution,* are almost always made with intent to deceive. Other words used in variable meanings, in most cases more or less dishonestly, are: *class, totalitarian, science, progressive, reactionary, bourgeois, equality.*

9   Now that I have made this catalogue of swindles and perversions, let me give another example of the kind of writing that they lead to. This time it must of its nature be an imaginary one. I am going to translate a passage of good English into modern English of the worst sort. Here is a well-known verse from *Ecclesiastes:*

> I returned and saw under the sun, that the race is not to the swift, nor the battle to the strong, neither yet bread to the wise, nor yet riches to men of understanding, nor yet favour to men of skill, but time and chance happeneth to them all.

10   Here it is in modern English:

> Objective consideration of contemporary phenomena compels the conclusion that success or failure in competitive activities exhibits no tendency to be commensurate with innate capacity, but that a considerable element of the unpredictable must invariably be taken into account.

11   This is a parody, but not a very gross one. Exhibit (3), above, for instance, contains several patches of the same kind of English. It will be seen that I have not made a full translation. The beginning and ending of the sentence follow the original meaning fairly closely, but in the middle the concrete illustrations — race, battle, bread — dissolve into the vague phrase "success or failure in competitive activities." This had to be so, because no modern writer of the kind I am discussing — no one capable of using phrases like "objective consideration of contemporary phenomena" — would ever tabulate his thoughts in that precise and detailed way. The whole tendency of modern prose is away from concreteness. Now analyse these two sentences a little more closely. The first contains forty-nine words but only sixty syllables, and all its words are those of everyday life. The second contains thirty-eight words of ninety syllables: eighteen of its words are from Latin roots, and one from Greek. The first sentence contains six vivid images, and only one phrase ("time and chance") that could be called vague. The second contains not a single fresh, arresting phrase, and in spite of its ninety syllables it gives only a shortened version of the meaning contained in the first. Yet without a

doubt it is the second kind of sentence that is gaining ground in modern English. I do not want to exaggerate. This kind of writing is not yet universal, and outcrops of simplicity will occur here and there in the worst-written page. Still, if you or I were told to write a few lines on the uncertainty of human fortunes, we should probably come much nearer to my imaginary sentence than to the one from *Ecclesiastes.*

As I have tried to show, modern writing at its worst does not   12 consist in picking out words for the sake of their meaning and inventing images in order to make the meaning clearer. It consists in gumming together long strips of words which have already been set in order by someone else, and making the results presentable by sheer humbug. The attraction of this way of writing is that it is easy. It is easier — even quicker, once you have the habit — to say *In my opinion it is not an unjustifiable assumption that* than to say *I think.* If you use ready-made phrases, you not only don't have to hunt about for words; you also don't have to bother with the rhythms of your sentences, since these phrases are generally so arranged as to be more or less euphonious. When you are composing in a hurry — when you are dictating to a stenographer, for instance, or making a public speech — it is natural to fall into a pretentious, Latinized style. Tags like *a consideration which we should do well to bear in mind* or *a conclusion to which all of us would readily assent* will save many a sentence from coming down with a bump. By using stale metaphors, similes and idioms, you save much mental effort, at the cost of leaving your meaning vague, not only for your reader but for yourself. This is the significance of mixed metaphors. The sole aim of a metaphor is to call up a visual image. When these images clash — as in *The Fascist octopus has sung its swan song, the jackboot is thrown into the melting pot* — it can be taken as certain that the writer is not seeing a mental image of the objects he is naming; in other words he is not really thinking. Look again at the examples I gave at the beginning of this essay. Professor Laski (1) uses five negatives in fifty-three words. One of these is superfluous, making nonsense of the whole passage, and in addition there is the slip *alien* for *akin,* making further nonsense, and several avoidable pieces of clumsiness which increase the general vagueness. Professor Hogben (2) plays ducks and drakes with a battery which is able to write prescriptions, and, while disapproving of the everyday phrase *put up with,* is unwilling to look *egregious* up in the dictionary and see what it means; (3), if one takes an uncharitable attitude towards it, is simply meaningless: probably one could work out its intended meaning by reading the whole of the article in which it occurs. In (4), the writer knows more or less what he wants to say, but an accumulation of stale phrases chokes him, like tea leaves blocking a sink. In (5), words and meaning have almost parted company. People who write in this manner usually have a general emotional meaning — they dislike one thing and want to express solidarity with another — but they are not interested in the detail of what they are saying. A scrupulous writer, in every sentence that he writes, will ask himself at least four questions, thus: What am I trying to say? What words will express it? What image or idiom will make it clearer? Is this image fresh enough to have an effect? And he will probably ask himself two more: Could I put it more shortly? Have I said anything that is avoidably ugly? But you are not obliged to go to all this trouble. You can shirk it by simply throwing your mind open and letting the ready-made phrases come crowding in. They will construct your sentences for you — even think your thoughts for you, to a certain extent — and at need they will perform the important service of partially concealing your meaning even from yourself. It is at this point that the special connection between politics and the debasement of language becomes clear.

13   In our time it is broadly true that political writing is bad writing. Where it is not true, it will generally be found that the writer is some kind of rebel, expressing his private opinions and not a "party line." Orthodoxy, of whatever color, seems to demand a lifeless, imitative style. The political dialects to be found in pamphlets, leading articles, manifestos, White Papers and the speeches of undersecretaries do, of course, vary from party to party, but they are all alike in that one almost never finds in them a fresh, vivid, home-made turn of speech. When one watches some tired hack on the platform mechanically repeating the familiar phrases — *bestial atrocities, iron heel, blood-stained tyranny, free people of the world, stand shoulder to shoulder* — one often has a curious feeling that one is not watching a live human being but some kind of dummy: a feeling which suddenly becomes stronger at moments when the light catches the speaker's spectacles and turns them into blank discs which seem to have no eyes behind them. And this is not altogether fanciful. A speaker who uses that kind of phraseology has gone some distance towards turning himself into a machine. The appropriate noises are coming out of his larynx, but his brain is not involved as it would be if he were choosing his words for himself. If the speech he is making is one that he is accustomed to make over and over again, he may be almost unconscious of what he is saying, as one is when one utters the responses in

church. And this reduced state of consciousness, if not indispensable, is at any rate favorable to political conformity.

In our time, political speech and writing are largely the defence of the indefensible. Things like the continuance of British rule in India, the Russian purges and deportations, the dropping of the atom bombs on Japan, can indeed be defended, but only by arguments which are too brutal for most people to face, and which do not square with the professed aims of political parties. Thus political language has to consist largely of euphemism, question-begging and sheer cloudy vagueness. Defenceless villages are bombarded from the air, the inhabitants driven out into the countryside, the cattle machine-gunned, the huts set on fire with incendiary bullets: this is called *pacification.* Millions of peasants are robbed of their farms and sent trudging along the roads with no more than they can carry: this is called *transfer of population* or *rectification of frontiers.* People are imprisoned for years without trial, or shot in the back of the neck or sent to die of scurvy in Arctic lumber camps: this is called *elimination of unreliable elements.* Such phraseology is needed if one wants to name things without calling up mental pictures of them. Consider for instance some comfortable English professor defending Russian totalitarianism. He cannot say outright, "I believe in killing off your opponents when you can get good results by doing so." Probably, therefore, he will say something like this: 14

"While freely conceding that the Soviet régime exhibits certain features which the humanitarian may be inclined to deplore, we must, I think, agree that a certain curtailment of the right to political opposition is an unavoidable concomitant of transitional periods, and that the rigors which the Russian people have been called upon to undergo have been amply justified in the sphere of concrete achievement." 15

The inflated style is itself a kind of euphemism. A mass of Latin words falls upon the facts like soft snow, blurring the outlines and covering up all the details. The great enemy of clear language is insincerity. When there is a gap between one's real and one's declared aims, one turns as it were instinctively to long words and exhausted idioms, like a cuttlefish squirting out ink. In our age there is no such thing as "keeping out of politics." All issues are political issues, and politics itself is a mass of lies, evasions, folly, hatred and schizophrenia. When the general atmosphere is bad, language must suffer. I should expect to find — this is a guess which I have not sufficient knowledge to verify — that the German, Russian and Italian languages have all deteriorated in the last ten or fifteen years, as a result of dictatorship. 16

17   But if thought corrupts language, language can also corrupt thought. A bad usage can spread by tradition and imitation, even among people who should and do know better. The debased language that I have been discussing is in some ways very convenient. Phrases like *a not unjustifiable assumption, leaves much to be desired, would serve no good purpose, a consideration which we should do well to bear in mind*, are a continuous temptation, a packet of aspirins always at one's elbow. Look back through this essay, and for certain you will find that I have again and again committed the very faults I am protesting against. By this morning's post I have received a pamphlet dealing with conditions in Germany. The author tells me that he "felt impelled" to write it. I open it at random, and here is almost the first sentence that I see: "[The Allies] have an opportunity not only of achieving a radical transformation of Germany's social and political structure in such a way as to avoid a nationalistic reaction in Germany itself, but at the same time of laying the foundations of a co-operative and unified Europe." You see, he "feels impelled" to write — feels, presumably, that he has something new to say — and yet his words, like cavalry horses answering the bugle, group themselves automatically into the familiar dreary pattern. This invasion of one's mind by ready-made phrases *(lay the foundations, achieve a radical transformation)* can only be prevented if one is constantly on guard against them, and every such phrase anaesthetizes a portion of one's brain.

18   I said earlier that the decadence of our language is probably curable. Those who deny this would argue, if they produced an argument at all, that language merely reflects existing social conditions, and that we cannot influence its development by any direct tinkering with words and constructions. So far as the general tone or spirit of a language goes, this may be true, but it is not true in detail. Silly words and expressions have often disappeared, not through any evolutionary process but owing to the conscious action of a minority. Two recent examples were *explore every avenue* and *leave no stone unturned*, which were killed by the jeers of a few journalists. There is a long list of flyblown metaphors which could similarly be got rid of if enough people would interest themselves in the job; and it should also be possible to laugh the *not un-* formation out of existence,[3] to reduce the amount of Latin and Greek in the average sentence, to drive out foreign phrases and strayed scientific words, and, in general, to make

---

[3] One can cure oneself of the *not un-* formation by memorizing this sentence: *A not unblack dog was chasing a not unsmall rabbit across a not ungreen field.*

pretentiousness unfashionable. But all these are minor points. The defence of the English language implies more than this, and perhaps it is best to start by saying what it does *not* imply.

To begin with it has nothing to do with archaism, with the sal- 19 vaging of obsolete words and turns of speech, or with the setting up of a "standard English" which must never be departed from. On the contrary, it is especially concerned with the scrapping of every word or idiom which has outworn its usefulness. It has nothing to do with correct grammar and syntax, which are of no importance so long as one makes one's meaning clear, or with the avoidance of American-isms, or with having what is called a "good prose style." On the other hand it is not concerned with fake simplicity and the attempt to make written English colloquial. Nor does it even imply in every case pre-ferring the Saxon word to the Latin one, though it does imply using the fewest and shortest words that will cover one's meaning. What is above all needed is to let the meaning choose the word, and not the other way about. In prose, the worst thing one can do with words is to surrender to them. When you think of a concrete object, you think wordlessly, and then, if you want to describe the thing you have been visualizing you probably hunt about till you find the exact words that seem to fit it. When you think of something abstract you are more inclined to use words from the start, and unless you make a conscious effort to prevent it, the existing dialect will come rushing in and do the job for you, at the expense of blurring or even changing your mean-ing. Probably it is better to put off using words as long as possible and get one's meaning as clear as one can through pictures or sensations. Afterwards one can choose — not simply *accept* — the phrases that will best cover the meaning, and then switch round and decide what impression one's words are likely to make on another person. This last effort of the mind cuts out all stale or mixed images, all prefabri-cated phrases, needless repetitions, and humbug and vagueness gen-erally. But one can often be in doubt about the effect of a word or a phrase, and one needs rules that one can rely on when instinct fails. I think the following rules will cover most cases:

(i) Never use a metaphor, simile or other figure of speech which you are used to seeing in print.

(ii) Never use a long word where a short one will do.

(iii) If it is possible to cut a word out, always cut it out.

(iv) Never use the passive where you can use the active.

(v) Never use a foreign phrase, a scientific word or a jargon word if you can think of an everyday English equivalent.

(vi) Break any of these rules sooner than say anything outright barbarous.

These rules sound elementary, and so they are, but they demand a deep change of attitude in anyone who has grown used to writing in the style now fashionable. One could keep all of them and still write bad English, but one could not write the kind of stuff that I quoted in those five specimens at the beginning of this article.

20   I have not here been considering the literary use of language, but merely language as an instrument for expressing and not for concealing or preventing thought. Stuart Chase and others have come near to claiming that all abstract words are meaningless, and have used this as a pretext for advocating a kind of political quietism. Since you don't know what Fascism is, how can you struggle against Fascism? One need not swallow such absurdities as this, but one ought to recognize that the present political chaos is connected with the decay of language, and that one can probably bring about some improvement by starting at the verbal end. If you simplify your English, you are freed from the worst follies of orthodoxy. You cannot speak any of the necessary dialects, and when you make a stupid remark its stupidity will be obvious, even to yourself. Political language — and with variations this is true of all political parties, from Conservatives to Anarchists — is designed to make lies sound truthful and murder respectable, and to give an appearance of solidity to pure wind. One cannot change this all in a moment, but one can at least change one's own habits, and from time to time one can even, if one jeers loudly enough, send some worn-out and useless phrase — some *jackboot, Achilles' heel, hotbed, melting pot, acid test, veritable inferno* or other lump of verbal refuse — into the dustbin where it belongs.

_____ **CONSIDERATIONS** _____

1. "Style is the man himself." How well, and in what ways, does Orwell's essay illustrate Buffon's aphorism? Select another author in the text, someone with a distinct style, and test it against Buffon's statement.

2. Assuming that Orwell's statement in Paragraph 2, "the fight against bad English is not frivolous and is not the exclusive concern of professional writers," is the conclusion of a syllogism, reconstruct the major and minor

premises of that syllogism by studying the steps Orwell takes to reach his conclusion.

3. Orwell documents his argument by quoting five passages by writers who wrote in the forties. From comparable sources, assemble a gallery of current specimens to help confirm or refute his contention that "the English language is in a bad way."

4. Orwell concludes with six rules. From the rest of his essay, how do you think he would define "anything outright barbarous" (in rule vi)?

5. Has Orwell broken some of his own rules? Point out and explain any examples you find. Look over his "Shooting an Elephant" and "A Hanging" as well as "Politics and the English Language."

6. In Paragraph 16, Orwell asserts that "The inflated style is itself a kind of euphemism." Look up the meaning of "euphemism" and compile examples from your local newspaper. Do you agree with Orwell that they are "swindles and perversions"? Note how Ambrose Bierce counts on our understanding of euphemisms in his Devil's Dictionary (pages 57–61).

*Two of George Orwell's best essays derive from his experience
as a colonial policeman, upholder of law and order for the British
empire. Many political thinkers derive an ideology from thought
and theory; Orwell's politics grew empirically from the life he
lived. He provides us models for learning by living — and for
learning by writing out of one's life.*

53

GEORGE ORWELL
Shooting an Elephant

1   In Moulmein, in Lower Burma, I was hated by large numbers of
people — the only time in my life that I have been important enough
for this to happen to me. I was sub-divisional police officer of the town,
and in an aimless, petty kind of way anti-European feeling was very
bitter. No one had the guts to raise a riot, but if a European woman
went through the bazaars alone somebody would probably spit betel
juice over her dress. As a police officer I was an obvious target and was
baited whenever it seemed safe to do so. When a nimble Burman
tripped me up on the football field and the referee (another Burman)
looked the other way, the crowd yelled with hideous laughter. This
happened more than once. In the end the sneering yellow faces of
young men that met me everywhere, the insults hooted after me when
I was at a safe distance, got badly on my nerves. The young Buddhist
priests were the worst of all. There were several thousands of them in
the town and none of them seemed to have anything to do except
stand on street corners and jeer at Europeans.

All this was perplexing and upsetting. For at that time I had 2
already made up my mind that imperialism was an evil thing and the
sooner I chucked up my job and got out of it the better. Theoretically
— and secretly, of course — I was all for the Burmese and all against
their oppressors, the British. As for the job I was doing, I hated it more
bitterly than I can perhaps make clear. In a job like that you see the
dirty work of Empire at close quarters. The wretched prisoners hud-
dling in the stinking cages of the lock-ups, the grey, cowed faces of the
long-term convicts, the scarred buttocks of the men who had been
flogged with bamboos — all these oppressed me with an intolerable
sense of guilt. But I could get nothing into perspective. I was young
and ill-educated and I had had to think out my problems in the utter
silence that is imposed on every Englishman in the East. I did not even
know that the British Empire is dying, still less did I know that it is a
great deal better than the younger empires that are going to supplant
it. All I knew was that I was stuck between my hatred of the empire I
served and my rage against the evil-spirited little beasts who tried to
make my job impossible. With one part of my mind I thought of the
British Raj as an unbreakable tyranny, as something clamped down, in
saecula saeculorum, upon the will of prostrate peoples; with another
part I thought that the greatest joy in the world would be to drive a
bayonet into a Buddhist priest's guts. Feelings like these are the normal by-products of imperialism; ask any Anglo-Indian official, if you
can catch him off duty.

One day something happened which in a roundabout way was 3
enlightening. It was a tiny incident in itself, but it gave me a better
glimpse than I had had before of the real nature of imperialism — the
real motives for which despotic governments act. Early one morning
the sub-inspector at a police station the other end of town rang me up
on the phone and said that an elephant was ravaging the bazaar. Would
I please come and do something about it? I did not know what I could
do, but I wanted to see what was happening and I got on to a pony and
started out. I took my rifle, an old .44 Winchester and much too small
to kill an elephant, but I thought the noise might be useful *in terro-
rem*. Various Burmans stopped me on the way and told me about the
elephant's doings. It was not, of course, a wild elephant, but a tame
one which had gone "must." It had been chained up, as tame elephants
always are when their attack of "must" is due, but on the previous
night it had broken its chain and escaped. Its mahout, the only person
who could manage it when it was in that state, had set out in pursuit,
but had taken the wrong direction and was now twelve hours' journey
away, and in the morning the elephant had suddenly reappeared in the

town. The Burmese population had no weapons and were quite help-less against it. It had already destroyed somebody's bamboo hut, killed a cow and raided some fruit-stalls and devoured the stock; also it had met the municipal rubbish van and, when the driver jumped out and took to his heels, had turned the van over and inflicted violences upon it.

4   The Burmese sub-inspector and some Indian constables were waiting for me in the quarter where the elephant had been seen. It was a very poor quarter, a labyrinth of squalid bamboo huts, thatched with palmleaf, winding all over a steep hillside. I remember that it was a cloudy, stuffy morning at the beginning of the rains. We began questioning the people as to where the elephant had gone and, as usual, failed to get any definite information. That is invariably the case in the East; a story always sounds clear enough at a distance, but the nearer you get to the scene of events the vaguer it becomes. Some of the people said that the elephant had gone in one direction, some said that he had gone in another, some professed not even to have heard of any elephant. I had almost made up my mind that the whole story was a pack of lies, when we heard yells a little distance away. There was a loud, scandalized cry of "Go away, child! Go away this instant!" and an old woman with a switch in her hand came round the corner of a hut, violently shooing away a crowd of naked children. Some more women followed, clicking their tongues and exclaiming; evidently there was something that the children ought not to have seen. I rounded the hut and saw a man's dead body sprawling in the mud. He was an Indian, a black Dravidian coolie, almost naked, and he could not have been dead many minutes. The people said that the elephant had come suddenly upon him round the corner of the hut, caught him with its trunk, put its foot on his back and ground him into the earth. This was the rainy season and the ground was soft, and his face had scored a trench a foot deep and a couple of yards long. He was lying on his belly with arms crucified and head sharply twisted to one side. His face was coated with mud, the eyes wide open, the teeth bared and grinning with an expression of unendurable agony. (Never tell me, by the way, that the dead look peaceful. Most of the corpses I have seen looked devilish.) The friction of the great beast's foot had stripped the skin from his back as neatly as one skins a rabbit. As soon as I saw the dead man I sent an orderly to a friend's house nearby to borrow an elephant rifle. I had already sent back the pony, not wanting it to go mad with fright and throw me if it smelt the elephant.

The orderly came back in a few minutes with a rifle and five 5 cartridges, and meanwhile some Burmans had arrived and told us that the elephant was in the paddy fields below, only a few hundred yards away. As I started forward practically the whole population of the quarter flocked out of the houses and followed me. They had seen the rifle and were all shouting excitedly that I was going to shoot the elephant. They had not shown much interest in the elephant when he was merely ravaging their homes, but it was different now that he was going to be shot. It was a bit of fun to them, as it would be to an English crowd; besides they wanted the meat. It made me vaguely uneasy. I had no intention of shooting the elephant — I had merely sent for the rifle to defend myself if necessary — and it is always unnerving to have a crowd following you. I marched down the hill, looking and feeling a fool, with the rifle over my shoulder and an ever-growing army of people jostling at my heels. At the bottom, when you got away from the huts, there was a metalled road and beyond that a miry waste of paddy fields a thousand yards across, not yet ploughed but soggy from the first rains and dotted with coarse grass. The elephant was standing eight yards from the road, his left side towards us. He took not the slightest notice of the crowd's approach. He was tearing up bunches of grass, beating them against his knees to clean them and stuffing them into his mouth.

I had halted on the road. As soon as I saw the elephant I knew 6 with perfect certainty that I ought not to shoot him. It is a serious matter to shoot a working elephant — it is comparable to destroying a huge and costly piece of machinery — and obviously one ought not to do it if it can possibly be avoided. And at that distance, peacefully eating, the elephant looked no more dangerous than a cow. I thought then and I think now that his attack of "must" was already passing off; in which case he would merely wander harmlessly about until the mahout came back and caught him. Moreover, I did not in the least want to shoot him. I decided that I would watch him for a little while to make sure that he did not turn savage again, and then go home.

But at that moment, I glanced round at the crowd that had fol- 7 lowed me. It was an immense crowd, two thousand at the least and growing every minute. It blocked the road for a long distance on either side. I looked at the sea of yellow faces above the garish clothes — faces all happy and excited over this bit of fun, all certain that the elephant was going to be shot. They were watching me as they would watch a conjuror about to perform a trick. They did not like me, but with the magical rifle in my hands I was momentarily worth watching. And suddenly I realized that I should have to shoot the elephant after all. The people expected it of me and I had got to do it; I could feel their two thousand wills pressing me forward, irresistibly. And it was at this moment, as I stood there with the rifle in my hands, that I first grasped the hollowness, the futility of the white man's dominion in the East. Here was I, the white man with his gun, standing in front of the unarmed native crowd — seemingly the leading actor of the piece; but in reality I was only an absurd puppet pushed to and fro by the will of those yellow faces behind. I perceived in this moment that when the white man turns tyrant it is his own freedom that he destroys. He becomes a sort of hollow, posing dummy, the conventionalized figure of a sahib. For it is the condition of his rule that he shall spend his life in trying to impress the "natives," and so in every crisis he has got to do what the "natives" expect of him. He wears a mask, and his face grows to fit it. I had got to shoot the elephant. I had committed myself to doing it when I sent for the rifle. A sahib has got to act like a sahib; he has got to appear resolute, to know his own mind and do definite things. To come all that way, rifle in hand, with two thousand people marching at my heels, and then to trail feebly away, having done nothing — no, that was impossible. The crowd would laugh at me. And my whole life, every white man's life in the East, was one long struggle not to be laughed at.

8   But I did not want to shoot the elephant. I watched him beating his bunch of grass against his knees, with that preoccupied grandmotherly air that elephants have. It seemed to me that it would be murder to shoot him. At that age I was not squeamish about killing animals, but I had never shot an elephant and never wanted to. (Somehow it always seems worse to kill a *large* animal.) Besides, there was the beast's owner to be considered. Alive, the elephant was worth at least a hundred pounds; dead, he would only be worth the value of his tusks, five pounds, possibly. But I had got to act quickly. I turned to some experienced-looking Burmans who had been there when we arrived, and asked them how the elephant had been behaving. They all said the same thing: he took no notice of you if you left him alone, but he might charge if you went too close to him.

9   It was perfectly clear to me what I ought to do. I ought to walk up to within, say, twenty-five yards of the elephant and test his behavior. If he charged, I could shoot; if he took no notice of me, it would be safe to leave him until the mahout came back. But also I knew that I was going to do no such thing. I was a poor shot with a rifle and the

ground was soft mud into which one would sink at every step. If the elephant charged and I missed him, I should have about as much chance as a toad under a steam-roller. But even then I was not thinking particularly of my own skin, only of the watchful yellow faces behind. For at that moment, with the crowd watching me, I was not afraid in the ordinary sense, as I would have been if I had been alone. A white man mustn't be frightened in front of "natives"; and so, in general, he isn't frightened. The sole thought in my mind was that if anything went wrong those two thousand Burmans would see me pursued, caught, trampled on and reduced to a grinning corpse like that Indian up the hill. And if that happened it was quite probable that some of them would laugh. That would never do. There was only one alternative. I shoved the cartridges into the magazine and lay down on the road to get a better aim.

The crowd grew very still, and a deep, low, happy sigh, as of   10
people who see the theatre curtain go up at last, breathed from innumerable throats. They were going to have their bit of fun after all. The rifle was a beautiful German thing with cross-hair sights. I did not then know that in shooting an elephant one would shoot to cut an imaginary bar running from ear-hole to ear-hole. I ought, therefore, as the elephant was sideways on, to have aimed straight at his ear-hole; actually I aimed several inches in front of this, thinking the brain would be further forward.

When I pulled the trigger I did not hear the bang or feel the kick   11
— one never does when a shot goes home — but I heard the devilish roar of glee that went up from the crowd. In that instant, in too short a time, one would have thought, even for the bullet to get there, a mysterious, terrible change had come over the elephant. He neither stirred nor fell, but every line of his body had altered. He looked suddenly stricken, shrunken, immensely old, as though the frightful impact of the bullet had paralysed him without knocking him down. At last, after what seemed a long time — it might have been five seconds, I dare say — he sagged flabbily to his knees. His mouth slobbered. An enormous senility seemed to have settled upon him. One could have imagined him thousands of years old. I fired again into the same spot. At the second shot he did not collapse but climbed with desperate slowness to his feet and stood weakly upright, with legs sagging and head drooping. I fired a third time. That was the shot that did for him. You could see the agony of it jolt his whole body and knock the last remnant of strength from his legs. But in falling he seemed for a moment to rise, for as his hind legs collapsed beneath

him he seemed to tower upward like a huge rock toppling, his trunk reaching skywards like a tree. He trumpeted, for the first and only time. And then down he came, his belly towards me, with a crash that seemed to shake the ground even where I lay.

12   I got up. The Burmans were already racing past me across the mud. It was obvious that the elephant would never rise again, but he was not dead. He was breathing very rhythmically with long rattling gasps, his great mound of a side painfully rising and falling. His mouth was wide open. I could see far down into caverns of pale pink throat. I waited a long time for him to die, but his breathing did not weaken. Finally I fired my two remaining shots into the spot where I thought his heart must be. The thick blood welled out of him like red velvet, but still he did not die. His body did not even jerk when the shots hit him, the tortured breathing continued without a pause. He was dying, very slowly and in great agony, but in some world remote from me where not even a bullet could damage him further. I felt I had got to put an end to that dreadful noise. It seemed dreadful to see the great beast lying there, powerless to move and yet powerless to die, and not even to be able to finish him. I sent back for my small rifle and poured shot after shot into his head and down his throat. They seemed to make no impression. The tortured gasps continued as steadily as the ticking of a clock.

13   In the end I could not stand it any longer and went away. I heard later that it took him half an hour to die. Burmans were bringing dahs and baskets even before I left, and I was told they had stripped his body almost to the bones by the afternoon.

14   Afterwards, of course, there were endless discussions about the shooting of the elephant. The owner was furious, but he was only an Indian and could do nothing. Besides, legally I had done the right thing, for a mad elephant has to be killed, like a mad dog, if its owner fails to control it. Among the Europeans opinion was divided. The older men said I was right, the younger men said it was a damn shame to shoot an elephant for killing a coolie, because the elephant was worth more than any damn Coringhee coolie. And afterwards I was very glad that the coolie had been killed; it put me legally in the right and it gave me sufficient pretext for shooting the elephant. I often wondered whether any of the others grasped that I had done it solely to avoid looking a fool.

____ CONSIDERATIONS _____

1. Some of Orwell's remarks about the Burmese make him sound like a racist; collect a half dozen of them on a separate sheet of paper, then look for lines or phrases that counter the first samples. Discuss your findings, particularly in terms of Orwell's purposes in his essay.

2. "In a job like that you see the dirty work of Empire at close quarters." If you ponder Orwell's capitalizing "Empire" (Paragraph 2) and then substitute other abstract terms for "Empire" — say, Government, Poverty, War, Hatred — you may discover one of the most important principles of effective writing, a principle beautifully demonstrated by Orwell's whole account.

3. In Paragraph 4, Orwell says, "the nearer you get to the scene of events the vaguer it becomes." Have you had any experience that would help you understand his remark? Would it hold true for the soldier caught in battle, a couple suffering a divorce, a football player caught in a pile-up on the scrimmage line?

4. Some years after his experience in Burma, Orwell became a well-known opponent of fascism. Explain how shooting the elephant taught him to detest totalitarianism.

5. "Somehow it always seems worse to kill a *large* animal," Orwell writes in Paragraph 8. Why? Are some lives more equal than others?

6. In Paragraph 10, Orwell describes his rifle as a "beautiful German thing." Does he use the word "beautiful" in the same way Don Sharp uses it in the last paragraph of his essay "Under the Hood"? Neither of the writers means "pulchritude" when he uses "beautiful." What synonyms might fit their sense of the word?

7. After two substantial paragraphs of agonizing detail, Orwell's elephant is still dying. Why does the writer inflict this punishment on the reader?

54

GEORGE ORWELL
A Hanging

1   It was in Burma, a sodden morning of the rains. A sickly light, like yellow tinfoil, was slanting over the high walls into the jail yard. We were waiting outside the condemned cells, a row of sheds fronted with double bars, like small animal cages. Each cell measured about ten feet by ten and was quite bare within except for a plank bed and a pot for drinking water. In some of them brown, silent men were squatting at the inner bars, with their blankets draped round them. These were the condemned men, due to be hanged within the next week or two.

2   One prisoner had been brought out of his cell. He was a Hindu, a puny wisp of a man, with a shaven head and vague liquid eyes. He had a thick, sprouting moustache, absurdly too big for his body, rather like the moustache of a comic man on the films. Six tall Indian warders were guarding him and getting him ready for the gallows. Two of them stood by with rifles and fixed bayonets, while the others handcuffed him, passed a chain through his handcuffs and fixed it to their belts, and lashed his arms tight to his sides. They crowded very close about him, with their hands always on him in a careful, caressing grip, as though all the while feeling him to make sure he was there. It was like men handling a fish which is still alive and may jump back into the water. But he stood quite unresisting, yielding his arms limply to the ropes, as though he hardly noticed what was happening.

3   Eight o'clock struck and a bugle call, desolately thin in the wet

air, floated from the distant barracks. The superintendent of the jail, who was standing apart from the rest of us, moodily prodding the gravel with his stick, raised his head at the sound. He was an army doctor, with a grey toothbrush moustache and a gruff voice. "For God's sake hurry up, Francis," he said irritably. "The man ought to have been dead by this time. Aren't you ready yet?"

Francis, the head jailer, a fat Dravidian in a white drill suit and   4
gold spectacles, waved his black hand. "Yes sir, yes sir," he bubbled. "All iss satisfactorily prepared. The hangman iss waiting. We shall proceed."

"Well, quick march, then. The prisoners can't get their breakfast   5
till this job's over."

We set out for the gallows. Two warders marched on either side   6
of the prisoner, with their rifles at the slope; two others marched close against him, gripping him by arm and shoulder, as though at once pushing and supporting him. The rest of us, magistrates and the like, followed behind. Suddenly, when we had gone ten yards, the procession stopped short without any order or warning. A dreadful thing had happened — a dog, come goodness knows whence, had appeared in the yard. It came bounding among us with a loud volley of barks and leapt round us wagging its whole body, wild with glee at finding so many human beings together. It was a large woolly dog, half Airedale, half pariah. For a moment it pranced round us, and then, before anyone could stop it, it had made a dash for the prisoner, and jumping up tried to lick his face. Everybody stood aghast, too taken aback even to grab the dog.

"Who let that bloody brute in here?" said the superintendent   7
angrily. "Catch it, someone!"

A warder detached from the escort, charged clumsily after the   8
dog, but it danced and gambolled just out of his reach, taking everything as part of the game. A young Eurasian jailer picked up a handful of gravel and tried to stone the dog away, but it dodged the stones and came after us again. Its yaps echoed from the jail walls. The prisoner, in the grasp of the two warders, looked on incuriously, as though this was another formality of the hanging. It was several minutes before someone managed to catch the dog. Then we put my handkerchief through its collar and moved off once more, with the dog still straining and whimpering.

It was about forty yards to the gallows. I watched the bare brown   9
back of the prisoner marching in front of me. He walked clumsily with his bound arms, but quite steadily, with that bobbing gait of the Indian

who never straightens his knees. At each step his muscles slid neatly into place, the lock of hair on his scalp danced up and down, his feet printed themselves on the wet gravel. And once, in spite of the men who gripped him by each shoulder, he stepped lightly aside to avoid a puddle on the path.

10   It is curious; but till that moment I had never realized what it means to destroy a healthy, conscious man. When I saw the prisoner step aside to avoid the puddle I saw the mystery, the unspeakable wrongness, of cutting a life short when it is in full tide. This man was not dying, he was alive just as we are alive. All the organs of his body were working — bowels digesting food, skin renewing itself, nails growing, tissues forming — all toiling away in solemn foolery. His nails would still be growing when he stood on the drop, when he was falling through the air with a tenth-of-a-second to live. His eyes saw the yellow gravel and the grey walls, and his brain still remembered, foresaw, reasoned — even about puddles. He and we were a party of men walking together, seeing, hearing, feeling, understanding the same world; and in two minutes, with a sudden snap, one of us would be gone — one mind less, one world less.

11   The gallows stood in a small yard, separate from the main grounds of the prison, and overgrown with tall prickly weeds. It was a brick erection like three sides of a shed, with planking on top, and above that two beams and a crossbar with the rope dangling. The hangman, a greyhaired convict in the white uniform of the prison, was waiting beside his machine. He greeted us with a servile crouch as we entered. At a word from Francis the two warders, gripping the prisoner more closely than ever, half led, half pushed him to the gallows and helped him clumsily up the ladder. Then the hangman climbed up and fixed the rope round the prisoner's neck.

12   We stood waiting, five yards away. The warders had formed in a rough circle round the gallows. And then, when the noose was fixed, the prisoner began crying out to his god. It was a high, reiterated cry of "Ram! Ram! Ram! Ram!" not urgent and fearful like a prayer or cry for help, but steady, rhythmical, almost like the tolling of a bell. The dog answered the sound with a whine. The hangman, still standing on the gallows, produced a small cotton bag like a flour bag and drew it down over the prisoner's face. But the sound, muffled by the cloth, still persisted, over and over again: "Ram! Ram! Ram! Ram! Ram!"

13   The hangman climbed down and stood ready, holding the lever. Minutes seemed to pass. The steady, muffled crying from the prisoner went on and on, "Ram! Ram! Ram!" never faltering for an instant. The superintendent, his head on his chest, was slowly poking the

ground with his stick; perhaps he was counting the cries, allowing the prisoner a fixed number — fifty, perhaps, or a hundred. Everyone had changed colour. The Indians had gone grey like bad coffee, and one or two of the bayonets were wavering. We looked at the lashed, hooded man on the drop, and listened to his cries — each cry another second of life; the same thought was in all our minds; oh, kill him quickly, get it over, stop that abominable noise!

Suddenly the superintendent made up his mind. Throwing up his head he made a swift motion with his stick. "Chalo!" he shouted almost fiercely. 14

There was a clanking noise, and then dead silence. The prisoner had vanished, and the rope was twisting on itself. I let go of the dog, and it galloped immediately to the back of the gallows; but when it got there it stopped short, barked, and then retreated into a corner of the yard, where it stood among the weeds, looking timorously out at us. We went round the gallows to inspect the prisoner's body. He was dangling with his toes pointed straight downwards, very slowly revolving, as dead as a stone. 15

The superintendent reached out with his stick and poked the bare brown body; it oscillated slightly. "*He's* all right," said the superintendent. He backed out from under the gallows, and blew out a deep breath. The moody look had gone out of his face quite suddenly. He glanced at his wrist-watch. "Eight minutes past eight. Well, that's all for this morning, thank God." 16

The warders unfixed bayonets and marched away. The dog, sobered and conscious of having misbehaved itself, slipped after them. We walked out of the gallows yard, past the condemned cells with their waiting prisoners, into the big central yard of the prison. The convicts, under the command of warders armed with lathis, were already receiving their breakfast. They squatted in long rows, each man holding a tin pannikin, while two warders with buckets marched round ladling out rice; it seemed quite a homely, jolly scene, after the hanging. An enormous relief had come upon us now that the job was done. One felt an impulse to sing, to break into a run, to snigger. All at once everyone began chatting gaily. 17

The Eurasian boy walking beside me nodded towards the way we had come, with a knowing smile: "Do you know, sir, our friend (he meant the dead man) when he heard his appeal had been dismissed, he pissed on the floor of his cell. From fright. Kindly take one of my cigarettes, sir. Do you not admire my new silver case, sir? From the boxwallah, two rupees eight annas. Classy European style." 18

Several people laughed — at what, nobody seemed certain. 19

20   Francis was walking by the superintendent, talking garrulously: "Well, sir, all has passed off with the utmost satisfactoriness. It was all finished — flick! Like that. It iss not always so — oah, no! I have known cases where the doctor wass obliged to go beneath the gallows and pull the prissoner's legs to ensure decease. Most disagreeable!"

21   "Wriggling about, eh? That's bad," said the superintendent.

22   "Ach, sir, it iss worse when they become refractory! One man, I recall, clung to the bars of hiss cage when we went to take him out. You will scarcely credit, sir, that it took six warders to dislodge him, three pulling at each leg. We reasoned with him, 'My dear fellow,' we said, 'think of all the pain and trouble you are causing to us!' But no, he would not listen! Ach, he wass very troublesome!"

23   I found that I was laughing quite loudly. Everyone was laughing. Even the superintendent grinned in a tolerant way. "You'd better all come out and have a drink," he said quite genially. "I've got a bottle of whiskey in the car. We could do with it."

24   We went through the big double gates of the prison into the road. "Pulling at his legs!" exclaimed a Burmese magistrate suddenly, and burst into a loud chuckling. We all began laughing again. At that moment Francis' anecdote seemed extraordinarily funny. We all had a drink together, native and European alike, quite amicably. The dead man was a hundred yards away.

___ CONSIDERATIONS ___

1. Many readers have described Orwell's "A Hanging" as a powerful condemnation of capital punishment. Study Orwell's technique in drawing from his readers the desired inference. It might be helpful to read another master of implication — Ernest Hemingway in his short story "Hills Like White Elephants."

2. Point out examples of Orwell's skillful use of detail to establish the place and the mood of "A Hanging." Adapt his technique to your purpose in your next essay.

3. What minor incident caused Orwell suddenly to see "the unspeakable wrongness . . . of cutting a life short"? Why?

4. What effect, in Paragraph 6, does the boisterous dog have on the players of this scene? On you, the reader? Explain in terms of the whole essay.

5. "One mind, one world less" is the way Orwell sums up the demise of the Hindu prisoner. Obviously, Orwell's statement is highly compressed, jamming into its short length many ideas, hopes, and fears. Write a short essay, opening up his aphorism so that your readers get some idea of what can be

packed into five short words. For additional examples of compressed expression, see Ambrose Bierce's "Devil's Dictionary," and any of the poems in this book.

6. The warden and others present were increasingly disconcerted by the prisoner's continued cry, "Ram! Ram! Ram! Ram!" But note Orwell's description of that cry in Paragraphs 12 and 13. Does that description give you a clue as to the nature of the man's cry? Why doesn't Orwell explain it?

Robert M. Pirsig (b. 1928), in his book Zen and the Art of Motorcycle Maintenance *(1974), describes a motorcycle journey he takes with his young son, and among passages of narrative and description, explains and argues ideas about education, technology, and thought. Pirsig also reminisces about the past. Especially he remembers the thoughts of one "Phaedrus" — the "he" of this essay — who is Pirsig's earlier self, before a mental breakdown and shock treatments altered his personality. Here, he remembers Phaedrus's Church of Reason lecture to his composition course students in a western university. The lecture argues the distinction between the university as we know it and the ideal university, starting with analogy and moving on to contrast. See how Pirsig uses analogy to analyze, to suggest the separation of material and ideal.*

55

ROBERT M. PIRSIG

The Church of Reason

1   That night, for the next day's lecture, he wrote out his defense of what he was doing. This was the Church of Reason lecture, which in contrast to his usual sketchy lecture notes, was very long and very carefully elaborated.

2   It begins with reference to a newspaper article about a country church building with an electric beer sign hanging right over the front entrance. The building had been sold and was being used as a bar. One can guess that some classroom laughter started at this point. The college was well-known for drunken partying and the image vaguely

fit. The article said a number of people had complained to the church officials about it. It had been a Catholic church, and the priest who had been delegated to respond to the criticism had sounded quite irritated about the whole thing. To him it had revealed an incredible ignorance of what a church really was. Did they think that bricks and boards and glass constituted a church? Or the shape of the roof? Here, posing as piety, was an example of the very materialism the church opposed. The building in question was not holy ground. It had been desanctified. That was the end of it. The beer sign resided over a bar, not a church, and those who couldn't tell the difference were simply revealing something about themselves.

Phaedrus said the same confusion existed about the University 3 and that was why loss of accreditation was hard to understand. The real University is not a material object. It is not a group of buildings that can be defended by police. He explained that when a college lost its accreditation, nobody came and shut down the school. There were no legal penalties, no fines, no jail sentences. Classes did not stop. Everything went on just as before. Students got the same education they would if the school didn't lose its accreditation. All that would happen, Phaedrus said, would simply be an official recognition of a condition that already existed. It would be similar to excommunication. What would happen is that the *real* University, which no legislature can dictate to and which can never be identified by any location of bricks or boards or glass, would simply declare that this place was no longer "holy ground." The real University would vanish from it, and all that would be left was the bricks and the books and the material manifestation.

It must have been a strange concept to all of the students, and I 4 can imagine him waiting for a long time for it to sink in, and perhaps then waiting for the question, What do you think the real University is?

His notes, in response to his question, state the following: 5

The real University, he said, has no specific location. It owns no 6 property, pays no salaries and receives no material dues. The real University is a state of mind. It is that great heritage of rational thought that has been brought down to us through the centuries and which does not exist at any specific location. It's a state of mind which is regenerated throughout the centuries by a body of people who traditionally carry the title of professor, but even that title is not part of the real University. The real University is nothing less than the continuing body of reason itself.

7   In addition to this state of mind, "reason," there's a legal entity which is unfortunately called by the same name but which is quite another thing. This is a nonprofit corporation, a branch of the state with a specific address. It owns property, is capable of paying salaries, of receiving money and of responding to legislative pressures in the process.

8   But this second university, the legal corporation, cannot teach, does not generate new knowledge or evaluate ideas. It is not the real University at all. It is just a church building, the setting, the location at which conditions have been made favorable for the real church to exist.

9   Confusion continually occurs in people who fail to see this difference, he said, and think that control of the church buildings implies control of the church. They see professors as employees of the second university who should abandon reason when told to and take orders with no backtalk, the same way employees do in other corporations.

10   They see the second university, but fail to see the first.

_____ **CONSIDERATIONS** _____

1. What are the telltale signs that the "real University" is present or absent on your campus?

2. What happens when a school loses its accreditation? How is accreditation maintained? Why?

3. Pirsig's definition of the "real University" puts a great deal of weight on rational thought. Do you agree with that emphasis?

4. Can you think of institutions other than the church and the university whose essence might be explained as in Pirsig's essay?

5. What techniques does Pirsig use that differ from those employed in other argumentative essays?

*Sylvia Plath (1932–1963) grew up in Massachusetts and gradu-
ated from Smith College. She was a precocious writer, publishing
professionally even as an undergraduate. Her first devotion was
to poetry but she also worked in fiction and the essay. On a Ful-
bright Fellowship to England she met and married the English
poet Ted Hughes; they had two children. Her first book of poetry,*
The Colossus, *was published in 1960, her novel* The Bell Jar *in
1963. The poems of* Ariel *(1965) are her best work — poems of
intense suffering and power, including "The Bee Meeting." In
February of 1963 she killed herself.*

    The journal entry that follows is from Johnny Panic and the
Bible of Dreams *(1978), a posthumous collection of short stories
and miscellaneous prose. Here we watch a young writer at work
— first on her journal — observant, careful, distinctive; then we
watch her refine her prose into the lines of the finished poem.*
The Collected Poems *appeared in 1981, and* The Journals of Sylvia Plath *in 1982.*

56

SYLVIA PLATH

Journal Entries:
Charlie Pollard and
the Beekeepers

JUNE 7 [1962]

The midwife stopped up to see Ted at noon to remind him that the   1
Devon beekeepers were having a meeting at six at Charlie Pollard's.
We were interested in starting a hive, so dumped the babies in bed and

jumped in the car and dashed down the hill past the old factory to Mill Lane, a row of pale orange stucco cottages on the Taw, which gets flooded whenever the river rises. We drove into the dusty, ugly paved parking lot under the gray peaks of the factory buildings, unused since 1928 and now only used for wool storage. We felt very new & shy, I hugging my bare arms in the cool of the evening, for I had not thought to bring a sweater. We crossed a little bridge to the yard where a group of miscellaneous Devonians were standing — an assortment of shapeless men in brown-speckled, bulgy tweeds, Mr. Pollard in white shirtsleeves, with his dark, nice brown eyes and oddly Jewy head, tan, balding, dark-haired. I saw two women, one very large, tall, stout, in a glistening aqua-blue raincoat, the other cadaverous as a librarian in a dun raincoat. Mr. Pollard glided toward us & stood for a moment on the bridge end, talking. He indicated a pile of hives, like white and green blocks of wood with little gables, & said we could have one, if we would like to fix it up. A small pale blue car pulled into the yard: the midwife. Her moony beam came at us through the windshield. Then the rector came pontificating across the bridge, & there was a silence that grew round him. He carried a curious contraption — a dark felt hat with a screen box built on under it, and cloth for a neckpiece under that. I thought the hat a clerical beekeeping hat, and that he must have made it for himself. Then I saw, on the grass, and in hands, everybody was holding a bee hat, some with netting of nylon, most with box screening, some with khaki round hats. I felt barer and barer. People became concerned. Have you no hat? Have you no coat? Then a dry little woman came up, Mrs. P, the secretary of the society, with tired, short blond hair. "I have a boiler suit." She went to her car and came back with a small white silk button-down smock, the sort pharmacist's assistants use. I put it on and buttoned it & felt more protected. Last year, said the midwife, Charlie Pollard's bees were bad-tempered and made everybody run. Everyone seemed to be waiting for someone. But then we all slowly filed after Charlie Pollard to his beehives. We threaded our way through neatly weeded allotment gardens, one with bits of tinfoil and a fan of black and white feathers on a string, very decorative, to scare the birds, and twiggy lean-tos over the plants. Black-eyed sweetpea-like blooms: broad beans, somebody said. The gray ugly backs of the factory. Then we came to a clearing, roughly scythed, with one hive, a double-brood hive, two layers. From this hive Charlie Pollard wanted to make three hives. I understood very little. The men gathered round the hive. Charlie Pollard started squirting smoke from a little funnel with a hand bellows attached to it round the entry at the bottom of the hive. "Too much smoke," hissed the large, blue-raincoated woman next to me. "What do you do if they sting?" I whispered, as the bees, now Charlie had lifted the top off the hive, were zinging out and dancing round as at the end of long elastics. (Charlie had produced a fashionable white straw Italian hat for me with a black nylon veil that collapsed perilously into my face in the least wind. The rector had tucked it into my collar, much to my surprise. "Bees always crawl up, never down," he said. I had drawn it down loose over my shoulders.) The woman said, "Stand behind me, I'll protect you." I did. (I had spoken to her husband earlier, a handsome, rather sarcastic man standing apart, silver hair, a military blue eye. Plaid tie, checked shirt, plaid vest, all different. Tweedy suit, navy blue beret. His wife, he had said, kept twelve hives & was the expert. The bees always stung him. His nose & lips, his wife later said.)

The men were lifting out rectangular yellow slides, crusted with 2 bees, crawling, swarming. I felt prickles all over me, & itches. I had one pocket & was advised to keep my hands in this and not move. "See all the bees round the rector's dark trousers!" whispered the woman. "They don't seem to like white." I was grateful for my white smock. The rector was somehow an odd man out, referred to now and then by Charlie jestingly: "Eh, rector?" "Maybe they want to join his church," one man, emboldened by the anonymity of the hats, suggested.

The donning of the hats had been an odd ceremony. Their ugli- 3 ness & anonymity very compelling, as if we were all party to a rite. They were brown or gray or faded green felt, mostly, but there was one white straw boater with a ribbon. All faces, shaded, became alike. Commerce became possible with complete strangers.

The men were lifting slides, Charlie Pollard squirting smoke, 4 into another box. They were looking for queen cells — long, pendulous, honey-colored cells from which the new queens would come. The blue-coated woman pointed them out. She was from British Guiana, had lived alone in the jungle for eighteen years, lost £25 on her first bees there — there had been no honey for them to eat. I was aware of bees buzzing and stalling before my face. The veil seemed hallucinatory. I could not see it for moments at a time. Then I became aware I was in a bone-stiff trance, intolerably tense, and shifted round to where I could see better. "Spirit of my death father, protect me!" I arrogantly prayed. A dark, rather nice, "unruly"-looking man came up through the cut grasses. Everyone turned, murmured, "O Mr. Jenner, we didn't think you were coming."

5   This, then, the awaited expert, the "government man" from Exeter. An hour late. He donned a white boiler suit and a very expert bee hat — a vivid green dome, square black screen box for head, joined with yellow cloth at the corners, and a white neckpiece. The men muttered, told what had been done. They began looking for the old queen. Slide after slide was lifted, examined on both sides. To no avail. Myriads of crawling, creeping bees. As I understood it from my blue bee-lady, the first new queen out would kill the old ones, so the new queen cells were moved to different hives. The old queen would be left in hers. But they couldn't find her. Usually the old queen swarmed before the new queen hatched. This was to prevent swarming. I heard words like "supersede," "queen excluder" (a slatted screen of metal only workers could crawl through). The rector slipped away unnoticed, then the midwife. "He used too much smoke" was the general criticism of Charlie Pollard. The queen hates smoke. She might have swarmed earlier. She might be hiding. She was not marked. It grew later. Eight. Eight-thirty. The hives were parceled up, queen excluders put on. An old beamy brown man wisely jutted a forefinger as we left. "She's in that one." The beekeepers clustered around Mr. Jenner with questions. The secretary sold chances for a bee festival.

FRIDAY, JUNE 8

6   Ted & I drove down to Charlie Pollard's about nine tonight to collect our hive. He was standing at the door of his cottage in Mill Lane, the corner one, in white shirtsleeves, collar open, showing dark chest hairs & a white mail-knit undershirt. His pretty blond wife smiled & waved. We went over the bridge to the shed, with its rotovator, orange, resting at the end. Talked of floods, fish, Ash Ridge: the Taw flooded his place over & over. He was wanting to move up, had an eye on the lodge at Ash Ridge, had hives up there. His father-in-law had been head gardener when they had six gardeners. Told of great heaters to dry hay artificially & turn it to meal: two thousand, four thousand, the machines cost, were lying up there now, hardly used. He hadn't been able to get any more flood insurance once he had claimed. Had his rugs cleaned, but they were flat: you can live with them, I can't, he told the inspector. Had to have the upholstered sofa & chairs all redone at the bottom. Walked down the first step from the second floor one night & put his foot in water. A big salmon inhabited his reach of the Taw. "To be honest with you," he said, over

& over. "To be honest with you." Showed us his big barny black offices. A honey ripener with a beautiful sweet-smelling, slow gold slosh of honey at the bottom. Loaned us a bee book. We loaded with our creaky old wood hive. He said if we cleaned it and painted it over Whitsun, he'd order a swarm of docile bees. Had showed us his beautiful red-gold Italian queen the day before, with her glossy green mark on the thorax, I think. He had made it. To see her the better. The bees were bad-tempered, though. She would lay a lot of docile bees. We said: Docile, be sure now, & drove home.

These few lines were typed at the top margin of the original MS:

Noticed: a surround of tall white cow parsley, pursy yellow gorse bloom, an old Christmas tree, white hawthorn, strong-smelling.

57

SYLVIA PLATH
The Bee Meeting

Who are these people at the bridge to meet me? They are the
    villagers ——
The rector, the midwife, the sexton, the agent for bees.
In my sleeveless summery dress I have no protection,
And they are all gloved and covered, why did nobody tell me?
5 They are smiling and taking out veils tacked to ancient hats.

I am nude as a chicken neck, does nobody love me?
Yes, here is the secretary of bees with her white shop smock,
Buttoning the cuffs at my wrists and the slit from my neck to my
    knees.
Now I am milkweed silk, the bees will not notice.
10 They will not smell my fear, my fear, my fear.

Which is the rector now, is it that man in black?
Which is the midwife, is that her blue coat?
Everybody is nodding a square black head, they are knights in visors,
Breastplates of cheesecloth knotted under the armpits.
15 Their smiles and their voices are changing. I am led through a
    beanfield.

Strips of tinfoil winking like people,
Feather dusters fanning their hands in a sea of bean flowers,

From *Ariel* by Sylvia Plath. Copyright © 1963 by Ted Hughes. Reprinted by permission of Harper & Row, Publishers, Inc. and Olwyn Hughes.

330

Creamy bean flowers with black eyes and leaves like bored hearts.
Is it blood clots the tendrils are dragging up that string?
No, no, it is scarlet flowers that will one day be edible. 20

Now they are giving me a fashionable white straw Italian hat
And a black veil that moulds to my face, they are making me one of
    them.
They are leading me to the shorn grove, the circle of hives.
Is it the hawthorn that smells so sick?
The barren body of hawthorn, etherizing its children. 25

Is it some operation that is taking place?
It is the surgeon my neighbours are waiting for,
This apparition in a green helmet,
Shining gloves and white suit.
Is it the butcher, the grocer, the postman, someone I know? 30

I cannot run, I am rooted, and the gorse hurts me
With its yellow purses, its spiky armoury.
I could not run without having to run forever.
The white hive is snug as a virgin,
Sealing off her brood cells, her honey, and quietly humming. 35

Smoke rolls and scarves in the grove.
The mind of the hive thinks this is the end of everything.
Here they come, the outriders, on their hysterical elastics.
If I stand very still, they will think I am cow parsley,
A gullible head untouched by their animosity, 40

Not even nodding, a personage in a hedgerow.
The villagers open the chambers, they are hunting the queen.
Is she hiding, is she eating honey? She is very clever.
She is old, old, old, she must live another year, and she knows it.
While in their fingerjoint cells the new virgins 45

Dream of a duel they will win inevitably,
A curtain of wax dividing them from the bride flight,
The upflight of the murderess into a heaven that loves her.
The villagers are moving the virgins, there will be no killing.
The old queen does not show herself, is she so ungrateful? 50

I am exhausted, I am exhausted ——
Pillar of white in a blackout of knives.
I am the magician's girl who does not flinch.
The villagers are untying their disguises, they are shaking hands.

55   Whose is that long white box in the grove, what have they accomplished, why am I cold?

_____ CONSIDERATIONS _____

1. To what extent did Sylvia Plath draw upon her notebook for material
in writing her poem, "The Bee Meeting"? Read both pieces carefully and list
any phrases, characters, events, and ideas that notebook and poem share. Note
changes in the material as it moved from notebook to poem.

2. Compare Plath's notebook entries with passages from other notebooks appearing in this book — those of Joan Didion, Anaïs Nin, and Thomas
Wolfe. Discuss differences and similarities. Compare your own daily writing
or journal.

3. Study the brief but graphic description of each of the people Plath
meets at the gathering of beekeepers. How do they differ? What do her observations reveal, other than the physical appearance of the subjects?

4. Study the details Plath notes of the places themselves — the parking
lot, the gardens. Do these details reveal Plath's feelings, or are they incidental?

5. "Commerce became possible with complete strangers," writes Plath
at the end of Paragraph 3. Consider this curious phenomenon: that strangers
will often speak more freely than will acquaintances. Can you explain this
behavior?

6. Reread Plath's notebook account, looking especially for points that
would allow you to explain either that Plath felt very much a part of the
beekeeping crowd or that she remained aloof, an interested but uninvolved
observer. It might be helpful to read Wendell Berry's "The Reactor and the
Garden."

Katherine Anne Porter (1890–1980) was born in Texas. The Collected Stores of Katherine Anne Porter *(1979) gathers her best-known work. She also published a novel* The Ship of Fools *(1962) and the* Collected Essays and Occasional Writings of Katherine Anne Porter *(1948). She writes about women and men, with a sharp eye for ironies of human behavior. Her sharp eye benefits from a clear prose style.*

58

KATHERINE ANNE PORTER
The Necessary Enemy

She is a frank, charming, fresh-hearted young woman who married for love. She and her husband are one of those gay, good-looking young pairs who ornament this modern scene rather more in profusion perhaps than ever before in our history. They are handsome, with a talent for finding their way in their world, they work at things that interest them, their tastes agree and their hopes. They intend in all good faith to spend their lives together, to have children and do well by them and each other — to be happy, in fact, which for them is the whole point of their marriage. And all in stride, keeping their wits about them. Nothing romantic, mind you; their feet are on the ground.

Unless they were this sort of person, there would be not much point to what I wish to say; for they would seem to be an example of the high-spirited, right-minded young whom the critics are always invoking to come forth and do their duty and practice all those sterling old-fashioned virtues which in every generation seem to be falling into disrepair. As for virtues, these young people are more or less on their own, like most of their kind; they get very little moral or other aid from their society; but after three years of marriage this very contemporary young woman finds herself facing the oldest and ugliest dilemma of marriage.

3   She is dismayed, horrified, full of guilt and forebodings because she is finding out little by little that she is capable of hating her husband, whom she loves faithfully. She can hate him at times as fiercely and mysteriously, indeed in terribly much the same way, as often she hated her parents, her brothers and sisters, whom she loves, when she was a child. Even then it had seemed to her a kind of black treacherousness in her, her private wickedness that, just the same, gave her her only private life. That was one thing her parents never knew about her, never seemed to suspect. For it was never given a name. They did and said hateful things to her and to each other as if by right, as if in them it was a kind of virtue. But when they said to her, "Control your feelings," it was never when she was amiable and obedient, only in the black times of her hate. So it was her secret, a shameful one. When they punished her, sometimes for the strangest reasons, it was, they said, only because they loved her — it was for her good. She did not believe this, but she thought herself guilty of something worse than ever they had punished her for. None of this really frightened her: the real fright came when she discovered that at times her father and mother hated each other; this was like standing on the doorsill of a familiar room and seeing in a lightning flash that the floor was gone, you were on the edge of a bottomless pit. Sometimes she felt that both of them hated her, but that passed, it was simply not a thing to be thought of, much less believed. She thought she had outgrown all this, but here it was again, an element in her own nature she could not control, or feared she could not. She would have to hide from her husband, if she could, the same spot in her feelings she had hidden from her parents, and for the same no doubt disreputable, selfish reason: she wants to keep his love.

4   Above all, she wants him to be absolutely confident that she loves him, for that is the real truth, no matter how unreasonable it sounds, and no matter how her own feelings betray them both at times. She depends recklessly on his love; yet while she is hating him, he might very well be hating her as much or even more, and it would serve her right. But she does not want to be served right, she wants to be loved and forgiven — that is, to be sure he would forgive her any-

thing, if he had any notion of what she had done. But best of all she would like not to have anything in her love that should ask for forgiveness. She doesn't mean about their quarrels — they are not so bad. Her feelings are out of proportion, perhaps. She knows it is perfectly natural for people to disagree, have fits of temper, fight it out; they learn quite a lot about each other that way, and not all of it disappointing either. When it passes, her hatred seems quite unreal. It always did.

Love. We are early taught to say it. I love you. We are trained to the thought of it as if there were nothing else, or nothing else worth having without it, or nothing worth having which it could not bring with it. Love is taught, always by precept, sometimes by example. Then hate, which no one meant to teach us, comes of itself. It is true that if we say I love you, it may be received with doubt, for there are times when it is hard to believe. Say I hate you, and the one spoken to believes it instantly, once for all. 5

Say I love you a thousand times to that person afterward and mean it every time, and still it does not change the fact that once we said I hate you, and meant that too. It leaves a mark on that surface love had worn so smooth with its eternal caresses. Love must be learned, and learned again and again; there is no end to it. Hate needs no instruction, but waits only to be provoked . . . hate, the unspoken word, the unacknowledged presence in the house, that faint smell of brimstone among the roses, that invisible tongue-tripper, that unkempt finger in every pie, that sudden oh-so-curiously *chilling* look — could it be boredom? — on your dear one's features, making them quite ugly. Be careful: love, perfect love, is in danger. 6

If it is not perfect, it is not love, and if it is not love, it is bound to be hate sooner or later. This is perhaps a not too exaggerated statement of the extreme position of Romantic Love, more especially in America, where we are all brought up on it, whether we know it or not. Romantic Love is changeless, faithful, passionate, and its sole end is to render the two lovers happy. It has no obstacles save those provided by the hazards of fate (that is to say, society), and such sufferings as the lovers may cause each other are only another word for delight: exciting jealousies, thrilling uncertainties, the ritual dance of courtship within the charmed closed circle of their secret alliance; all *real* troubles come from without, they face them unitedly in perfect confidence. Marriage is not the end but only the beginning of true happiness, cloudless, changeless to the end. That the candidates for this 7 blissful condition have never seen an example of it, nor ever knew anyone who had, makes no difference. That is the ideal and they will achieve it.

8   How did Romantic Love manage to get into marriage at last, where it was most certainly never intended to be? At its highest it was tragic; the love of Héloïse and Abélard. At its most graceful, it was the homage of the trouvère for his lady. In its most popular form, the adulterous strayings of solidly married couples who meant to stray for their own good reasons, but at the same time do nothing to upset the property settlements or the line of legitimacy; at its most trivial, the pretty trifling of shepherd and shepherdess.

9   This was generally condemned by church and state and a word of fear to honest wives whose mortal enemy it was. Love within the sober, sacred realities of marriage was a matter of personal luck, but in any case, private feelings were strictly a private affair having, at least in theory, no bearing whatever on the fixed practice of the rules of an institution never intended as a recreation ground for either sex. If the couple discharged their religious and social obligations, furnished forth a copious progeny, kept their troubles to themselves, maintained public civility and died under the same roof, even if not always on speaking terms, it was rightly regarded as a successful marriage. Apparently this testing ground was too severe for all but the stoutest spirits; it too was based on an ideal, as impossible in its way as the ideal Romantic Love. One good thing to be said for it is that society took responsibility for the conditions of marriage, and the sufferers within its bonds could always blame the system, not themselves. But Romantic Love crept into the marriage bed, very stealthily, by centuries, bringing its absurd notions about love as eternal springtime and marriage as a personal adventure meant to provide personal happiness. To a Western romantic such as I, though my views have been much modified by painful experience, it still seems to me a charming work of the human imagination, and it is a pity its central notion has been taken too literally and has hardened into a convention as cramping and enslaving as the older one. The refusal to acknowledge the evils in ourselves which therefore are implicit in any human situation is as extreme and unworkable a proposition as the doctrine of total depravity; but somewhere between them, or maybe beyond them, there does exist a possibility for reconciliation between our desires for impossible satisfactions and the simple unalterable fact that we also desire to be unhappy and that we create our own sufferings; and out of these sufferings we salvage our fragments of happiness.

Our young woman who has been taught that an important part 10 of her human nature is not real because it makes trouble and interferes with her peace of mind and shakes her self-love, has been very badly taught; but she has arrived at a most important stage of her re-education. She is afraid her marriage is going to fail because she has not love enough to face its difficulties; and this because at times she feels a painful hostility toward her husband, and cannot admit its reality because such an admission would damage in her own eyes her view of what love should be, an absurd view, based on her vanity of power. Her hatred is real as her love is real, but her hatred has the advantage at present because it works on a blind instinctual level, it is lawless; and her love is subjected to a code of ideal conditions, impossible by their very nature of fulfillment, which prevents its free growth and deprives it of its right to recognize its human limitations and come to grips with them. Hatred is natural in a sense that love, as she conceives it, a young person brought up in the tradition of Romantic Love, is not natural at all. Yet it did not come by hazard, it is the very imperfect expression of the need of the human imagination to create beauty and harmony out of chaos, no matter how mistaken its notion of these things may be, nor how clumsy its methods. It has conjured love out of the air, and seeks to preserve it by incantations; when she spoke a vow to love and honor her husband until death, she did a very reckless thing, for it is not possible by an act of the will to fulfill such an engagement. But it was the necessary act of faith performed in defense of a mode of feeling, the statement of honorable intention to practice as well as she is able the noble, acquired faculty of love, that very mysterious overtone to sex which is the best thing in it. Her hatred is part of it, the necessary enemy and ally.

____ CONSIDERATIONS ____

1. How do the flat opening statements of Porter's essay establish its tone? What patterns of sentence construction can you find?

2. In Paragraph 5 Porter remarks on one's need to reiterate love, which "may be received with doubt," while hate is believed "instantly, once and for all." How does Porter resolve this paradox in the final paragraph?

3. In Paragraph 8, Porter mentions "the love of Héloïs and Abélard." Who were they, and why does Porter bring them into the essay?

4. Porter takes care to maintain distance from her subject, but in Paragraph 9 she becomes directly personal and expresses an opinion. Why?

5. In Paragraph 4 Porter writes "But best of all she would like not to have anything in her love that should ask for forgiveness." Does the title of her essay help to explain this sentence? Elaborate.

6. In an essay, compare and contrast the modern version of "an institution never intended as a recreation ground for either sex" (Paragraph 9) with its original form.

7. Porter resorts to several devices — diction, direct address, and informal speech — to lighten what would otherwise be a dense essay. Find examples of each of these devices.

James C. Rettie (1904–1969) was born and grew up on a ranch in eastern Oregon; he attended Willamette University in Oregon, Yale University, and the University of London. He was an economist of natural resources, and conservation was the passion of his life. He acted as economic advisor to Stewart Udall, who was Secretary of the Interior under Presidents Kennedy and Johnson.

Rettie wrote this essay in 1938 while working as an ecologist for the United States Forest Service. Although in his government work he produced hundreds of documents and reports, he wrote nothing else that resembles this essay. It first appeared in a Department of Agriculture Bulletin, and was reprinted in Cornet Magazine *in March of 1951.*

59

JAMES C. RETTIE

"But a Watch in the Night": A Scientific Fable[1]

1   Out beyond our solar system there is a planet called Copernicus. It came into existence some four or five billion years before the birth of our Earth. In due course of time it became inhabited by a race of intelligent men.

2   About 750 million years ago the Copernicans had developed the motion picture machine to a point well in advance of the stage that we have reached. Most of the cameras that we now use in motion picture work are geared to take twenty-four pictures per second on a continuous strip of film. When such film is run through a projector, it throws a series of images on the screen and these change with a

---

[1] From the Bible, Psalm 90, apparently either slightly altered or using a translation other than the King James version, which reads:

Lord, thou has been our dwelling place
In all generations.
Before the mountains were brought forth,
Or ever thou hadst formed the earth and the world,
Even from everlasting to everlasting, thou art God.
Thou turnest man to destruction;
And sayest, "Return, ye children of men."
For a thousand years in thy sight
Are but as yesterday when it is past,
And as a watch in the night. . . .

                                       — Ed.

rapidity that gives the visual impression of normal movement. If a motion is too swift for the human eye to see it in detail, it can be captured and artificially slowed down by means of the slow-motion camera. This one is geared to take many more shots per second — ninety-six or even more than that. When the slow-motion film is projected at the normal speed of twenty-four pictures per second, we can see just how the jumping horse goes over a hurdle.

What about motion that is too slow to be seen by the human eye? That problem has been solved by the use of the time-lapse camera. In this one, the shutter is geared to take only one shot per second, or one per minute, or even one per hour — depending upon the kind of movement that is being photographed. When the time-lapse film is projected at the normal speed of twenty-four pictures per second, it is possible to see a bean sprout growing up out of the ground. Time-lapse films are useful in the study of many types of motion too slow to be observed by the unaided human eye.

The Copernicans, it seems, had time-lapse cameras some 757 million years ago and they also had superpowered telescopes that gave them a clear view of what was happening upon this Earth. They decided to make a film record of the life history of Earth and to make it on the scale of one picture per year. The photography has been in progress during the last 757 million years.

In the near future, a Copernican interstellar expedition will arrive upon our Earth and bring with it a copy of the time-lapse film. Arrangements will be made for showing the entire film in one continuous run. This will begin at midnight of New Year's eve and continue day and night without a single stop until midnight of December 31. The rate of projection will be twenty-four pictures per second. Time on the screen will thus seem to move at the rate of twenty-four years per second; 1,440 years per minute; 86,400 years per hour; approximately two million years per day; and 62 million years per month. The normal life-span of individual man will occupy about three seconds. The full period of Earth history that will be unfolded on the screen (some 757 million years) will extend from what the geologists call Pre-Cambrian times up to the present. This will, by no means, cover the full time-span of the Earth's geological history but it will embrace the period since the advent of living organisms.

During the months of January, February and March the picture will be desolate and dreary. The shape of the land masses and the oceans will bear little or no resemblance to those that we know. The violence of geological erosion will be much in evidence. Rains will pour down on the land and promptly go booming down to the seas. There will be no clear streams anywhere except where the rains fall upon hard rock. Everywhere on the steeper ground the stream channels will be filled with boulders hurled down by rushing waters. Raging torrents and dry stream beds will keep alternating in quick succession. High mountains will seem to melt like so much butter in the sun. The shifting of land into the seas, later to be thrust up as new mountains, will be going on at a grand scale.

7   Early in April there will be some indication of the presence of single-celled living organisms in some of the warmer and sheltered coastal waters. By the end of the month it will be noticed that some of these organisms have become multicellular. A few of them, including the Trilobites, will be encased in hard shells.

8   Toward the end of May, the first vertebrates will appear, but they will still be aquatic creatures. In June about 60 percent of the land area that we know as North America will be under water. One broad channel will occupy the space where the Rocky Mountains now stand. Great deposits of limestone will be forming under some of the shallower seas. Oil and gas deposits will be in process of formation — also under shallow seas. On land there will still be no sign of vegetation. Erosion will be rampant, tearing loose particles and chunks of rock and grinding them into sand and silt to be spewed out by the streams into bays and estuaries.

9   About the middle of July the first land plants will appear and take up the tremendous job of soil building. Slowly, very slowly, the mat of vegetation will spread, always battling for its life against the power of erosion. Almost foot by foot, the plant life will advance, lacing down with its root structures whatever pulverized rock material it can find. Leaves and stems will be giving added protection against the loss of the soil foothold. The increasing vegetation will pave the way for the land animals that will live upon it.

10   Early in August the seas will be teeming with fish. This will be what geologists call the Devonian period. Some of the races of these fish will be breathing by means of lung tissue instead of through gill tissues. Before the month is over, some of the lung fish will go ashore and take on a crude lizard-like appearance. Here are the first amphibians.

11   In early September the insects will put in their appearance. Some will look like huge dragon flies and will have a wingspread of 24 inches. Large portions of the land masses will now be covered with heavy vegetation that will include the primitive spore-propagating

trees. Layer upon layer of this plant growth will build up, later to appear as the coal deposits. About the middle of this month, there will be evidence of the first seed-bearing plants and the first reptiles. Heretofore, the land animals will have been amphibians that could reproduce their kind only by depositing a soft egg mass in quiet waters. The reptiles will be shown to be freed from the aquatic bond because they can reproduce by means of a shelled egg in which the embryo and its nurturing liquids are sealed in and thus protected from destructive evaporation. Before September is over, the first dinosaurs will be seen — creatures destined to dominate the animal realm for about 140 million years and then to disappear.

In October there will be a series of mountain uplifts along what 12 is now the eastern coast of the United States. A creature with feathered limbs — half bird and half reptile in appearance — will take itself into the air. Some small and rather unpretentious animals will be seen to bring forth their young in a form that is a miniature replica of the parents and to feed these young on milk secreted by mammary glands in the female parent. The emergence of this mammalian form of animal life will be recognized as one of the great events in geologic time. October will also witness the high water mark of the dinosaurs — creatures ranging in size from that of the modern goat to monsters like Brontosaurus that weighed some 40 tons. Most of them will be placid vegetarians, but a few will be hideous-looking carnivores, like Allosaurus and Tyrannosaurus. Some of the herbivorous dinosaurs will be clad in body armor for protection against their flesh-eating comrades.

November will bring pictures of a sea extending from the Gulf of 13 Mexico to the Arctic in space now occupied by the Rocky Mountains. A few of the reptiles will take to the air on bat-like wings. One of these, called Pteranodon, will have a wingspread of 15 feet. There will be a rapid development of the modern flowering plants, modern trees, and modern insects. The dinosaurs will disappear. Toward the end of the month there will be a tremendous land disturbance in which the Rocky Mountains will rise out of the sea to assume a dominating place in the North American landscape.

As the picture runs on into December it will show the mammals 14 in command of the animal life. Seed-bearing trees and grasses will have covered most of the land with a heavy mantle of vegetation. Only the areas newly thrust up from the sea will be barren. Most of the streams will be crystal clear. The turmoil of geologic erosion will be confined to localized areas. About December 25 will begin the cutting of the Grand Canyon of the Colorado River. Grinding down through layer after layer of sedimentary strata, this stream will finally expose deposits laid down in Pre-Cambrian times. Thus in the walls of that canyon will appear geological formations dating from recent times to the period when the earth had no living organisms upon it.

15   The picture will run on through the latter days of December and even up to its final day with still no sign of mankind. The spectators will become alarmed in the fear that man has somehow been left out. But not so; sometime about noon on December 31 (one million years ago) will appear a stooped, massive creature of man-like proportions. This will be Pithecanthropus, the Java ape man. For tools and weapons he will have nothing but crude stone and wooden clubs. His children will live a precarious existence threatened on the one side by hostile animals and on the other by tremendous climatic changes. Ice sheets — in places 4000 feet deep — will form in the northern parts of North America and Eurasia. Four times this glacial ice will push southward to cover half the continents. With each advance the plant and animal life will be swept under or pushed southward. With each recession of the ice, life will struggle to reestablish itself in the wake of the retreating glaciers. The wooly mammoth, the musk ox, and the caribou all will fight to maintain themselves near the ice line. Sometimes they will be caught and put into cold storage — skin, flesh, blood, bones and all.

16   The picture will run on through supper time with still very little evidence of man's presence on the Earth. It will be about 11 o'clock when Neanderthal man appears. Another half hour will go by before the appearance of Cro-Magnon man living in caves and painting crude animal pictures on the walls of his dwelling. Fifteen minutes more will bring Neolithic man, knowing how to chip stone and thus produce sharp cutting edges for spears and tools. In a few minutes more it will appear that man has domesticated the dog, the sheep and, possibly, other animals. He will then begin the use of milk. He will also learn the arts of basket weaving and the making of pottery and dugout canoes.

17   The dawn of civilization will not come until about five or six minutes before the end of the picture. The story of the Egyptians, the Babylonians, the Greeks, and the Romans will unroll during the fourth, the third and the second minute before the end. At 58 minutes and 43 seconds past 11:00 P.M. (just 1 minute and 17 seconds before the end) will come the beginning of the Christian era. Columbus will discover the new world 20 seconds before the end. The Declaration of

Independence will be signed just 17 seconds before the final curtain comes down.

In those few moments of geologic time will be the story of all that has happened since we became a nation. And what a story it will be! A human swarm will sweep across the face of the continent and take it away from the . . . red men. They will change it far more radically than it has ever been changed before in a comparable time. The great virgin forests will be seen going down before ax and fire. The soil, covered for aeons by its protective mantle of trees and grasses, will be laid bare to the ravages of water and wind erosion. Streams that had been flowing clear will, once again, take up a load of silt and push it toward the seas. Humus and mineral salts, both vital elements of productive soil, will be seen to vanish at a terrifying rate. The railroads and highways and cities that will spring up may divert attention, but they cannot cover up the blight of man's recent activities. In great sections of Asia, it will be seen that man must utilize cow dung and every scrap of available straw or grass for fuel to cook his food. The forests that once provided wood for this purpose will be gone without a trace. The use of these agricultural wastes for fuel, in place of returning them to the land, will be leading to increasing soil impoverishment. Here and there will be seen a dust storm darkening the landscape over an area a thousand miles across. Man-creatures will be shown counting their wealth in terms of bits of printed paper representing other bits of a scarce but comparatively useless yellow metal that is kept buried in strong vaults. Meanwhile, the soil, the only real wealth that can keep mankind alive on the face of this Earth is savagely being cut loose from its ancient moorings and washed into the seven seas.

We have just arrived upon this Earth. How long will we stay?   19

——— **CONSIDERATIONS** ————————————————

1. Rettie's essay, opening somewhat like a science-fiction story, is an ingenious example of the extended analogy. What are the advantages and disadvantages of such a device?

2. Rettie's Copernican film spins out a large segment of evolutionary history. Compare it with any other account of evolution readily available, such as that in a biology text or encyclopedia. How do different styles and purposes affect the presentation of similar material?

3. An unusual feature of Rettie's style is that he writes almost entirely in the future tense. Why? What tense do most writers use? Why?

4. In Paragraph 12, Rettie mentions the emergence of mammals as an event that "will be recognized as one of the great events in geologic time." Recognized by whom? Might the answer to that question go a long way toward understanding why Rettie describes the event as "great"? Would the Copernican audiences of Rettie's imaginary film necessarily use the same adjective?

5. Do our feelings and ideas have "ancestral forms" and evolutionary histories, as our bodies seem to have? What device might an inventive writer employ to discuss such a topic?

6. "How long will we stay?" asks Rettie at the close of his hypothetical movie depicting 757 million years of earth history. The question is a rhetorical one because it is asked not so much to elicit an answer as to force a moment of reflection against the backdrop of his 750-million-year movie. What kinds of reflection would be appropriate?

*Richard Rodriguez (b. 1944) grew up in Sacramento, Califor-
nia, where his parents had immigrated from Mexico. Hunger of
Memory (1982) is a memoir of assimilation, recounting his gradual separation from family and culture as he moved through high
school to Stanford University for his B.A. and onward for a Ph.D.
in English literature. Although Rodriguez regrets his losses, he
largely praises the journey undertaken. This essay comes from
Harper's Magazine, March 1984, which posed the question "Does
America Still Exist?" to a number of authors.*

60

RICHARD RODRIGUEZ

Does America Still Exist?

For the children of immigrant parents the knowledge comes eas- 1
ier. America exists everywhere in the city — on billboards, frankly in
the smell of French fries and popcorn. It exists in the pace: traffic
lights, the assertions of neon, the mysterious bong-bong-bong through
the atriums of department stores. America exists as the voice of the
crowd, a menacing sound — the high nasal accent of American
English.

When I was a boy in Sacramento (California, the fifties), people 2
would ask me, "Where you from?" I was born in this country, but I
knew the question meant to decipher my darkness, my looks.

My mother once instructed me to say, "I am an American of 3
Mexican descent." By the time I was nine or ten, I wanted to say, but
dared not reply, "I am an American."

Immigrants come to America and, against hostility or mere lone- 4 liness, they recreate a homeland in the parlor, tacking up postcards or calendars of some impossible blue — lake or sea or sky. Children of immigrant parents are supposed to perch on a hyphen between two countries. Relatives assume the achievement as much as anyone. Relatives are, in any case, surprised when the child begins losing old ways. One day at the family picnic the boy wanders away from their spiced food and faceless stories to watch other boys play baseball in the distance.

5   There is sorrow in the American memory, guilty sorrow for having left something behind — Portugal, China, Norway. The American story is the story of immigrant children and of their children — children no longer able to speak to grandparents. The memory of exile becomes inarticulate as it passes from generation to generation, along with wedding rings and pocket watches — like some mute stone in a wad of old lace. Europe. Asia. Eden.

6   But, it needs to be said, if this is a country where one stops being Vietnamese or Italian, this is a country where one begins to be an American. America exists as a culture and a grin, a faith and a shrug. It is clasped in a handshake, called by a first name.

7   As much as the country is joined in a common culture, however, Americans are reluctant to celebrate the process of assimilation. We pledge allegiance to diversity. America was born Protestant and bred Puritan, and the notion of community we share is derived from a seventeenth-century faith. Presidents and the pages of ninth-grade civics readers yet proclaim the orthodoxy: We are gathered together — but as individuals, with separate pasts, distinct destinies. Our society is as paradoxical as a Puritan congregation: We stand together, alone.

8   Americans have traditionally defined themselves by what they refused to include. As often, however, Americans have struggled, turned in good conscience at last to assert the great Protestant virtue of tolerance. Despite outbreaks of nativist frenzy, America has remained an immigrant country, open and true to itself.

9   Against pious emblems of rural America — soda fountain, Elks hall, Protestant church, and now shopping mall — stands the coldhearted city, crowded with races and ambitions, curious laughter, much that is odd. Nevertheless, it is the city that has most truly represented America. In the city, however, the millions of singular lives have had no richer notion of wholeness to describe them than the idea of pluralism.

10   *"Where you from?" the American asks the immigrant child. "Mexico," the boy learns to say.*

11   Mexico, the country of my blood ancestors, offers formal contrast

to the American achievement. If the United States was formed by Protestant individualism, Mexico was shaped by a medieval Catholic dream of one world. The Spanish journeyed to Mexico to plunder, and they may have gone, in God's name, with an arrogance peculiar to those who intend to convert. But through the conversion, the Indian converted the Spaniard. A new race was born, the *mestizo*, wedding European to Indian. José Vasconcelos, the Mexican philosopher, has celebrated this New World creation, proclaiming it the "cosmic race."

Centuries later, in a San Francisco restaurant, a Mexican-American lawyer of my acquaintance says, in English, over *salade niçoise*, that he does not intend to assimilate into gringo society. His claim is echoed by a chorus of others (Italian-Americans, Greeks, Asians) in this era of ethnic pride. The melting pot has been retired, clanking, into the museum of quaint disgrace, alongside Aunt Jemima and the Katzenjammer Kids. But resistance to assimilation is characteristically American. It only makes clear how inevitable the process of assimilation actually is.   12

For generations, this has been the pattern. Immigrant parents have sent their children to school (simply, they thought) to acquire the "skills" to survive in the city. The child returned home with a voice his parents barely recognized or understood, couldn't trust, and didn't like.   13

In Eastern cities — Philadelphia, New York, Boston, Baltimore — class after class gathered immigrant children to women (usually women) who stood in front of rooms full of children, changing children. So also for me in the 1950s. Irish-Catholic nuns. California. The old story. The hyphen tipped to the right, away from Mexico and toward a confusing but true American identity.   14

I speak now in the chromium American accent of my grammar school classmates — Billy Reckers, Mike Bradley, Carol Schmidt, Kathy O'Grady. . . . I believe I became like my classmates, became German, Polish, and (like my teachers) Irish. And because assimilation is always reciprocal, my classmates got something of me. (I mean sad eyes; belief in the Indian Virgin; a taste for sugar skulls on the Feast of the Dead.) In the blending, we became what our parents could never have been, and we carried America one revolution further.   15

"Does America still exist?" Americans have been asking the question for so long that to ask it again only proves our continuous link. But perhaps the question deserves to be asked with urgency — now. Since the black civil rights movement of the 1960s, our tenuous notion of a shared public life has deteriorated notably.   16

The struggle of black men and women did not eradicate racism,   17 but it became the great moment in the life of America's conscience. Water hoses, bulldogs, blood — the images, rendered black, white, rectangular, passed into living rooms.

18   It is hard to look at a photograph of a crowd taken, say, in 1890 or in 1930 and not notice the absence of blacks. (It becomes an impertinence to wonder if America *still* exists.)

19   In the sixties, other groups of Americans learned to champion their rights by analogy to the black civil rights movement. But the heroic vision faded. Dr. Martin Luther King Jr. had spoken with Pauline eloquence of a nation that would unite Christian and Jew, old and young, rich and poor. Within a decade, the struggles of the 1960s were reduced to a bureaucratic competition for little more than pieces of a representational pie. The quest for a portion of power became an end in itself. The metaphor for the American city of the 1970s was a committee: one black, one woman, one person under thirty . . .

20   If the small town had sinned against America by too neatly defining who could be an American, the city's sin was a romantic secession. One noticed the romanticism in the antiwar movement — certain demonstrators who demonstrated a lack of tact or desire to persuade and seemed content to play secular protestants. One noticed the romanticism in the competition among members of "minority groups" to claim the status of Primary Victim. To Americans unconfident of their common identity, minority standing became a way of asserting individuality. Middle-class Americans — men and women clearly not the primary victims of social oppression — brandished their suffering with exuberance.

21   The dream of a single society probably died with *The Ed Sullivan Show*. The reality of America persists. Teenagers pass through big-city high schools banded in racial groups, their collars turned up to a uniform shrug. But then they graduate to jobs at the phone company or in banks, where they end up working alongside people unlike themselves. Typists and tellers walk out together at lunchtime.

22   It is easier for us as Americans to believe the obvious fact of our separateness — easier to imagine the black and white Americas prophesied by the Kerner report (broken glass, street fires) — than to recognize the reality of a city street at lunchtime. Americans are wedded by proximity to a common culture. The panhandler at one corner is related to the pamphleteer at the next who is related to the banker who is kin to the Chinese old man wearing an MIT sweatshirt. In any true national history, Thomas Jefferson begets Martin Luther King Jr. who begets the Gray Panthers. It is because we lack a vision of our-

selves entire — the city street is crowded and we are each preoccupied with finding our own way home — that we lack an appropriate hymn.

Under my window now passes a little white girl softly rehearsing   23
to herself a Motown obbligato.

_____ CONSIDERATIONS _____

1. Compare Rodriguez's use of short paragraphs (for example, Paragraphs 3, 10, and 18) with paragraphs from Katherine Anne Porter's "The Necessary Enemy" (pages 333–337). How does a writer know when to end a paragraph?

2. Rodriguez frequently uses a figure of speech called the oxymoron, as in phrases like "We stand together, alone" (Paragraph 7) or "brandished their suffering with exuberance" (Paragraph 20). Can you find others? What does this technique contribute to our understanding of the way he sees American society?

3. The reference to the "Pauline eloquence" of Dr. Martin Luther King, Jr. (Paragraph 19) demonstrates one source of Rodriguez's varied diction. What do you make of the last two words in this essay?

4. Rodriguez shows his skill in using contrast to highlight a point, for example, in pairing off his Mexican heritage "shaped by a medieval Catholic dream of one world" with that of the United States "formed by Protestant individualism" (Paragraph 11). What other contrasts can you identify in this essay?

5. The immigrant child's plight 'perched' "on a hyphen between two countries" (Paragraph 4) is seen by Rodriguez as the natural pattern of cultural assimilation. What does he suggest in the final paragraphs is the strength of such a process?

6. Compare Rodriguez's idea of his own assimilation into "gringo society" (Paragraph 15) with that of Richard Wright's in "The Library Card" (pages 467–475.)

*Carl Sagan (b. 1934) is an astronomer and writer, whose thir-
teen-part* Cosmos *series appeared on public television in 1980.
His books include* Intelligent Life in the Universe *(1966),* Other
Worlds *(1975),* The Dragons of Eden *(1977), for which he received
a Pulitzer Prize,* Broca's Brain *(1979), and* Cosmos *(1980). He is
director of the Laboratory for Planetary Studies and David Dun-
can Professor of Astronomy and Space Sciences at Cornell University.*

61

CARL SAGAN
The Measure of Eratosthenes

1   The earth is a place. It is by no means the only place. It is not
even a typical place. No planet or star or galaxy can be typical, because
the cosmos is mostly empty. The only typical place is within the vast,
cold, universal vacuum, the everlasting night of intergalactic space, a
place so strange and desolate that, by comparison, planets and stars
and galaxies seem achingly rare and lovely.

2   If we were randomly inserted into the cosmos, the chance that
we would find ourselves on or near a planet would be less than one in
a billion trillion trillion (10^{33}, a one followed by 33 zeros). In everyday
life, such odds are called compelling. Worlds are precious.

3   The discovery that the earth is a *little* world was made, as so
many important human discoveries were, in the ancient Near East, in
a time some humans call the third century B.C., in the greatest metrop-
olis of the age, the Egyptian city of Alexandria.

4   Here there lived a man named Eratosthenes. One of his envious

contemporaries called him "Beta," the second letter of the Greek
alphabet, because, he said, Eratosthenes was the world's second best
in everything. But it seems clear that, in almost everything, Eratos-
thenes was "alpha."

He was an astronomer, historian, geographer, philosopher, poet,   5
theater critic, and mathematician. His writings ranged from "Astron-
omy" to "On Freedom from Pain." He was also the director of the
great library of Alexandria, where one day he read, in a papyrus book,
that in the southern frontier outpost of Syene (now Aswan), near the
first cataract of the Nile, at noon on June 21 vertical sticks cast no
shadows. On the summer solstice, the longest day of the year, as the
hours crept toward midday, the shadows of the temple columns grew
shorter. At noon, they were gone. A reflection of the sun could then
be seen in the water at the bottom of a deep well. The sun was directly
overhead.

It was an observation that someone else might easily have   6
ignored. Sticks, shadows, reflections in wells, the position of the sun
— of what possible importance could such simple, everyday matters
be? But Eratosthenes was a scientist, and his musings on these com-
monplaces changed the world: in a way, they made the world.

Eratosthenes had the presence of mind to do an experiment —   7
actually to observe whether *in Alexandria* vertical sticks cast shadows
near noon on June 21. And, he discovered, sticks do.

Eratosthenes asked himself how, at the same moment, a stick in   8
Syene could cast no shadow and a stick in Alexandria, far to the north,
could cast a pronounced shadow.

Consider a map of ancient Egypt with two vertical sticks of equal   9
length, one stuck in Alexandria, the other in Syene. Suppose that, at a
certain moment, neither stick casts any shadow at all. This is perfectly
easy to understand — provided the earth is flat. The sun would then
be directly overhead. If the two sticks cast shadows of equal length,
that also would make sense on a flat earth: the sun's rays would then
be inclined at the same angle to the two sticks. But how could it be
that at the same instant there was no shadow at Syene and a substan-
tial shadow at Alexandria?

The only possible answer, he saw, was that the surface of the   10
earth is curved. Not only that: the greater the curvature, the greater
the difference in the shadow lengths. The sun is so far away that its
rays are parallel when they reach the earth. Sticks placed at different
angles to the sun's rays cast shadows of different lengths. For the
observed difference in the shadow lengths, the distance between Alex-

andria and Syene had to be about seven degrees along the surface of the earth; that is, if you imagine the sticks extending down to the center of the earth, they would intersect there at an angle of seven degrees.

11   Seven degrees is something like one-fiftieth of 360 degrees, the full circumference of the earth. Eratosthenes knew that the distance between Alexandria and Syene was approximately 800 kilometers, because he had hired a man to pace it out.

12   Eight hundred kilometers times 50 is 40,000 kilometers; so that must be the circumference of the earth. (Or, if you like to measure things in miles, the distance between Alexandria and Syene is about 500 miles, and 500 miles times 50 is 25,000 miles.)

13   This is the right answer.

14   Eratosthenes' only tools were sticks, eyes, feet, and brains, plus a taste for experiment. With them he deduced the circumference of the earth with an error of only a few percent, a remarkable achievement for 2,200 years ago. He was the first person accurately to measure the size of a planet.

_____ **CONSIDERATIONS** _____

1. Sagan's short essay is a tribute to the power of deduction, the thought process that made Sherlock Holmes famous. How does deduction differ from induction?

2. The great Alexandrian library has long been described as one of the truly great human accomplishments. But what happened to it? Is there any truth to the story that Arabian conquerors shoveled it into furnaces to heat the public baths for six months?

3. Sagan's explanation of Eratosthenes's deductions is a good example of process analysis, which attempts to show how something works. Select some process that you know well — how to change a tire, how to derive the square root of a number, how to make a sunsuit, how to talk to a computer, how to tune a violin — and write a process essay. Study Sagan's techniques for making the process lively.

4. Eratosthenes was, according to Sagan, a "scientist" (Paragraph 6), but nearly 2,000 years would have to pass before the word "scientist" would be invented. (See the Oxford English Dictionary for the comparatively recent history of that word.) What did Sagan have in mind when he applied the term to Eratosthenes?

5. Sagan's essay begins with a series of short, simple sentences, and Paragraph 13 contains only one sentence five words long. College writers are usually urged to avoid such brevity. Does Sagan use those constructions successfully?

E. F. Schumacher (1911–1977) was born in Germany and attended Oxford University in 1930 as a Rhodes Scholar. Later he taught economics at Columbia University in New York, and in Great Britain he became economic advisor to the National Coal Board from 1950 to 1970. He invented the notion of intermediate technology for developing countries. Small is Beautiful (1973), from which we take "Production in Service to Life," is subtitled "Economics as if People Mattered." This book brought Schumacher's ideas to the public, and its title added a phrase to the language.

62

E. F. SCHUMACHER
Production in Service to Life

The idea of unlimited economic growth, more and more until   1
everybody is saturated with wealth, needs to be seriously questioned
on at least two counts: the availability of basic resources and, alter-
natively or additionally, the capacity of the environment to cope with
the degree of interference implied.

It is only necessary to assert that something would reduce the   2
'standard of living,' and every debate is instantly closed. That soul-
destroying, meaningless, mechanical, monotonous, moronic work is
an insult to human nature which must necessarily and inevitably
produce either escapism or aggression, and that no amount of 'bread
and circuses' can compensate for the damage done — these are facts
which are neither denied nor acknowledged but are met with an
unbreakable conspiracy of silence — because to deny them would be

too obviously absurd and to acknowledge them would condemn the central preoccupation of modern society as a crime against humanity.

3   It is hardly an exaggeration to say that, with increasing affluence, economics has moved into the very centre of public concern, and economic performance, economic growth, economic expansion, and so forth have become the abiding interest, if not the obsession, of all modern societies. In the current vocabulary of condemnation there are few words as final and conclusive as the word 'uneconomic.' If an activity has been branded as uneconomic, its right to existence is not merely questioned but energetically denied. Anything that is found to be an impediment to economic growth is a shameful thing, and if people cling to it, they are thought of as either saboteurs or fools. Call a thing immoral or ugly, soul-destroying or a degradation of man, a peril to the peace of the world or to the well-being of future generations; as long as you have not shown it to be 'uneconomic' you have not really questioned its right to exist, grow, and prosper.

4   But what does it *mean* when we say something is uneconomic? ... The answer to this question cannot be in doubt: something is uneconomic when it fails to earn an adequate profit in terms of money. The method of economics does not, and cannot, produce any other meaning.

5   The judgment of economics, in other words, is an extremely *fragmentary* judgment; out of the large number of aspects which in real life have to be seen and judged together before a decision can be taken, economics supplies only one — whether a thing yields a money profit *to those who undertake it* or not.

6   Do not overlook the words 'to those who undertake it.' It is a great error to assume, for instance, that the methodology of economics is normally applied to determine whether an activity carried on by a group within society yields a profit to society as a whole. Even nationalised industries are not considered from this more comprehensive point of view. Every one of them is given a financial target — which is, in fact, an obligation — and is expected to pursue this target without regard to any damage it might be inflicting on other parts of the economy.

7   Economics, moreover, deals with goods in accordance with their market value and not in accordance with what they really are. The same rules and criteria are applied to primary goods, which man has to win from nature, and secondary goods, which presuppose the existence of primary goods and are manufactured from them. All goods are treated the same, because the point of view is fundamentally that of

private profit-making, and this means that it is inherent in the methodology of economics *to ignore man's dependence on the natural world.*

To press non-economic values into the framework of the economic calculus, economists use the method of cost/benefit analysis. This is generally thought to be an enlightened and progressive development, as it is at least an attempt to take account of costs and benefits which might otherwise be disregarded altogether. In fact, however, it is a procedure by which the higher is reduced to the level of the lower and the priceless is given a price. It can therefore never serve to clarify the situation and lead to an enlightened decision. All it can do is lead to self-deception or the deception of others; for to undertake to measure the immeasurable is absurd and constitutes but an elaborate method of moving from preconceived notions to foregone conclusions; all one has to do to obtain the desired results is to impute suitable values to the immeasurable costs and benefits. The logical absurdity, however, is not the greatest fault of the undertaking: what is worse, and destructive of civilization, is the pretence that everything has a price or, in other words, that money is the highest of all values.

8

Having established by his purely quantitative methods that the Gross National Product of a country has risen by, say, five percent, the economist-turned-econometrician is unwilling, and generally unable, to face the question of whether this is to be taken as a good thing or a bad thing. He would lose all his certainties if he even entertained such a question: Growth of GNP must be a good thing, irrespective of what has grown and who, if anyone, has benefited. The idea that there could be pathological growth, unhealthy growth, disruptive or destructive growth is to him a perverse idea which must not be allowed to surface.

9

It is of course true that quality is much more difficult to 'handle' than quantity, just as the exercise of judgment is a higher function than the ability to count and calculate. Quantitative differences can be more easily grasped and certainly more easily defined than qualitative differences; their concreteness is beguiling and gives them the appearance of scientific precision, even when this precision has been purchased by the suppression of vital differences of quality. The great majority of economists is still pursuing the absurd ideal of making their 'science' as scientific and precise as physics, as if there were no qualitative difference between mindless atoms and men made in the image of God.

10

There is universal agreement that a fundamental source of

11

wealth is human labour. Now, the modern economist has been brought up to consider 'labour' or work as little more than a necessary evil. From the point of view of the employer, it is in any case simply an item of cost, to be reduced to a minimum if it cannot be eliminated altogether, say, by automation. From the point of view of the workman, it is a 'disutility'; to work is to make a sacrifice of one's leisure and comfort, and wages are a kind of compensation for the sacrifice. Hence the ideal from the point of view of the employer is to have output without employees, and the ideal from the point of view of the employee is to have income without employment.

12   While the materialist is mainly interested in goods, the Buddhist is mainly interested in liberation. But Buddhism is 'The Middle Way' and therefore in no way antagonistic to physical well-being. It is not wealth that stands in the way of liberation but the attachment to wealth; not the enjoyment of pleasurable things but the craving for them. The keynote of Buddhist economics, therefore, is simplicity and non-violence. From an economist's point of view, the marvel of the Buddhist way of life is the utter rationality of its pattern — amazingly small means leading to extraordinarily satisfactory results.

13   For the modern economist this is very difficult to understand. He is used to measuring the 'standard of living' by the amount of annual consumption, assuming all the time that a man who consumes more is 'better off' than a man who consumes less. A Buddhist economist would consider this approach excessively irrational: since consumption is merely a means to human well-being, the aim should be to obtain the maximum of well-being with the minimum of consumption.

14   Buddhist economics is the systematic study of how to attain given ends with the minimum means.

15   The economics of giantism and automation is a leftover of nineteenth-century conditions and nineteenth-century thinking and it is totally incapable of solving any of the real problems of today. An entirely new system of thought is needed, a system based on attention to people, and not primarily attention to goods — (the goods will look after themselves!). It could be summed up in the phrase, 'production by the masses, rather than mass production.'

16   What is the meaning of democracy, freedom, human dignity, standard of living, self-realisation, fulfillment? Is it a matter of goods, or of people? Of course it is a matter of people. But people can be themselves only in small comprehensible groups. Therefore we must learn to think in terms of an articulated structure that can cope with

a multiplicity of small-scale units. If economic thinking cannot grasp this it is useless. If it cannot get beyond its vast abstractions, the national income, the rate of growth, capital/output ratio, input-output analysis, labour mobility, capital accumulation; if it cannot get beyond all this and make contact with the human realities of poverty, frustration, alienation, despair, breakdown, crime, escapism, stress, congestion, ugliness, and spiritual death, then let us scrap economics and start afresh.

When I first began to travel the world, visiting rich and poor 17 countries alike, I was tempted to formulate the first law of economics as follows: 'The amount of real leisure a society enjoys tends to be in inverse proportion to the amount of labour-saving machinery it employs.' It might be a good idea for the professors of economics to put this proposition into their examination papers and ask their pupils to discuss it. However that may be, the evidence is very strong indeed. If you go from easy-going England to, say, Germany or the United States, you find that people there live under much more strain than here. And if you move to a country like Burma, which is very near to the bottom of the league table of industrial progress, you find that people have an enormous amount of leisure really to enjoy them-selves. Of course, as there is so much less labour-saving machinery to help them, they 'accomplish' much less than we do; but that is a different point. The fact remains that the burden of living rests much more lightly on their shoulders than on ours.

The strength of the idea of private enterprise lies in its terrifying 18 simplicity. It suggests that the totality of life can be reduced to one aspect — profits. The businessman, as a private individual, may still be interested in other aspects of life — perhaps even in goodness, truth and beauty — but *as a businessman* he concerns himself only with profits.

Everything becomes crystal clear after you have reduced reality 19 to one — one only — of its thousand aspects. You know what to do — whatever produces profits; you know what to avoid — whatever reduces them or makes a loss. And there is at the same time a perfect measuring rod for the degree of success or failure. Let no one befog the issue by asking whether a particular action is conducive to the wealth and well-being of society, whether it leads to moral, aesthetic, or cultural enrichment. Simply find out whether it pays; simply investigate whether there is an alternative that pays better. If there is, choose the alternative.

It is no accident that successful businessmen are often astonish- 20 ingly primitive; they live in a world made primitive by this process of reduction. They fit into this simplified version of the world and are satisfied with it. And when the real world occasionally makes its existence known and attempts to force upon their attention a different one of its facets, one not provided for in their philosophy, they tend to become quite helpless and confused. They feel exposed to incalculable dangers and 'unsound' forces and freely predict general disaster. As a result, their judgments on actions dictated by a more comprehensive outlook on the meaning and purpose of life are generally quite worthless.

21   General evidence of material progress would suggest that the *modern* private enterprise system is — or has been — the most perfect instrument for the pursuit of personal enrichment. The *modern* private enterprise system ingeniously employs the human urges of greed and envy as its motive power, but manages to overcome the most blatant deficiencies of *laissez-faire* by means of Keynesian economic management, a bit of redistributive taxation, and the 'countervailing power' of the trade unions.

22   Can such a system conceivably deal with the problems we are now having to face? The answer is self-evident: greed and envy demand continuous and limitless economic growth of a material kind, without proper regard for conservation, and this type of growth cannot possibly fit into a finite environment. We must therefore study the essential nature of the private enterprise system and the possibilities of evolving an alternative system which might fit the new situation.

23   We shrink back from the truth if we believe that the destructive forces of the modern world can be 'brought under control' simply by mobilizing more resources — of wealth, education, and research — to fight pollution, to preserve wildlife, to discover new sources of energy, and to arrive at more effective agreements on peaceful coexistence. Needless to say, wealth, education, research, and many other things are needed for any civilization, but what is most needed today is a revision of the ends which these means are meant to serve. And this implies, above all else, the development of a life-style which accords to material things their proper, legitimate place, which is secondary and not primary.

24   The 'logic of production' is neither the logic of life nor that of society. It is a small and subservient part of both. The destructive forces unleashed by it cannot be brought under control, unless the 'logic of production' itself is brought under control — so that destruc-

tive forces cease to be unleashed. It is of little use trying to suppress terrorism if the production of deadly devices continues to be deemed a legitimate employment of man's creative powers. Nor can the fight against pollution be successful if the patterns of production and consumption continue to be of a scale, a complexity, and a degree of violence which, as is becoming more and more apparent, do not fit into the laws of the universe, to which man is just as much subject as the rest of creation. Equally, the chance of mitigating the rate of resource depletion or of bringing harmony into the relationships between those in possession of wealth and power and those without is non-existent as long as there is no idea anywhere of enough being good and more-than-enough being evil.

—— CONSIDERATIONS ——————————————

1. In Paragraph 16, Schumacher asks the meaning of such terms as "democracy," "freedom," and "human dignity" as though these abstract words have single, universally accepted definitions. He might better ask why it is so difficult to define any of them satisfactorily. Look up the meaning of "referent" for a clue to the undefinable nature of such terms.

2. Schumacher follows the question noted above with still another: "Is it a matter of goods, or of people?" Is he really asking a question, or is he stating an assumption in the form of a question? The latter is a common argumentative device called the "rhetorical question." Study the rhetorical question as used by Schumacher and other writers and speakers and determine how it works.

3. In your knowledge of the world, would you agree with Schumacher that "In the current vocabulary of condemnation there are few words as final and conclusive as the word 'uneconomic' "? Does Schumacher provide support for his statement? Could you insert, in Paragraph 3 or 4, two or three concrete instances?

4. Look carefully at Schumacher's Paragraph 8. Then read the closing paragraph of Caroline Bird's "Where College Fails Us" (pages 62–72). Does Bird provide an example of what Schumacher discusses? Explain.

5. Schumacher's essay is composed mostly of abstract and general statements — propositions, a logician might call them — on which the author builds still more propositions; they are all arranged to persuade readers to accept his conclusions. Schumacher argues deductively in contrast to the largely inductive argument of, say, Jefferson's "Declaration of Independence" (pages 208–213). Look up terms, deduction and induction, and then re-examine each method of arguing as represented by Schumacher and Jefferson. What are the respective strengths and weaknesses of each method?

63

WILLIAM SHAKESPEARE

That time of year thou mayst in me behold

That time of year thou mayst in me behold
When yellow leaves, or none, or few, do hang
Upon those boughs which shake against the cold,
Bare ruined choirs, where late the sweet birds sang.
5   In me thou see'st the twilight of such day
As after sunset fadeth in the west;
Which by and by black night doth take away,
Death's second self, that seals up all in rest.
In me thou see'st the glowing of such fire,
10   That on the ashes of his youth doth lie,
As the deathbed whereon it must expire,
Consumed with that which it was nourished by.
This thou perceiv'st, which makes thy love more strong,
To love that well which thou must leave ere long.

Don Sharp (b. 1938) has taught in Alaska, Hawaii, and Australia, and once owned and operated a garage in Pennsylvania called Discriminating Services. He now lives in Massachusetts, where he writes for magazines and works on old cars. This essay won the Ken Purdy Award for Excellence in Automobile Journalism in 1981

64

DON SHARP
Under the Hood

The owner of this 1966 Plymouth Valiant has made the rounds 1
of car dealers. They will gladly sell him a new car — the latest model
of government regulation and industrial enterprise — for $8,000, but
they don't want his clattering, emphysemic old vehicle in trade. It
isn't worth enough to justify the paperwork, a classified ad, and space
on the used-car lot. "Sell it for junk," they tell him. "Scrap iron is high
now, and they'll give you $25 for it."

The owner is hurt. He likes this car. It has served him well for 2
90,000-odd miles. It has a functional shape and he can get in and out
of it easily. He can roll down his window in a light rain and not get
his shoulder wet. The rear windows roll down, and he doesn't need an
air conditioner. He can see out of it fore, aft, and abeam. He can hazard
it on urban parking lots without fear of drastic, insurance-deductible
casualty loss. His teenage children reject it as passé, so it is always
available to him. It has no buzzers, and the only flashing lights are
those he controls himself when signaling a turn. The owner, clearly

one of a vanishing tribe, brings the car to a kindred spirit and asks me to rebuild it.

3   We do not discuss the cost. I do not advertise my services and my sign is discreet. My shop is known by word of mouth, and those who spread the word emphasize my house rule: "A blank check and a free hand." That is, I do to your car what I think it needs and you pay for it; you trust me not to take advantage, I guarantee you good brakes, sound steering, and prompt starting, and you pay without quarrel. This kind of arrangement saves a lot of time spent in making estimates and a lot of time haggling over the bill. It also imposes a tremendous burden of responsibility on me and on those who spread the word, and it puts a burden of trust on those who deliver their cars into my custody.

4   A relationship of that sort is about as profound as any that two people can enjoy, even if it lasts no longer than the time required to reline a set of brakes. I think of hometown farmers who made share-cropping deals for the season on a handshake; then I go into a large garage and see the white-coated service writer noting the customer's every specification, calling attention to the fine print at the bottom of the work order, and requiring a contractual signature before even a brake-light bulb is replaced. I perceive in their transaction that ignorance of cause and effect breeds suspicion, and I wonder who is the smaller, the customer or the service writer, and how they came to be so small of spirit.

5   Under the hood of this ailing Valiant, I note a glistening line of seeping oil where the oil pan meets the engine block. For thousands of miles, a piece of cork — a strip of bark from a Spanish tree — has stood firm between the pan and the block against churning oil heated to nearly 200 degrees, oil that sought vainly to escape its duty and was forced back to work by a stalwart gasket. But now, after years of perseverance, the gasket has lost its resilience and the craven oil escapes. Ecclesiastes allows a time for all things, and the time for this gasket has passed.

6   Higher up, between the block casting that forms the foundation of the engine and the cylinder-head casting that admits fresh air and exhausts oxidized air and fuel, is the head gasket, a piece of sheet metal as thin as a matchbook cover that has confined the multiple fires built within the engine to their proper domains. Now, a whitish-gray deposit betrays an eroded area from which blue flame spits every time the cylinder fires. The gasket is "blown."

Let us stop and think of large numbers. In the four-cycle engines 7
that power all modern cars, a spark jumps a spark-plug gap and sets off
a fire in a cylinder every time the crankshaft goes around twice. The
crankshaft turns the transmission shaft, which turns the driveshaft,
which turns the differential gears, which turn the rear axles, which
turn the wheels (what could Aquinas have done with something like
that, had he addressed himself to the source of the spark or to the final
destination of the wheels?). In 100,000 miles — a common life for
modern engines — the engine will make some 260 million turns, and
in half of those turns, 130 million of them, a gasoline-fueled fire with
a maximum temperature of 2,000 degrees (quickly falling to about
1,200 degrees) is built in each cylinder. The heat generated by the fire
raises the pressure in the cylinder to about 700 pounds per square inch,
if only for a brief instant before the piston moves and the pressure
falls. A head gasket has to contend with heat and pressure like this all
the time the engine is running, and, barring mishap, it will put up
with it indefinitely.

This Plymouth has suffered mishap. I know it as soon as I raise 8
the hood and see the telltale line of rust running across the underside
of the hood: the mark of overheating. A water pump bearing or seal
gave way, water leaked out, and was flung off the fan blades with
enough force to embed particles of rust in the undercoating. Without
cooling water, the engine grew too hot, and that's why the head gasket
blew. In an engine, no cause exists without an effect. Unlike a court
of law, wherein criminals are frequently absolved of wrongdoing, no
engine component is without duty and responsibility, and failure cannot be mitigated by dubious explanations such as parental neglect or
a crummy neighborhood.

Just as Sherlock Holmes would not be satisfied with one clue if 9
he could find others, I study the oil filter. The block and oil pan are
caked with seepings and drippings, but below the filter the caking is
visibly less thick and somewhat soft. So: once upon a time, a careless
service-station attendant must have ruined the gasket while installing
a new oil filter. Oil en route to the bearings escaped and washed away
the grime that had accumulated. Odds are that the oil level fell too
low and the crankshaft bearings were starved for oil.

Bearings are flat strips of metal, formed into half-circles about as 10
thick as a matchbook match and about an inch wide. The bearing
surface itself — the surface that *bears* the crankshaft and that *bears*
the load imposed by the fire-induced pressure above the piston — is

half as thick. Bearing metal is a drab, gray alloy, the principal component of which is *babbitt*, a low-friction metal porous enough to absorb oil but so soft that it must be allowed to withstand high pressures. (I like to think that Sinclair Lewis had metallurgy in mind when he named his protagonist George Babbitt.) When the fire goes off above the piston and the pressure is transmitted to the crankshaft via the connecting rod, the babbitt-alloyed bearing pushes downward with a force of about 3,500 pounds per square inch. And it must not give way, must not be peened into foil and driven from its place in fragments.

11   Regard the fleshy end joint of your thumb and invite a 100-pound woman (or a pre-teen child, if no such woman be near to hand) to stand on it. Multiply the sensation by thirty-five and you get an idea of what the bearing is up against. Of course, the bearing enjoys a favorable handicap in the comparison because it works in a metal-to-metal environment heated to 180 degrees or so. The bearing is equal to its task so long as it is protected from direct metal-to-metal contact by a layer of lubricating oil, oil that must be forced into the space between the bearing and the crankshaft against that 3,500 pounds of force. True, the oil gets a lot of help from hydrodynamic action as the spinning crankshaft drags oil along with it, but lubrication depends primarily on a pump that forces oil through the engine at around 40 pounds of pressure.

12   If the oil level falls too low, the oil pump sucks in air. The oil gets as frothy as whipped cream and doesn't flow. In time, oil pressure will fall so low that the "idiot" light on the dashboard will flash, but long before then the bearing may have run "dry" and suffered considerable amounts of its metal to be peened away by those 3,500-pound hammer blows. "Considerable" may mean only .005 inches, or about the thickness of one sheet of 75-percent-cotton, 25-pound-per-ream dissertation bond — not much metal, but enough to allow oil to escape from the bearing even after the defective filter gasket is replaced and the oil supply replenished. From the time of oil starvation onward, the beaten bearing is a little disaster waiting to spoil a vacation or a commute to an important meeting.

13   Curious, that an unseen .005 inches of drab, gray metal worthy only to inspire the name of a poltroonish bourgeois should enjoy more consequence for human life than almost any equal thickness of a randomly chosen doctoral dissertation. Life is full of ironies.

14   The car I confront does not have an "idiot" light. It has an old-fashioned oil-pressure gauge. As the driver made his rounds from con-

dominium to committee room, he could — if he cared or was ever so alert — monitor the health of his engine bearings by noting the oil pressure. Virtually all cars had these gauges in the old days, but they began to disappear in the mid-'50s, and nowadays hardly any cars have them. In eliminating oil-pressure gauges, the car makers pleaded that, in their dismal experience, people didn't pay much attention to gauges. Accordingly, Detroit switched to the warning light, which was cheaper to manufacture anyway (and having saved a few bucks on the mechanicals, the manufacturer could afford to etch a design in the opera windows; this is called "progress"). Curious, in the midst of all this, that Chrysler Corporation, the maker of Plymouths and the victim of so much bad management over the past fifteen years, should have been the one car manufacturer to constantly assert, via a standard-equipment oil-pressure gauge, a faith in the awareness, judgment, and responsibility of drivers. That Chrysler did so may have something to do with its current problems.

The other car makers were probably right. Time was when most 15 men knew how to replace their own distributor points, repair a flat tire, and install a battery. Women weren't assumed to know as much, but they were expected to know how to put a gear lever in neutral, set a choke and throttle, and crank a car by hand if the battery was dead. Now, odds are that 75 percent of men and a higher percentage of women don't even know how to work the jacks that come with their cars. To be sure, a bumper jack is an abominable contraption — the triumph of production economies over good sense — but it will do what it is supposed to do, and the fact that most drivers cannot make one work says much about the way motorists have changed over the past forty years.

About all that people will watch on the downslide of this century 16 is the fuel gauge, for they don't like to be balked in their purpose. A lack of fuel will stop a car dead in its tracks and categorically prevent the driver from arriving at the meeting to consider tenure for a male associate professor with a black grandfather and a Chinese mother. Lack of fuel will stall a car in mid-intersection and leave dignity and image prey to the honks and curses of riffraff driving taxicabs and beer trucks, so people watch the fuel gauge as closely as they watch a pubescent daughter or a bearish stock.

But for the most part, once the key goes into the ignition, people 17 assign responsibility for the car's smooth running to someone else — to anybody but themselves. If the engine doesn't start, that's not because the driver has abused it, but because the manufacturer was remiss or the mechanic incompetent. (Both suspicions are reasonable, but they do not justify the driver's spineless passivity.) The driver considers himself merely a client of the vehicle. He proudly disclaims, at club and luncheon, any understanding of the dysfunctions of the machine. He must so disclaim, for to admit knowledge or to seek it actively would require an admission of responsibility and fault. To be wrong about inflation or the political aspirations of the Albanians doesn't cost anybody anything, but to claim to know why the car won't start and then to be proved wrong is both embarrassing and costly.

18   Few people would remove $500 from someone's pocket without a qualm and put it in their own. Yet, the job-lot run of mechanics do it all the time. Mechanics and drivers are alike: they gave up worrying long ago about the intricacies and demands of cause and effect. The mechanics do not attend closely to the behavior of the vehicle. Rather, they consult a book with flow-charts that says, "Try this, and if it doesn't work, try that." Or they hook the engine up to another machine and read gauges or cathode-ray-tube squiggles, but without realizing that gauges and squiggles are not reality but only tools used to aid perception of reality. A microscope is also a wonderful tool, but you still have to comprehend what you're looking for; else, like James Thurber, you get back the reflection of your own eye.

19   Mechanics, like academics and bureaucrats, have retreated too far from the realities of their tasks. An engine runs badly. They consult the book. The book says to replace part A. They replace A. The engine still runs badly, but the mechanic can deny the fact as handily as a socialist can deny that minimum-wage laws eventually lead to unemployment. Just as the driver doesn't care to know why his oil pressure drops from 40 to 30 to 20 pounds and then to zero, so the mechanic cares little for the casuistic distinctions that suggest that part A is in good order but that some subtle conjunction of wholesome part B with defective part C may be causing the trouble. (I don't know about atheists in foxholes, but I doubt that many Jesuits are found among incompetent mechanics.)

20   And why should the mechanic care? He gets paid in any event. From the mechanic's point of view, he should get paid, for he sees a federal judge hire academic consultants to advise about busing, and after the whites have fled before the imperious column of yellow buses and left the schools blacker than ever, the judge hires the con-

sultants again to find out why the whites moved out. The consultant gets paid in public money, whatever effects his actions have, even when he causes things he said would never happen.

Consider the garden-variety Herr Doktor who has spent a pleasant series of warm fall weekends driving to a retreat in the Catskills; his car has started with alacrity and run well despite a stuck choke. Then, when the first blue norther of the season sends temperatures toward zero, the faithful machine must be haggled into action and proceeds haltingly down the road, gasping and backfiring. "Needs a new carburetor," the mechanic says, and, to be sure, once a new carburetor is installed, the car runs well again. Our Herr Doktor is happy. His car did not run well; it got a new carburetor and ran well again; ergo, the carburetor was at fault. Q.E.D. 21

Curious that in personal matters the classic *post hoc* fallacy should be so readily accepted when it would be mocked in academic debate. Our Herr Doktor should know, or at least suspect, that the carburetor that functioned so well for the past several months could hardly have changed its nature overnight, and we might expect of him a more diligent inquiry into its problems. But "I'm no mechanic," he chuckles to his colleagues, and they nod agreeably. Such skinned-knuckle expertise would be unfitting in a man whose self-esteem is equivalent to his uselessness with a wrench. Lilies of the postindustrial field must concern themselves with weighty matters beyond the ken of greasy laborers who drink beer at the end of a workday. 22

Another example will illustrate the point. A battery cable has an end that is designed to connect to a terminal on the battery. Both cable-end and battery-terminal surfaces look smooth, but aren't. Those smooth surfaces are pitted and peaked, and only the peaks touch each other. The pits collect water from the air, and the chemistry of electricity-carrying metals causes lead oxides to form in the pits. The oxides progressively insulate the cable end and battery terminal from each other until the day that turning the key produces only a single, resounding *clunk* and no more. The road service mechanic installs a new $75 battery and collects $25 for his trouble. Removing the cables from the old battery cleans their ends somewhat, so things work for a few days, and then the car again fails to start. The mechanic installs a $110 alternator, applies a $5 charge to the battery, and collects another $25; several days later he gives the battery another $5 charge, installs a $75 starter, and collects $25 more. In these instances, to charge the battery — to send current backwards from cable end to battery terminal — disturbs the oxides and temporarily improves their 23 conductivity. Wriggling the charger clamps on the cable ends probably helps too. On the driver's last $25 visit, the mechanic sells another $5 battery charge and a pair of $25 battery cables. Total bill: $400, and all the car needed was to have its cable ends and battery terminals cleaned. The mechanic wasn't necessarily a thief. Perhaps, like academic education consultants, he just wasn't very smart — and his ilk abound; they are as plentiful as the drivers who will pay generously for the privilege of an aristocratic disdain of elementary cause and effect in a vehicular electrical system.

24   After a tolerably long practice as a mechanic, I firmly believe that at least two-thirds of the batteries, starters, alternators, ignition coils, carburetors, and water pumps that are sold are not needed. Batteries, alternators, and starters are sold because battery-cable ends are dirty. A maladjusted or stuck automatic choke is cured by a new carburetor. Water pumps and alternators are sold to correct problems from loose fan belts. In the course of the replacement, the fan belt gets properly tightened, so the original problem disappears in the misguided cure, with mechanic and owner never the wiser.

25   I understand the venality (and laziness and ignorance) of mechanics, and I understand the shop owner's need to pay a salary to someone to keep up with the IRS and OSHA forms. The shop marks up parts by 50 to 100 percent. When the car with the faulty choke comes in the door, the mechanic must make a choice: he can spend fifteen minutes fixing it and charge a half-hour's labor, or he can spend a half-hour replacing the carburetor (and charge for one hour) with one he buys for $80 and sells for $135. If the shop is a profit-making enterprise, the mechanic can hardly be blamed for selling the unneeded new carburetor, especially if the customer will stand still to be fleeced. Whether the mechanic acts from ignorance or larceny (the odds are about equal), the result is still a waste, one that arises from the driver's refusal to study the cause and effect of events that occur under the hood of his car.

26   The willingness of a people to accept responsibility for the machines they depend on is a fair barometer of their sense of individual worth and of the moral strength of a culture. According to popular reports, the Russian working folk are a sorrowfully vodka-besotted lot; likewise, reports are that Russian drivers abuse their vehicles atrociously. In our unhappy country, as gauges for battery-charging (ammeters), cooling-water temperature, and oil pressure disappeared from the dashboards, they were replaced by a big-brotherly series of

cacophonous buzzers and flashing lights, buzzers and lights mandated by regulatory edict for the sole purpose of reminding the driver that the government considers him a hopeless fool. Concurrent with these developments has come social agitation and law known as "consumer protection," which is, in fact, an extension of the philosophy that people are morons for whom the government must provide outpatient care. People pay handsome taxes to be taught that they are not responsible and do not need to be. This is a long way from what the Puritans paid their tithes for, and, Salem witch trials aside, the Puritans got a better product for their money.

What is astounding and dismaying is how quickly people came to believe in their own incompetence. In 1951, Eric Hoffer noted in *The True Believer* that a leader so disposed could make free people into slaves easier than he could turn slaves into free people (cf. Moses). Hoffer must be pained by the accuracy of his perception.   27

I do not claim that Everyman can be his own expert mechanic, for I know that precious few can. I do claim that disdain for the beautiful series of cause-and-effect relationships ("beautiful" in the way that provoked Archimedes to proclaim "Eureka!") that move machines, and particularly the automobile, measures not only a man's wit but also a society's morals.   28

_____ **CONSIDERATIONS** _____

1. At the end of Paragraph 4, Sharp poses a question. What sentence toward the end of his essay answers this question? Is that sentence the thesis of his essay? What do you think of his choice of a moral barometer?

2. What would James Thurber think of Sharp's use of "which" in Paragraph 7? (See Thurber's short essay "Which.")

3. In Paragraphs 10, 11, and 12, Sharp offers an exposition of a process. Study his success in explaining technical matters without lapsing into terminology too specialized for the general reader.

4. Sharp calls a particular device on the dashboard an "idiot light." Why? Does this epithet connect with other parts of his essay?

5. Sharp refers (in Paragraph 9) to Sherlock Holmes's renowned skill in deduction, and (in Paragraph 22) to a common logical fallacy called *post hoc ergo propter hoc*. Consult a good dictionary for the meaning of this Latin phrase.

William Stafford (b. 1914) is a poet who grew up in Kansas and taught for many years at Lewis and Clark College in Oregon. Traveling through the Dark *won the National Book Award in 1963, and in 1977, Stafford collected his poems into one volume called* Stories That Could Be True. A Glass Face in the Rain *followed in 1982. His essays appear in* Writing the Australian Crawl *(1978).*

Stafford's poetry and his account of writing his poetry look simple. In a way, they are simple, but their simplicity deepens as you look at it. His poetry is simple and deep, rather than complex and superficial. Reading about his way of writing, you feel the style of the man as intensely in his prose as in his poems.

65

WILLIAM STAFFORD

A Way of Writing

1   A writer is not so much someone who has something to say as he is someone who has found a process that will bring about new things he would not have thought of if he had not started to say them. That is, he does not draw on a reservoir; instead, he engages in an activity that brings to him a whole succession of unforeseen stories, poems, essays, plays, laws, philosophies, religions, or — but wait!

2   Back in school, from the first when I began to try to write things, I felt this richness. One thing would lead to another; the world would give and give. Now, after twenty years or so of trying, I live by that certain richness, an idea hard to pin, difficult to say, and perhaps offensive to some. For there are strange implications in it.

From *Field: Contemporary Poetry and Poetics*, #2. Spring 1970. Reprinted by permission of *Field*, Oberlin College, Oberlin, Ohio.

One implication is the importance of just plain receptivity. When 3
I write, I like to have an interval before me when I am not likely to be
interrupted. For me, this means usually the early morning, before others are awake. I get pen and paper, take a glance out the window (often
it is dark out there), and wait. It is like fishing. But I do not wait very
long, for there is always a nibble — and this is where receptivity
comes in. To get started I will accept anything that occurs to me.
Something always occurs, of course, to any of us. We can't keep from
thinking. Maybe I have to settle for an immediate impression: it's
cold, or hot, or dark, or bright, or in between! Or — well, the possibilities are endless. If I put down something, that thing will help the next
thing come, and I'm off. If I let the process go on, things will occur to
me that were not at all in my mind when I started. These things, odd
or trivial as they may be, are somehow connected. And if I let them
string out, surprising things will happen.

If I let them string out. . . . Along with initial receptivity, then, 4
there is another readiness: I must be willing to fail. If I am to keep on
writing, I cannot bother to insist on high standards. I must get into
action and not let anything stop me, or even slow me much. By "standards" I do not mean "correctness" — spelling, punctuation, and so
on. These details become mechanical for anyone who writes for a
while. I am thinking about what many people would consider "important" standards, such matters as social significance, positive values,
consistency, etc. I resolutely disregard these. Something better,
greater, is happening! I am following a process that leads so wildly and
originally into new territory that no judgment can at the moment be
made about values, significance, and so on. I am making something
new, something that has not been judged before. Later others — and
maybe I myself — will make judgments. Now, I am headlong to discover. Any distraction may harm the creating.

So, receptive, careless of failure, I spin out things on the page. 5
And a wonderful freedom comes. If something occurs to me, it is all
right to accept it. It has one justification: it occurs to me. No one else
can guide me. I must follow my own weak, wandering, diffident
impulses.

A strange bonus happens. At times, without my insisting on it, 6
my writings become coherent; the successive elements that occur to
me are clearly related. They lead by themselves to new connections.
Sometimes the language, even the syllables that happen along, may
start a trend. Sometimes the materials alert me to something waiting
in my mind, ready for sustained attention. At such times, I allow

myself to be eloquent, or intentional, or for great swoops (treacherous! not to be trusted!) reasonable. But I do not insist on any of that; for I know that back of my activity there will be the coherence of my self, and that indulgence of my impulses will bring recurrent patterns and meanings again.

7   This attitude toward the process of writing creatively suggests a problem for me, in terms of what others say. They talk about "skills" in writing. Without denying that I do have experience, wide reading, automatic orthodoxies and maneuvers of various kinds, I still must insist that I am often baffled about what "skill" has to do with the precious little area of confusion when I do not know what I am going to say and then I find out what I am going to say. That precious interval I am unable to bridge by skill. What can I witness about it? It remains mysterious, just as all of us must feel puzzled about how we are so inventive as to be able to talk along through complexities with our friends, not needing to plan what we are going to say, but never stalled for long in our confident forward progress. Skill? If so, it is the skill we all have, something we must have learned before the age of three or four.

8   A writer is one who has become accustomed to trusting that grace, or luck, or — skill.

9   Yet another attitude I find necessary: most of what I write, like most of what I say in casual conversation, will not amount to much. Even I will realize, and even at the time, that it is not negotiable. It will be like practice. In conversation I allow myself random remarks — in fact, as I recall, that is the way I learned to talk — , so in writing I launch many expendable efforts. A result of this free way of writing is that I am not writing for others, mostly; they will not see the product at all unless the activity eventuates in something that later appears to be worthy. My guide is the self, and its adventuring in the language brings about communication.

10   This process-rather-than-substance view of writing invites a final, dual reflection:

1. Writers may not be special — sensitive or talented in any usual sense. They are simply engaged in sustained use of a language skill we all have. Their "creations" come about through confident reliance on stray impulses that will, with trust, find occasional patterns that are satisfying.

2. But writing itself is one of the great, free human activities. There is scope for individuality, and elation, and discovery, in writing. For the person who follows with trust and forgiveness what occurs to

him, the world remains always ready and deep, an inexhaustible environment, with the combined vividness of an actuality and flexibility of a dream. Working back and forth between experience and thought, writers have more than space and time can offer. They have the whole unexplored realm of human vision.

A sample daily-writing sheet and the poem as revised.

15 December 1969
At the fountain on Main Street I saw
our shadows. It did not drink, but
waited on cement and water while I drank.
There were two people and but one shadow.
Two people in love there but one shadow.
I looked at Fred, returned that a bird
flying past made a shadow on the sky.
There is a place in the air where our house
used to be. Once I crawled through
grassblades to hear the sounds of their shadows.
One of the shadows moved, and it was
the earth where a mole was passing.
I could hear little paws in the dirt,
and fur brush along the tunnel, and even,
somehow, the mole shadow.
Out in places like Wyoming some of the shadows
are cut out and pasted on fossils.
There are mountains that erode when
clouds drag across them. ~~I hear~~ You can hear
the tick of the light breaking edges off white stones.
In my prayers I let yesterday begin
and then go behind this hour now. Every heart
pumps from a well full of shadows.
In churches their hearts pump from wells
full of shadows. sermons
In churches they pump sermons from
wells full of shadows.

Shadows

I

Out in places like Wyoming some of the shadows

are cut out and pasted on fossils.

There are mountains that erode when
clouds drag across them. You can hear the tick

~~the tick~~ of the light breaking edges off white stones.

At a ~~the~~ fountain on Main Street I saw

our shadow. It did not drink but

waited on cement and water while I drank.

There were two people and but one shadow.

I looked up so hard outward that a bird

flying past made a shadow on the sky.

There is a place in the air where our house

~~used to be.~~

Once I crawled through grassblades to hear

the sounds of their shadows. One of the shadows

moved, and it was the earth where a mole

was passing. I could hear little

paws in the dirt, and fur brush along

the tunnel, and even, somehow, the mole shadow.

In churches when ~~their~~ hearts pump sermons

from wells full of shadows.

In my prayers I let yesterday begin

and then go behind this hour now.

SHADOWS

Out in places like Wyoming some of the shadows
are cut out and pasted on fossils.
There are mountains that erode when
clouds drag across them. You hear the tick
of sunlight breaking edges off white stones.

At a fountain on Main Street I saw
our shadow. It did not drink but
waited on cement and water while I drank.
There were two people and but one shadow.
I looked up so hard outward that a bird
flying past made a shadow on the sky.
There is a place in the air where
our old house used to be.

Once I crawled through grassblades to hear
the sounds of their shadows. One shadow
moved, and it was the earth where a mole
was passing. I could hear little
paws in the dirt, and fur brush along
the tunnel, and even, somehow, the mole shadow.

In my prayers I let yesterday begin
and then go behind this hour now,
in churches where hearts pump sermons
from wells full of shadows.

—— **CONSIDERATIONS** ——————————————

1. Stafford is clearly and openly talking about himself — how *he* writes, what writing means to *him* — and yet most readers agree that he successfully avoids the egotism or self-consciousness that sours many first-person essays. Compare his style with three or four other first-person pieces in this book to see how he does it.

2. In his first paragraph, Stafford tells of an idea that might be called writing as discovery. Thinking back through your own writing, can you recall this experience — when, after struggling to write an essay or letter that you *had* to write, you discovered something you *wanted* to write? What did you do about it? More important, what might you do next time it happens?

3. What, according to Stafford, is more important to a writer than "social significance, or positive values, or consistency"?

4. Stafford is talking about writing a poem. How do his discoveries and conclusions bear on *your* problems in writing an essay? Be specific.

5. Do the opening and closing paragraphs differ in style? If so, what is the difference, and why does Stafford allow it?

6. Study the three versions of Stafford's poem "Shadows." Do you find anything that belies the easygoing impression his essay gives of Stafford at work? Explain.

Jonathan Swift (1667–1745), the author of Gulliver's Travels, *was a priest, a poet, and a master of English prose. Some of his strongest satire took the form of reasonable defense of the unthinkable, like his argument in favor of abolishing Christianity in the British Isles. Born in Dublin, he was angry all his life at England's misuse and mistreatment of the subject Irish people. In 1729, he made this modest proposal for solving the Irish problem.*

66

JONATHAN SWIFT
A Modest Proposal

FOR PREVENTING THE CHILDREN OF POOR PEOPLE IN IRELAND FROM BEING A BURDEN TO THEIR PARENTS OR COUNTRY, AND FOR MAKING THEM BENEFICIAL TO THE PUBLIC

It is a melancholy object to those who walk through this great 1 town or travel in the country, when they see the streets, the roads, and cabin doors, crowded with beggars of the female sex, followed by three, four, or six children, all in rags and importuning every passenger for an alms. These mothers, instead of being able to work for their honest livelihood, are forced to employ all their time in strolling to beg sustenance for their helpless infants, who, as they grow up, either turn thieves for want of work, or leave their dear native country to fight for the Pretender in Spain, or sell themselves to the Barbadoes.

I think it is agreed by all parties that this prodigious number of 2 children in the arms, or on the backs, or at the heels of their mothers, and frequently of their fathers, is in the present deplorable state of the kingdom a very great additional grievance; and therefore whoever could find out a fair, cheap, and easy method of making these children

379

sound, useful members of the commonwealth would deserve so well of the public as to have his statue set up for a preserver of the nation.

3   But my intention is very far from being confined to provide only for the children of professed beggars; it is of a much greater extent, and shall take in the whole number of infants at a certain age who are born of parents in effect as little able to support them as those who demand our charity in the streets.

4   As to my own part, having turned my thoughts for many years upon this important subject, and maturely weighed the several schemes of other projectors, I have always found them grossly mistaken in their computation. It is true, a child just dropped from its dam may be supported by her milk for a solar year, with little other nourishment; at most not above the value of two shillings, which the mother may certainly get, or the value in scraps, by her lawful occupation of begging; and it is exactly at one year old that I propose to provide for them in such a manner as instead of being a charge upon their parents or the parish, or wanting food and raiment for the rest of their lives, they shall on the contrary contribute to the feeding, and partly to the clothing, of many thousands.

5   There is likewise another great advantage in my scheme, that it will prevent those voluntary abortions, and that horrid practice of women murdering their bastard children, alas, too frequent among us, sacrificing the poor innocent babes, I doubt, more to avoid the expense than the shame, which would move tears and pity in the most savage and inhuman breast.

6   The number of souls in this kingdom being usually reckoned one million and a half, of these I calculate there may be about two hundred thousand couples whose wives are breeders; from which number I subtract thirty thousand couples who are able to maintain their own children, although I apprehend there cannot be so many under the present distress of the kingdom; but this being granted, there will remain an hundred and seventy thousand breeders. I again subtract fifty thousand for those women who miscarry, or whose children die by accident or disease within the year. There only remain an hundred and twenty thousand children of poor parents actually born. The question therefore is, how this number shall be reared and provided for, which, as I have already said, under the present situation of affairs, is utterly impossible by all the methods hitherto proposed. For we can neither employ them in handicraft or agriculture; we neither build houses (I mean in the country) nor cultivate land. They can very seldom pick up a livelihood by stealing till they arrive at six years old,

except where they are of towardly parts; although I confess they learn the rudiments much earlier, during which time they can however be looked upon only as probationers, as I have been informed by a principal gentleman in the country of Cavan, who protested to me that he never knew above one or two instances under the age of six, even in a part of the kingdom so renowned for the quickest proficiency in that art.

I am assured by our merchants that a boy or a girl before twelve   7 years old is no salable commodity; and even when they come to this age they will not yield above three pounds, or three pounds and half a crown at most on the Exchange; which cannot turn to account either to the parents or the kingdom, the charge of nutriment and rags having been at least four times that value.

I shall now therefore humbly propose my own thoughts, which I   8 hope will not be liable to the least objection.

I have been assured by a very knowing American of my acquain-   9 tance in London, that a young healthy child well nursed is at a year old a most delicious, nourishing, and wholesome food, whether stewed, roasted, baked, or boiled; and I make no doubt that it will equally serve in a fricassee or a ragout.

I do therefore humbly offer it to public consideration that of the   10 hundred and twenty thousand children, already computed, twenty thousand may be reserved for breed, whereof only one fourth part to be males, which is more than we allow to sheep, black cattle, or swine; and my reason is that these children are seldom the fruits of marriage, a circumstance not much regarded by our savages, therefore one male will be sufficient to serve four females. That the remaining hundred thousand may at a year old be offered in sale to the persons of quality and fortune through the kingdom, always advising the mother to let them suck plentifully in the last month, so as to render them plump and fat for a good table. A child will make two dishes at an entertainment for friends; and when the family dines alone, the fore or hind quarter will make a reasonable dish, and seasoned with a little pepper or salt will be very good boiled on the fourth day, especially in the winter.

I have reckoned upon a medium that a child just born will weigh   11 twelve pounds, and in a solar year if tolerably nursed increaseth to twenty-eight pounds.

I grant this food will be somewhat dear, and therefore very proper   12 for landlords, who, as they have already devoured most of the parents, seem to have the best title to the children.

13   Infant's flesh will be in season throughout the year, but more plentiful in March, and a little before and after. For we are told by a grave author, an eminent French physician, that fish being a prolific diet, there are more children born in Roman Catholic countries about nine months after Lent than at any other season; therefore, reckoning a year after Lent, the markets will be more glutted than usual, because the number of popish infants is at least three to one in this kingdom; and therefore it will have one other collateral advantage, by lessening the number of Papists among us.

14   I have already computed the charge of nursing a beggar's child (in which list I reckon all cottagers, laborers, and four fifths of the farmers) to be about two shillings per annum, rags included; and I believe no gentleman would repine to give ten shillings for the carcass of a good fat child, which, as I have said, will make four dishes of excellent nutritive meat, when he hath only some particular friend or his own family to dine with him. Thus the squire will learn to be a good landlord, and grow popular among the tenants; the mother will have eight shillings net profit, and be fit for work till she produces another child.

15   Those who are more thrifty (as I must confess the times require) may flay the carcass; the skin of which artificially dressed will make admirable gloves for ladies, and summer boots for fine gentlemen.

16   As to our city of Dublin, shambles may be appointed for this purpose in the most convenient parts of it, and butchers we may be assured will not be wanting; although I rather recommend buying the children alive, and dressing them hot from the knife as we do roasting pigs.

17   A very worthy person, a true lover of his country, and whose virtues I highly esteem, was lately pleased in discoursing on this matter to offer a refinement upon my scheme. He said that many gentlemen of his kingdom, having of late destroyed their deer, he conceived that the want of venison might be well supplied by the bodies of young lads and maidens, not exceeding fourteen years of age nor under twelve, so great a number of both sexes in every county being now ready to starve for want of work and service; and these to be disposed of by their parents, if alive, or otherwise by their nearest relations. But with due deference to so excellent a friend and so deserving a patriot, I cannot be altogether in his sentiments; for as to the males, my American acquaintance assured me from frequent experience that their flesh was generally tough and lean, like that of our schoolboys, by continual exercise, and their taste disagreeable; and to fatten them

would not answer the charge. Then as to the females, it would, I think with humble submission, be a loss to the public, because they soon would become breeders themselves: and besides, it is not improbable that some scrupulous people might be apt to censure such a practice (although indeed very unjustly) as a little bordering upon cruelty; which, I confess, hath always been with me the strongest objection against any project, how well soever intended.

But in order to justify my friend, he confessed that this expedient was put into his head by the famous Psalmanazar, a native of the island Formosa, who came from thence to London above twenty years ago, and in conversation told my friend that in his country when any young person happened to be put to death, the executioner sold the carcass to persons of quality as a prime dainty; and that in his time the body of a plump girl of fifteen, who was crucified for an attempt to poison the emperor, was sold to his Imperial Majesty's prime minister of state, and other great mandarins of the court, in joints from the gibbet, at four hundred crowns. Neither indeed can I deny that if the same use were made of several plump young girls in this town, who without one single groat to their fortunes cannot stir abroad without a chair, and appear at the playhouse and assemblies in foreign fineries which they never will pay for, the kingdom would not be the worse. 18

Some persons of a desponding spirit are in great concern about that vast number of poor people who are aged, diseased, or maimed, and I have been desired to employ my thoughts what course may be taken to ease the nation of so grievous an encumbrance. But I am not in the least pain upon that matter, because it is very well known that they are every day dying and rotting by cold and famine, and filth and vermin, as fast as can be reasonably expected. And as to the younger laborers, they are now in almost as hopeful a condition. They cannot get work, and consequently pine away for want of nourishment to a degree that if at any time they are accidentally hired to common labor, they have not strength to perform it; and thus the country and themselves are happily delivered from the evils to come. 19

I have too long digressed, and therefore shall return to my subject. I think the advantages by the proposal which I have made are obvious and many, as well as of the highest importance. 20

For first, as I have already observed, it would greatly lessen the number of Papists, with whom we are yearly overrun, being the principal breeders of the nation as well as our most dangerous enemies; and who stay at home on purpose to deliver the kingdom to the Pre- 21 tender, hoping to take their advantage by the absence of so many good Protestants, who have chosen rather to leave their country than to stay at home and pay tithes against their conscience to an Episcopal curate.

22   Secondly, the poorer tenants will have something valuable of their own, which by law may be made liable to distress, and help to pay their landlord's rent, their corn and cattle being already seized and money a thing unknown.

23   Thirdly, whereas the maintenance of an hundred thousand children, from two years old and upwards, cannot be computed at less than ten shillings a piece per annum, the nation's stock will be thereby increased fifty thousand pounds per annum, besides the profit of a new dish introduced to the tables of all gentlemen of fortune in the kingdom who have any refinement in taste. And the money will circulate among ourselves, the goods being entirely of our own growth and manufacture.

24   Fourthly, the constant breeders, besides the gain of eight shillings sterling per annum by the sale of their children, will be rid of the charge of maintaining them after the first year.

25   Fifthly, this food would likewise bring great custom to taverns, where the vintners will certainly be so prudent as to procure the best receipts for dressing it to perfection, and consequently have their houses frequented by all the fine gentlemen, who justly value themselves upon their knowledge in good eating; and a skillful cook, who understands how to oblige his guests, will contrive to make it as expensive as they please.

26   Sixthly, this would be a great inducement to marriage, which all wise nations have either encouraged by rewards or enforced by laws and penalties. It would increase the care and tenderness of mothers toward their children, when they were sure of a settlement for life to the poor babes, provided in some sort by the public, to their annual profit instead of expense. We should see an honest emulation among the married women, which of them could bring the fattest child to the market. Men would become as fond of their wives during the time of their pregnancy as they are now of their mares in foal, their cows in calf, or sows when they are ready to farrow; nor offer to beat or kick them (as is too frequent a practice) for fear of a miscarriage.

27   Many other advantages might be enumerated. For instance, the addition of some thousand carcasses in our exportation of barreled beef, the propagation of swine's flesh, and improvements in the art of making good bacon, so much wanted among us by the great destruc-

tion of pigs, too frequent at our tables, which are no way comparable in taste or magnificence to a well-grown, fat, yearling child, which roasted whole will make a considerable figure at a lord mayor's feast or any other public entertainment. But this and many others I omit, being studious of brevity.

Supposing that one thousand families in this city would be constant customers for infants' flesh, besides others who might have it at merry meetings, particularly weddings and christenings, I compute that Dublin would take off annually about twenty thousand carcasses, and the rest of the kingdom (where probably they will be sold somewhat cheaper) the remaining eighty thousand. 28

I can think of no one objection that will possibly be raised against this proposal, unless it should be urged that the number of people will be thereby much lessened in the kingdom. This I freely own, and it was indeed one principal design in offering it to the world. I desire the reader will observe, that I calculate my remedy for this one individual kingdom of Ireland and for no other that ever was, is, or I think ever can be upon earth. Therefore let no man talk to me of other expedients: of taxing our absentees at five shillings a pound: of using neither clothes nor household furniture except what is of our own growth and manufacture; of utterly rejecting the materials and instruments that promote foreign luxury: of curing the expensiveness of pride, vanity, idleness, and gaming in our women: of introducing a vein of parsimony, prudence, and temperance: of learning to love our country, in the want of which we differ even from Laplanders and the inhabitants of Topinamboo: of quitting our animosities and factions, nor acting any longer like the Jews, who were murdering one another at the very moment their city was taken: of being a little cautious not to sell our country and conscience for nothing: of teaching landlords to have at least one degree of mercy toward their tenants: lastly, of putting a spirit of honesty, industry, and skill into our shopkeepers; who, if a resolution could now be taken to buy only our native goods, would immediately unite to cheat and exact upon us in the price, the measure, and the goodness, nor could ever yet be brought to make one fair proposal of just dealing, though often and earnestly invited to it. 29

Therefore, I repeat, let no man talk to me of these and the like expedients, till he hath at least some glimpse of hope that there will ever be some hearty and sincere attempt to put them in practice. 30

But as to myself, having been wearied out for many years with offering vain, idle, visionary thoughts, and at length utterly despairing of success, I fortunately fell upon this proposal, which, as it is wholly 31 new, so it hath something solid and real, of no expense and little trouble, full in our own power, and whereby we can incur no danger in disobliging England. For this kind of commodity will not bear exportation, the flesh being of too tender a consistence to admit a long continuance in salt, although perhaps I could name a country which would be glad to eat up our whole nation without it.

32   After all, I am not so violently bent upon my own opinion as to reject any offer proposed by wise men, which shall be found equally innocent, cheap, easy, and effectual. But before something of that kind shall be advanced in contradiction to my scheme, and offering a better, I desire the author or authors will be pleased maturely to consider two points. First, as things now stand, how they will be able to find food and raiment for an hundred thousand useless mouths and backs. And secondly, there being a round million of creatures in human figure throughout this kingdom, whose sole subsistence put into a common stock would leave them in debt two millions of pounds sterling, adding those who are beggars by profession to the bulk of farmers, cottagers, and laborers, with their wives and children who are beggars in effect; I desire those politicians who dislike my overture, and may perhaps be so bold to attempt an answer, that they will first ask the parents of these mortals whether they would not at this day think it a great happiness to have been sold for food at a year old in this manner I prescribe, and thereby have avoided such a perpetual scene of misfortunes as they have since gone through by the oppression of landlords, the impossibility of paying rent without money or trade, the want of common sustenance, with neither house nor clothes to cover them from the inclemencies of the weather, and the most inevitable prospect of entailing the like or greater miseries upon their breed forever.

33   I profess, in the sincerity of my heart, that I have not the least personal interest in endeavoring to promote this necessary work, having no other motive than the public good of my country, by advancing our trade, providing for infants, relieving the poor, and giving some pleasure to the rich. I have no children by which I can propose to get a single penny; the youngest being nine years old, and my wife past childbearing.

_____ **CONSIDERATIONS** _____

1. The biggest risk a satirist runs is that his reader will not understand that he is reading satire; that he will be too literal-minded. Can you imagine

a reader missing the satiric nature of Swift's "A Modest Proposal"? It has happened many times. What might such a reader think of the author? Consider the same problem with regard to Ambrose Bierce (pages 57–61), Calvin Trillen (pages 413–416), Wright Morris (pages 252–257), or Stephen Jay Gould (pages 161–166).

2. One clue to the satire is Swift's choice of diction in certain passages. In Paragraph 4, for example, note the phrase, "just dropped from its dam," in reference to a newborn child. How do these words make a sign to the reader? Look for other such words.

3. What words and phrases does Swift use to give the impression of straightforward seriousness?

4. How does Swift turn his satirical talent against religious intolerance?

5. What is the chief target of his satire toward the end of the essay?

6. If you have read Swift's *Gulliver's Travels* only in the version usually offered to children, you are in for a surprise when you read the complete, unexpurgated *Gulliver's Travels*, a devastating satire of British political, moral, and religious values.

Studs Terkel (b. 1912) has been an actor on stage and television, and has conducted a successful radio interview show in Chicago. His best known books, collections of interviews, are Division Street America *(1966),* Hard Times *(1970), and* Working *(1974) — from which we take this example of American speech. In 1977, he published* Talking to Myself, *his autobiography, and in 1980* American Dreams Lost and Found.

67

STUDS TERKEL

Phil Stallings, Spot Welder

1   *He is a spot-welder at the Ford assembly plant on the far South Side of Chicago. He is twenty-seven years old; recently married. He works the third shift: 3:30 P.M. to midnight.*

2   *"I start the automobile, the first welds. From there it goes to another line, where the floor's put on, the roof, the trunk hood, the doors. Then it's put on a frame. There is hundreds of lines.*

3   *"The welding gun's got a square handle, with a button on the top for high voltage and a button on the bottom for low. The first is to clamp the metal together. The second is to fuse it.*

4   *"The gun hangs from a ceiling, over tables that ride on a track. It travels in a circle, oblong, like an egg. You stand on a cement platform, maybe six inches from the ground."*

5   I stand in one spot, about two- or three-feet area, all night. The only time a person stops is when the line stops. We do about thirty-

two jobs per car, per unit. Forty-eight units an hour, eight hours a day. Thirty-two times forty-eight times eight. Figure it out. That's how many times I push that button.

The noise, oh it's tremendous. You open your mouth and you're 6 liable to get a mouthful of sparks. (Shows his arms.) That's a burn, these are burns. You don't compete against the noise. You go to yell and at the same time you're straining to maneuver the gun to where you have to weld.

You got some guys that are uptight, and they're not sociable. It's 7 too rough. You pretty much stay to yourself. You get involved with yourself. You dream, you think of things you've done. I drift back continuously to when I was a kid and what me and my brothers did. The things you love most are the things you drift back into.

Lots of times I worked from the time I started to the time of the 8 break and I never realized I had even worked. When you dream, you reduce the chances of friction with the foreman or with the next guy.

It don't stop. It just goes and goes and goes. I bet there's men who 9 have lived and died out there, never seen the end of that line. And they never will — because it's endless. It's like a serpent. It's just all body, no tail. It can do things to you . . . (Laughs.)

Repetition is such that if you were to think about the job itself, 10 you'd slowly go out of your mind. You'd let your problems build up, you'd get to a point where you'd be at the fellow next to you — his throat. Every time the foreman came by and looked at you, you'd have something to say. You just strike out at anything you can. So if you involve yourself by yourself, you overcome this.

I don't like the pressure, the intimidation. How would you like 11 to go up to someone and say, "I would like to go to the bathroom?" If the foreman doesn't like you, he'll make you hold it, just ignore you. Should I leave this job to go to the bathroom I risk being fired. The line moves all the time.

I work next to Jim Grayson and he's preoccupied. The guy on my 12 left, he's a Mexican, speaking Spanish, so it's pretty hard to understand him. You just avoid him. Brophy, he's a young fella, he's going to college. He works catty-corner from me. Him and I talk from time to time. If he ain't in the mood, I don't talk. If I ain't in the mood, he knows it.

Oh sure, there's tension here. It's not always obvious, but the 13 whites stay with the whites and the coloreds stay with the coloreds. When you go into Ford, Ford says, "Can you work with other men?" This stops a lot of trouble, 'cause when you're working side by side with a guy, they can't afford to have guys fighting. When two men don't socialize, that means two guys are gonna do more work, know what I mean?

14   I don't understand how come more guys don't flip. Because you're nothing more than a machine when you hit this type of thing. They give better care to that machine than they will to you. They'll have more respect, give more attention to that machine. And you *know* this. Somehow you get the feeling that the machine is better than you are. (Laughs.)

15   You really begin to wonder. What price do they put on me? Look at the price they put on the machine. If that machine breaks down, there's somebody out there to fix it right away. If I break down, I'm just pushed over to the other side till another man takes my place. The only thing they have on their mind is to keep that line running.

16   I'll do the best I can. I believe in an eight-hour pay for an eight-hour day. But I will not try to outreach my limits. If I can't cut it, I just don't do it. I've been there three years and I keep my nose pretty clean. I never cussed anybody or anything like that. But I've had some real brushes with foremen.

17   What happened was my job was overloaded. I got cut and it got infected. I got blood poisoning. The drill broke. I took it to the foreman's desk. I says, "Change this as soon as you can." We were running specials for XL hoods. I told him I wasn't a repair man. That's how the conflict began. I says, "If you want, take me to the Green House." Which is a superintendent's office — disciplinary station. This is when he says, "Guys like you I'd like to see in the parking lot."

18   One foreman I know, he's about the youngest out here, he has this idea: I'm it and if you don't like it, you know what you can do. Anything this other foreman says, he usually overrides. Even in some cases, the foremen don't get along. They're pretty hard to live with, even with each other.

19   Oh yeah, the foreman's got somebody knuckling down on him, putting the screws to him. But a foreman is still free to go to the bathroom, go get a cup of coffee. He doesn't face the penalties. When I first went in there, I kind of envied foremen. Now, I wouldn't have a foreman's job. I wouldn't give 'em the time of the day.

20   When a man becomes a foreman, he has to forget about even being human, as far as feelings are concerned. You see a guy there bleeding to death. So what, buddy? That line's gotta keep goin'. I can't live like that. To me, if a man gets hurt, first thing you do is get him some attention.

About the blood poisoning. It came from the inside of a hood 21
rubbin' against me. It caused quite a bit of pain. I went down to the
medics. They said it was a boil. Got to my doctor that night. He said
blood poisoning. Running fever and all this. Now I've smartened up.

They have a department of medics. It's basically first aid. There's 22
no doctor on our shift, just two or three nurses, that's it. They've got
a door with a sign on it that says Lab. Another door with a sign on it:
Major Surgery. But my own personal opinion, I'm afraid of 'em. I'm
afraid if I were to get hurt, I'd get nothin' but back talk. I got hit square
in the chest one day with a bar from a rack and it cut me down this
side. They didn't take x-rays or nothing. Sent me back on the job. I
missed three and a half days two weeks ago. I had bronchitis. They
told me I was all right. I didn't have a fever. I went home and my
doctor told me I couldn't go back to work for two weeks. I really
needed the money, so I had to go back the next day. I woke up still
sick, so I took off the rest of the week.

I pulled a muscle on my neck, straining. This gun, when you grab 23
this thing from the ceiling, cable, weight, I mean you're pulling everything. Your neck, your shoulders, and your back. I'm very surprised
more accidents don't happen. You have to lean over, at the same time
holding down the gun. This whole edge here is sharp. I go through a
shirt every two weeks, it just goes right through. My coveralls catch
on fire. I've had gloves catch on fire. (Indicates arms.) See them little
holes? That's what sparks do. I've got burns across here from last
night.

I know I could find better places to work. But where could I get 24
the money I'm making? Let's face it, $4.32 an hour. That's real good
money now. Funny thing is, I don't mind working at body construction. To a great degree, I enjoy it. I love using my hands — more than
I do my mind. I love to be able to put things together and see something in the long run. I'll be the first to admit I've got the easiest job
on the line. But I'm against this thing where I'm being held back. I'll
work like a dog until I get what I want. The job I really want is utility.

It's where I can stand and say I can do any job in this department, 25
and nobody has to worry about me. As it is now, out of say, sixty jobs,
I can do almost half of 'em. I want to get away from standing in one
spot. Utility can do a different job every day. Instead of working right
there for eight hours I could work over there for eight, I could work
the other place for eight. Every day it would change. I would be around
more people. I go out on my lunch break and work on the fork truck
for a half-hour — to get the experience. As soon as I got it down pretty

good, the foreman in charge says he'll take me. I don't want the other guys to see me. When I hit that fork lift, you just stop your thinking and you concentrate. Something right there in front of you, not in the past, not in the future. This is real healthy.

26   I don't eat lunch at work. I may grab a candy bar, that's enough. I wouldn't be able to hold it down. The tension your body is put under by the speed of the line . . . When you hit them brakes, you just can't stop. There's a certain momentum that carries you forward. I could hold the food, but it wouldn't set right.

27   Proud of my work? How can I feel pride in a job where I call a foreman's attention to a mistake, a bad piece of equipment, and he'll ignore it. Pretty soon you get the idea they don't care. You keep doing this and finally you're titled a troublemaker. So you just go about your work. You *have* to have pride. So you throw it off to something else. And that's my stamp collection.

28   I'd break both my legs to get into social work. I see all over so many kids really gettin' a raw deal. I think I'd go into juvenile. I tell kids on the line, "Man, go out there and get that college." Because it's too late for me now.

29   When you go into Ford, first thing they try to do is break your spirit. I seen them bring a tall guy where they needed a short guy. I seen them bring a short guy where you have to stand on two guys' backs to do something. Last night, they brought a fifty-eight-year-old man to do the job I was on. That man's my father's age. I know damn well my father couldn't do it. To me, this is humanely wrong. A job should be a job, not a death sentence.

30   The younger worker, when he gets uptight, he talks back. But you take an old fellow, he's got a year, two years, maybe three years to go. If it was me, I wouldn't say a word, I wouldn't care what they did. 'Cause, baby, for another two years I can stick it out. I can't blame this man. I respect him because he had enough will power to stick it out for thirty years.

31   It's gonna change. There's a trend. We're getting younger and younger men. We got this new Thirty and Out. Thirty years seniority and out. The whole idea is to give a man more time, more time to slow down and live. While he's still in his fifties, he can settle down in a camper and go out and fish. I've sat down and thought about it. I've got twenty-seven years to go. (Laughs.) That's why I don't go around causin' trouble or lookin' for a cause.

32   The only time I get involved is when it affects me or it affects a

man on the line in a condition that could be me. I don't believe in lost causes, but when it all happened . . . (He pauses, appears bewildered.)

The foreman was riding the guy. The guy either told him to go 33 away or pushed him, grabbed him . . . You can't blame the guy — Jim Grayson. I don't want nobody stickin' their finger in my face. I'd've probably hit him beside the head. The whole thing was: Damn it, it's about time we took a stand. Let's stick up for the guy. We stopped the line. (He pauses, grins.) Ford lost about twenty units. I'd figure about five grand a unit — whattaya got? (Laughs.)

I said, "Let's all go home." When the line's down like that, you 34 can go up to one man and say, "You gonna work?" If he says no, they can fire him. See what I mean? But if nobody was there, who the hell were they gonna walk up to and say, "Are you gonna work?" Man, there woulda been nobody there! If it were up to me, we'd gone home.

Jim Grayson, the guy I work next to, he's colored. Absolutely. 35 That's the first time I've seen unity on that line. Now it's happened once, it'll happen again. Because everybody just sat down. Believe you me. (Laughs.) It stopped at eight and it didn't start till twenty after eight. Everybody and his brother were down there. It was really nice to see, it really was.

——— CONSIDERATIONS ———

1. Terkel is famous for his ability to catch the voice of the people he interviews. Study the language of Phil Stallings and list some of the features of his voice.

2. In addition to diction, what about this selection takes it out of the category of "essay"?

3. How does Stallings indicate his opinion that the company puts a higher value on its machines than on its men?

4. Does Stalling agree with what Caroline Bird says in her essay on the value of college (pages 62–72)?

5. What occurrence on the line, described toward the end of the interview, reveals Stallings's social consciousness?

6. Interview someone you find interesting.

Lewis Thomas (b. 1913) received his M.D. from Harvard Medical School in 1937, and since 1973 has headed the Memorial Sloan-Kettering Cancer Center in New York City. In 1971 he began to contribute meticulous essays to the New England Journal of Medicine, since collected in The Lives of a Cell *(1974) and* Late Night Thoughts on Listening to Mahler's Ninth Symphony *(1983) from which we take "On Smell." He has also written a memoir of his life as a doctor,* The Youngest Science *(1983) in which he reprints a poem that he published as a young man in* The Atlantic Monthly. *When he writes about the sense of smell, he brings a poet's language to a scientist's observation.*

68

LEWIS THOMAS
On Smell

1   The vacuum cleaner turned on in the apartment's back bedroom emits a high-pitched lament indistinguishable from the steam alarm on the teakettle in the kitchen, and the only way of judging whether to run to the stove is to consult one's watch: there is a time of day for the vacuum cleaner, another time for the teakettle. The telephone in the guest bedroom sounds like the back-door bell, so you wait for the second or third ring before moving. There is a random crunching sound in the vicinity of the front door, resembling an assemblage of people excitedly taking off galoshes, but when listened to carefully it is recognizable as a negligible sound, needing no response, made by the ancient elevator machinery in the wall alongside the door. So it goes. We learn these things from day to day, no trick to it. Sometimes the

sounds around our lives become novel confusions, harder to sort out: the family was once given a talking crow named Byron for Christmas, and this animal imitated every nearby sound with such accuracy that the household was kept constantly on the fly, answering doors and telephones, oiling hinges, looking out the window for falling bodies, glancing into empty bathrooms for the sources of flushing.

We are not so easily misled by vision. Most of the things before our eyes are plainly there, not mistakable for other things except for the illusions created for pay by professional magicians and, sometimes, the look of the lights of downtown New York against a sky so black as to make it seem a near view of eternity. Our eyes are not easy to fool. 2

Smelling is another matter. I should think we might fairly gauge the future of biological science, centuries ahead, by estimating the time it will take to reach a complete, comprehensive understanding of odor. It may not seem a profound enough problem to dominate all the life sciences, but it contains, piece by piece, all the mysteries. Smoke: tobacco burning, coal smoke, wood-fire smoke, leaf smoke. Most of all, leaf smoke. This is the only odor I can *will* back to consciousness just by thinking about it. I can sit in a chair, thinking, and call up clearly to mind the smell of burning autumn leaves, coded and stored away somewhere in a temporal lobe, firing off explosive signals into every part of my right hemisphere. But nothing else: if I try to recall the thick smell of Edinburgh in winter, or the accidental burning of a plastic comb, or a rose, or a glass of wine, I cannot do this; I can get a clear picture of any face I feel like remembering, and I can hear whatever Beethoven quartet I want to recall, but except for the leaf bonfire I cannot really remember a smell in its absence. To be sure, I know the odor of cinnamon or juniper and can name such things with accuracy when they turn up in front of my nose, but I cannot imagine them into existence. 3

The act of smelling something, anything, is remarkably like the act of thinking itself. Immediately, at the very moment of perception, you can feel the mind going to work, sending the odor around from place to place, setting off complex repertoires throughout the brain, polling one center after another for signs of recognition, old memories, connections. This is as it should be, I suppose, since the cells that do the smelling are themselves proper brain cells, the only neurones whose axones carry information picked up at first hand in the outside world. Instead of dendrites they have cilia, equipped with receptors for all sorts of chemical stimuli, and they are in some respects as myste- 4 rious as lymphocytes. There are reasons to believe that each of these neurones has its own specific class of receptors; like lymphocytes, each cell knows in advance what it is looking for; there are responder and nonresponder cells for different classes of odorant. And they are also the only brain neurones that replicate themselves; the olfactory receptor cells of mice turn over about once every twenty-eight days. There may be room for a modified version of the clonal-selection theory to explain olfactory learning and adaptation. The olfactory receptors of mice can smell the difference between self and nonself, a discriminating gift coded by the same H-2 gene locus governing homograft rejection. One wonders whether lymphocytes in the mucosa may be carrying along this kind of genetic information to donate to new generations of olfactory receptor cells as they emerge from basal cells.

5   The most medically wonderful of all things about these brain cells is that they do not become infected, not very often anyway, despite their exposure to all the microorganisms in the world of the nose. There must exist, in the mucus secretions bathing this surface of the brain, the most extraordinary antibiotics, including eclectic antiviral substances of some sort.

6   If you are looking about for things to even out the disparity between the brains of ordinary animals and the great minds of ourselves, the superprimate humans, this apparatus is a good one to reflect on in humility. Compared to the common dog, or any rodent in the field, we are primitive, insensitive creatures, biological failures. Heaven knows how much of the world we are missing.

7   I suppose if we tried we could improve ourselves. There are, after all, some among our species with special gifts for smelling — perfume makers, tea tasters, whiskey blenders — and it is said that these people can train themselves to higher and higher skills by practicing. Perhaps, instead of spending the resources of our huge cosmetic industry on chemicals for the disguising or outright destruction of odors we should be studying ways to enhance the smell of nature, facing up to the world.

8   In the meantime, we should be hanging on to some of the few great smells left to us, and I would vote for the preservation of leaf bonfires, by law if necessary. This one is pure pleasure, fetched like music intact out of numberless modular columns of neurones filled chockablock with all the natural details of childhood, firing off memories in every corner of the brain. An autumn curbside bonfire has everything needed for education: danger, surprise (you know in advance that if you poke the right part of the base of leaves with the

right kind of stick, a blinding flare of heat and fragrance will follow instantly, but it is still an astonishment when it happens), risk, and victory over odds (if you jump across at precisely the right moment the flare and sparks will miss your pants), and above all the aroma of comradeship (if you smell that odor in the distance you know that there are friends somewhere in the next block, jumping and exulting in their leaves, maybe catching fire).

It was a mistake to change this, smoke or no smoke, carbon dioxide and the greenhouse effect or whatever; it was a loss to give up the burning of autumn leaves. Now, in our haste to protect the environment (which is us, when you get down to it), we rake them up and cram them into great black plastic bags, set out at the curb like wrapped corpses, carted away by the garbage truck to be buried somewhere or dumped in the sea or made into fuel or alcohol or whatever it is they do with autumn leaves these days. We should be giving them back to the children to burn.

9

——— CONSIDERATIONS ———————————————————

1. In this essay, Thomas approaches his real subject slowly, talking with apparent casualness first about the precision of our hearing, then of our sight, and finally, in Paragraph 3, introducing his actual topic. What are the advantages and disadvantages of such an approach?

2. In what way does Paragraph 4 differ from all the other paragraphs of Thomas's essay?

3. Ease of reading is affected by the writer's ability to help the reader move smoothly from one paragraph to the next by the use of transitional words and phrases. Note the first sentences of both Paragraphs 2 and 3 and also of Paragraphs 7 and 8. Identify the words or phrases that form a bridge between paragraphs. Do you find any comparable transitional aid between Paragraphs 5 and 6?

4. Thomas says that his memory can evoke only one odor — that of burning leaves. What odors can you recall? Why those and not others? Build an essay about childhood on the basis of smells and the experiences they can suddenly bring to mind.

5. Thomas's concluding paragraph argues that when we ban the burning of fall leaves we sacrifice an emotional value for a practical one. Is this what E. F. Schumacher describes in his "Production in Service to Life" (pages 355–361)? How might a conservationist deeply concerned about air pollution — see, for example, Wendell Berry's "The Reactor and the Garden" (pages 48–56) — respond to Thomas's advice that we should give the leaves back to the children to burn?

"Ceti" comes from Lives of a Cell, *Thomas's first collection of essays, which won a National Book Award in 1975. His scientific mind, like the best minds in any field, extends itself by language to investigate everything human and to speculate beyond the human.*

69

LEWIS THOMAS
Ceti

1   Tau Ceti is a relatively nearby star that sufficiently resembles our sun to make its solar system a plausible candidate for the existence of life. We are, it appears, ready to begin getting in touch with Ceti, and with any other interested celestial body in more remote places, out to the edge. CETI is also, by intention, the acronym of the First International Conference on Communication with Extraterrestrial Intelligence, held in 1972 in Soviet Armenia under the joint sponsorship of the National Academy of Sciences of the United States and the Soviet Academy, which involved eminent physicists and astronomers from various countries, most of whom are convinced that the odds for the existence of life elsewhere are very high, with a reasonable probability that there are civilizations, one place or another, with technologic mastery matching or exceeding ours.

2   On this assumption, the conferees thought it likely that radio-astronomy would be the generally accepted mode of interstellar communication, on grounds of speed and economy. They made a formal recommendation that we organize an international cooperative program, with new and immense radio telescopes, to probe the reaches of

deep space for electromagnetic signals making sense. Eventually, we would plan to send out messages on our own and receive answers, but at the outset it seems more practical to begin by catching snatches of conversation between others.

So, the highest of all our complex technologies in the hardest of our sciences will soon be engaged, full scale, in what is essentially biologic research — and with some aspects of social science, at that.   3

The earth has become, just in the last decade, too small a place. We have the feeling of being confined — shut in; it is something like outgrowing a small town in a small county. The views of the dark, pocked surface of Mars, still lifeless to judge from the latest photographs, do not seem to have extended our reach; instead, they bring closer, too close, another unsatisfactory feature of our local environment. The blue noonday sky, cloudless, has lost its old look of immensity. The word is out that the sky is not limitless; it is finite. It is, in truth, only a kind of local roof, a membrane under which we live, luminous but confusingly refractile when suffused with sunlight; we can sense its concave surface a few miles over our heads. We know that it is tough and thick enough so that when hard objects strike it from the outside they burst into flames. The color photographs of the earth are more amazing than anything outside: we live inside a blue chamber, a bubble of air blown by ourselves. The other sky beyond, absolutely black and appalling, is wide-open country, irresistible for exploration.   4

Here we go, then. An extraterrestrial embryologist, having a close look at us from time to time, would probably conclude that the morphogenesis of the earth is coming along well, with the beginnings of a nervous system and fair-sized ganglions in the form of cities, and now with specialized, dish-shaped sensory organs, miles across, ready to receive stimuli. He may well wonder, however, how we will go about responding. We are evolving into the situation of a Skinner pigeon in a Skinner box, peering about in all directions, trying to make connections, probing.   5

When the first word comes in from outer space, finally, we will probably be used to the idea. We can already provide a quite good explanation for the origin of life, here or elsewhere. Given a moist planet with methane, formaldehyde, ammonia, and some usable minerals, all of which abound, exposed to lightning or ultraviolet irradiation at the right temperature, life might start off almost anywhere. The tricky, unsolved thing is how to get the polymers to arrange in membranes and invent replication. The rest is clear going. If they   6 follow our protocol, it will be anaerobic life at first, then photosynthesis and the first exhalation of oxygen, then respiring life and the great burst of variation, then speciation, and, finally, some kind of consciousness. It is easy, in the telling.

7   I suspect that when we have recovered from the first easy acceptance of signs of life from elsewhere, and finished nodding at each other, and finished smiling, we will be in shock. We have had it our way, relatively speaking, being unique all these years, and it will be hard to deal with the thought that the whole, infinitely huge, spinning, clocklike apparatus around us is itself animate, and can sprout life whenever the conditions are right. We will respond, beyond doubt, by making connections after the fashion of established life, floating out our filaments, extending pili, but we will end up feeling smaller than ever, as small as a single cell, with a quite new sense of continuity. It will take some getting used to.

8   The immediate problem, however, is a much more practical, down-to-earth matter, and must be giving insomnia to the CETI participants. Let us assume that there is, indeed, sentient life in one or another part of remote space, and that we will be successful in getting in touch with it. What on earth are we going to talk about? If, as seems likely, it is a hundred or more light years away, there are going to be some very long pauses. The barest amenities, on which we rely for opening conversations — Hello, are you there?, from us, followed by Yes, hello, from them — will take two hundred years at least. By the time we have our party we may have forgotten what we had in mind.

9   We could begin by gambling on the rightness of our technology and just send out news of ourselves, like a mimeographed Christmas letter, but we would have to choose our items carefully, with durability of meaning in mind. Whatever information we provide must still make sense to us two centuries later, and must still seem important, or the conversation will be an embarrassment to all concerned. In two hundred years it is, as we have found, easy to lose the thread.

10   Perhaps the safest thing to do at the outset, if technology permits, is to send music. This language may be the best we have for explaining what we are like to others in space, with least ambiguity. I would vote for Bach, all of Bach, streamed out into space, over and over again. We would be bragging, of course, but it is surely excusable for us to put the best possible face on at the beginning of such an acquaintance. We can tell the harder truths later. And, to do ourselves justice, music would give a fairer picture of what we are really like than some of the other things we might be sending, like *Time*, say, or a history of the

U.N. or Presidential speeches. We could send out our science, of course, but just think of the wincing at this end when the polite comments arrive two hundred years from now. Whatever we offer as today's items of liveliest interest are bound to be out of date and irrelevant, maybe even ridiculous. I think we should stick to music.

Perhaps, if the technology can be adapted to it, we should send some paintings. Nothing would better describe what this place is like, to an outsider, than the Cézanne demonstrations that an apple is really part fruit, part earth.   11

What kinds of questions should we ask? The choices will be hard, and everyone will want his special question first. What are your smallest particles? Did you think yourselves unique? Do you have colds? Have you anything quicker than light? Do you always tell the truth? Do you cry? There is no end to the list.   12

Perhaps we should wait a while, until we are sure we know what we want to know, before we get down to detailed questions. After all, the main question will be the opener: Hello, are you there? If the reply should turn out to be Yes, hello, we might want to stop there and think about that, for quite a long time.   13

—— CONSIDERATIONS ——————————

1. If you were to decide on our first communication with life in outer space, what message would you send? Why?

2. Why must people working on interplanetary communication keep time in mind?

3. Like Loren Eiseley (see pages 115–117), Thomas skillfully uses figurative language to help us see what he is talking about. Consider, for example, his description of our sky in Paragraph 4.

4. Point out some stylistic features in Thomas's essay that account for the highly informal, even jaunty tone.

5. Thomas touches on the shock we will feel when we have proof that mankind is not, after all, unique. What does he mean by saying "we will end up feeling smaller than ever, as small as a single cell, with quite a new sense of continuity"?

6. Why Bach rather than the Beatles or Bob Dylan?

7. How seriously do science fiction stories like *Star Wars* confront the questions raised by Thomas?

*While Thomas brings a poet's imagery to scientific matters, he
also brings to the study of language his wit and imagination. The
effect is like a scientist's microscope, with its power to multiply,
that turns the tiny into the huge.*

70

LEWIS THOMAS
Notes on Punctuation

1   There are no precise rules about punctuation (Fowler lays out
some general advice (as best he can under the complex circumstances
of English prose (he points out, for example, that we possess only four
stops (the comma, the semicolon, the colon and the period (the question mark and exclamation point are not, strictly speaking, stops; they
are indicators of tone (oddly enough, the Greeks employed the semicolon for their question mark (it produces a strange sensation to read
a Greek sentence which is a straightforward question: Why weepest
thou; (instead of Why weepest thou? (and, of course, there are parentheses (which are surely a kind of punctuation making this whole
matter much more complicated by having to count up the left-handed
parentheses in order to be sure of closing with the right number (but
if the parentheses were left out, with nothing to work with but the
stops, we would have considerably more flexibility in the deploying of
layers of meaning than if we tried to separate all the clauses by physical barriers (and in the latter case, while we might have more precision
and exactitude for our meaning, we would lose the essential flavor of
language, which is its wonderful ambiguity)))))))))))).

2   The commas are the most helpful and usable of all the stops. It

From *The Medusa and the Snail* by Lewis Thomas. Copyright © 1979 by Lewis
Thomas. Reprinted by permission of Viking Penguin Inc.

is highly important to put them in place as you go along. If you try to come back after doing a paragraph and stick them in the various spots that tempt you you will discover that they tend to swarm like minnows into all sorts of crevices whose existence you hadn't realized and before you know it the whole long sentence becomes immobilized and lashed up squirming in commas. Better to use them sparingly, and with affection, precisely when the need for each one arises, nicely, by itself.

I have grown fond of semicolons in recent years. The semicolon   3
tells you that there is still some question about the preceding full sentence; something needs to be added; it reminds you sometimes of the Greek usage. It is almost always a greater pleasure to come across a semicolon than a period. The period tells you that that is that; if you didn't get all the meaning you wanted or expected, anyway you got all the writer intended to parcel out and now you have to move along. But with a semicolon there you get a pleasant little feeling of expectancy; there is more to come; read on; it will get clearer.

Colons are a lot less attractive, for several reasons: firstly, they   4
give you the feeling of being rather ordered around, or at least having your nose pointed in a direction you might not be inclined to take if left to yourself, and, secondly, you suspect you're in for one of those sentences that will be labeling the points to be made: firstly, secondly and so forth, with the implication that you haven't sense enough to keep track of a sequence of notions without having them numbered. Also, many writers use this system loosely and incompletely, starting out with number one and number two as though counting off on their fingers but then going on and on without the succession of labels you've been led to expect, leaving you floundering about searching for the ninthly or seventeenthly that ought to be there but isn't.

Exclamation points are the most irritating of all. Look! they say,   5
look at what I just said! How amazing is my thought! It is like being forced to watch someone else's small child jumping up and down crazily in the center of the living room shouting to attract attention. If a sentence really has something of importance to say, something quite remarkable, it doesn't need a mark to point it out. And if it is really, after all, a banal sentence needing more zing, the exclamation point simply emphasizes its banality!

Quotation marks should be used honestly and sparingly, when   6
there is a genuine quotation at hand, and it is necessary to be very rigorous about the words enclosed by the marks. If something is to be quoted, the *exact* words must be used. If part of it must be left out

because of space limitations, it is good manners to insert three dots to indicate the omission, but it is unethical to do this if it means connecting two thoughts which the original author did not intend to have tied together. Above all, quotation marks should not be used for ideas that you'd like to disown, things in the air so to speak. Nor should they be put in place around clichés; if you want to use a cliché you must take full responsibility for it yourself and not try to job it off on anon., or on society. The most objectionable misuse of quotation marks, but one which illustrates the dangers of misuse in ordinary prose, is seen in advertising, especially in advertisements for small restaurants, for example "just around the corner," or "a good place to eat." No single, identifiable, citable person ever really said, for the record, "just around the corner," much less "a good place to eat," least likely of all for restaurants of the type that use this type of prose.

7   The dash is a handy device, informal and essentially playful, telling you that you're about to take off on a different tack but still in some way connected with the present course — only you have to remember that the dash is there, and either put a second dash at the end of the notion to let the reader know that he's back on course, or else end the sentence, as here, with a period.

8   The greatest danger in punctuation is for poetry. Here it is necessary to be as economical and parsimonious with commas and periods as with the words themselves, and any marks that seem to carry their own subtle meanings, like dashes and little rows of periods, even semicolons and question marks, should be left out altogether rather than inserted to clog up the thing with ambiguity. A single exclamation point in a poem, no matter what else the poem has to say, is enough to destroy the whole work.

9   The things I like best in T. S. Eliot's poetry, especially in the *Four Quartets,* are the semicolons. You cannot hear them, but they are there, laying out the connections between the images and the ideas. Sometimes you get a glimpse of a semicolon coming, a few lines farther on, and it is like climbing a steep path through woods and seeing a wooden bench just at a bend in the road ahead, a place where you can expect to sit for a moment, catching your breath.

10   Commas can't do this sort of thing; they can only tell you how the different parts of a complicated thought are to be fitted together, but you can't sit, not even take a breath, just because of a comma,

_____ **CONSIDERATIONS** _____

1. Why so many parentheses at the end of Thomas's first paragraph? How many are there? Why that number precisely? What is this author up to?

2. Read Thomas's little lesson in punctuation in conjunction with James Thurber's "Which." Compare.

3. One of the blemishes in the works of beginning writers is often the faulty use of quotation marks. See Thomas's advice in Paragraph 6. Then look in newspapers, magazines, and your own papers for examples.

4. Both Thomas and Thurber allude to the best known of several available handbooks of usage: *A Dictionary of Modern English Usage,* by H. W. Fowler. It has been a trusted standby for writers through its many editions. It is also opinionated, sophisticated, and tartly amusing. Discover its worth for yourself by consulting a copy in your college library.

5. Thomas is obviously very conscious of the punctuation in this essay. It might be interesting to look at his punctuation in some of the other essays collected in *The Lives of a Cell* and *The Medusa and the Snail,* to see whether he follows his own advice.

6. Many students have commented that a humorous approach to grammar has not only proved more interesting but a surer way of learning the concept or convention involved than the customary humorless presentation. After reading Thomas and Thurber, try your hand at explaining, in a jocular way, a point of grammar that you have had some trouble with, such as pronoun reference, subject and verb agreement, dangling participles, or the like.

Henry David Thoreau (1817–1862) is one of the greatest Amer-
ican writers, and Walden *one of the great American books. Tho-*
reau attended Concord Academy, in the Massachusetts town
where he was born and lived. Then he went to Harvard and com-
pleted his formal education, which was extensive in mathemat-
ics, literature, Greek, Latin, and French — and included
smatterings of Spanish and Italian and some of the literature of
India and China. He and his brother founded a school that lasted
four years, and then he was a private tutor to a family. He also
worked for his father, manufacturing pencils. But mostly Tho-
reau walked, meditated, observed nature, and wrote.

A friend of Ralph Waldo Emerson's, Thoreau was influenced
by the older man, and by Transcendentalism — a doctrine that
recognized the unity of man and nature. For Thoreau, an idea
required testing by life itself; it never remained merely mental.
In his daily work on his journals, and in the books he carved
from them — A Week on the Concord and Merrimack Rivers
(1849) as well as Walden *(1854) — he observed the detail of daily*
life, human and natural, and he speculated on the universal laws
he could derive from this observation.

"To know it by experience, and be able to give a true account of
it" — these words could be carved on Thoreau's gravestone. "To
give a true account" he became a great writer, a master of obser-
vation. This passage comes from his journal; the daily-disci-
plined writing from which Thoreau later shaped his finished
books. He writes about the bream — a small, silvery, flattish,
freshwater fish — not so much by describing it as by recounting
his reaction to it and by ruminating on the relationship between
people and the natural world.

71

HENRY DAVID THOREAU
Thinking Like a Bream

November 30, 1858:

I cannot but see still in my mind's eye those little striped breams poised in Walden's glaucous water. They balance all the rest of the world in my estimation at present, for this is the bream that I have just found, and for the time I neglect all its brethren and am ready to kill the fatted calf on its account. For more than two centuries have men fished here and have not distinguished this permanent settler of the township. It is not like a new bird, a transient visitor that may not be seen again for years, but there it dwells and has dwelt permanently, who can tell how long? When my eyes first rested on Walden the striped bream was poised in it, though I did not see it, and when Tahatawan paddled his canoe there. How wild it makes the pond and the township to find a new fish in it! America renews her youth here. But in my account of this bream I cannot go a hair's breadth beyond the mere statement that it exists, — the miracle of its existence, my contemporary and neighbor, yet so different from me! I can only poise my thought there by its side and try to think like a bream for a moment. I can only think of precious jewels, of music, poetry, beauty, and the mystery of life. I only see the bream in its orbit, as I see a star, but I care not to measure its distance or weight. The bream, appreciated, floats in the pond as the centre of the system, another image of God. Its life no man can explain more than he can his own. I want you to perceive the mystery of the bream. I have a contemporary in Walden. It has fins where I have legs and arms. I have a friend among the fishes, at least a new acquaintance. Its character will interest me, I trust, not its clothes and anatomy. I do not want it to eat. Acquaintance with it is to make my life more rich and eventful. It is as if a poet or an anchorite had moved into the town, whom I can see from

407

time to time and think of yet oftener. Perhaps there are a thousand of these striped bream which no one had thought of in that pond, — not their mere impressions in stone, but in the full tide of the bream life.

2   Though science may sometimes compare herself to a child picking up pebbles on the seashore, that is a rare mood with her; ordinarily her practical belief is that it is only a few pebbles which are *not* known, weighed and measured. A new species of fish signifies hardly more than a new name. See what is contributed in the scientific reports. One counts the fin-rays, another measures the intestines, a third daguerreotypes a scale, etc., etc.; otherwise there's nothing to be said. As if all but this were done, and these were very rich and generous contributions to science. Her votaries may be seen wandering along the shore of the ocean of truth, with their backs to that ocean, ready to seize on the shells which are cast up. You would say that the scientific bodies were terribly put to it for objects and subjects. A dead specimen of an animal, if it is only well preserved in alcohol, is just as good for science as a living one preserved in its native element.

3   What is the amount of my discovery to me? It is not that I have got one in a bottle, that it has got a name in a book, but that I have a little fishy friend in the pond. How was it when the youth first discovered fishes? Was it the number of their fin-rays or their arrangement, or the place of the fish in some system that made the boy dream of them? Is it these things that interest mankind in the fish, the inhabitant of the water? No, but a faint recognition of a living contemporary, a provoking mystery. One boy thinks of fishes and goes a-fishing from the same motive that his brother searches the poets for rare lines. It is the poetry of fishes which is their chief use; their flesh is their lowest use. The beauty of the fish, that is what it is best worth the while to measure. Its place in our systems is of comparatively little importance. Generally the boy loses some of his perception and his interest in the fish; he degenerates into a fisherman or an ichthyologist.

_____ **CONSIDERATIONS** _____

1. Thoreau's excitement in describing the bream was generated by his discovery of a species living unnoticed in Walden Pond. But why, according to him, can he do no more than say that it exists? Why is that statement sufficient?

2. What kind of truth — scientific? philosophic? economic? aesthetic? — can you find in Thoreau's statement that the bream "is the center of the

system, another image of God"? Look at his sentence in Paragraph 1 carefully. Why pay particular attention to the word "appreciated," which is set off by commas.

3. In a short essay explain, on the basis of Thoreau's essay, why he would probably agree with Lewis Thomas's advice (in "On Smell," Paragraph 9, page 397) that we should throw out laws forbidding the burning of fall leaves.

4. Why, in his closing statement, does Thoreau consider both the fisherman and the ichthyologist deplorable?

5. "Mystery" is an important word in Thoreau's essay. What is there about the way scientists work that limits their appreciation of the mystery of creation?

James Thurber (1894–1961) was born in Columbus, Ohio, the scene of many of his funniest stories. He graduated from Ohio State University, and after a period as a newspaper man in Paris, began to work for The New Yorker. *For years his comic writing and his cartoons — drawings of sausage-shaped dogs and of men and women forever at battle — were fixtures of that magazine. His collection of essays, short stories, and cartoons include* The Owl in the Attic and Other Perplexities *(1931),* The Seal in the Bedroom and Other Predicaments *(1932),* My Life and Hard Times *(1933),* Men, Women, and Dogs *(1943), and* Alarms and Diversions *(1957). He also wrote an account of life on* The New Yorker *staff,* The Years with Ross *(1959).* Selected Letters of James Thurber *appeared in 1981.*

An elegant stylist, Thurber was always fussy about language. "Which" is an example not only of his fascination with language — which became obsessive at times — but also of his humor.

72

JAMES THURBER
Which

1   The relative pronoun "which" can cause more trouble than any other word, if recklessly used. Foolhardy persons sometimes get lost in which-clauses and are never heard of again. My distinguished contemporary, Fowler, cites several tragic cases, of which the following is one: "It was rumoured that Beaconsfield intended opening the Conference with a speech in French, his pronounciation of which language leaving everything to be desired . . ." That's as much as Mr. Fowler quotes because, at his age, he was afraid to go any farther. The young

410

man who originally got into that sentence was never found. His fate, however, was not as terrible as that of another adventurer who became involved in a remarkable which-mire. Fowler has followed his devious course as far as he safely could on foot: "Surely what applies to games should also apply to racing, the leaders of which being the very people from whom an example might well be looked for . . ." Not even Henry James could have successfully emerged from a sentence with "which," "whom," and "being" in it. The safest way to avoid such things is to follow in the path of the American author, Ernest Hemingway. In his youth he was trapped in a which-clause one time and barely escaped with his mind. He was going along on solid ground until he got into this: "It was the one thing of which, being very much afraid — for whom has not been warned to fear such things — he . . ." Being a young and powerfully built man, Hemingway was able to fight his way back to where he had started, and begin again. This time he skirted the treacherous morass in this way: "He was afraid of one thing. This was the one thing. He had been warned to fear such things. Everybody has been warned to fear such things." Today Hemingway is alive and well, and many happy writers are following along the trail he blazed.

What most people don't realize is that one "which" leads to 2 another. Trying to cross a paragraph by leaping from "which" to "which" is like Eliza crossing the ice. The danger is in missing a "which" and falling in. A case in point is this: "He went up to a pew which was in the gallery, which brought him under a colored window which he loved and always quieted his spirit." The writer, worn out, missed the last "which" — the one that should come just before "always" in that sentence. But supposing he had got it in! We would have: "He went up to a pew which was in the gallery, which brought him under a colored window which he loved and which always quieted his spirit." Your inveterate whicher in this way gives the effect of tweeting like a bird or walking with a crutch, and is not welcome in the best company.

It is well to remember that one "which" leads to two and that 3 two "whiches" multiply like rabbits. You should never start out with the idea that you can get by with one "which." Suddenly they are all around you. Take a sentence like this: "It imposes a problem which we either solve, or perish." On a hot night, or after a hard day's work, a man often lets himself get by with a monstrosity like that, but suppose he dictates that sentence bright and early in the morning. It comes to him typed out by his stenographer and he instantly senses that something is the matter with it. He tries to reconstruct the sentence, still clinging to the "which," and gets something like this: "It imposes a problem which we either solve, or which, failing to solve, we must perish on account of." He goes to the water-cooler, gets a drink, sharpens his pencil, and grimly tries again. "It imposes a problem which we either solve or which we don't solve . . ." He begins once more: "It imposes a problem which we either solve, or which we do not solve, and from which . . ." The more times he does it the more "whiches" he gets. The way out is simple: "We must either solve this problem, or perish." Never monkey with "which." Nothing except getting tangled up in a typewriter ribbon is worse.

____ CONSIDERATIONS ____

1. James Thurber concentrates on one word from an important class of function words. These relative pronouns often complicate life for the writer wishing to write clear sentences more complex than "I see Spot. Spot is a dog. Spot sees me." What other words belong to this class? Do you find any of them tripping you up in your sentences?

2. A grammar lesson may seem a peculiar place to find humor, but humor is Thurber's habit, whatever his subject. How does he make his treatment of the relative pronoun "which" entertaining?

3. Compare Fowler's book with an American version such as Wilson Follett's *Modern American Usage.* This could lead you into a study of the concept of usage as the ultimate authority in establishing conventions of grammar, spelling, definition, and punctuation.

4. "One 'which' leads to another" is a play on the old saying, "One drink leads to another." Consider how changing one word can revive a thought that George Orwell would call a hackneyed phrase. See how it is done by substituting a key word in several familiar sayings.

5. The two writers Thurber mentions, Henry James and Ernest Hemingway, are not idly chosen. Why not?

Calvin Trillin (b. 1935) left his native Kansas City to go to Yale University; he now lives in New York and writes for The New Yorker. *He writes about murder trials, pop food, and American places. Some of his essays are collected in* U. S. Journal *(1971) and in his hamburger trilogy:* American Fried *(1974),* Alice Let's Eat *(1978) and* Third Helpings *(1983). He also writes a humorous, mostly political column for* The Nation, *collected in* Uncivil Liberties *(1982), from which we (literally) take this essay.*

73

CALVIN TRILLIN
Literally

September 12, 1981

My problem with country living began innocently enough when 1 our well ran dry and a neighbor said some pump priming would be necessary.

"I didn't come up here to discuss economics," I said. Actually, I 2 don't discuss economics in the city either. As it happens, I don't understand economics. There's no use revealing that, though, to every Tom, Dick and Harry who interrupts his dinner to try to get your water running, so I said, "I come up here to get away from that sort of thing." My neighbor gave me a puzzled look.

"He's talking about the water pump," Alice told me. "It needs 3 priming."

I thought that experience might have been just a fluke — until, 4 on a fishing trip with the same neighbor, I proudly pulled in a fish with what I thought was a major display of deep-sea angling skill, only to hear a voice behind me say, "It's just a fluke."

5   "This is dangerous," I said to Alice, while helping her weed the vegetable garden the next day. I had thought our problem was limited to the pump-priming ichthyologist down the road, but that morning at the post office I had overheard a farmer say that since we seemed to be in for a few days of good weather he intended to make his hay while the sun was shining. "These people are robbing me of aphorisms," I said, taking advantage of the discussion to rest for a while on my hoe. "How can I encourage the children to take advantage of opportunities by telling them to make hay while the sun shines if they think that means making hay while the sun shines?"

6   "Could you please keep weeding those peas while you talk," she said. "You've got a long row to hoe."

7   I began to look at Alice with new eyes. By that, of course, I don't mean that I actually went to a discount eye outlet, acquired two new eyes (20/20 this time), replaced my old eyes with the new ones and looked at Alice. Having to make that explanation is just the sort of thing I found troubling. What I mean is that I was worried about the possibility of Alice's falling into the habit of rural literalism herself. My concern was deepened a few days later by a conversation that took place while I was in one of our apple trees, looking for an apple that was not used as a *dacha* by the local worms. "I just talked to the Murrays, and they say that the secret is picking up windfalls," Alice said.

8   "Windfalls?" I said. "Could it be that Jim Murray has taken over Exxon since last time I saw him? Or do the Murrays have a natural-gas operation in the back forty I didn't know about?"

9   "Not those kinds of windfalls," Alice said. "The apples that fall from the tree because of the wind. They're a breeding place for worms."

10   "There's nothing wrong with our apples," I said, reaching for a particularly plump one.

11   "Be careful," she said. "You may be getting yourself too far out on a limb."

12   "You may be getting yourself out on a limb yourself," I said to Alice at breakfast the next morning.

13   She looked around the room. "I'm sitting at the kitchen table," she said.

14   "I meant it symbolically," I said. "The way it was meant to be meant. This has got to stop. I won't have you coming in from the

garden with small potatoes in your basket and saying that what you found was just small potatoes. 'Small potatoes' doesn't mean small potatoes.''

"Small potatoes doesn't mean small potatoes?" 15

"I refuse to discuss it," I said. "The tide's in, so I'm going fishing, 16 and I don't want to hear any encouraging talk about that fluke not being the only fish in the ocean."

"I was just going to ask why you have to leave before you finish 17 your breakfast," she said.

"Because time and tide wait for no man," I said. "And I mean it." 18

Had she trapped me into saying that? Or was it possible that I 19 was falling into the habit myself? Was I, as I waited for a bite, thinking that there were plenty of other fish in the sea? Then I had a bite — then another. I forgot about the problem until after I had returned to the dock and done my most skillful job of filleting.

"Look!" I said, holding up the carcass of one fish proudly, as Alice 20 approached the dock. "It's nothing but skin and bones."

The shock of realizing what I had said caused me to stumble 21 against my fish-cleaning table and knock the fillets off the dock. "Now we won't have anything for dinner," I said.

"Don't worry about it," Alice said. "I have other fish to fry." 22

"That's not right!" I shouted. "That's not what that means. It 23 means you have something better to do."

"It can also mean that I have other fish to fry," she said. "And I 24 do. I'll just get that other fish you caught out of the freezer. Even though it was just a fluke."

I tried to calm myself. I apologized to Alice for shouting and 25 offered to help her pick vegetables from the garden for dinner.

"I'll try to watch my language," she said, as we stood among the 26 peas.

"It's all right, really," I said. 27

"I was just going to say that tonight it seems rather slim pick- 28 ings," she said. "Just about everything has gone to seed."

"Perfectly all right," I said, wandering over toward the garden 29 shed, where some mud seemed to be caked in the eaves. I pushed at the mud with a rake, and a swarm of wasps burst out at me. I ran for the house, swatting at wasps with my hat. Inside, I suddenly had the feeling that some of them had managed to crawl up the legs of my jeans, and I tore the jeans off. Alice found me there in the kitchen, standing quietly in what the English call their smalls.

"That does it," I said. "We're going back to the city." 30

31   "Just because of a few stings?"

32   "Can't you see what happened?" I said. "They scared the pants off me."

_____ CONSIDERATIONS _____

1. Trillin uses clichés such as "rest for a while on my hoe" (Paragraph 4) and "too far out on a limb" (Paragraph 10) set against their literal meaning. Such a strategy can leave the writer open to misinterpretation. Explain.

2. Note that Trillin uses dialogue to organize the flow of his thought. See other writers included in the text who make important use of dialogue — Hemingway, for example — and in your next paper, try to use dialogue.

3. What expressions used by Trillin *figuratively* do you *not* understand, and thus miss the joke: "some pump priming," "just a fluke," "small potatoes," and "windfall"? How can you learn their meaning?

4. In this lighthearted piece, Trillin addresses no serious thought, but there is a lesson here for the literal-minded who fail to recognize satire when they see it. See Swift's "A Modest Proposal" (pages 379–386), Stephen J. Gould's "Phyletic Size Decrease in Hershey Bars" (pages 161–166), and Woody Allen's "Death Knocks" (pages 12–20) for examples of satires that often confound the literal-minded reader.

5. Prepare a list of clichés drawn from your experience, similar to those used by Trillin, and write a satiric essay.

John Updike (b. 1932) grew up in Pennsylvania and went to Harvard, where he edited the humor magazine, the Lampoon. *On a fellowship year at Oxford, Updike sold a poem to* The New Yorker *and began his long relationship with that magazine. First he worked on the staff of* The New Yorker, *contributing to "The Talk of the Town." When he quit to free-lance, he continued to write stories, poems, reviews, and articles for the magazine.* The Poorhouse Fair *(1959), his first novel, appeared in the same year as his first collection of stories,* The Same Door, *from which we take "Ace in the Hole." This story appears to be the seed of his second novel,* Rabbit, Run *(1960) — also about an ex-basketball star with a deteriorating marriage.*

Updike has published stories, novels, poems, and three miscellaneous collections, Assorted Prose *(1965),* Picked-up Pieces *(1975), and* Hugging the Shore *(1983). Among his best-known novels are* The Centaur *(1963) and* The Witches of Eastwick *(1984). In "Ace in the Hole," Updike writes with his usual precision and finish, and with a final image that illuminates everything that has gone before it, gilding the dross of the present with a recollected gold.*

_74

JOHN UPDIKE
Ace in the Hole

No sooner did his car touch the boulevard heading home than Ace flicked on the radio. He needed the radio, especially today. In the seconds before the tubes warmed up, he said aloud, doing it just to hear a human voice, "Jesus. She'll pop her lid." His voice, though 1 familiar, irked him; it sounded thin and scratchy, as if the bones in his head were picking up static. In a deeper register Ace added, "She'll murder me." Then the radio came on, warm and strong, so he stopped worrying. The Five Kings were doing "Blueberry Hill"; to hear them made Ace feel so sure inside that from the pack pinched between the car roof and the sun shield he plucked a cigarette, hung it on his lower lip, snapped a match across the rusty place on the dash, held the flame in the instinctive spot near the tip of his nose, dragged, and blew out the match, all in time to the music. He rolled down the window and snapped the match so it spun end-over-end into the gutter. "Two points," he said, and cocked the cigarette toward the roof of the car, sucked powerfully, and exhaled two plumes through his nostrils. He was beginning to feel like himself, Ace Anderson, for the first time that whole day, a bad day. He beat time on the accelerator. The car jerked crazily. "On Blueberry Hill," he sang, "my heart stood still. The wind in the wil-low tree" — he braked for a red light — "played love's suh-*weet* melodee —"

2   "Go, Dad, bust your lungs!" a kid's voice blared. The kid was riding in a '52 Pontiac that had pulled up beside Ace at the light. The profile of the driver, another kid, was dark over his shoulder.

3   Ace looked over at him and smiled slowly, just letting one side of his mouth lift a little. "Shove it," he said, good-naturedly, across the little gap of years that separated them. He knew how they felt, young and mean and shy.

4   But the kid, who looked Greek, lifted his thick upper lip and spat out the window. The spit gleamed on the asphalt like a half-dollar.

5   "Now isn't that pretty?" Ace said, keeping one eye on the light. "You miserable wop. You are *mis*erable." While the kid was trying to think of some smart comeback, the light changed. Ace dug out so hard he smelled burned rubber. In his rear-view mirror he saw the Pontiac lurch forward a few yards, then stop dead, right in the middle of the intersection.

6   The idea of them stalling their fat tin Pontiac kept him in a good humor all the way home. He decided to stop at his mother's place and pick up the baby, instead of waiting for Evey to do it. His mother must have seen him drive up. She came out on the porch holding a plastic spoon and smelling of cake.

7   "You're out early," she told him.

8   "Friedman fired me," Ace told her.

9   "Good for you," his mother said. "I always said he never treated you right." She brought a cigarette out of her apron pocket and tucked

it deep into one corner of her mouth, the way she did when something pleased her.

Ace lighted it for her. "Friedman was O.K. personally," he said. 10 "He just wanted too much for his money. I didn't mind working Saturdays, but until eleven, twelve Friday nights was too much. Everybody as a right to some leisure."

"Well, I don't dare think what Evey will say, but I, for one, thank 11 dear God you had the brains to get out of it. I always said that job had no future to it — no future of any kind, Freddy."

"I guess," Ace admitted. "But I wanted to keep at it, for the 12 family's sake."

"Now, I know I shouldn't be saying this, but any time Evey — 13 this is just between us — any time Evey thinks she can do better, there's room for you *and* Bonnie right in your father's house." She pinched her lips together. He could almost hear the old lady think, *There, I've said it.*

"Look, Mom, Evey tries awfully hard, and anyway you know she can't work that way. Not that *that* — I mean, she's a realist, too . . ." He let the rest of the thought fade as he watched a kid across the street dribbling a basketball around a telephone pole that had a backboard and net nailed on it.

"Evey's a wonderful girl of her own kind. But I've always said, and your father agrees, Roman Catholics ought to marry among themselves. Now I know I've said it before, but when they get out in the greater world —"

"*No*, Mom." 16

She frowned, smoothed herself, and said, "Your name was in the 17 paper today."

Ace chose to let that go by. He kept watching the kid with the 18 basketball. It was funny how, though the whole point was to get the ball up into the air, kids grabbed it by the sides and squeezed. Kids just didn't think.

"Did you hear?" his mother asked. 19

"Sure, but so what?" Ace said. His mother's lower lip was com- 20 ing at him, so he changed the subject. "I guess I'll take Bonnie."

His mother went into the house and brought back his daughter, 21 wrapped in a blue blanket. The baby looked dopey. "She fussed all day," his mother complained. "I said to your father, 'Bonnie is a dear little girl, but without a doubt she's her mother's daughter.' You were the best-natured boy."

"Well I *had* everything," Ace said with an impatience that made 22 his mother blink. He nicely dropped his cigarette into a brown flow-erpot on the edge of the porch and took his daughter into his arms. She was getting heavier, solid. When he reached the end of the cement walk, his mother was still on the porch, waving to him. He was so close he could see the fat around her elbow jiggle, and he only lived a half block up the street, yet here she was, waving to him as if he was going to Japan.

23   At the door of his car, it seemed stupid to him to drive the measly half block home. His old coach, Bob Behn, used to say never to ride where you could walk. Cars were the death of legs. Ace left the ignition keys in his pocket and ran along the pavement with Bonnie laughing and bouncing at his chest. He slammed the door of his landlady's house open and shut, pounded up the two flights of stairs, and was panting so hard when he reached the door of his apartment that it took him a couple of seconds to fit the key into the lock.

24   The run must have tuned Bonnie up. As soon as he lowered her into the crib, she began to shout and wave her arms. He didn't want to play with her. He tossed some blocks and a rattle into the crib and walked into the bathroom, where he turned on the hot water and began to comb his hair. Holding the comb under the faucet before every stroke, he combed his hair forward. It was so long, one strand curled under his nose and touched his lips. He whipped the whole mass back with a single pull. He tucked in the tufts around his ears, and ran the comb straight back on both sides of his head. With his fingers he felt for the little ridge at the back where the two sides met. It was there, as it should have been. Finally, he mussed the hair in front enough for one little lock to droop over his forehead, like Alan Ladd. It made the temple seem lower than it was. Every day, his hair-line looked higher. He had observed all around him how blond men went bald first. He remembered reading somewhere, though, that bald-ness shows virility.

25   On his way to the kitchen he flipped the left-hand knob of the television. Bonnie was always quieter with the set on. Ace didn't see how she could understand much of it, but it seemed to mean some-thing to her. He found a can of beer in the refrigerator behind some brownish lettuce and those hot dogs Evey never got around to cooking. She'd be home any time. The clock said 5:12. She'd pop her lid.

26   Ace didn't see what he could do but try and reason with her. "Evey," he'd say, "you ought to thank God I got out of it. It had no future to it at all." He hoped she wouldn't get too mad, because when she was mad he wondered if he should have married her, and doubting that made him feel crowded. It was bad enough, his mother always

crowding him. He punched the two triangles in the top of the beer can, the little triangle first, and then the big one, the one he drank from. He hoped Evey wouldn't say anything that couldn't be forgotten. What women didn't seem to realize was that there were things you knew but shouldn't say.

He felt sorry he had called the kid in the car a wop. 27

Ace balanced the beer on a corner where two rails of the crib met 28
and looked under the chairs for the morning paper. He had trouble finding his name, because it was at the bottom of a column on an inside sports page, in a small article about the county basketball statistics:

> "Dusty" Tremwick, Grosvenor Park's sure-fingered center, copped the individual scoring honors with a season's grand (and we do mean grand) total of 376 points. This is within eighteen points of the all-time record of 394 racked up in the 1949–1950 season by Olinger High's Fred Anderson.

Ace angrily sailed the paper into an armchair. Now it was Fred Anderson; it used to be Ace. He hated being called Fred, especially in print, but then the sportswriters were all office boys anyway, Behn used to say.

"Do not just ask for shoe polish," a man on television said, "but 30
ask for *Emu Shoe Gloss,* the *only* polish that absolutely *guarantees* to make your shoes look shinier than new." Ace turned the sound off, so that the man moved his mouth like a fish blowing bubbles. Right away, Bonnie howled, so Ace turned it up loud enough to drown her out and went into the kitchen, without knowing what he wanted there. He wasn't hungry; his stomach was tight. It used to be like that when he walked to the gymnasium alone in the dark before a game and could see the people from town, kids and parents, crowding in at the lighted doors. But once he was inside, the locker room would be bright and hot, and the other guys would be there, laughing it up and towel-slapping, and the tight feeling would leave. Now there were whole days when it didn't leave.

A key scratched at the door lock. Ace decided to stay in the 31
kitchen. Let *her* find *him*. Her heels clicked on the floor for a step or two; then the television set went off. Bonnie began to cry. "Shut up, honey," Evey said. There was a silence.

"I'm home," Ace called. 32

"No kidding. I thought Bonnie got the beer by herself." 33

Ace laughed. She was in a sarcastic mood, thinking she was Lau- 34 ren Bacall. That was all right, just so she kept funny. Still smiling, Ace eased into the living room and got hit with, "What are *you* smirking about? Another question: What's the idea running up the street with Bonnie like she was a football?"

35   "You saw that?"

36   "Your mother told me."

37   "You saw her?"

38   "Of course I saw her. I dropped by to pick up Bonnie. What the hell do you think? — I read her tiny mind?"

39   "Take it easy," Ace said, wondering if Mom had told her about Friedman.

40   "Take it easy? Don't coach *me*. Another question: Why's the car out in front of her place? You give the car to her?"

41   "Look, I parked it there to pick up Bonnie, and I thought I'd leave it there."

42   "Why?"

43   "Whaddeya mean, why? I just did. I just thought I'd walk. It's not that far, you know."

44   "No, I don't know. If you'd been on your feet all day long a block would look like one hell of a long way."

45   "Okay. I'm sorry."

46   She hung up her coat and stepped out of her shoes and walked around the room picking up things. She stuck the newspaper in the wastebasket.

47   Ace said, "My name was in the paper today."

48   "They spell it right?" She shoved the paper deep into the basket with her foot. There was no doubt; she knew about Friedman.

49   "They called me Fred."

50   "Isn't that your name? What *is* your name anyway? Hero J. Great?"

51   There wasn't any answer, so Ace didn't try any. He sat down on the sofa, lighted a cigarette, and waited.

52   Evey picked up Bonnie. "Poor thing stinks. What does your mother do, scrub out the toilet with her?"

53   "Can't you take it easy? I know you're tired."

54   "You should. I'm always tired."

55   Evey and Bonnie went into the bathroom; when they came out, Bonnie was clean and Evey was calm. Evey sat down in an easy chair beside Ace and rested her stocking feet on his knees. "Hit me," she said, twiddling her fingers for the cigarette.

56   The baby crawled up to her chair and tried to stand, to see what

he gave her. Leaning over close to Bonnie's nose, Evey grinned, smoke leaking through her teeth, and said, "Only for grownups, honey."

"Eve," Ace began, "there was no future in that job. Working all Saturday, and then Friday nights on top of it."

"I know. Your mother told *me* all that, too. All I want from you is what happened."   58

She was going to take it like a sport, then. He tried to remember how it *did* happen. "It wasn't my fault," he said. "Friedman told me to back this '51 Chevvy into the line that faces Church Street. He just bought it from an old guy this morning who said it only had thirteen thousand on it. So in I jump and start her up. There was a knock in the engine like a machine gun. I almost told Friedman he'd bought a squirrel, but you know I cut that smart stuff out ever since Palotta laid me off."   59

"You told me that story. What happens in this one?"   60

"Look, Eve. I *am* telling ya. Do you want me to go out to a movie or something?"   61

"Suit yourself."   62

"So I jump in the Chevvy and snap it back in line, and there was a kind of scrape and thump. I get out and look and Friedman's running over, his arms going like *this*" — Ace whirled his own arms and laughed — "and here was the whole back fender of a '49 Merc mashed in. Just looked like somebody took a planer and shaved off the bulge, you know, there at the back." He tried to show her with his hands. "The Chevvy, though, didn't have a dent. It even gained some paint. But *Friedman*, to *hear* him — Boy, they can rave when their pocketbook's hit. He said" — Ace laughed again — "never mind."   63

Evey said, "You're proud of yourself."   64

"No, listen. I'm not happy about it. But there wasn't a thing I could *do*. It wasn't my driving at all. I looked over on the other side, and there was just two or three inches between the Chevvy and a Buick. *Nobody* could have gotten into that hole. Even if it had hair on it." He thought this was pretty good.   65

She didn't. "You could have looked."   66

"There just wasn't the *space.* Friedman said stick it in; I stuck it in."   67

"But you could have looked and moved the other cars to make more room."

"I guess that would have been the smart thing."   69

"I guess, too. Now what?"   70

"What do you mean?"   71

72   "I mean now what? Are you going to give up? Go back to the Army? Your mother? Be a basketball pro? What?"

73   "You know I'm not tall enough. Anybody under six-six they don't want."

74   "Is that so? Six-six? Well, please listen to this, Mr. Six-Foot-Five-and-a-Half: I'm fed up. I'm ready as Christ to let you run." She stabbed her cigarette into an ashtray on the arm of the chair so hard the ashtray jumped to the floor. Evey flushed and shut up.

75   What Ace hated most in their arguments was these silences after Evey had said something so ugly she wanted to take it back. "Better ask the priest first," he murmured.

76   She sat right up. "If there's one thing I don't want to hear about from you it's priests. You let the priests to me. You don't know a damn thing about it. Not a damn thing."

77   "Hey, look at Bonnie," he said, trying to make a fresh start with his tone.

78   Evey didn't hear him. "If you think," she went on, "if for one rotten moment you think, Mr. Fred, that the be-all and end-all of my life is you and your hot-shot stunts —"

79   "Look, Mother," Ace pleaded, pointing at Bonnie. The baby had packed up the ashtray and put it on her head for a hat and was waiting for praise.

80   Evey glanced down sharply at the child. "Cute," she said. "Cute as her daddy."

81   The ashtray slid from Bonnie's head and she patted where it had been and looked around puzzled.

82   "Yeah, but watch," Ace said. "Watch her hands. They're really terrific hands."

83   "You're nuts," Evey said.

84   "No, honest. Bonnie's great. She's a natural. Get the rattle for her. Never mind, I'll get it." In two steps, Ace was at Bonnie's crib, picking the rattle out of the mess of blocks and plastic rings and beanbags. He extended the rattle toward his daughter, shaking it delicately. Made wary by this burst of attention, Bonnie reached with both hands; like two separate animals they approached from opposite sides and touched the smooth rattle simultaneously. A smile bubbled up on her face. Ace tugged weakly. She held on, and then tugged back. "She's a natural," Ace said, "and it won't do her any good because she's a girl. Baby, we got to have a boy."

85   "I'm not your baby," Evey said, closing her eyes.

86   Saying "Baby" over and over again, Ace backed up to the radio and, without turning around, switched on the volume knob. In the

moment before the tubes warmed up, Evey had time to say, "Wise up, Freddy. What shall we do?"

The radio came in on something slow: dinner music. Ace picked   87
Bonnie up and set her in the crib. "Shall we dance?" he asked his wife, bowing.

"I want to talk."   88

"Baby. It's the cocktail hour."   89

"This is getting us no place," she said, rising from her chair, though.

"Fred Junior. I can see him now," he said, seeing nothing.   91

"We will have no Juniors."   92

In her crib, Bonnie whimpered at the sight of her mother being   93
seized. Ace fitted his hand into the natural place on Evey's back and she shuffled stiffly into his lead. When, with a sudden injection of saxophones, the tempo quickened, he spun her out carefully, keeping the beat with his shoulders. Her hair brushed his lips as she minced in, then swung away, to the end of his arm; he could feel her toes dig into the carpet. He flipped his own hair back from his eyes. The music ate through his skin and mixed with the nerves and small veins; he seemed to be great again, and all the other kids were around them, in a ring, clapping time.

_____ **CONSIDERATIONS** _____

1. Updike often uses minute physical observations. Do you find any of these in "Ace in the Hole"? How do they contribute to the story's effect?

2. How old is Ace? What information in the story prompts you to make a guess? What kind of age do you mean — chronological, mental, emotional? How important is his age to the story?

3. What are Ace's *real* interests: wife? child? job? future career? How does Updike help you discriminate between Ace's casual and lasting interests?

4. Which is most important to Ace — the past, the present, or the future? Cite evidence. Of what thematic significance is this question?

5. If you were a marriage counselor, would you have any advice for this young couple? Would you say that their marriage is in trouble? What are the chances that they would even consider consulting a marriage counselor? For your answers use the story itself.

6. What importance has play had in Ace's life? What particulars in the story reveal his attitude toward play, sport, games, fun, diversions, recreation?

7. Compare the reactions of Ace's mother and his wife to losing the job. How do their different attitudes toward this event reveal important things about Ace's life at this time?

Gore Vidal (b. 1925) entered the army after graduation from Phillips Exeter Academy and never attended college. He published his first novel the year he turned twenty-one. He has run for Congress, lived in Europe, and has written plays and essays but chiefly novels, including Julian *(1964),* Myra Breckinridge *(1968),* Burr *(1973),* Kalki *(1979), and* Lincoln *(1984).*

75

GORE VIDAL
Drugs

1   It is possible to stop most drug addiction in the United States within a very short time. Simply make all drugs available and sell them at cost. Label each drug with a precise description of what effect — good and bad — the drug will have on the taker. This will require heroic honesty. Don't say that marijuana is addictive or dangerous when it is neither, as millions of people know — unlike "speed," which kills most unpleasantly, or heroin, which is addictive and difficult to kick.

2   For the record, I have tried — once — almost every drug and liked none, disproving the popular Fu Manchu theory that a single whiff of opium will enslave the mind. Nevertheless many drugs are bad for certain people to take and they should be told why in a sensible way.

3   Along with exhortation and warning, it might be good for our citizens to recall (or learn for the first time) that the United States was the creation of men who believed that each man has the right to do what he wants with his own life as long as he does not interfere with

his neighbor's pursuit of happiness (that his neighbor's idea of happiness is persecuting others does confuse matters a bit).

This is a startling notion to the current generation of Americans. 4
They reflect a system of public education which has made the Bill of Rights, literally, unacceptable to a majority of high school graduates (see the annual Purdue reports) who now form the "silent majority" — a phrase which that underestimated wit Richard Nixon took from Homer who used it to describe the dead.

Now one can hear the warning rumble begin: if everyone is 5
allowed to take drugs everyone will and the GNP will decrease, the Commies will stop us from making everyone free, and we shall end up a race of Zombies, passively murmuring "groovie" to one another. Alarming thought. Yet it seems most unlikely that any reasonably sane person will become a drug addict if he knows in advance what addiction is going to be like.

Is everyone reasonably sane? No. Some people will always 6
become drug addicts just as some people will always become alcoholics, and it is just too bad. Every man, however, has the power (and should have the legal right) to kill himself if he chooses. But since most men don't, they won't be mainliners either. Nevertheless, forbidding people things they like or think they might enjoy only makes them want those things all the more. This psychological insight is, for some mysterious reason, perennially denied our governors.

It is a lucky thing for the American moralist that our country has 7
always existed in a kind of time-vacuum: we have no public memory of anything that happened before last Tuesday. No one in Washington today recalls what happened during the years alcohol was forbidden to the people by a Congress that thought it had a divine mission to stamp out Demon Rum — launching, in the process, the greatest crime wave in the country's history, causing thousands of deaths from bad alcohol, and creating a general (and persisting) contempt among the citizenry for the laws of the United States.

The same thing is happening today. But the government has 8
learned nothing from past attempts at prohibition, not to mention repression.

Last year when the supply of Mexican marijuana was slightly 9
curtailed by the Feds, the pushers got the kids hooked on heroin and deaths increased dramatically, particularly in New York. Whose fault? Evil men like the Mafiosi? Permissive Dr. Spock? Wild-eyed Dr. Leary? No.

The Government of the United States was responsible for those 10 deaths. The bureaucratic machine has a vested interest in playing cops and robbers. Both the Bureau of Narcotics and the Mafia want strong laws against the sale and use of drugs because if drugs are sold at cost there would be no money in it for anyone.

11   If there was no money in it for the Mafia, there would be no friendly playground pushers, and addicts would not commit crimes to pay for the next fix. Finally, if there was no money in it, the Bureau of Narcotics would wither away, something they are not about to do without a struggle.

12   Will anything sensible be done? Of course not. The American people are as devoted to the idea of sin and its punishment as they are to making money — and fighting drugs is nearly as big a business as pushing them. Since the combination of sin and money is irresistible (particularly to the professional politician), the situation will only grow worse.

_____ **CONSIDERATIONS** _____

1. One mark of the experienced arguer is his ability to anticipate and thus neutralize his opponent's rebuttal. Where does Vidal do this? How effective is his attempt?

2. Vidal's argument (Paragraphs 10, 11, and 12) that "the bureaucratic machine has a vested interest in playing cops and robbers" rests on his implication that lawmen are at least as interested in preserving their jobs as they are in preserving law and order. Does he present any evidence to support this argument? What kind of evidence could he offer? How could you support a counterargument?

3. Vidal contends that every man "should have the legal right to kill himself." How far would he (or you) extend that "right"? To all varieties of suicide, for instance?

4. In Paragraph 3, Vidal introduces lightly a serious dilemma that often emerges in any discussion of individual liberty. See Richard Rodriguez's "Does America Still Exist?" (pages 347–351) for an example of the same problem. Then write your own solution.

5. Is the slang term "groovie" — usually spelled "groovy" — still current? Linguists often study slang because it changes faster than standard language. For the same reason, geneticists study fruit flies because the quick turnover of generations allows them to investigate principles of genetics within a brief period of time. In what way(s) do changes in slang parallel changes in English in general?

6. Given Vidal's belief in freedom of the individual, how do you think he would approach the question of gun control?

Eudora Welty (b. 1909) lives in her native Jackson, Mississippi, where she continues to write, deliberately and slowly, her perfect stories and novels. A Curtain of Green *(1941) was her first volume of collected stories. Her novels include* Losing Battles *(1970) and* The Optimist's Daughter *(1972), which won her a Pulitzer Prize. In 1980* The Collected Stories of Eudora Welty *was published, and in 1984, a reminiscence,* One Writer's Beginning.

Here is one of her stories, followed by a useful essay she wrote about it years later, which appears in her book The Eye of the Story *(1978).*

76

EUDORA WELTY
A Worn Path

It was December — a bright frozen day in the early morning. Far out in the country there was an old Negro woman with her head tied in a red rag, coming along a path through the pinewoods. Her name was Phoenix Jackson. She was very old and small and she walked slowly in the dark pine shadows, moving a little from side to side in her steps, with the balanced heaviness and lightness of a pendulum in a grandfather clock. She carried a thin, small cane made from an umbrella, and with this she kept tapping the frozen earth in front of her. This made a grave and persistent noise in the still air, that seemed meditative, like the chirping of a solitary little bird.

She wore a dark striped dress reaching down to her shoetops, and an equally long apron of bleached sugar sacks, with a full pocket; all neat and tidy, but every time she took a step she might have fallen over her shoelaces, which dragged from her unlaced shoes. She looked straight ahead. Her eyes were blue with age. Her skin had a pattern all its own of numberless branching wrinkles and as though a whole little tree stood in the middle of her forehead, but a golden color ran underneath, and the two knobs of her cheeks were illuminated by a yellow burning under the dark. Under the red rag her hair came down on her neck in the frailest of ringlets, still black, and with an odor like copper.

3   Now and then there was a quivering in the thicket. Old Phoenix said, "Out of my way, all you foxes, owls, beetles, jack rabbits, coons, and wild animals! . . . Keep out from under these feet, little bobwhites. . . . Keep the big wild hogs out of my path. Don't let none of those come running my direction. I got a long way." Under her small black-freckled hand her cane, limber as a buggy whip, would switch at the brush as if to rouse up any hiding things.

4   On she went. The woods were deep and still. The sun made the pine needles almost too bright to look at, up where the wind rocked. The cones dropped as light as feathers. Down in the hollow was the mourning dove — it was not too late for him.

5   The path ran up a hill. "Seem like there is chains about my feet, time I get this far," she said, in the voice of argument old people keep to use with themselves. "Something always take a hold on this hill — pleads I should stay."

6   After she got to the top she turned and gave a full, severe look behind her where she had come. "Up through pines," she said at length. "Now down through oaks."

7   Her eyes opened their widest and she started down gently. But before she got to the bottom of the hill a bush caught her dress.

8   Her fingers were busy and intent, but her skirts were full and long, so that before she could pull them free in one place they were caught in another. It was not possible to allow the dress to tear. "I in the thorny bush," she said. "Thorns, you doing your appointed work. Never want to let folks past — no sir. Old eyes thought you was a pretty little *green* bush."

9   Finally, trembling all over, she stood free, and after a moment dared to stoop for her cane.

10   "Sun so high!" she cried, leaning back and looking, while the thick tears went over her eyes. "The time getting all gone here."

11   At the foot of this hill was a place where a log was laid across the creek.

12   "Now comes the trial," said Phoenix.

13   Putting her right foot out, she mounted the log and shut her eyes.

Lifting her skirt, leveling her cane fiercely before her, like a festival figure in some parade, she began to march across. Then she opened her eyes and she was safe on the other side.

"I wasn't as old as I thought," she said. 14

But she sat down to rest. She spread her skirts on the bank around 15
her and folded her hands over her knees. Up above her was a tree in a pearly cloud of mistletoe. She did not dare to close her eyes, and when a little boy brought her a little plate with a slice of marble-cake on it she spoke to him. "That would be acceptable," she said. But when she went to take it there was just her own hand in the air.

So she left that tree, and had to go through a barbed-wire fence. 16
There she had to creep and crawl, spreading her knees and stretching her fingers like a baby trying to climb the steps. But she talked loudly to herself: she could not let her dress be torn now, so late in the day, and she could not pay for having her arm or leg sawed off if she got caught fast where she was.

At last she was safe through the fence and risen up out in the 17
clearing. Big dead trees, like black men with one arm, were standing in the purple stalks of the withered cotton field. There sat a buzzard.

"Who you watching?" 18

In the furrow she made her way along. 19

"Glad this not the season for bulls," she said, looking sideways, 20
"and the good Lord made his snakes to curl up and sleep in the winter. A pleasure I don't see no two-headed snake coming around that tree, where it come once. It took a while to get by him, back in the summer."

She passed through the old cotton and went into a field of dead 21
corn. It whispered and shook, and was taller than her head. "Through the maze now," she said, for there was no path.

Then there was something tall, black, and skinny there, moving 22
before her.

At first she took it for a man. It could have been a man dancing 23
in the field. But she stood still and listened, and it did not make a sound. It was as silent as a ghost.

"Ghost," she said sharply, "who be you the ghost of? For I have 24
heard of nary death close by."

But there was no answer, only the ragged dancing in the wind. 25

She shut her eyes, reached out her hand, and touched a sleeve. 26
She found a coat and inside that an emptiness, cold as ice.

"You scarecrow," she said. Her face lighted. "I ought to be shut 27
up for good," she said with laughter. "My senses is gone. I too old. I

the oldest people I ever know. Dance, old scarecrow," she said, "while I dancing with you."

28   She kicked her foot over the furrow, and with mouth drawn down shook her head once or twice in a little strutting way. Some husks blew down and whirled in streamers about her skirts.

29   Then she went on, parting her way from side to side with the cane, through the whispering field. At last she came to the end, to a wagon track, where the silver grass blew between the red ruts. The quail were walking around like pullets, seeming all dainty and unseen.

30   "Walk pretty," she said. "This the easy place. This the easy going."

31   She followed the track, swaying through the quiet bare fields, through the little strings of trees silver in their dead leaves, past cabins silver from weather, with the doors and windows boarded shut, all like old women under a spell sitting there. "I walking in their sleep," she said, nodding her head vigorously.

32   In a ravine she went where a spring was silently flowing through a hollow log. Old Phoenix bent and drank. "Sweetgum makes the water sweet," she said, and drank more. "Nobody knows who made this well, for it was here when I was born."

33   The track crossed a swampy part where the moss hung as white as lace from every limb. "Sleep on, alligators, and blow your bubbles." Then the track went into the road.

34   Deep, deep the road went down between the high green-colored banks. Overhead the live-oaks met, and it was as dark as a cave.

35   A black dog with a lolling tongue came up out of the weeds by the ditch. She was meditating, and not ready, and when he came at her she only hit him a little with her cane. Over she went in the ditch, like a little puff of milk-weed.

36   Down there, her senses drifted away. A dream visited her, and she reached her hand up, but nothing reached down and gave her a pull. So she lay there and presently went to talking. "Old woman," she said to herself, "that black dog come up out of the weeds to stall you off, and now there he sitting on his fine tail, smiling at you."

37   A white man finally came along and found her — a hunter, a young man, with his dog on a chain.

38   "Well, Granny!" he laughed. "What are you doing there?"

39   "Lying on my back like a June-bug waiting to be turned over, mister," she said, reaching up her hand.

40   He lifted her up, gave her a swing in the air, and set her down, "Anything broken, Granny?"

"No sir, them old dead weeds is springy enough," said Phoenix, 41
when she had got her breath. "I thank you for your trouble."

"Where do you live, Granny?" he asked, while the two dogs were 42
growling at each other.

"Away back yonder, sir, behind the ridge. You can't even see it 43
from here."

"On your way home?" 44

"No, sir, I going to town." 45

"Why that's too far! That's as far as I walk when I come out 46
myself, and I get something for my trouble." He patted the stuffed bag
he carried, and there hung down a little closed claw. It was one of the
bobwhites, with its beak hooked bitterly to show it was dead. "Now
you go on home, Granny!"

"I bound to go to town, mister," said Phoenix. "The time come 47
around."

He gave another laugh, filling the whole landscape. "I know you 48
colored people! Wouldn't miss going to town to see Santa Claus!"

But something held Old Phoenix very still. The deep lines in her 49
face went into a fierce and different radiation. Without warning she
had seen with her own eyes a flashing nickel fall out of the man's
pocket on to the ground.

"How old are you, Granny?" he was saying. 50

"There is no telling, mister," she said, "no telling." 51

Then she gave a little cry and clapped her hands, and said, "Git 52
on away from here, dog! Look! Look at that dog!" She laughed as if in
admiration. "He ain't scared of nobody. He a big black dog." She whispered, "Sick him!"

"Watch me get rid of that cur," said the man. "Sick him, Pete! 53
Sick him!"

Phoenix heard the dogs fighting and heard the man running and 54
throwing sticks. She even heard a gunshot. But she was slowly bending
forward by that time, further and further forward, the lids stretched
down over her eyes, as if she were doing this in her sleep. Her chin
was lowered almost to her knees. The yellow palm of her hand came
out from the fold of her apron. Her fingers slid down and along the
ground under the piece of money with the grace and care they would
have in lifting an egg from under a sitting hen. Then she slowly
straightened up, she stood erect, and the nickel was in her apron
pocket. A bird flew by. Her lips moved. "God watching me the whole
time. I come to stealing."

The man came back, and his own dog panted about them. "Well, 55

I scared him off that time," he said, and then he laughed and lifted his gun and pointed it at Phoenix.

56   She stood straight and faced him.

57   "Doesn't the gun scare you?" he said, still pointing it.

58   "No, sir, I seen plenty go off closer by, in my day, and for less what I done," she said, holding utterly still.

59   He smiled, and shouldered the gun. "Well, Granny," he said, "you must be a hundred years old, and scared of nothing. I'd give you a dime if I had any money with me. But you take my advice and stay home, and nothing will happen to you."

60   "I bound to go on my way, mister," said Phoenix. She inclined her head in the red rag. Then they went in different directions, but she could hear the gun shooting again and again over the hill.

61   She walked on. The shadows hung from the oak trees to the road like curtains. Then she smelled wood-smoke, and smelled the river, and she saw a steeple and the cabins on their steep steps. Dozens of little black children whirled around her. There ahead was Natchez shining. Bells were ringing. She walked on.

62   In the paved city it was Christmas time. There were red and green electric lights strung and crisscrossed everywhere, and all turned on in the daytime. Old Phoenix would have been lost if she had not distrusted her eyesight and depended on her feet to know where to take her.

63   She paused quietly on the sidewalk, where people were passing by. A lady came along in the crowd, carrying an armful of red-, green-, and silver-wrapped presents; she gave off perfume like the red roses in hot summer, and Phoenix stopped her.

64   "Please, missy, will you lace up my shoe?" She held up her foot.

65   "What do you want, Grandma?"

66   "See my shoe," said Phoenix. "Do all right for out in the country, but wouldn't look right to go in a big building."

67   "Stand still then, Grandma," said the lady. She put her packages down carefully on the sidewalk beside her and laced and tied both shoes tightly.

68   "Can't lace 'em with a cane," said Phoenix. "Thank you, missy. I doesn't mind asking a nice lady to tie up my shoe when I gets out on the street."

69   Moving slowly and from side to side, she went into the stone building and into a tower of steps, where she walked up and around and around until her feet knew to stop.

70   She entered a door, and there she saw nailed up on the wall the

document that had been stamped with the gold seal and framed in the gold frame which matched the dream that was hung up in her head.

"Here I be," she said. There was a fixed and ceremonial stiffness over her body. 71

"A charity case, I suppose," said an attendant who sat at the desk before her. 72

But Phoenix only looked above her head. There was sweat on her face; the wrinkles shone like a bright net. 73

"Speak up, Grandma," the woman said. "What's your name? We must have your history, you know. Have you been here before? What seems to be the trouble with you?" 74

Old Phoenix only gave a twitch to her face as if a fly were bothering her. 75

"Are you deaf?" cried the attendant. 76

But then the nurse came in. 77

"Oh, that's just old Aunt Phoenix," she said. "She doesn't come for herself — she has a little grandson. She makes these trips just as regular as clockwork. She lives away back off the Old Natchez Trace." She bent down. "Well, Aunt Phoenix, why don't you just take a seat? We won't keep you standing after your long trip." She pointed. 78

The old woman sat down, bolt upright in the chair. 79

"Now, how is the boy?" asked the nurse. 80

Old Phoenix did not speak. 81

"I said, how is the boy?" 82

But Phoenix only waited and stared straight ahead, her face very solemn and withdrawn into rigidity. 83

"Is his throat any better?" asked the nurse. "Aunt Phoenix, don't you hear me? Is your grandson's throat any better since the last time you came for the medicine?" 84

With her hand on her knees, the old woman waited, silent, erect and motionless, just as if she were in armor. 85

"You mustn't take up our time this way, Aunt Phoenix," the nurse said. "Tell us quickly about your grandson, and get it over. He isn't dead, is he?" 86

At last there came a flicker and then a flame of comprehension across her face, and she spoke. 87

"My grandson. It was my memory had left me. There I sat and forgot why I made my long trip." 88

"Forgot?" The nurse frowned. "After you came so far?" 89

Then Phoenix was like an old woman begging a dignified forgiveness for waking up frightened in the night. "I never did go to school 90

— I was too old at the Surrender," she said in a soft voice. "I'm an old woman without an education. It was my memory fail me. My little grandson, he is just the same, and I forgot it in the coming."

91   "Throat never heals, does it?" said the nurse, speaking in a loud, sure voice to Old Phoenix. By now she had a card with something written on it, a little list. "Yes. Swallowed lye. When was it — January — two — three years ago — "

92   Phoenix spoke unasked now. "No, missy, he not dead, he just the same. Every little while his throat begin to close up again, and he not able to swallow. He not get his breath. He not able to help himself. So the time come around, and I go on another trip for soothing medicine."

93   "All right. The doctor said as long as you came to get it you could have it," said the nurse. "But it's an obstinate case."

94   "My little grandson, he sit up there in the house all wrapped up, waiting by himself," Phoenix went on. "We is the only two left in the world. He suffer and it don't seem to put him back at all. He got a sweet look. He going to last. He wear a little patch quilt and peep out, holding his mouth open like a little bird. I remembers so plain now. I not going to forget him again, no, the whole enduring time. I could tell him from all the others in creation."

95   "All right." The nurse was trying to hush her now. She brought her a bottle of medicine. "Charity," she said, making a check mark in a book.

96   Old Phoenix held the bottle close to her eyes and then carefully put it into her pocket.

97   "I thank you," she said.

98   "It's Christmas time, Grandma," said the attendant. "Could I give you a few pennies out of my purse?"

99   "Five pennies is a nickel," said Phoenix stiffly.

100   "Here's a nickel," said the attendant.

101   Phoenix rose carefully and held out her hand. She received the nickel and then fished the other nickel out of her pocket and laid it beside the new one. She stared at her palm closely, with her head on one side.

102   Then she gave a tap with her cane on the floor.

103   "This is what come to me to do," she said. "I going to the store and buy my child a little windmill they sells, made out of paper. He going to find it hard to believe there such a thing in the world. I'll march myself back where he waiting, holding it straight up in this hand."

She lifted her free hand, gave a little nod, turned round, and   104
walked out of the doctor's office. Then her slow step began on the
stairs, going down.

____ **CONSIDERATIONS** _____

1. Some features of Old Phoenix's long journey might bring to mind
Everyman's difficult travel through life. Do specific passages suggest that Old
Phoenix's journey is symbolic or archetypal?

2. Would you say that Old Phoenix is senile? Is she in excellent control
of her thoughts? What evidence can you find for your answer?

3. Is the grandson alive or dead? After you answer this question, read
Welty's own comments on the story in the next selection.

4. Who was the little boy with the slice of marble-cake? Why does he
appear and disappear so abruptly?

5. Eudora Welty makes no comment in the story on Old Phoenix's
encounter with the white man. Do the details of that encounter reveal anything about relations between whites and blacks?

6. What do you learn of Old Phoenix's sense of morality, and sense of
humor, and feeling of personal worth?

77

EUDORA WELTY
The Point of the Story

1   A story writer is more than happy to be read by students; the fact that these serious readers think and feel something in response to his work he finds life-giving. At the same time he may not always be able to reply to their specific questions in kind. I wondered if it might clarify something, for both the questioners and myself, if I set down a general reply to the question that comes to me most often in the mail, from both students and their teachers, after some classroom discussion. The unrivaled favorite is this: "Is Phoenix Jackson's grandson really *dead?*" It refers to a short story I wrote years ago called "A Worn Path," which tells of a day's journey an old woman makes on foot from deep in the country into town and into a doctor's office on behalf of her little grandson; he is at home, periodically ill, and periodically she comes for his medicine; they give it to her as usual, she receives it and starts the journey back.

2   I had not meant to mystify readers by withholding any fact; it is not a writer's business to tease. The story is told through Phoenix's mind as she undertakes her errand. As the author at one with the character as I tell it, I must assume that the boy is alive. As the reader, you are free to think as you like, of course: the story invites you to believe that no matter what happens, Phoenix for as long as she is able to walk and can hold to her purpose will make her journey. The *possibility* that she would keep on even if he were dead is there in her devotion and its single-minded, single-track errand. Certainly the *artistic* truth, which should be good enough for the fact, lies in Phoenix's

From *The New York Times Book Review,* March 5, 1978. © 1978 by The New York Times Company. Reprinted by permission.

own answer to that question. When the nurse asks, "He isn't dead, is he?" she speaks for herself: "He still the same. He going to last."

The grandchild is the incentive. But it is the journey, the going 3 of the errand, that is the story, and the question is not whether the grandchild is in reality alive or dead. It doesn't affect the outcome of the story or its meaning from start to finish. But it is not the question itself that has struck me as much as the idea, almost without exception implied in the asking, that for Phoenix's grandson to be dead would somehow make the story "better."

It's *all right*, I want to say to the students who write to me, for 4 things to be what they appear to be, and for words to mean what they say. It's all right, too, for words and appearances to mean more than one thing — ambiguity is a fact of life. A fiction writer's responsibility covers not only what he presents as the facts of a given story but what he chooses to stir up as their implications; in the end, these implications, too, become facts, in the larger, fictional sense. But it is not all right, not in good faith, for things not to mean what they say.

The grandson's plight was real and it made the truth of the story, 5 which is the story of an errand of love carried out. If the child no longer lived, the truth would persist in the "wornness" of the path. But his being dead can't increase the truth of the story, can't affect it one way or the other. I think I signal this, because the end of the story has been reached before old Phoenix gets home again: she simply starts back. To the question "Is the grandson really dead?" I could reply that it doesn't make any difference. I could also say that I did not make him up in order to let him play a trick on Phoenix. But my best answer would be: "Phoenix is alive."

The origin of a story is sometimes a trustworthy clue to the 6 author — or can provide him with the clue — to its key image; maybe in this case it will do the same for the reader. One day I saw a solitary old woman like Phoenix. She was walking; I saw her, at middle distance, in a winter country landscape, and watched her slowly make her way across my line of vision. That sight of her made me write the story. I invented an errand for her, but that only seemed a living part of the figure she was herself; what errand other than for someone else could be making her go? And her going was the first thing, her persisting in her landscape was the real thing, and the first and the real were what I wanted and worked to keep. I brought her up close enough, by imagination, to describe her face, make her present to the eyes, but the full-length figure moving across the winter fields was the indelible one and the image to keep, and the perspective extending into the vanishing distance the true one to hold in mind.

7   I invented for my character as I wrote, some passing adventures — some dreams and harassments and a small triumph or two, some jolts to her pride, some flights of fancy to console her, one or two encounters to scare her, a moment that gave her cause to feel ashamed, a moment to dance and preen — for it had to be a journey, and all these things belonged to that, parts of life's uncertainty.

8   A narrative line is in its deeper sense, of course, the tracing out of a meaning, and the real continuity of a story lies in this probing forward. The real dramatic force of a story depends on the strength of the emotion that has set it going. The emotional value is the measure of the reach of the story. What gives any such content to "A Worn Path" is not its circumstances but its subject: the deep-grained habit of love.

9   What I hoped would come clear was that in the whole surround of this story, the world it threads through, the only certain thing at all is the worn path. The habit of love cuts through confusion and stumbles or contrives its way out of difficulty, it remembers the way even when it forgets, for a dumbfounded moment, its reason for being. The path is the thing that matters.

10   Her victory — old Phoenix's — is when she sees the diploma in the doctor's office, when she finds "nailed up on the wall the document that had been stamped with the gold seal and framed in the gold frame, which matched the dream that was hung up in her head." The return with the medicine is just a matter of retracing her own footsteps. It is the part of the journey, and of the story, that can now go without saying.

11   In the matter of function, old Phoenix's way might even do as a sort of parallel to your way of work if you are a writer of stories. The way to get there is the all-important, all-absorbing problem, and this problem is your reason for undertaking the story. Your only guide, too, is your sureness about your subject, about what this subject is. Like Phoenix, you work all your life to find your way, through all the obstructions and the false appearances and the upsets you may have brought on yourself, to reach a meaning — using inventions of your imagination, perhaps helped out by your dreams and bits of good luck. And finally too, like Phoenix, you have to assume that what you are working in aid of is life, not death.

12   But you would make the trip anyway — wouldn't you? — just on hope.

_____ **CONSIDERATIONS** _____

1. Welty says that Old Phoenix's return trip is "the part of the journey, and of the story, that can now go without saying." If you were writing this story would you choose a different place to end it? Would you follow Old Phoenix all the way back into the hills? Would you show the grandson? Why?

2. How does Welty feel about writers who intentionally mystify their readers?

3. Does "A Worn Path" illustrate what Welty means when she says, "A narrative line is in its deeper sense . . . the tracing out of a meaning"?

4. In Paragraph 4, Welty touches on the "factuality" of a work of fiction. This introduces a fascinating (if maddening) question: what is the difference between fiction and nonfiction?

5. Another southern writer, William Faulkner, wrote a short novel, *As I Lay Dying*, that can be read as a fuller version of "A Worn Path." It too is based on "an errand of love," as Welty puts it. Read the novel and discuss its parallels with Welty's story.

6. What do you think of Welty's response to the question about her story? Does it help you understand and appreciate the story? Does it avoid the initial question?

E. B. White (b. 1899) was born in Mount Vernon, New York, graduated from Cornell in 1921, and joined the staff of The New Yorker *in 1926. For many years, he wrote the brief essay which led off that magazine's "The Talk of the Town" and edited other "Talk" segments. In 1929, White collaborated with James Thurber on a book called* Is Sex Necessary? *and from time to time he has published collections of essays and poems, most of them taken from* The New Yorker *and* Harper's. *Some of his best-known collections are* One Man's Meat *(1942),* The Second Tree from the Corner *(1953), and* The Points of My Compass *(1962). He is also the author of children's books, most notably* Stuart Little *(1945) and* Charlotte's Web *(1952), and the celebrated book on prose,* The Elements of Style *(with William Strunk, Jr., 1959).*

In 1937, White retired from The New Yorker *and moved to a farm in Maine, where he continued to write those minimal, devastating comments attached to the proofhacks and other errors printed at the ends of* The New Yorker's *columns. And he continues his slow, consistent writing of superb prose. In recent years, the collected* Letters of E. B. White *(1976), and* Essays of E. B. White *(1977), and* Poems and Sketches of E. B. White *(1981), have reconfirmed this country's infatuation with the versatile author. A special citation from the Pulitzer Prize Committee in 1978 celebrated the publication of White's letters.*

78

E. B. WHITE
Once More to the Lake

One summer, along about 1904, my father rented a camp on a 1
lake in Maine and took us all there for the month of August. We all
got ringworm from some kittens and had to rub Pond's Extract on our
arms and legs night and morning, and my father rolled over in a canoe
with all his clothes on; but outside of that the vacation was a success
and from then on none of us ever thought there was any place in the
world like that lake in Maine. We returned summer after summer —
always on August 1st for one month. I have since become a salt-water
man, but sometimes in summer there are days when the restlessness
of the tides and the fearful cold of the sea water and the incessant
wind that blows across the afternoon and into the evening make me
wish for the placidity of a lake in the woods. A few weeks ago this
feeling got so strong I bought myself a couple of bass hooks and a
spinner and returned to the lake where we used to go, for a week's
fishing and to revisit old haunts.

I took along my son, who had never had any fresh water up his 2
nose and who had seen lily pads only from train windows. On the
journey over to the lake I began to wonder what it would be like. I
wondered how time would have marred this unique, this holy spot —
the coves and streams, the hills that the sun set behind, the camps
and the paths behind the camps. I was sure that the tarred road would
have found it out and I wondered in what other ways it would be
desolated. It is strange how much you can remember about places like
that once you allow your mind to return into the grooves that lead

back. You remember one thing, and that suddenly reminds you of another thing. I guess I remembered clearest of all the early mornings, when the lake was cool and motionless, remembered how the bedroom smelled of the lumber it was made of and of the wet woods whose scent entered through the screen. The partitions in the camp were thin and did not extend clear to the top of the rooms, and as I was always the first up I would dress softly so as not to wake the others, and sneak out into the sweet outdoors and start out in the canoe, keeping close along the shore in the long shadows of the pines. I remembered being very careful never to rub my paddle against the gunwale for fear of disturbing the stillness of the cathedral.

3   The lake had never been what you would call a wild lake. There were cottages sprinkled around the shores, and it was in farming country although the shores of the lake were quite heavily wooded. Some of the cottages were owned by nearby farmers, and you would live at the shore and eat your meals at the farmhouse. That's what our family did. But although it wasn't wild, it was a fairly large and undisturbed lake and there were places in it which, to a child at least, seemed infinitely remote and primeval.

4   I was right about the tar: it led to within half a mile of the shore. But when I got back there, with my boy, and we settled into a camp near a farmhouse and into the kind of summertime I had known, I could tell that it was going to be pretty much the same as it had been before — I knew it, lying in bed the first morning, smelling the bedroom, and hearing the boy sneak quietly out and go off along the shore in a boat. I began to sustain the illusion that he was I, and therefore, by simple transposition, that I was my father. This sensation persisted, kept cropping up all the time we were there. It was not an entirely new feeling, but in this setting it grew much stronger. I seemed to be living a dual existence. I would be in the middle of some simple act, I would be picking up a bait box or laying down a table fork, or I would be saying something, and suddenly it would be not I but my father who was saying the words or making the gesture. It gave me a creepy sensation.

5   We went fishing the first morning. I felt the same damp moss covering the worms in the bait can, and saw the dragonfly alight on the tip of my rod as it hovered a few inches from the surface of the water. It was the arrival of this fly that convinced me beyond any doubt that everything was as it always had been, that the years were a mirage and there had been no years. The small waves were the same, chucking the rowboat under the chin as we fished at anchor, and the

boat was the same boat, the same color green and the ribs broken in the same places, and under the floor-boards the same fresh-water leavings and débris — the dead hellgrammite, the wisps of moss, the rusty discarded fishhook, the dried blood from yesterday's catch. We stared silently at the tips of our rods, at the dragonflies that came and went. I lowered the tip of mine into the water, tentatively, pensively dislodging the fly, which darted two feet away, poised, darted two feet back, and came to rest again a little farther up the rod. There had been no years between the ducking of this dragonfly and the other one — the one that was part of memory. I looked at the boy, who was silently watching his fly, and it was my hands that held his rod, my eyes watching. I felt dizzy and didn't know which rod I was at the end of.

We caught two bass, hauling them in briskly as though they were 6 mackerel, pulling them over the side of the boat in a businesslike manner without any landing net, and stunning them with a blow on the back of the head. When we got back for a swim before lunch, the lake was exactly where we had left it, the same number of inches from the dock, and there was only the merest suggestion of a breeze. This seemed an utterly enchanted sea, this lake you could leave to its own devices for a few hours and come back to, and find that it had not stirred, this constant and trustworthy body of water. In the shallows, the dark, water-soaked sticks and twigs, smooth and old, were undulating in clusters on the bottom against the clean ribbed sand, and the track of the mussel was plain. A school of minnows swam by, each minnow with its small individual shadow, doubling the attendance, so clear and sharp in the sunlight. Some of the other campers were in swimming, along the shore, one of them with a cake of soap, and the water felt thin and clear and unsubstantial. Over the years there had been this person with the cake of soap, this cultist, and here he was. There had been no years.

Up to the farmhouse to dinner through the teeming, dusty field, 7 the road under our sneakers was only a two-track road. The middle track was missing, the one with the marks of the hooves and splotches of dried, flaky manure. There had always been three tracks to choose from in choosing which track to walk in; now the choice was narrowed down to two. For a moment I missed terribly the middle alternative. But the way led past the tennis court, and something about the way it lay there in the sun reassured me; the tape had loosened along the backline, the alleys were green with plantains and other weeds, and the net (installed in June and removed in September) sagged in the dry noon, and the whole place steamed with midday heat and hunger and emptiness. There was a choice of pie for dessert, and one was blueberry and one was apple, and the waitresses were the same country girls, there having been no passage of time, only the illusion of it as in a dropped curtain — the waitresses were still fifteen; their hair had been washed, that was the only difference — they had been to the movies and seen the pretty girls with the clean hair.

8   Summertime, oh summertime, pattern of life indelible, the fade-proof lake, the woods unshatterable, the pasture with the sweetfern and the juniper forever and ever, summer without end; this was the background, and the life along the shore was the design, the cottages with their innocent and tranquil design, their tiny docks with the flagpole and the American flag floating against the white clouds in the blue sky, the little paths over the roots of the trees leading from camp to camp and the paths leading back to the outhouses and the can of lime for sprinkling, and at the souvenir counters at the store the miniature birch-bark canoes and the post cards that showed things looking a little better than they looked. This was the American family at play, escaping the city heat, wondering whether the newcomers in the camp at the head of the cove were "common" or "nice," wondering whether it was true that the people who drove up for Sunday dinner at the farmhouse were turned away because there wasn't enough chicken.

9   It seemed to me, as I kept remembering all this, that those times and those summers had been infinitely precious and worth saving. There had been jollity and peace and goodness. The arriving (at the beginning of August) had been so big a business in itself, at the railway station the farm wagon drawn up, the first smell of the pine-laden air, the first glimpse of the smiling farmer, and the great importance of the trunks and your father's enormous authority in such matters, and the feel of the wagon under you for the long ten-mile haul, and at the top of the last long hill catching the first view of the lake after eleven months of not seeing this cherished body of water. The shouts and cries of the other campers when they saw you, and the trunks to be unpacked, to give up their rich burden. (Arriving was less exciting nowadays, when you sneaked up in your car and parked it under a tree near the camp and took out the bags and in five minutes it was all over, no fuss, no loud wonderful fuss about trunks.)

10   Peace and goodness and jollity. The only thing that was wrong now, really, was the sound of the place, an unfamiliar nervous sound of the outboard motors. This was the note that jarred, the one thing that would sometimes break the illusion and set the years moving. In those other summertimes all motors were inboard; and when they

were at a little distance, the noise they made was a sedative, an ingredient of summer sleep. They were one-cylinder and two-cylinder engines, and some were make-and-break and some were jump-spark, but they all made a sleepy sound across the lake. The one-lungers throbbed and fluttered, and the twin-cylinder ones purred and purred and that was a quiet sound too. But now the campers all had outboards. In the daytime, in the hot mornings, these motors made a petulant, irritable sound; at night, in the still evening when the afterglow lit the water, they whined about one's ears like mosquitoes. My boy loved our rented outboard, and his great desire was to achieve singlehanded mastery over it, and authority, and he soon learned the trick of choking it a little (but not too much), and the adjustment of the needle valve. Watching him I would remember the things you could do with the old one-cylinder engine with the heavy flywheel, how you could have it eating out of your hand if you got really close to it spiritually. Motor boats in those days didn't have clutches, and you would make a landing by shutting off the motor at the proper time and coasting in with a dead rudder. But there was a way of reversing them, if you learned the trick, by cutting the switch and putting it on again exactly on the final dying revolution of the flywheel, so that it would kick back against compression and begin reversing. Approaching a dock in a strong following breeze, it was difficult to slow up sufficiently by the ordinary coasting method, and if a boy felt he had complete mastery over his motor, he was tempted to keep it running beyond its time and then reverse it a few feet from the dock. It took a cool nerve, because if you threw the switch a twentieth of a second too soon you could catch the flywheel when it still had speed enough to go up past center, and the boat would leap ahead, charging bull-fashion at the dock.

We had a good week at the camp. The bass were biting well and   11
the sun shone endlessly, day after day. We would be tired at night and lie down in the accumulated heat of the little bedrooms after the long hot day and the breeze would stir almost imperceptibly outside and the smell of the swamp drift in through the rusty screens. Sleep would come easily and in the morning the red squirrel would be on the roof, tapping out his gay routine. I kept remembering everything, lying in bed in the mornings — the small steamboat that had a long rounded stern like the lip of a Ubangi, and how quietly she ran on the moonlight sails, when the older boys played their mandolins and the girls sang and we ate doughnuts dipped in sugar, and how sweet the music was on the water in the shining light, and what it had felt like to think

about girls then. After breakfast we would go up to the store and the things were in the same place — the minnows in a bottle, the plugs and spinners disarranged and pawed over by the youngsters from the boys' camp, the fig newtons and the Beeman's gum. Outside, the road was tarred and cars stood in front of the store. Inside, all was just as it had always been, except there was more Coca-Cola and not so much Moxie and root beer and birch beer and sarsaparilla. We would walk out with a bottle of pop apiece and sometimes the pop would backfire up our noses and hurt. We explored the streams, quietly, where the turtles slid off the sunny logs and dug their way into the soft bottom; and we lay on the town wharf and fed worms to the tame bass. Everywhere we went I had trouble making out which was I, the one walking at my side, the one walking in my pants.

12   One afternoon while we were there at that lake a thunderstorm came up. It was like the revival of an old melodrama that I had seen long ago with childish awe. The second-act climax of the drama of the electrical disturbance over a lake in America had not changed in any important respect. This was the big scene, still the big scene. The whole thing was so familiar, the first feeling of oppression and heat and a general air around camp of not wanting to go very far away. In midafternoon (it was all the same) a curious darkening of the sky, and a lull in everything that had made life tick; and then the way the boats suddenly swung the other way at their moorings with the coming of a breeze out of the new quarter, and the premonitory rumble. Then the kettle drum, then the snare, then the bass drum and cymbals, then crackling light against the dark, and the gods grinning and licking their chops in the hills. Afterward the calm, the rain steadily rustling in the calm lake, the return of light and hope and spirits, and the campers running out in joy and relief to go swimming in the rain, their bright cries perpetuating the deathless joke about how they were getting simply drenched, and the children screaming with delight at the new sensation of bathing in the rain, and the joke about getting drenched linking the generations in a strong indestructible chain. And the comedian who waded in carrying an umbrella.

13   When the others went swimming my son said he was going in too. He pulled his dripping trunks from the line where they had hung all through the shower, and wrung them out. Languidly, and with no thought of going in, I watched him, his hard little body, skinny and bare, saw him wince slightly as he pulled up around his vitals the small, soggy, icy garment. As he buckled the swollen belt suddenly my groin felt the chill of death.

_____ **CONSIDERATIONS** _____

1. A master of the personal essay, E. B. White transforms an exercise in memory into something universal, timeless, and profound. Study Paragraph 4 to see how.

2. White rejuvenates bits and pieces of language that have become worn and lackluster through repetition. Can you find an example of this technique in Paragraph 2?

3. White notes many changes at the old summer place, but he is more moved by the sameness. Locate examples of his feeling of sameness and consider how these examples contribute to his themes.

4. The author expresses a predictable dislike of outboard motors on the otherwise quiet lake. Does he avoid stereotype when he writes about motors elsewhere in this essay?

5. What is the chief device White uses in his description of the thunderstorm in Paragraph 12?

6. How is the last sentence of the essay a surprise? How has White prepared us for it?

When E. B. White reprinted a few brief essays from The New York's *"Talk of the Town," he called them editorials, and we follow him. He also mentioned that he signed his name to them "hesitantly, for it is questionable whether anyone can properly assume authorship of material which is published anonymously." Yet when we read them they do not seem anonymous; White's singular prose style announces itself.*

79

E. B. WHITE

The Wild Flag

April 19, 1943

1   The time is at hand to revive the discussion of companionate marriage, for it is now apparent that the passion of nations will shortly lead to some sort of connubial relationship, either a companionate one (as in the past) or a lawful one (which would be something new). If you observe closely the courtship among nations, if you read each morning the many protestations of affection and the lively plans for consummation, you will find signs that the drift is still toward an illicit arrangement based on love, respect, and a strong foreign policy. Countries appear to be on the verge of making new and solemn compacts with each other, of renewing old pledges. If it is to be this and no more, we predict that they will lie together in rapture for a while and then bust up as usual. The companionate idea is appealing to nations because it is familiar, because it demands little, and because it is exciting to the blood. The mention of a license and the thought of

relinquishing something of one's independence come hard to the sovereign ear and mind. Even at this woebegone time it seems questionable whether the grim institution of marriage will be embraced by the world's states, which have always practiced free love and are used to its excesses and its tragic violence.

Our advice to the nations who call themselves united is to go out 2 and buy rings. If there is to be love-in-bloom at the war's end, we should prefer to see it legal this time, if only for a change. The history of the modern world is the story of nations having affairs with each other. These affairs have been based on caprice and on ambition; they have been oiled with diplomacy and intrigue and have been unsanctified by law, there having been no law covering the rights and obligations of the contracting parties. The result has been chaotic and there still is no law. We are informed, almost hourly, that a new world order is in the making, yet most of the talk is of policy and almost none of the talk is of law.

America and China are in love. England and Russia are seen 3 frequently together in public. France, Norway, the Netherlands, Greece, Poland, Czechoslovakia — each is groping for the other's hand in the darkness of the newsreel. What is going to come of this romantic and wonderful condition — a few stolen kisses, a key to an apartment somewhere, a renewal of individual vows and general irresponsibility? Considering how eager the nations are to lie down with each other, it seems to us time for a brief notice to be inserted in the world's paper, inviting interested parties to a preliminary meeting, a sociable if you want, to talk over the whole situation and perhaps even discuss the end of policy and laxity in their love life and the beginning of law and of force. The notice should be carefully worded and should be at least as honest as those wistful little ads which the lovelorn and the lonely place in the classified columns. It should conclude with that desperate yet somehow very hopeful phrase 'Object, matrimony.'

_____ **CONSIDERATIONS** _____

1. One of E. B. White's techniques is to mix different dictions in the same piece. In Paragraph 1, for example, he uses general and abstract words, such as "companionate marriage," "connubial relationship," "protestations of affection." But there is one phrase in the same paragraph that brings us down to earth with a refreshing thump. Find it and comment on its utility in this passage.

2. White's entire editorial is an exercise in analogy or the extended metaphor. Sort out the essential parts of the metaphor — the vehicle and the tenor — to see how consistently he maintains that figurative device. Then try your hand at the same technique with a substantial paragraph on a topic of your own choice. You might get ideas for topics by looking into *Letters of E. B. White,* edited by Dorothy Lobrano Guth (Harper & Row, 1976).

3. Despite his characteristic playfulness with language, White's editorial is distinctly an argumentative essay. State his thesis in literal terms. What institution has been formed to further that thesis since White's editorial?

4. White has a knack for using commonplace detail to help us understand something far more important. Study the phrase in Paragraph 3, ". . . each is groping for the other's hand in the darkness of the newsreel." Why "groping"? Why "darkness"? Why "newsreel"?

Thomas Wolfe *(1900–1938) wrote enormous autobiographical novels, most notably* Look Homeward, Angel *(1929) and* Of Time and the River *(1935), and two published posthumously,* The Web and the Rock *(1939) and* You Can't Go Home Again *(1940). He was born and grew up in Asheville, North Carolina, entered the University of North Carolina at fifteen, attended Harvard, and taught at New York University. Wolfe was a huge man, and he wrote hugely. His novels were unending journals of total recall. He sometimes wrote twenty thousand words — the equivalent of about sixty pages in* A Writer's Reader — *at one sitting. Patient editors, especially Maxwell Perkins at Scribner's, spent months carving each of his novels from packing cases full of disorganized manuscript. The finished novels were highly emotional, lyrical accounts of childhood, youth, and early manhood. Wolfe wrote one book about his unique method of writing,* The Story of a Novel *(1936). He died of complications following an attack of pneumonia, two weeks before he would have turned thirty-eight.*

The journal from which these selections come was written shortly before his final illness and death. He had given a talk at Purdue University in Indiana, and then had traveled to the Pacific Northwest looking for some relatives on his mother's side. He took a notebook with him, thinking that later he might work his notes up into a book. Only these notes survive, presented here line by line, transcribed from the novelist's nearly illegible handwriting.

Brilliant descriptions, intense evocation — and no discipline or structure. Of course one would not expect discipline or structure from any writer in an unedited, posthumously published journal. This journal may serve as a model for students who wish to learn to write rapidly — in order to loosen up and to accumulate detail and color, idea and recollection — before applying to their writing the formal disciplines of sentence, paragraph, and essay.

80

THOMAS WOLFE
Journal Entries

MONDAY JUNE 20 (CRATER LAKE)

1   Left Portland, University Club, 8:15 sharp —
Fair day, bright sunlight, no cloud in sky —
Went South by East through farmlands of upper
Willamette and around base of Mount Hood
which was glowing in brilliant sun — Then
climbed and crossed Cascades, and came down
with suddenness of knife into the dry lands of the
Eastern slope — Then over high plateau and
through bare hills and canyons and irrigated
farmlands here and there, low valley, etc., and
into Bend at 12:45 — 200 miles in 4½
hours —

2   Then lunch at hotel and view of the 3 Sisters and
the Cascade range — then up to the Pilot Butte
above the town — the great plain stretching
infinite away — and unapproachable the great line
of the Cascades with their snowspired sentinels
Hood, Adams, Jefferson, 3 sisters, etc, and out of
Bend at 3 and then through the vast and level
pinelands — somewhat reminiscent of the South

Reprinted from *A Western Journal: A Daily Log of the Great Parks Trip, June 20–July 2, 1938* by Thomas Wolfe by permission of the University of Pittsburgh Press. © 1967 by Paul Gitlin, Administrator, C.T.A.

for 100 miles then down through the noble pines
to the vast plainlike valley of the Klamath? — the
virgin land of Canaan all again — the far-off
ranges — infinite — Oregon and the Promised
Land — then through the valley floor — past Indian
reservation — Capt Jack — the Modocs — the great
trees open approaching vicinity of the Park —
the entrance and the reservation — the forester —
the houses — the great snow patches underneath
the trees — then the great climb upwards — the
foresting, administration — up and up again —
through the passes the great plain behind and at
length the incredible crater of the lake — the hotel
and a certain cheerlessness in spite of cordialness
— dry tongues vain-licking for a feast — the return,
the cottages, the college boys and girls who serve
and wait — the cafeteria and the souvenirs —
the great crater fading coldly in incredible
cold light — at

    length departure — and the forest rangers down   3
below — long, long talks — too long with them
about "our wonders," etc — then by darkness the
sixty or seventy miles down the great dim
expanse of Klamath Lake, the decision to stay
here for the night — 3 beers, a shower, and this,
reveille at 5:30 in the morning — and so to bed!
    First day: 404 miles

    The gigantic unconscious humor of the situation   4
— C "making every national park" without
seeing any of them — the main thing is to "make
them" — and so on and on tomorrow

TUESDAY JUNE 21, 1938 (YOSEMITE)

    Dies Irae: Wakened at 5:30 — dragged weary   5
bones erect, dressed, closed baggage, was ready
shortly before six, and we were off again "on
the dot" — at six oclock. So out of Klamath,

the lakes red, and a thread of silver river in
the desert, and immediately

6   the desert, sage brush, and bare, naked, hills,
giant-molded, craterous, cupreous, glaciated
blasted — a demonic heath with reaches of great
pine, and volcanic glaciation, cupreous, fiendish,
desert, blasted — the ruins of old settlers homesteads, ghost towns and the bleak little facades
of long forgotten postoffices lit bawdily by blazing
rising sun and the winding mainstreet, the
deserted station of the incessant railway — all
dominated now by the glittering snow — pale
masses of

7   Mount Shasta — pine lands, canyons, sweeps and
rises, the naked crateric hills and the volcanic
lava masses and then Mount Shasta omnipresent
— Mount Shasta all the time — always Mt. Shasta
— and at last the town named Weed (with a
divine felicity) — and breakfast at Weed at 7:45 —
and the morning bus from Portland and the
tired people tumbling out and *in* for breakfast

8   and away from Weed and towering Shasta at
8:15 — and up and climbing and at length into
the passes of the lovely timbered Siskiyous
and now down into canyon of the Sacramento
in among the lovely timbered Siskiyous and all
through the morning down and down and down
the canyon, and the road snaking, snaking
always with a thousand little punctual gashes,
and the freight trains and the engines turned
backward with the cabs in *front*

9   down below along the lovely Sacramento snaking
snaking snaking — and at last into the town of
Redding and the timber fading, hills fading,
cupreous lavic masses fading — and almost at
once the mighty valley of the Sacramento — as
broad as a continent — and all through the morn-

ing through the great floor of that great plain
like valley — the vast fields thick with straw
grass lighter

than Swedes hair — and infinitely far and   10
unapproachable the towns down the mountain
on both sides — and great herds of fat brown
steers in straw light fields — a dry land, with
a strange hot heady fragrance and fertility —
and at last no mountains at all but the great
sun-bright, heat-hazed, straw-light plain and
the straight marvel of the road on which the
car rushes

on like magic and no sense of speed at 60 miles   11
an hour — At 11:30 a brief halt at — to look at
the hotel — and great palms now, and spanish
tiles and arches and pilasters and a patio in
the hotel and swimming pool — and on again and
on again across the great, hot, straw light plain,
and great fields mown new and scattered with
infinite bundles of baled hay and

occasional clumps of greenery and pastures and   12
houses and barns where water is and as Sacramento
nears a somewhat greener land, more unguent,
and better houses now, and great fat herds of
steers innumerable and lighter and more sun —
ovenhot towns and at length through the heat-
haze the slopes of Sacramento and over an
enormous viaduct across a flat

and marshy land and planes flying, and then   13
the far flung filling stations, hot dog stores,
3 Little Pigs, and Bar B-Q's of a California
town and then across the Sacramento into town —
the turn immediate and houses new and mighty
palms and trees and people walking. and the
State house with its gold leaf dome
and spaghetti at the first Greeks that we find,
and on out again immediate —

14   pressing on — past state house — and past street
by street of leafy trees and palms and pleasant houses and out from
town now — but traffic
flashing past now — and loaded trucks and
whizzing cars — no more the lovely 50 mile
stretches and 60 miles an hour — but down across
the backbone of the state — and the whole backbone
of the state — cars and towns and farms
and people
flashing by — and still that same vast
billowy plain — no light *brown* now — the
San Joaquin Valley now — and bursting with
Gods plenty — orchards — peaches — apricots —
and vineyards — orange groves — Gods plenty of
the best — and glaring little towns sown thick
with fruit packing houses — ovenhot, glittering
in the hot and shining air — town

15   after town — each in the middle of Gods plenty —
and at length the turn at — toward Yosemite —
90 miles away — the barren, crateric, lavic, volcanic
blasted hills — but signs now telling us we can't
get in now across the washed out road save
behind the conductor — and now too late — already
5 of six and the last conductor leaves

16   at six and we still 50 miles away — and telephone
calls now to rangers, superintendents and so
forth, a filling station and hot cabins, and the
end of a day of blazing heat and the wind
stirring in the sycamores about the cabins, and
on again now, and almost immediately the broken
ground, the straw light mouldings, the rises to
the crater hills and soon

17   among them — climbing, climbing into timber —
and down down down into pleasant timbered
mountain folds — get no sensation yet and winding
in and out — and little hill towns here and there
and climbing, climbing, climbing, mountain

lodges, cabins, houses, and so on, and now in
terrific mountain folds, close packed, precipitous,
lapped together and down and over, down again

    along breath taking curves and steepnesses and   18
sheer drops down below into a canyon cut a
mile below by great knifes blade — and at the
bottom the closed gate — the little store — calls upon
the phone again, and darkness and the sending
notes, and at last success — upon our own heads
be the risk but we may enter — and we do —
and so slowly up

    we go along the washed out road — finding it   19
not near so dangerous as we feared — and at
length past the bad end and the closed gate and
release — and up now climbing and the sound of
mighty waters in the gorge and the sheer black-
nesses of beetling masses and the stars — and
presently the entrance and the rangers house —
a free pass now — and up and up — and boles of
trees terrific, cloven rock above the road

    and over us and dizzy masses night black as a   20
cloud, a sense of the imminent terrific and at
length the valley of the Yosemite; roads forking
darkly, but the perfect sign — and now a smell
of smokes and of gigantic tentings and enormous
trees and gigantic cliff walls night black all
around and above the sky-bowl of starred night —
and Currys Lodge and

    smoky gaiety and wonder — hundreds of young
faces and voices — the offices, buildings, stores,
the dance floor crowded with its weary hundreds
and the hundreds of tents and cabins and the
absurdity of the life and the immensity of all —
and 1200 little shop girls and stenogs and new-
weds and schoolteachers and boys — all, God
bless their

22   little lives, necking, dancing, kissing, feeling,
and embracing in the great darkness of the giant
redwood trees — and the sound of the dark gigantic fall
of water — and so to bed!
      And 535 miles today!

_____ CONSIDERATIONS _____

1. Judging from the kinds of things he recorded in his journal, what were Wolfe's chief interests during the journey? What was he searching for? Why did he bother to keep a journal?

2. How many periods can you find in this selection? How does that number help account for the sense of speed and constant motion we get from the journal? What other characteristics of Wolfe's prose here contribute to that sense?

3. Does Wolfe depend much in his journal on figurative language, or is this selection chiefly literal and matter-of-fact?

4. How much of a typical American tourist was Wolfe? How often does he break out of such a stereotype? As you consider these questions, think of the phrases "see America first," "the American dream," and "middle-class values."

5. Write journal entries of your own about a trip you've made, imitating Wolfe's style. How do an imitation and a parody differ?

6. It would seem only fair to look at a sample of Wolfe's finished, published work. Try the opening pages of *Look Homeward, Angel,* or *You Can't Go Home Again,* or *Of Time and the River.* Do you find any similarities between his finished work and his rough notebook? Does anything suggest that he might have used a good deal of journal material in his novels?

Virginia Woolf (1882–1941) is best known as a novelist. The
Voyage Out *appeared in 1915, followed by* Night and Day *(1919),*
Jacob's Room *(1922),* Mrs. Dalloway *(1925),* To The Lighthouse
(1927), Orlando *(1928),* The Waves *(1931),* The Years *(1937), and*
Between the Acts, *published shortly after her death. Daughter of
Sir Leslie Stephen, Victorian critic and essayist who edited the*
Dictionary of National Biography, *she was educated at home,
and began her literary career as a critic for the* Times Literary
Supplement. *She wrote essays regularly until her death; four volumes of her* Collected Essays *appeared in the United States in
1967. More recently, her publishers have issued six volumes of
her collected letters, and her diary is being published.*

*With her sister Vanessa, a painter, her husband Leonard Woolf,
an editor and writer, and Vanessa's husband Clive Bell, an art
critic, Woolf lived at the center of the Bloomsbury group — artists and intellectuals who gathered informally to talk and to
amuse each other, and whose unconventional ideas and habits,
when they were known, shocked the stolid British public. John
Maynard Keynes, the economist, was a member of the varied
group, which also included the biographer Lytton Strachey, the
novelist E. M. Forster, and eventually the American poet living in
England, T. S. Eliot. With her husband, Virginia Woolf founded
The Hogarth Press, a small firm dedicated to publishing superior
works. Among its authors were T. S. Eliot and Woolf herself.*

Virginia Woolf, *a recent biography by her nephew Quentin
Bell, gives an intimate picture of the whole group. Of all the
Bloomsbury people, Woolf was perhaps the most talented.
Through most of her life, she struggled against recurring mental
illness, which brought intense depression and suicidal impulses.
When she was fifty-nine she drowned herself in the River Ouse.
The following famous passage from* A Room of One's Own *(1929)
presents a feminist argument by means of a memorable supposi-
tion.*

81

VIRGINIA WOOLF
If Shakespeare Had Had a Sister

1   It is a perennial puzzle why no woman wrote a word of that
extraordinary [Elizabethan] literature when every other man, it
seemed, was capable of song or sonnet. What were the conditions in
which women lived, I asked myself; for fiction, imaginative work that
is, is not dropped like a pebble upon the ground, as science may be;
fiction is like a spider's web, attached ever so lightly perhaps, but still
attached to life at all four corners. Often the attachment is scarcely
perceptible; Shakespeare's plays, for instance, seem to hang there complete by themselves. But when the web is pulled askew, hooked up at
the edge, torn in the middle, one remembers that these webs are not
spun in mid-air by incorporeal creatures, but are the work of suffering
human beings, and are attached to grossly material things, like health
and money and the house we live in. . . .

2   But what I find . . . is that nothing is known about women before
the eighteenth century. I have no model in my mind to turn about this
way and that. Here am I asking why women did not write poetry in
the Elizabethan age, and I am not sure how they were educated;
whether they were taught to write; whether they had sitting-rooms to
themselves; how many women had children before they were twenty-
one; what, in short, they did from eight in the morning till eight at
night. They had no money, evidently; according to Professor Trevelyan they were married whether they liked it or not before they were
out of the nursery, at fifteen or sixteen very likely. It would have been
extremely odd, even upon this showing, had one of them suddenly

written the plays of Shakespeare, I concluded, and I thought of that old gentleman, who is dead now, but was a bishop, I think, who declared that it was impossible for any woman, past, present, or to come, to have the genius of Shakespeare. He wrote to the papers about it. He also told a lady who applied to him for information that cats do not as a matter of fact go to heaven, though they have, he added, souls of a sort. How much thinking those old gentlemen used to save one! How the borders of ignorance shrank back at their approach! Cats do not go to heaven. Women cannot write the plays of Shakespeare.

Be that as it may, I could not help thinking, as I looked at the works of Shakespeare on the shelf, that the bishop was right at least in this; it would have been impossible, completely and entirely, for any woman to have written the plays of Shakespeare in the age of Shakespeare. Let me imagine, since facts are so hard to come by, what would have happened had Shakespeare had a wonderfully gifted sister, called Judith, let us say. Shakespeare himself went, very probably — his mother was an heiress — to the grammar school, where he may have learnt Latin — Ovid, Virgil and Horace — and the elements of grammar and logic. He was, it is well known, a wild boy who poached rabbits, perhaps shot a deer, and had, rather sooner than he should have done, to marry a woman in the neighbourhood, who bore him a child rather quicker than was right. That escapade sent him to seek his fortune in London. He had, it seemed, a taste for the theatre; he began by holding horses at the stage door. Very soon he got work in the theatre, became a successful actor, and lived at the hub of the universe, meeting everybody, knowing everybody, practising his art on the boards, exercising his wits in the streets, and even getting access to the palace of the queen. Meanwhile his extraordinarily gifted sister, let us suppose, remained at home. She was as adventurous, as imaginative, as agog to see the world as he was. But she was not sent to school. She had no chance of learning grammar and logic, let alone of reading Horace and Virgil. She picked up a book now and then, one of her brother's perhaps, and read a few pages. But then her parents came in and told her to mend the stockings or mind the stew and not moon about with books and papers. They would have spoken sharply but kindly, for they were substantial people who knew the conditions of life for a woman and loved their daughter — indeed, more likely than not she was the apple of her father's eye. Perhaps she scribbled some pages up in an apple loft on the sly, but was careful to hide them or set fire to them. Soon, however, before she was out of her teens, she was to be betrothed to the son of a neighbouring wool-stapler. She

3

cried out that marriage was hateful to her, and for that she was severely beaten by her father. Then he ceased to scold her. He begged her instead not to hurt him, not to shame him in this matter of her marriage. He would give her a chain of beads or a fine petticoat, he said; and there were tears in his eyes. How could she disobey him? How could she break his heart? The force of her own gift alone drove her to it. She made up a small parcel of her belongings, let herself down by a rope one summer's night and took the road to London. She was not seventeen. The birds that sang in the hedge were not more musical than she was. She had the quickest fancy, a gift like her brother's, for the tune of words. Like him, she had a taste for the theatre. She stood at the stage door; she wanted to act, she said. Men laughed in her face. The manager — a fat, loose-lipped man — guffawed. He bellowed something about poodles dancing and women acting — no woman, he said, could possibly be an actress. He hinted — you can imagine what. She could get no training in her craft. Could she even seek her dinner in a tavern or roam the streets at midnight? Yet her genius was for fiction and lusted to feed abundantly upon the lives of men and women and the study of their ways. At last — for she was very young, oddly like Shakespeare the poet in her face, with the same grey eyes and rounded brows — at last Nick Greene the actor-manager took pity on her; she found herself with child by that gentleman and so — who shall measure the heat and violence of the poet's heart when caught and tangled in a woman's body? — killed herself one winter's night and lies buried at some cross-roads where the omnibuses now stop outside the Elephant and Castle.

4   That, more or less, is how the story would run, I think, if a woman in Shakespeare's day had had Shakespeare's genius. But for my part, I agree with the deceased bishop, if such he was — it is unthinkable that any woman in Shakespeare's day should have had Shakespeare's genius. For genius like Shakespeare's is not born among labouring, uneducated, servile people. It was not born in England among the Saxons and the Britons. It is not born today among the working classes. How, then, could it have been born among women whose work began, according to Professor Trevelyan, almost before they were out of the nursery, who were forced to it by their parents and held to it by all the power of law and custom?

⎯⎯ CONSIDERATIONS ⎯⎯⎯⎯⎯⎯⎯⎯⎯⎯⎯⎯⎯⎯⎯⎯⎯⎯⎯⎯⎯⎯

1. In Paragraph 3, Woolf develops at length an imaginary sister of Shakespeare. Why does the writer call that sister Judith rather than Priscilla or Elizabeth or Megan? A quick look at Shakespeare's biography will give you the answer and alert you to a mischievous side of Woolf.

2. At the end of Paragraph 2, Woolf says, "How the borders of ignorance shrank back at their approach!" Is this a straight statement, or does she mean something other than what the words say? Study the differences among the following terms, what are often used mistakenly as synonyms: sarcasm, satire, irony, wit, humor, cynicism, invective, the sardonic.

3. Woolf's essay consists of four paragraphs, one of which accounts for more than half of the composition. Can you find a justification for this disproportionately long paragraph?

4. Concoct an imaginary biography like Woolf's account of Judith: for example, Mozart's daughter, Napoleon's father, the brother of Jesus Christ, the Queen of Luxembourg, Tolstoi's nephew or niece. Have a point to make.

5. ". . . for fiction . . . is not dropped like a pebble upon the ground, as science may be . . ." (Paragraph 1). In what sense is science dropped like a pebble upon the ground? What is the point of this odd comparison?

6. If you were to invite three authors from this book to an informal discussion of Woolf's essay, which would you select? Why? Make your selections on the basis of some relationship between their ideas and hers. What sort of outcome would you expect from such a conversation? Write a page of this dialogue.

7. Woolf wrote in the informal idiom of an educated Englishwoman of the 1920s; there are a number of differences between her language and ours. Circle a half dozen such differences and contrast British English with American English.

Richard Wright (1908–1960) was born on a plantation in Natchez, Mississippi. A restless and unruly child, at fifteen he left home and supported himself doing unskilled work, gradually improving his employment until he became a clerk in a post office. In this essay from his autobiography Black Boy *(1944) he writes about an occasion that transformed his life. By chance he became obsessed with the notion of reading H. L. Mencken, the iconoclastic editor and essayist. (See Mencken's "Gamalielese" on pages 245–248.) He schemed and plotted to borrow Mencken's books from the library, and when he succeeded, his career as a writer began.*

Determined to be a writer, Richard Wright worked on the Federal Writers' Project, wrote for the New Masses, *and finally won a prize from* Story *magazine for a short novel called* Uncle Tom's Children. *The following year, he was awarded a Guggenheim Fellowship, and in 1940 he published his novel* Native Son, *which has become an American classic. In 1946 he emigrated to Paris, where he lived until his death. His later novels included* The Outsider *(1953) and* The Long Dream *(1958). In 1977, his publisher issued the second half of* Black Boy, *entitled* American Hunger.

82

RICHARD WRIGHT
The Library Card

One morning I arrived early at work and went into the bank   1
lobby where the Negro porter was mopping. I stood at a counter and
picked up the Memphis *Commercial Appeal* and began my free reading of the press. I came finally to the editorial page and saw an article
dealing with one H. L. Mencken. I knew by hearsay that he was the
editor of the *American Mercury*, but aside from that I knew nothing
about him. The article was a furious denunciation of Mencken, concluding with one, hot, short sentence: Mencken is a fool.

I wondered what on earth this Mencken had done to call down   2
upon him the scorn of the South. The only people I had ever heard
denounced in the South were Negroes, and this man was not a Negro.
Then what ideas did Mencken hold that made a newspaper like the
Commercial Appeal castigate him publicly? Undoubtedly he must be
advocating ideas that the South did not like. Were there, then, people
other than Negroes who criticized the South? I knew that during the
Civil War the South had hated northern whites, but I had not encountered such hate during my life. Knowing no more of Mencken than I
did at that moment, I felt a vague sympathy for him. Had not the
South, which had assigned me the role of a non-man, cast at him its
hardest words?

Now, how could I find out about this Mencken? There was a   3
huge library near the riverfront, but I knew that Negroes were not
allowed to patronize its shelves any more than they were the parks
and playgrounds of the city. I had gone into the library several times
to get books for the white men on the job. Which of them would now

help me to get books? And how could I read them without causing concern to the white men with whom I worked? I had so far been successful in hiding my thoughts and feelings from them, but I knew that I would create hostility if I went about the business of reading in a clumsy way.

4   I weighed the personalities of the men on the job. There was Don, a Jew; but I distrusted him. His position was not much better than mine and I knew that he was uneasy and insecure; he had always treated me in an offhand, bantering way that barely concealed his contempt. I was afraid to ask him to help me get books; his frantic desire to demonstrate a racial solidarity with the whites against Negroes might make him betray me.

5   Then how about the boss? No, he was a Baptist and I had the suspicion that he would not be quite able to comprehend why a black boy would want to read Mencken. There were other white men on the job whose attitudes showed clearly that they were Kluxers or sympathizers, and they were out of the question.

6   There remained only one man whose attitude did not fit into an anti-Negro category, for I had heard the white men refer to him as a "Pope lover." He was an Irish Catholic and was hated by the white Southerners. I knew that he read books, because I had got him volumes from the library several times. Since he, too, was an object of hatred, I felt that he might refuse me but would hardly betray me. I hesitated, weighing and balancing the imponderable realities.

7   One morning I paused before the Catholic fellow's desk.

8   "I want to ask you a favor," I whispered to him.

9   "What is it?"

10   "I want to read. I can't get books from the library. I wonder if you'd let me use your card?"

11   He looked at me suspiciously.

12   "My card is full most of the time," he said.

13   "I see," I said and waited, posing my question silently.

14   "You're not trying to get me into trouble, are you, boy?" he asked, staring at me.

15   "Oh, no, sir."

16   "What book do you want?"

17   "A book by H. L. Mencken."

18   "Which one?"

19   "I don't know. Has he written more than one?"

20   "He has written several."

21   "I didn't know that."

"What makes you want to read Mencken?" 22

"Oh, I just saw his name in the newspaper," I said. 23

"It's good of you to want to read," he said. "But you ought to read 24
the right things."

I said nothing. Would he want to supervise my reading? 25

"Let me think," he said. "I'll figure out something." 26

I turned from him and he called me back. He stared at me quiz- 27
zically.

"Richard, don't mention this to the other white men," he said. 28

"I understand," I said. "I won't say a word." 29

A few days later he called me to him. 30

"I've got a card in my wife's name," he said. "Here's mine." 31

"Thank you, sir." 32

"Do you think you can manage it?" 33

"I'll manage fine," I said. 34

"If they suspect you, you'll get in trouble," he said. 35

"I'll write the same kind of notes to the library that you wrote 36
when you sent me for books," I told him. "I'll sign your name."

He laughed. 37

"Go ahead. Let me see what you get," he said. 38

That afternoon I addressed myself to forging a note. Now, what 39
were the names of books written by H. L. Mencken? I did not know
any of them. I finally wrote what I thought would be a foolproof note:
Dear Madam: Will you please let this nigger boy — I used the word
"nigger" to make the librarian feel that I could not possibly be the
author of the note — *have some books by H. L. Mencken?* I forged the
white man's name.

I entered the library as I had always done when on errands for 40
whites, but I felt that I would somehow slip up and betray myself. I
doffed my hat, stood a respectful distance from the desk, looked as
unbookish as possible, and waited for the white patrons to be taken
care of. When the desk was clear of people, I still waited. The white
librarian looked at me.

"What do you want, boy?" 41

As though I did not possess the power of speech, I stepped forward 42
and simply handed her the forged note, not parting my lips.

"What books by Mencken does he want?" she asked. 43

"I don't know, ma'am," I said, avoiding her eyes. 44

"Who gave you this card?" 45

"Mr. Falk," I said. 46

"Where is he?" 47

48   "He's at work, at the M—— Optical Company," I said. "I've been in here for him before."

49   "I remember," the woman said. "But he never wrote notes like this."

50   Oh, God, she's suspicious. Perhaps she would not let me have the books? If she had turned her back at that moment, I would have ducked out the door and never gone back. Then I thought of a bold idea.

51   "You can call him up, ma'am," I said, my heart pounding.

52   "You're not using these books, are you?" she asked pointedly.

53   "Oh, no, ma'am. I can't read."

54   "I don't know what he wants by Mencken," she said under her breath.

55   I knew now that I had won; she was thinking of other things and the race question had gone out of her mind. She went to the shelves. Once or twice she looked over her shoulder at me, as though she was still doubtful. Finally she came forward with two books in her hand.

56   "I'm sending him two books," she said. "But tell Mr. Falk to come in next time, or send me the names of the books he wants. I don't know what he wants to read."

57   I said nothing She stamped the card and handed me the books. Not daring to glance at them, I went out of the library, fearing that the woman would call me back for further questioning. A block away from the library I opened one of the books and read a title: *A Book of Prefaces*. I was nearing my nineteenth birthday and I did not know how to pronounce the word "preface." I thumbed the pages and saw strange words and strange names. I shook my head, disappointed. I looked at the other book; it was called *Prejudices*. I knew what that word meant; I had heard it all my life. And right off I was on guard against Mencken's books. Why would a man want to call a book *Prejudices?* The word was so stained with all my memories of racial hate that I could not conceive of anybody using it for a title. Perhaps I had made a mistake about Mencken? A man who had prejudices must be wrong.

58   When I showed the books to Mr. Falk, he looked at me and frowned.

59   "That librarian might telephone you," I warned him.

60   "That's all right," he said. "But when you're through reading those books, I want you to tell me what you get out of them."

61   That night in my rented room, while letting the hot water run over my can of pork and beans in the sink, I opened *A Book of Prefaces*

and began to read. I was jarred and shocked by the style, the clear, clean sweeping sentences. Why did he write like that? And how did one write like that? I pictured the man as a raging demon, slashing with his pen, consumed with hate, denouncing everything American, extolling everything European or German, laughing at the weaknesses of people, mocking God, authority. What was this? I stood up, trying to realize what reality lay behind the meaning of the words . . . Yes, this man was fighting, fighting with words. He was using words as a weapon, using them as one would use a club. Could words be weapons? Well, yes, for here they were. Then, maybe, perhaps, I could use them as a weapon? No. It frightened me. I read on and what amazed me was not what he said, but how on earth anybody had the courage to say it.

Occasionally I glanced up to reassure myself that I was alone in   62
the room. Who were these men about whom Mencken was talking so passionately? Who was Anatole France? Joseph Conrad? Sinclair Lewis, Sherwood Anderson, Dostoevski, George Moore, Gustave Flaubert, Maupassant, Tolstoy, Frank Harris, Mark Twain, Thomas Hardy, Arnold Bennett, Stephen Crane, Zola, Norris, Gorky, Bergson, Ibsen, Balzac, Bernard Shaw, Dumas, Poe, Thomas Mann, O. Henry, Dreiser, H. G. Wells, Gogol, T. S. Eliot, Gide, Baudelaire, Edgar Lee Masters, Stendhal, Turgenev, Huneker, Nietzsche, and scores of others? Were these men real? Did they exist or had they existed? And how did one pronounce their names?

I ran across many words whose meanings I did not know, and I   63
either looked them up in a dictionary or, before I had a chance to do that, encountered the word in a context that made its meaning clear. But what strange world was this? I concluded the book with the conviction that I had somehow overlooked something terribly important in life. I had once tried to write, had once reveled in feeling, had let my crude imagination roam, but the impulse to dream had been slowly beaten out of me by experience. Now it surged up again and I hungered for books, new ways of looking and seeing. It was not a matter of believing or disbelieving what I read, but of feeling something new, of being affected by something that made the look of the world different.

As dawn broke I ate my pork and beans, feeling dopey, sleepy. I   64
went to work, but the mood of the book would not die; it lingered, coloring everything I saw, heard, did. I now felt that I knew what the white men were feeling. Merely because I had read a book that had spoken of how they lived and thought, I identified myself with that

book. I felt vaguely guilty. Would I, filled with bookish notions, act in a manner that would make the whites dislike me?

65   I forged more notes and my trips to the library became frequent. Reading grew into a passion. My first serious novel was Sinclair Lewis's *Main Street.* It made me see my boss, Mr. Gerald, and identify him as an American type. I would smile when I saw him lugging his golf bags into the office. I had always felt a vast distance separating me from the boss, and now I felt closer to him, though still distant. I felt now that I knew him, that I could feel the very limits of his narrow life. And this had happened because I had read a novel about a mythical man called George F. Babbitt.

66   The plots and stories in the novels did not interest me so much as the point of view revealed. I gave myself over to each novel without reserve, without trying to criticize it; it was enough for me to see and feel something different. And for me, everything was something different. Reading was like a drug, a dope. The novels created moods in which I lived for days. But I could not conquer my sense of guilt, my feeling that the white men around me knew that I was changing, that I had begun to regard them differently.

67   Whenever I brought a book to the job, I wrapped it in newspaper — a habit that was to persist for years in other cities and under other circumstances. But some of the white men pried into my packages when I was absent and they questioned me.

68   "Boy, what are you reading those books for?"

69   "Oh, I don't know, sir."

70   "That's deep stuff you're reading, boy."

71   "I'm just killing time, sir."

72   "You'll addle your brains if you don't watch out."

73   I read Dreiser's *Jennie Gerhardt* and *Sister Carrie* and they revived in me a vivid sense of my mother's suffering; I was overwhelmed. I grew silent, wondering about the life around me. It would have been impossible for me to have told anyone what I derived from these novels, for it was nothing less than a sense of life itself. All my life had shaped me for the realism, the naturalism of the modern novel, and I could not read enough of them.

74   Steeped in new moods and ideas, I bought a ream of paper and tried to write; but nothing would come, or what did come was flat beyond telling. I discovered that more than desire and feeling were necessary to write and I dropped the idea. Yet I still wondered how it was possible to know people sufficiently to write about them? Could I ever learn about life and people? To me, with my vast ignorance, my

Jim Crow station in life, it seemed a task impossible of achievement. I now knew what being a Negro meant. I could endure the hunger. I had learned to live with hate. But to feel that there were feelings denied me, that the very breath of life itself was beyond my reach, that more than anything else hurt, wounded me. I had a new hunger.

In buoying me up, reading also cast me down, made me see what   75 was possible, what I had missed. My tension returned, new, terrible, bitter, surging, almost too great to be contained. I no longer *felt* that the world about me was hostile, killing; I *knew* it. A million times I asked myself what I could do to save myself, and there were no answers. I seemed forever condemned, ringed by walls.

I did not discuss my reading with Mr. Falk, who had lent me his   76 library card; it would have meant talking about myself and that would have been too painful. I smiled each day, fighting desperately to maintain my old behavior, to keep my disposition seemingly sunny. But some of the white men discerned that I had begun to brood.

"Wake up there, boy!" Mr. Olin said one day.   77

"Sir!" I answered for the lack of a better word.   78

"You act like you've stolen something," he said.   79

I laughed in the way I knew he expected me to laugh, but I   80 resolved to be more conscious of myself, to watch my every act, to guard and hide the new knowledge that was dawning within me.

If I went north, would it be possible for me to build a new life   81 then? But how could a man build a life upon vague, unformed yearnings? I wanted to write and I did not even know the English language. I bought English grammars and found them dull. I felt that I was getting a better sense of the language from novels than from grammars. I read hard, discarding a writer as soon as I felt that I had grasped his point of view. At night the printed page stood before my eyes in sleep.

Mrs. Moss, my landlady, asked me one Sunday morning: 82

"Son. what is this you keep on reading?"   83

"Oh, nothing. Just novels."   84

"What you get out of 'em?"   85

"I'm just killing time," I said.   86

"I hope you know your own mind," she said in a tone which   87 implied that she doubted if I had a mind.

I knew of no Negroes who read the books I liked and I wondered   88 if any Negroes ever thought of them. I knew that there were Negro doctors, lawyers, newspapermen, but I never saw any of them. When I read a Negro newspaper I never caught the faintest echo of my preoccupation in its pages. I felt trapped and occasionally, for a few days, I would stop reading. But a vague hunger would come over me for books, books that opened up new avenues of feeling and seeing, and again I would forge another note to the white librarian. Again I would read and wonder as only the naïve and unlettered can read and wonder, feeling that I carried a secret, criminal burden about with me each day.

89   That winter my mother and brother came and we set up house-keeping, buying furniture on the installment plan, being cheated and yet knowing no way to avoid it. I began to eat warm food and to my surprise found that regular meals enabled me to read faster. I may have lived through many illnesses and survived them, never suspecting that I was ill. My brother obtained a job and we began to save toward the trip north, plotting our time, setting tentative dates for departure. I told none of the white men on the job that I was planning to go north; I knew that the moment they felt I was thinking of the North they would change toward me. It would have made them feel that I did not like the life I was living, and because my life was completely conditioned by what they said or did, it would have been tantamount to challenging them.

90   I could calculate my chances for life in the South as a Negro fairly clearly now.

91   I could fight the southern whites by organizing with other Negroes, as my grandfather had done. But I knew that I could never win that way; there were many whites and there were but few blacks. They were strong and we were weak. Outright black rebellion could never win. If I fought openly I would die and I did not want to die. News of lynchings were frequent.

92   I could submit and live the life of a genial slave, but that was impossible. All of my life had shaped me to live by my own feelings, and thoughts. I could make up to Bess and marry her and inherit the house. But that, too, would be the life of a slave; if I did that, I would crush to death something within me, and I would hate myself as much as I knew the whites already hated those who had submitted. Neither could I ever willingly present myself to be kicked, as Shorty had done. I would rather have died than do that.

93   I could drain off my restlessness by fighting with Shorty and Harrison. I had seen many Negroes solve the problem of being black by transferring their hatred of themselves to others with a black skin and fighting them. I would have to be cold to do that, and I was not cold and I could never be.

94   I could, of course, forget what I had read, thrust the whites out of

my mind, forget them; and find release from anxiety and longing in sex and alcohol. But the memory of how my father had conducted himself made that course repugnant. If I did not want others to violate my life, how could I voluntarily violate it myself?

I had no hope whatever of being a professional man. Not only had I been so conditioned that I did not desire it, but the fulfillment of such an ambition was beyond my capabilities. Well-to-do Negroes lived in a world that was almost as alien to me as the world inhabited by whites. 95

What, then, was there? I held my life in my mind, in my consciousness each day, feeling at times that I would stumble and drop it, spill it forever. My reading had created a vast sense of distance between me and the world in which I lived and tried to make a living, and that sense of distance was increasing each day. My days and nights were e long, quiet, continuously contained dream of terror, tension, and anxiety. I wondered how long I could bear it. 96

———— CONSIDERATIONS ————————————————

1. How do you heat a can of beans if you don't have a hot plate or a stove? How is Wright's answer to this question an autobiographical fact that might affect your appreciation of his essay?

2. In Paragraph 65, Wright says of himself, "Reading grew into a passion." You don't have to look too far in the lives of other writers to find similar statements about reading. Reread the first paragraph of the Preface to this book, and think about the importance of reading to your prospects of improving as a writer. See also Ralph Ellison's "On Becoming a Writer" (pages 118–125).

3. Compare what Wright had to endure to use the public library with your own introduction to the same institution. How do you account for the motivation Wright needed to break the barriers between him and freedom to read?

4. The word Wright uses throughout to refer to his own race is no longer widely accepted. Why? What other words have been used at other times in American history? What difference does a name make?

5. Notice how Wright uses dialogue in this essay. How do you decide when to use dialogue? What are its purposes?

6. The authors mentioned by Wright in his essay would make a formidable reading program for anyone. If you were to lay out such a program for yourself, what titles would you include? Why?

A Rhetorical Index

The various writing patterns — argument and persuasion, description, exposition, and narration — are amply illustrated in the many essays, stories, journal entries, and poems in *A Writer's Reader*. If any classification of writing according to type is suspect — because good writers inevitably merge the types — this index offers one plausible arrangement. Anyone looking for models or examples for study and imitation may well begin here.

A word about subcategories: We index two sorts of argument — formal and implicit — because some selections are obvious attempts to defend a stated proposition, often in high style, whereas others argue indirectly, informally, or diffusely, but persuasively nonetheless. Under "Description" we index not only whole selections, but also sections within selections that primarily describe persons, places, or miscellaneous phenomena. We call "Expository" selections those that clearly show the various rhetorical patterns of development: example, classification, cause and effect, comparison and contrast, process analysis, and definition. Again, both whole selections and separate paragraphs are listed. "Narration" categorizes memoirs, essays, stories, and nonfiction nonautobiographical narratives.

We have starred short selections (under 1,200 words). Numbers in parentheses refer to paragraph numbers within selections. At the end, we list the non-essay materials in the *Reader* — journal entries, short stories, poems, and drama.

ARGUMENT AND PERSUASION

Formal, Overt
    BERRY, *A Good Scythe,* 39–42
    BERRY, *In Defense of Literacy,* 44–47
    BERRY, *The Reactor and the Garden,* 48–55
    BIRD, *Where College Fails Us,* 62–72

GOULD, *The Politics of Census*, 154–159
GOULD, *Phyletic Size Decrease in Hershey Bars*, 161–166
GOULD, *Wide Hats and Narrow Minds*, 167–172
JACOBS, *Paradoxes of Size*, 201–206
JEFFERSON, *The Declaration of Independence*, 208–213
LAKOFF, *You Are What You Say*, 214–220
LAWRENCE, *Pornography*, 223–226
*MARVELL, *To His Coy Mistress*, 243–244
MENCKEN, *Gamalielese*, 245–248
O'CONNOR, *The Total Effect and the Eighth Grade*, 263–266
ORWELL, *Politics and the English Language*, 294–306
*PIRSIG, *The Church of Reason*, 322–324
PORTER, *The Necessary Enemy*, 333–337
SCHUMACHER, *Production in Service to Life*, 355–361
SWIFT, *A Modest Proposal*, 379–386
*VIDAL, *Drugs*, 426–428
*WELTY, *The Point of the Story*, 438–440

Informal, Subdued, Oblique, Elliptical, Implied
BALDWIN, *Autobiographical Notes*, 33–37
*BIERCE, *Some Devil's Definitions*, 57–60
DOUGLASS, *Plantation Life*, 109–113
EPHRON, *A Few Words about Breasts*, 126–133
*FROST, *The Gift Outright*, 149
GANSBURG, *38 Who Saw Murder Didn't Call the Police*, 150–153
*HUGHES, *Salvation*, 192–194
*LINCOLN, *The Gettysburg Address*, 228–229
*MORGAN, *Exam-Week Unrealities*, 250–251
O'CONNOR, *From Flannery O'Connor's Letters*, 284–290
ORWELL, *Shooting an Elephant*, 308–314
ORWELL, *A Hanging*, 316–320
RODRIGUEZ, *Does America Still Exist?* 347–351
SHARP, *Under the Hood*, 363–371
STAFFORD, *A Way of Writing*, 372–377
TERKEL, *Phil Stallings, Spot Welder*, 388–393
*THOMAS, *On Smell*, 394–397
THOMAS, *Ceti*, 398–401
*THOMAS, *Notes on Punctuation*, 402–404
*THURBER, *Which*, 410–412
*WHITE, *The Wild Flag*, 450–451
*WOOLF, *If Shakespeare Had Had a Sister*, 462–464

DESCRIPTION

Abstract Conditions, Institutions, Phenomena, Events, Creatures
    AUSTIN, *The Scavengers*, 27–31
    BERRY, *A Good Scythe*, 39–42
    *BISHOP, *The Fish*, 73–75
    *BLEIBTREU, *The Moment of Being*, 76–78
    CONROY, *A Yo-Yo Going Down*, 84–91
    *DICKINSON, *There's a certain Slant of light*, 92–93
    DILLARD, *Sojourner*, 105–108
    DOUGLASS, *Plantation Life*, 109–113
    ELLISON, *On Becoming a Writer*, 118–125
    EPHRON, *A Few Words about Breasts*, 126–133
    GANSBURG, *38 Who Saw Murder Didn't Call the Police*, 150–153
    GOULD, *The Politics of Census*, 154–159
    GOULD, *Phyletic Size Decrease in Hershey Bars*, 161–166
    HAINES, *Lost*, 174–177
    JACOBS, *Paradoxes of Size*, 201–206
    MENCKEN, *Gamalielese*, 245–248
    MORRIS, *Odd Balls*, 252–257
    *NIN, *Journal Entry*, 260–261
    ORWELL, *Politics and the English Language*, 294–306
    ORWELL, *Shooting an Elephant*, 308–314
    ORWELL, *A Hanging*, 316–320
    *PIRSIG, *The Church of Reason*, 322–324
    PLATH, *Journal Entries*, 325–329
    PORTER, *The Necessary Enemy*, 333–337
    SCHUMACHER, *Production in Service to Life*, 355–361
    *SHAKESPEARE, *That time of year thou mayst in me behold*, 362
    SHARP, *Under the Hood*, 363–371
    STAFFORD, *A Way of Writing*, 372–377
    *THOMAS, *On Smell*, 394–397
    THOMAS, *Ceti*, 398–401
    *THOMAS, *Notes on Punctuation*, 402–404
    *THOREAU, *Thinking Like a Bream*, 407–408
    *THURBER, *Which*, 410–412
    WHITE, *Once More to the Lake*, 443–448
    *WHITE, *The Wild Flag*, 450–451
    *WOOLF, *If Shakespeare Had Had a Sister*, 462–464

Persons
    ADAMS, *Winter and Summer*, 1–6
    ANGELOU, *Mr. Red Leg*, 21–26

CATTON, *Grant and Lee*, 79–82
CONROY, *A Yo-Yo Going Down* (12–69), 84–91
*DOUGLASS, *Plantation Life* (5–6), 109–113
*HELLMAN, *Runaway* (1–2), 178–184
HEMINGWAY, *Hills Like White Elephants*, 186–190
*HUGHES, *Salvation*, 192–194
O'CONNOR, *A Good Man Is Hard to Find*, 267–281
PLATH, *Journal Entries*, 325–329
TERKEL, *Phil Stallings, Spot Welder*, 388–393
UPDIKE, *Ace in the Hole*, 417–425
WELTY, *A Worn Path*, 429–437
*WOOLF, *If Shakespeare Had Had a Sister*, 462–464

Places
ADAMS, *Winter and Summer*, 1–6
AGEE, *Knoxville: Summer 1915*, 7–11
AUSTIN, *The Scavengers*, 27–31
*DILLARD, *Strangers to Darkness*, 102–104
DOUGLASS, *Plantation Life*, 109–113
*EISELEY, *More Thoughts on Wilderness*, 115–117
HEMINGWAY, *Hills Like White Elephants*, 186–190
*MAILER, *A Walk on the Moon* (18), 235–241
*THOMAS, *Ceti* (4), 398–401
WHITE, *Once More to the Lake*, 443–448
*WOLFE, *Journal Entries*, 454–460

EXPOSITION

Analogy (see Comparison, Contrast, Analogy)

Cause and Effect
*ADAMS, *Winter and Summer* (7–8), 1–6
*FROST, *The Gift Outright*, 149
GOULD, *The Politics of Census*, 154–159
GOULD, *Phyletic Size Decrease in Hershey Bars*, 161–166
JACOBS, *Paradoxes of Size*, 201–206
JEFFERSON, *The Declaration of Independence*, 208–213
LAKOFF, *You Are What You Say*, 214–220
LAWRENCE, *Pornography*, 223–226
*MARVELL, *To His Coy Mistress*, 243–244
O'CONNOR, *The Total Effect and the Eighth Grade*, 263–266
RETTIE, *"But a Watch in the Night": A Scientific Fable*, 340–345
*SAGAN, *The Measure of Eratosthenes*, 352–354

*SHARP, *Under the Hood,* 363–371
SWIFT, *A Modest Proposal,* 379–386
*VIDAL, *Drugs,* 426–428
*WOOLF, *If Shakespeare Had Had a Sister,* 462–464

Classification and Division
    ADAMS, *Winter and Summer,* 1–6
    AUSTIN, *The Scavengers,* 27–31
    McPHEE, *Ancestors of the Jump Shot,* 230–233
    MORRIS, *Odd Balls,* 252–257
    ORWELL, *Politics and the English Language,* 294–306
    *THOMAS, *Notes on Punctuation,* 402–404

Comparison, Contrast, Analogy
    ADAMS, *Winter and Summer,* 1–6
    AGEE, *Knoxville: Summer 1915,* 7–11
    BERRY, *A Good Scythe,* 39–42
    BERRY, *The Reactor and the Garden,* 48–55
    *BLEIBTREU, *The Moment of Being,* 76–78
    CATTON, *Grant and Lee,* 79–82
    DILLARD, *Sojourner,* 105–108
    *JACOBS, *Paradoxes of Size (1–4),* 201–206
    LAKOFF, *You Are What You Say,* 214–220
    McPHEE, *Ancestors of the Jump Shot,* 230–233
    *MAILER, *A Walk on the Moon (11–12),* 235–241
    *MORGAN, *Exam-Week Unrealities,* 250–251
    MORRIS, *Odd Balls,* 252–257
    *PIRSIG, *The Church of Reason,* 322–324
    RETTIE, *"But a Watch in the Night": A Scientific Fable,* 340–345
    RODRIGUEZ, *Does America Still Exist?* 347–351
    *SCHUMACHER, *Production in Service to Life (12–17),* 355–361
    *SHAKESPEARE, *That time of year thou mayst in me behold,* 362
    *SHARP, *Under the Hood (8–9),* 363–371
    *THOMAS, *Ceti (5),* 398–401
    WELTY, *A Worn Path,* 429–437
    *WELTY, *The Point of the Story,* 438–440
    *WHITE, *The Wild Flag,* 450–451
    *WOOLF, *If Shakespeare Had Had a Sister,* 462–464

Definition
    *BERRY, *In Defense of Literacy (2),* 44–47
    *BIERCE, *Some Devil's Definitions,* 57–60
    *BIRD, *Where College Fails Us (5–6),* 62–72
    *DILLARD, *Sojourner (10–16),* 105–108

*FEIFFER, *Superman,* 145–148
*FROST, *The Gift Outright,* 149
 GOULD, *The Politics of Census,* 154–159
 LAKOFF, *You Are What You Say,* 214–220
 LAWRENCE, *Pornography,* 223–226
 MENCKEN, *Gamalielese,* 245–248
 MORRIS, *Odd Balls,* 252–257
*PIRSIG, *The Church of Reason,* 322–324
 PORTER, *The Necessary Enemy,* 333–337
 RETTIE, *"But a Watch in the Night": A Scientific Fable,* 340–345
 RODRIGUEZ, *Does America Still Exist?* 347–351
 SCHUMACHER, *Production in Service to Life,* 355–361
*SHARP, *Under the Hood (10),* 363–371
 STAFFORD, *A Way of Writing,* 372–377
*THOMAS, *On Smell,* 394–397
*THOMAS, *Notes on Punctuation,* 402–404

Example
 BIRD, *Where College Fails Us,* 62–72
*BLEIBTREU, *The Moment of Being,* 76–78
 DIDION, *On Keeping a Notebook,* 94–100
 GOULD, *Phyletic Size Decrease in Hershey Bars,* 161–166
 GOULD, *Wide Hats and Narrow Minds,* 167–172
 JACOBS, *Paradoxes of Size,* 201–206
 JEFFERSON, *The Declaration of Independence,* 208–213
 LAKOFF, *You Are What You Say,* 214–220
 MENCKEN, *Gamalielese,* 245–248
 MORRIS, *Odd Balls,* 252–257
 ORWELL, *Politics and the English Language,* 294–306
 PORTER, *The Necessary Enemy,* 333–337
 RETTIE, *"But a Watch in the Night": A Scientific Fable,* 340–345
 RODRIGUEZ, *Does America Still Exist?* 347–351
*SAGAN, *The Measure of Eratosthenes,* 352–354
*SHARP, *Under the Hood (21–23),* 363–371
 STAFFORD, *A Way of Writing,* 372–377
*THOMAS, *Notes on Punctuation,* 402–404

Process Analysis
 CONROY, *A Yo-Yo Going Down,* 84–91
*DILLARD, *Sojourner (3–8),* 105–108
*EISELEY, *More Thoughts on Wilderness,* 115–117
 McPHEE, *Ancestors of the Jump Shot,* 230–233
 MAILER, *A Walk on the Moon,* 235–241
 MORRIS, *Odd Balls,* 252–257

RETTIE, *"But a Watch in the Night": A Scientific Fable*, 340–345
•SAGAN, *The Measure of Eratosthenes*, 352–354
•SHARP, *Under the Hood (10–12)*, 363–371
STAFFORD, *A Way of Writing*, 372–377
•THOMAS, *On Smell (4)*, 394–397

NARRATION

Autobiography and Memoir
ADAMS, *Winter and Summer*, 1–6
AGEE, *Knoxville: Summer 1915*, 7–11
ANGELOU, *Mr. Red Leg*, 21–26
BALDWIN, *Autobiographical Notes*, 33–37
CONROY, *A Yo-Yo Going Down*, 84–91
ELLISON, *On Becoming a Writer*, 118–125
EPHRON, *A Few Words about Breasts*, 126–133
HAINES, *Lost*, 174–177
HELLMAN, *Runaway*, 178–184
HUGHES, *Salvation*, 192–194
ORWELL, *Shooting an Elephant*, 308–314
ORWELL, *A Hanging*, 316–320
PLATH, *Journal Entries*, 325–329
TERKEL, *Phil Stallings, Spot Welder*, 388–393
WHITE, *Once More to the Lake*, 443–448
WRIGHT, *The Library Card*, 467–475
Fiction
FAULKNER, *A Rose for Emily*, 135–143
HEMINGWAY, *Hills Like White Elephants*, 186–190
HUGHES, *Feet Live Their Own Life*, 197–199
O'CONNOR, *A Good Man Is Hard to Find*, 267–281
UPDIKE, *Ace in the Hole*, 417–425
WELTY, *A Worn Path*, 429–437

Nonfiction
GANSBURG, *38 Who Saw Murder Didn't Call the Police*, 150–153
MAILER, *A Walk on the Moon*, 235–241
RETTIE, *"But a Watch in the Night": A Scientific Fable*, 340–345

JOURNALS, DIARIES, NOTEBOOKS, SHORT TAKES

BIERCE, *Some Devil's Definitions*, 57–60
DIDION, *On Keeping a Notebook*, 94–100

NIN, *Journal Entry*, 260–261
PLATH, *Journal Entries*, 325–329
THOREAU, *Thinking Like a Bream*, 407–408
TRILLIN, *Literally*, 413–416
WHITE, *The Wild Flag*, 450–451
WOLFE, *Journal Entries*, 454–460

SHORT STORIES

FAULKNER, *A Rose for Emily*, 135–143
HEMINGWAY, *Hills Like White Elephants*, 186–190
HUGHES, *Feet Live Their Own Life*, 197–199
O'CONNOR, *A Good Man Is Hard to Find*, 267–281
UPDIKE, *Ace in the Hole*, 417–425
WELTY, *A Worn Path*, 429–437

POEMS

BISHOP, *The Fish*, 73–75
DICKINSON, *There's a certain Slant of light*, 92–93
FROST, *The Gift Outright*, 149
HUGHES, *Two Poems*, 195–196
MARVELL, *To His Coy Mistress*, 243–244
PLATH, *The Bee Meeting*, 330–332
SHAKESPEARE, *That time of year thou mayst in me behold*, 362
STAFFORD, *Shadows*, 377

DRAMA

ALLEN, *Death Knocks*, 12–19

A Thematic Index

BIOGRAPHY, AUTOBIOGRAPHY, TRUE STORIES

ADAMS, *Winter and Summer*, 1–6
AGEE, *Knoxville: Summer 1915*, 7–11
ANGELOU, *Mr. Red Leg*, 21–26
BALDWIN, *Autobiographical Notes*, 33–37
CATTON, *Grant and Lee*, 79–82
CONROY, *A Yo-Yo Going Down*, 84–91
DOUGLASS, *Plantation Life*, 109–113
ELLISON, *On Becoming a Writer*, 118–125
EPHRON, *A Few Words about Breasts*, 126–133
HAINES, *Lost*, 174–177
HELLMAN, *Runaway*, 178–184
HUGHES, *Salvation*, 192–194
NIN, *Journal Entry*, 260–261
ORWELL, *Shooting an Elephant*, 308–314
ORWELL, *A Hanging*, 316–320
WHITE, *Once More to the Lake*, 443–448
WRIGHT, *The Library Card*, 467–475

CHILDHOOD, GROWING UP, RITES OF PASSAGE

ADAMS, *Winter and Summer*, 1–6
AGEE, *Knoxville: Summer 1915*, 7–11
ANGELOU, *Mr. Red Leg*, 21–26
CONROY, *A Yo-Yo Going Down*, 84–91
ELLISON, *On Becoming a Writer*, 118–125
EPHRON, *A Few Words about Breasts*, 126–133
HELLMAN, *Runaway*, 178–184
HUGHES, *Salvation*, 192–194
THOMAS, *On Smell*, 394–397

WHITE, *Once More to the Lake*, 443–448
WRIGHT, *The Library Card*, 467–475

CONTESTS, STRUGGLES, WINS AND LOSSES

ADAMS, *Winter and Summer*, 1–6
ALLEN, *Death Knocks*, 12–19
ANGELOU, *Mr. Red Leg*, 21–26
BISHOP, *The Fish*, 73–75
CATTON, *Grant and Lee*, 79–82
CONROY, *A Yo-Yo Going Down*, 84–91
FAULKNER, *A Rose for Emily*, 135–143
GANSBURG, *38 Who Saw Murder Didn't Call the Police*, 150–153
GOULD, *The Politics of Census*, 154–159
HELLMAN, *Runaway*, 178–184
HEMINGWAY, *Hills Like White Elephants*, 186–190
HUGHES, *Salvation*, 192–194
HUGHES, *Two Poems*, 195–196
MARVELL, *To His Coy Mistress*, 243–244
NIN, *Journal Entry*, 260–261
O'CONNOR, *A Good Man Is Hard to Find*, 267–281
O'CONNOR, *From Flannery O'Connor's Letters*, 284–290
ORWELL, *Shooting an Elephant*, 308–314
ORWELL, *A Hanging*, 316–320
PORTER, *The Necessary Enemy*, 333–337
TERKEL, *Phil Stallings, Spot Welder*, 388–393
UPDIKE, *Ace in the Hole*, 417–425
WELTY, *A Worn Path*, 429–437
WRIGHT, *The Library Card*, 467–475

EDUCATION, THE GETTING OF WISDOM

ADAMS, *Winter and Summer*, 1–6
ANGELOU, *Mr. Red Leg*, 21–26
BALDWIN, *Autobiographical Notes*, 33–37
BERRY, *A Good Scythe*, 39–42
BERRY, *In Defense of Literacy*, 44–47
BIERCE, *Some Devil's Definitions*, 57–60
BIRD, *Where College Fails Us*, 62–72
HELLMAN, *Runaway*, 178–184
MORGAN, *Exam-Week Unrealities*, 250–251
O'CONNOR, *The Total Effect and the Eighth Grade*, 263–266

ORWELL, *Shooting an Elephant*, 308–314
PIRSIG, *The Church of Reason*, 322–324
PORTER, *The Necessary Enemy*, 333–337
WELTY, *The Point of the Story*, 438–440
WRIGHT, *The Library Card*, 467–475

EPIPHANY, IMAGINATION, VISION

DICKINSON, *There's a certain Slant of light*, 92–93
DIDION, *On Keeping a Notebook*, 94–100
DILLARD, *Strangers to Darkness*, 102–104
DILLARD, *Sojourner*, 105–108
EISELEY, *More Thoughts on Wilderness*, 115–117
HAINES, *Lost*, 174–177
MAILER, *A Walk on the Moon*, 235–241
NIN, *Journal Entry*, 260–261
O'CONNOR, *A Good Man Is Hard to Find*, 267–281
PIRSIG, *The Church of Reason*, 322–324
STAFFORD, *A Way of Writing*, 372–377
THOMAS, *On Smell*, 394–397
THOMAS, *Ceti*, 398–401
THOREAU, *Thinking Like a Bream*, 407–408
WOLFE, *Journal Entries*, 454–460

FAMILIES, PARENTS AND OFFSPRING

ADAMS, *Winter and Summer*, 1–6
AGEE, *Knoxville: Summer 1915*, 7–11
FAULKNER, *A Rose for Emily*, 135–143
HELLMAN, *Runaway*, 178–184
O'CONNOR, *A Good Man Is Hard to Find*, 267–281
SWIFT, *A Modest Proposal*, 379–386
UPDIKE, *Ace in the Hole*, 417–425
WHITE, *Once More to the Lake*, 443–448
WOOLF, *If Shakespeare Had Had a Sister*, 462–464

FREEDOM AND RESTRAINT, OPPRESSORS AND OPPRESSED

ADAMS, *Winter and Summer*, 1–6
ANGELOU, *Mr. Red Leg*, 21–26

DOUGLASS, *Plantation Life*, 109–113
ELLISON, *On Becoming a Writer*, 118–125
FROST, *The Gift Outright*, 149
JEFFERSON, *The Declaration of Independence*, 208–213
LAWRENCE, *Pornography*, 223–226
ORWELL, *Shooting an Elephant*, 308–314
TERKEL, *Phil Stallings, Spot Welder*, 388–393
VIDAL, *Drugs*, 426–428
WOOLF, *If Shakespeare Had Had a Sister*, 462–464
WRIGHT, *The Library Card*, 467–475

HEROES, LEADERS, PERFORMERS

ADAMS, *Winter and Summer*, 1–6
ANGELOU, *Mr. Red Leg*, 21–26
CATTON, *Grant and Lee*, 79–82
CONROY, *A Yo-Yo Going Down*, 84–91
FEIFFER, *Superman*, 145–148
McPHEE, *Ancestors of the Jump Shot*, 230–233
MAILER, *A Walk on the Moon*, 235–241
ORWELL, *Shooting an Elephant*, 308–314
WELTY, *A Worn Path*, 429–437

HISTORY, THE POWER OF THE PAST

ADAMS, *Winter and Summer*, 1–6
AGEE, *Knoxville: Summer 1915*, 7–11
CATTON, *Grant and Lee*, 79–82
EISELEY, *More Thoughts on Wilderness*, 115–117
FAULKNER, *A Rose for Emily*, 135–143
FROST, *The Gift Outright*, 149
HUGHES, *Feet Live Their Own Life*, 197–199
JEFFERSON, *The Declaration of Independence*, 208–213
LINCOLN, *The Gettysburg Address*, 228–229
McPHEE, *Ancestors of the Jump Shot*, 230–233
O'CONNOR, *The Total Effect and the Eighth Grade*, 263–266
RETTIE, *"But a Watch in the Night": A Scientific Fable*, 340–345
THOMAS, *Ceti*, 398–401
WHITE, *Once More to the Lake*, 443–448
WHITE, *The Wild Flag*, 450–451
WOOLF, *If Shakespeare Had Had a Sister*, 462–464

HUMOR, WIT, SATIRE

ALLEN, *Death Knocks*, 12–19
ANGELOU, *Mr. Red Leg*, 21–26
BIERCE, *Some Devil's Definitions*, 57–60
DIDION, *On Keeping a Notebook*, 94–100
EPHRON, *A Few Words about Breasts*, 126–133
FEIFFER, *Superman*, 145–148
GOULD, *Phyletic Size Decrease in Hershey Bars*, 161–166
HUGHES, *Feet Live Their Own Lives*, 197–199
MARVELL, *To His Coy Mistress*, 243–244
MENCKEN, *Gamalielese*, 245–248
MORRIS, *Odd Balls*, 252–257
O'CONNOR, *A Good Man Is Hard to Find*, 267–281
SWIFT, *A Modest Proposal*, 379–386
THOMAS, *Notes on Punctuation*, 402–404
THURBER, *Which*, 410–412
TRILLIN, *Literally*, 413–416
WHITE, *Once More to the Lake*, 443–448
WHITE, *The Wild Flag*, 450–451

THE IMPORTANCE OF PLACE, "ROOTS"

ADAMS, *Winter and Summer*, 1–6
AGEE, *Knoxville: Summer 1915*, 7–11
ANGELOU, *Mr. Red Leg*, 21–26
BALDWIN, *Autobiographical Notes*, 33–37
CATTON, *Grant and Lee*, 79–82
DILLARD, *Strangers to Darkness*, 102–104
DOUGLASS, *Plantation Life*, 109–113
EISELEY, *More Thoughts on Wilderness*, 115–117
ELLISON, *On Becoming a Writer*, 118–125
FAULKNER, *A Rose for Emily*, 135–143
FROST, *The Gift Outright*, 149
HEMINGWAY, *Hills Like White Elephants*, 186–190
HUGHES, *Feet Live Their Own Life*, 197–199
LINCOLN, *The Gettysburg Address*, 228–229
RODRIGUEZ, *Does America Still Exist?* 347–351
THOMAS, *Ceti*, 398–401
WHITE, *Once More to the Lake*, 443–448
WOLFE, *Journal Entries*, 454–460
WRIGHT, *The Library Card*, 467–475

INDIVIDUALITY, PRIVACY, SOLITUDE

AGEE, *Knoxville: Summer 1915*, 7–11
DICKINSON, *There's a certain Slant of light*, 92–93
DIDION, *On Keeping a Notebook*, 94–100
DILLARD, *Strangers to Darkness*, 102–104
FAULKNER, *A Rose for Emily*, 135–143
HUGHES, *Salvation*, 192–194
PLATH, *Journal Entries*, 325–329
PLATH, *The Bee Meeting*, 330–332
WRIGHT, *The Library Card*, 467–475

MEN AND WOMEN, LOVE, SEXUALITY

EPHRON, *A Few Words about Breasts*, 126–133
FAULKNER, *A Rose for Emily*, 135–143
HELLMAN, *Runaway*, 178–184
HEMINGWAY, *Hills Like White Elephants*, 186–190
HUGHES, *Two Poems*, 195–196
LAKOFF, *You Are What You Say*, 214–220
LAWRENCE, *Pornography*, 223–226
MARVELL, *To His Coy Mistress*, 243–244
PORTER, *The Necessary Enemy*, 333–337
SHAKESPEARE, *That time of year thou mayst in me behold*, 362
STAFFORD, *Shadows*, 377
UPDIKE, *Ace in the Hole*, 417–425
WOOLF, *If Shakespeare Had Had a Sister*, 462–464

MUTABILITY, AGING, DEATH

ALLEN, *Death Knocks*, 12–19
AUSTIN, *The Scavengers*, 27–31
EISELEY, *More Thoughts on Wilderness*, 115–117
FAULKNER, *A Rose for Emily*, 135–143
GOULD, *Phyletic Size Decrease in Hershey Bars*, 161–166
HAINES, *Lost*, 174–177
MARVELL, *To His Coy Mistress*, 243–244
NIN, *Journal Entry*, 260–261
ORWELL, *A Hanging*, 316–320
RETTIE, *"But a Watch in the Night": A Scientific Fable*, 340–345
SHAKESPEARE, *That time of year thou mayst in me behold*, 362

WELTY, *A Worn Path*, 429–437
WHITE, *Once More to the Lake*, 443–448

NATURE, ENVIRONMENT, WONDERS OF CREATION

AGEE, *Knoxville: Summer 1915*, 7–11
AUSTIN, *The Scavengers*, 27–31
BLEIBTREU, *The Moment of Being*, 76–78
DILLARD, *Strangers to Darkness*, 102–104
DILLARD, *Sojourner*, 105–108
EISELEY, *More Thoughts on Wilderness*, 115–117
FROST, *The Gift Outright*, 149
HAINES, *Lost*, 174–177
MAILER, *A Walk on the Moon*, 235–241
RETTIE, *"But a Watch in the Night": A Scientific Fable*, 340–345
SAGAN, *The Measure of Eratosthenes*, 352–354
THOMAS, *On Smell*, 394–397
THOMAS, *Ceti*, 398–401
THOREAU, *Thinking Like a Bream*, 407–408
WHITE, *Once More to the Lake*, 443–448
WOLFE, *Journal Entries*, 454–460

PLAY, GAMES, SPORTING LIFE

AGEE, *Knoxville: Summer 1915*, 7–11
ALLEN, *Death Knocks*, 12–19
CONROY, *A Yo-Yo Going Down*, 84–91
McPHEE, *Ancestors of the Jump Shot*, 230–233
MORRIS, *Odd Balls*, 252–257
UPDIKE, *Ace in the Hole*, 417–425

REBELS AND CONFORMISTS

BALDWIN, *Autobiographical Notes*, 33–37
BIERCE, *Some Devil's Definitions*, 57–60
BIRD, *Where College Fails Us*, 62–72
DOUGLASS, *Plantation Life*, 109–113
FAULKNER, *A Rose for Emily*, 135–143
FEIFFER, *Superman*, 145–148

GANSBURG, *38 Who Saw Murder Didn't Call the Police*, 150–153
HELLMAN, *Runaway*, 178–184
HUGHES, *Salvation*, 192–194
JEFFERSON, *The Declaration of Independence*, 208–213
TERKEL, *Phil Stallings, Spot Welder*, 388–393
VIDAL, *Drugs*, 426–428
WELTY, *A Worn Path*, 429–437
WRIGHT, *The Library Card*, 467–475

RELIGION, GOD, FAITH, SPIRITUAL LIFE

DILLARD, *Strangers to Darkness*, 102–104
DILLARD, *Sojourner*, 105–108
EISELEY, *More Thoughts on Wilderness*, 115–117
HUGHES, *Salvation*, 192–194
O'CONNOR, *A Good Man Is Hard to Find*, 267–281
O'CONNOR, *From Flannery O'Connor's Letters*, 284–290
THOREAU, *Thinking Like a Bream*, 407–408

SCIENTIFIC INQUIRY AND DISCOVERY

AUSTIN, *The Scavengers*, 27–31
BLEIBTREU, *The Moment of Being*, 76–78
DILLARD, *Strangers to Darkness*, 102–104
DILLARD, *Sojourner*, 105–108
EISELEY, *More Thoughts on Wilderness*, 115–117
GOULD, *Phyletic Size Decrease in Hershey Bars*, 161–166
GOULD, *Wide Hats and Narrow Minds*, 167–172
MAILER, *A Walk on the Moon*, 235–241
RETTIE, *"But a Watch in the Night": A Scientific Fable*, 340–345
SAGAN, *The Measure of Eratosthenes*, 352–354
THOMAS, *On Smell*, 394–397
THOMAS, *Ceti*, 398–401
THOREAU, *Thinking Like a Bream*, 407–408

THE SOCIAL FABRIC, GOVERNMENT, FAMILY OF MAN

ANGELOU, *Mr. Red Leg*, 21–26
BALDWIN, *Autobiographical Notes*, 33–37
BERRY, *The Reactor and the Garden*, 48–55

DOUGLASS, *Plantation Life*, 109–113
ELLISON, *On Becoming a Writer*, 118–125
GANSBURG, *38 Who Saw Murder Didn't Call the Police*, 150–153
GOULD, *The Politics of Census*, 154–159
GOULD, *Wide Hats and Narrow Minds*, 167–172
JACOBS, *Paradoxes of Size*, 201–206
JEFFERSON, *The Declaration of Independence*, 208–213
LAKOFF, *You Are What You Say*, 214–220
LINCOLN, *The Gettysburg Address*, 228–229
ORWELL, *Shooting an Elephant*, 308–314
ORWELL, *A Hanging*, 316–320
PLATH, *Journal Entries*, 325–329
RODRIGUEZ, *Does America Still Exist?* 347–351
SCHUMACHER, *Production in Service to Life*, 355–361
SHARP, *Under the Hood*, 363–371
SWIFT, *A Modest Proposal*, 379–386
WHITE, *The Wild Flag*, 450–451
WOOLF, *If Shakespeare Had Had a Sister*, 462–464
WRIGHT, *The Library Card*, 467–475

WORKING

BERRY, *A Good Scythe*, 39–42
BERRY, *The Reactor and the Garden*, 48–55
BIRD, *Where College Fails Us*, 62–72
MAILER, *A Walk on the Moon*, 235–241
ORWELL, *Shooting an Elephant*, 308–314
SCHUMACHER, *Production in Service to Life*, 355–361
SHARP, *Under the Hood*, 363–371
STAFFORD, *A Way of Writing*, 372–377
TERKEL, *Phil Stallings, Spot Welder*, 388–393
UPDIKE, *Ace in the Hole*, 417–425
WELTY, *A Worn Path*, 429–437
WOOLF, *If Shakespeare Had Had a Sister*, 462–464

WRITING, LANGUAGE, RHETORIC, AND STYLE

BALDWIN, *Autobiographical Notes*, 33–37
BERRY, *In Defense of Literacy*, 44–47
BIERCE, *Some Devil's Definitions*, 57–60
DIDION, *On Keeping a Notebook*, 94–100
ELLISON, *On Becoming a Writer*, 118–125

LAKOFF, *You Are What You Say*, 214–220
LAWRENCE, *Pornography*, 223–226
MENCKEN, *Gamalielese*, 245–248
O'CONNOR, *The Total Effect and the Eighth Grade*, 263–266
ORWELL, *Politics and the English Language*, 294–306
STAFFORD, *A Way of Writing*, 372–377
THOMAS, *Notes on Punctuation*, 402–404
THURBER, *Which*, 410–412
TRILLIN, *Literally*, 413–416
WELTY, *The Point of the Story*, 438–440

To the Student

Part of our job as educational publishers is to try to improve the textbooks we publish. Thus, when revising we take into account the experience of both instructors and students with the previous edition. At some time in the future your instructor will be asked to comment extensively on *A Writer's Reader*, Fourth Edition, but right now we want to hear from you. After all, though your instructor assigned this book, you are the one for whom it is intended (and the one who paid for it).

Please help us by completing this questionnaire and returning it to College English Developmental Group, Little, Brown and Company, 34 Beacon Street, Boston, Mass. 02106.

School_____ Course Title_____

Instructor's Name_____

Other Books Assigned_____

Tell us about the readings.

	KEEP	DROP	DID NOT READ
ADAMS, *Winter and Summer*	____	____	____
AGEE, *Knoxville, Summer 1915*	____	____	____
ALLEN, *Death Knocks*	____	____	____
ANGELOU, *Mr. Red Leg*	____	____	____
AUSTIN, *The Scavengers*	____	____	____

(OVER)

	KEEP	DROP	DID NOT READ
BALDWIN, *Autobiographical Notes*	___	___	___
BERRY, *A Good Scythe*	___	___	___
BERRY, *In Defense of Literacy*	___	___	___
BERRY, *The Reactor and the Garden*	___	___	___
BIERCE *Some Devil's Definitions*	___	___	___
BIRD, *Where College Fails Us*	___	___	___
BISHOP, *The Fish*	___	___	___
BLEIBTREU, *The Moment of Being*	___	___	___
CATTON, *Grant and Lee . . .*	___	___	___
CONROY, *A Yo-Yo Going Down*	___	___	___
DICKINSON, *There's a certain Slant of light*	___	___	___
DIDION, *On Keeping a Notebook*	___	___	___
DILLARD, *Strangers to Darkness*	___	___	___
DILLARD, *Sojourners*	___	___	___
DOUGLASS, *Plantation Life*	___	___	___
EISELEY, *More Thoughts on Wilderness*	___	___	___
ELLISON, *On Becoming a Writer*	___	___	___
EPHRON, *A Few Words about Breasts*	___	___	___
FAULKNER, *A Rose for Emily*	___	___	___
FEIFFER, *Superman*	___	___	___
FROST, *The Gift Outright*	___	___	___
GANSBERG, *38 Who Saw Murder . . .*	___	___	___
GOULD, *The Politics of Census*	___	___	___
GOULD, *The Phyletic Size Decrease . . .*	___	___	___
GOULD, *Wide Hats and Narrow Minds*	___	___	___
HAINES, *Lost*	___	___	___
HELLMAN, *Runaway*	___	___	___
HEMINGWAY, *Hills Like White Elephants*	___	___	___
HUGHES, *Salvation*	___	___	___
HUGHES, *Two Poems*	___	___	___
HUGHES, *Feet Live Their Own Life*	___	___	___
JACOBS, *Paradoxes of Size*	___	___	___
JEFFERSON, *The Declarations . . .*	___	___	___
LAKOFF, *You Are What You Say*	___	___	___
LINCOLN, *The Gettysburg Address*	___	___	___
McPHEE, *Ancestors of the Jump Shot*	___	___	___
MAILER, *A Walk on the Moon*	___	___	___

	KEEP	DROP	DID NOT READ
MARVELL, *To His Coy Mistress*	___	___	___
MENCKEN, *Gamalielese*	___	___	___
MORGAN, *Exam-Week Unrealities*	___	___	___
MORRIS, *Odd Balls*	___	___	___
NIN, *Journal Entry*	___	___	___
O'CONNOR, *The Total Effect and the Eighth Grade*	___	___	___
O'CONNOR, *A Good Man Is Hard to Find*	___	___	___
O'CONNOR, *From Flannery O'Connor's Letters*	___	___	___
ORWELL, *Politics and the English Language*	___	___	___
ORWELL, *Shooting an Elephant*	___	___	___
ORWELL, *A Hanging*	___	___	___
PIRSIG, *The Church of Reason*	___	___	___
PLATH, *Journal Entries . . .*	___	___	___
PLATH, *The Bee Meeting*	___	___	___
PORTER, *The Necessary Enemy*	___	___	___
RETTIE, *"But a Watch in the Night"*	___	___	___
RODRIGUEZ, *Does America Still Exist?*	___	___	___
SAGAN, *The Measure of Eratosthenes*	___	___	___
SCHUMACHER, *Production in Service to Life*	___	___	___
SHAKESPEARE, *That time of year . . .*	___	___	___
SHARP, *Under the Hood*	___	___	___
STAFFORD, *A Way of Writing*	___	___	___
SWIFT, *A Modest Proposal*	___	___	___
TERKEL, *Phil Stallings, Spot Welder*	___	___	___
THOMAS, *On Smell*	___	___	___
THOMAS, *Ceti*	___	___	___
THOMAS, *Notes on Punctuation*	___	___	___
THOREAU, *Thinking Like a Bream*	___	___	___
THURBER, *Which*	___	___	___
TRILLIN, *Literally*	___	___	___
UPDIKE, *Ace in the Hole*	___	___	___
VIDAL, *Drugs*	___	___	___

(OVER)

	KEEP	DROP	DID NOT READ
WELTY, *A Worn Path*	___	___	___
WELTY, *The Point of the Story*	___	___	___
WHITE, *Once More to the Lake*	___	___	___
WHITE, *Editorial*	___	___	___
WOLFE, *Journal Entries*	___	___	___
WOOLF, *If Shakespeare Had Had a Sister*	___	___	___
WRIGHT, *The Library Card*	___	___	___

Did you use the Rhetorical and Thematic Indexes? _____

How might they be improved? _____

_____

_____

Were the Introductions and Considerations that accompany each

selection helpful? _____ How might they be improved? _____

_____

_____

Should we add more stories and poems? _____

Please add any further comments or suggestions. _____

_____

_____

_____

Date _____ Your Name _____

_____

Mailing Address